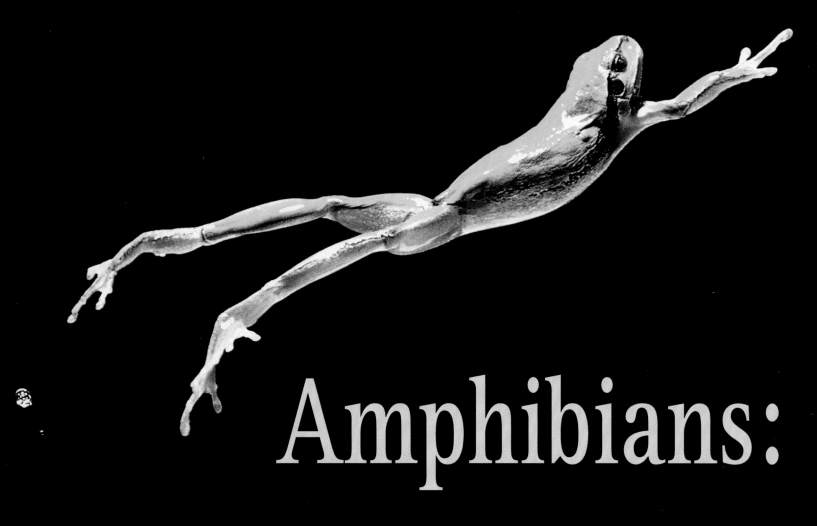

Amphibians:

The World of Frogs,
Toads, Salamanders
and Newts

Robert Hofrichter, Editor

FIREFLY BOOKS

A FIREFLY BOOK

Published by Firefly Books (U.S.) Inc., 2000

First Printing

U.S. Cataloguing-in-Publication Data

Amphibians : the world of frogs, toads, salamanders and newts
/Robert Hofrichter, editor. –1st ed.
[264] p. : color. Ill., maps ; cm.
Includes index.
1. Amphibians.   I. Hofrichter, Robert, ed.   II. Title.
ISBN 1-55209-541-X
597.8   21   2000   CIP

First published in the United States in 2000 by
Firefly Books (U.S.) Inc.
P.O. Box 1338, Ellicott Station
Buffalo, New York
14205

Originally published in German in 1998 by Weltbild Verlag GmbH, Augsburg

Published in Canada in 2000 by Key Porter Books

Printed and bound in Canada

Illustrations: Martin Gregus, L.E.B.O. advertising GmbH, Preßburg
Layout: Zuzana Kotrus-Miskolczi, L.E.B.O. advertising GmbH, Preßburg
and Michael Stiehl, Leipzig
Cover design: Peter Maher
Electronic formatting: Jean Lightfoot Peters

Front cover photographs (l–r): Roman Rozinek, Rolf Bechter, Robert Hofrichter (x 2), Wolfgang Petz, (center) Bavaria Bildagentur
Back cover photographs: Robert Hofrichter
Cover (front): Red-eyed (tree) frogs (*Agalychnis callydrias*, Hylidae)
Cover (back): Red-eyed (tree) frog (*Agalychnis callydrias*, Hylidae) from Central America, fire salamander (*Salamandra salamandra*, Salamandridae) and two juvenile emerald-green tree frogs (*Pelodryas caerulea*, Hylidae).
Page 1: *Dendrobates azureus* (Dendrobatidae)
(Photo: Photo Press / Möhn)
Page 2/3: Common tree frog (*Hyla arborea*, Hylidae) (photo: Silvestris / NHPA / Dalton).
Page 5: *Gastrotheca walkeri* (Hylidae)
(Photo: K.- H. Jungfer)
Page 6/7: *Pachymedusa dacnicolor* (Hylidae) from Mexico on a leaf, photograph taken against the light.
(Photo: R. Hofrichter)
Page 8: Hybrid edible frog (*Rana kl esculenta*) (Photo: N. Wimmer).

Contributors

Dr. Robert Hofrichter (ed.)
Dr. Alfred Goldschmid
Dr. Alois Lametschwandtner
Dr. Franz Uiblein
Dr. Robert Schabetsberger

Institute of Zoology, University of Salzburg

Dr. Zbyněk Roček DrSc
*Geological Institute,
Academy of Science of Czechoslovakia
and Chair of Zoology at Karls University,
Prague*

Dr. Ulrich Sinsch
*Institute of Biology, University of
Koblenz-Landau*

Prof. Dr. Jakob Parzefall
*Institute of Zoology and Zoological
Museum, University of Hamburg*

Dr. Joachim Kuhn
Doris Gutser (Eng.)
*Environmental Research Centre, Leipzig-
Halle*

Dr. Walter Hödl
Dr. Heinz Tunner
Robert Jehle (M.A.)
Thomas Schmuck (M.A.)
Institute of Zoology, University of Vienna

Dr. Milan Kminiak CSc
*Institute for Landscape Ecology,
Comenius University, Bratislava*

Dr. Franz Tiedemann
Dr. Heinz Grillitsch
Gerald Benyr (M.A.)
*Museum of Natural History,
Herpetological collection in the 1st zoo-
logical dept., Vienna*

Dr. Britta Grillitsch
*Institute for Hydrobiology, University of
Veterinary Medicine, Vienna*

Dr. Miloš Kaležič
*Institute for Zoology, University of
Beograd*

Dr. Frank Glaw
  National Zoological Collection, Munich

Dr. Günter Fachbach
Dr. Helmut Faber
  Institute for Zoology, University of Graz

Karl-Heinz Jungfer
  *German association of herpetology and the
science of terrarium keeping, AG Anuren*

Martin Kyek (M.A.)
  *Institute for Ecology in the House of
Nature, Salzburg*

Dr. Alain Dubois
  Museum of Natural History, Paris

Dr. Andreas Haßl
  *Clinical Institute for Hygiene, University of
Vienna*

Christian Proy
  Austrian Herpetological Association

Dr. Peter Weygoldt
  Institute of Zoology, University of Freiburg

Dr. Werner Himstedt
  *Institute of Zoology, Technical University of
Darmstadt*

Josef Schmuck (Eng.)
  *D.C.S.P.–Documentation Centre for Species
Protection, Graz*

Rudolf Malkmus
  *The Senkenberg Society for Research in
Natural History, Frankfurt/Main*

Dr. Wolfgang Walkowiak
  Institute of Zoology, University of Cologne

Dr. Wolfgang Böhme
Dr. Miguel Vences
Jörn Köhler
Stefan Lötters
  *Department of Herpetology, Zoological
Research Institute and Alexander Koenig
Museum, Bonn*

Contents

Robert Hofrichter # Foreword

Ugly toads, poisonous European sala-manders, frogs croaking loudly, tree frogs in pickle jars, the frog king in fairy tales, frog legs as a gastronomic treat, frogs as road kill and (recently) as an advertising gimmick for a certain telephone company—these are just some of the associations that immediately spring to mind at the mention of amphibians. But the world of amphib-ians encompasses much more. It is a world full of wonders, of unusual and extreme adaptations, and also of unsolved mysteries. In survival and reproduction strategies, amphibians not only match but surpass in variety all

other vertebrates. And as the stunning images in this book illustrate, the amphibian world is also one of beauty. Many tropical tree and poison-dart frogs are more dazzling in appearance than some of the world's most colorful birds. This book, we hope, will enchant readers so that they will never again associate words such as "ugly" and "dis-gusting" with frogs, realizing that such descriptions are founded on superstition and prejudice.

Amphibian skin has no scales, hair, or feathers; instead, it is warty and slip-pery, evoking disgust in some people.

*Australian tree frogs (*Pelodryas caerulea Hylidae, *previously called* Litoria caerulea) *are popular among owners of terrariums.*

As a result, people have generally found amphibians to be less attractive than feathered or hairy vertebrates. Over 200 years ago, Carl von Linnaeus, the founder of modern zoological nomen-clature, spoke of "ugly, disgusting crea-tures... whose creator failed to try to make more of them." The best treatment for "Linnaeus' syndrome"—as it might be called—is simply to take a frog in one's hand. Even "ugly" toads feel soft and pleasing to the touch, and most signs of the syndrome disappear after only an hour of such "therapy."

When modern natural science was still in its infancy, amphibians were assigned a rather subordinate role. Together with reptiles, they were regarded as "lower" forms of terrestrial vertebrates, in contrast to the "higher" life forms—birds and mammals. Urodela (salamanders), Anura (frogs and toads) and reptiles—all tossed into the collective category called "herpeton" (from Greek: things that crawl)—represented the "lower house" among land vertebrates, while birds and mammals represented the "upper house." Amphibians got this negative connotation because of their cold-bloodedness, a physiological trait they share with reptiles and which separates them from birds and mammals, which are warm-blooded.

Historically the study of the two fundamentally different vertebrate classes, amphibians and reptiles, was combined into one scientific field called herpetology. However, the differences between the two groups outweigh any commonalities they may have. While amphibian eggs have no protective skin—amphibians, like fishes, are so-called anamniotes—and require water or at least a moist environment for successful development, reptile eggs have a hard, protective shell. Reptiles, like birds and mammals, are so-called amniotes. Their embryos are in a liquid-filled egg, encased in several protective layers even in dry environments. The skin of amphibians and reptiles is also fundamentally different: while amphibian skin is unprotected, soft and water-permeable, reptile skin is characterized by dryness and keratinous scales.

For a long time negative attitudes toward reptiles and amphibians relegated herpetological research to the back seat, a handicap that has thankfully been overcome. Herpetology now enjoys unprecedented popularity, not least of all thanks to the countless hobbyists who keep terrariums, and to naturalists, herpetologists and other scientists who devote their time to these fascinating creatures worldwide. Over the course of time, amphibians have colonized most areas of the globe with the exception of polar regions, and the oceans, whose high saline content they are unable to tolerate. Since they require moisture and warmth, amphib-

ian diversity is greatest in tropical and subtropical regions. Having conquered land, amphibians evolved at an astonishing rate and in amazing variety, and recent representatives impress with the diversity of their adaptations on all levels: morphology, physiology, ecology, ethology and reproduction.

The three recent amphibian orders have gone through a long and distinct development, and the differences between them are correspondingly profound. Aside from general morphology, the greatest differences lie in their methods of movement: frogs leap, newts crawl and caecilians dig. Methods of communication are similarly diversified, with frogs most often communicating acoustically; reproduction is yet another highly diversified area—almost all frogs reproduce by external fertilization, while salamanders often reproduce by internal fertilization (by means of spermatophores) and caecilians rely exclusively on the male copulatory organ for internal fertilization.

Caecilians (whose appearance has more in common with a giant earthworm than with frogs, toads or salamanders) are the order that is least known. The largest caecilian species reaches a length of 5 feet (1.5 m)! Among newts, too, there are such giants. The Japanese giant salamander, which in captivity can reach an age of 60 years, grows to more than 5 feet 3 inches (1.6 m) long and looks like a prehistoric monster. In geological times, when amphibians were at their peak in development, their species even included terrifying predators as long as a mid-sized crocodile,

e.g., *Eryops* (up to 2 yards/2 m) and *Mastodonsaurus* (up to 13 feet/4 m).

As I've said, Urodela and Anura need water. Nevertheless, there are species that live in desert and semi-desert regions. Burrowing deep into sand, they remain in a cocoon-like condition for years, until the next rainfall. Accordingly, their reproductive cycle must happen within a very short period of time. Other frogs use skin secretions to build foam nests in tree branches to create the right spawning substrate for their eggs. Some Anura seem to have sprung from the imagination of a science-fiction author—for example, those that are able to imitate dried leaves and camouflage themselves on the forest floor. Yet others impress with eccentric coloring, signaling to potential predators: Careful, I am poisonous!

Just how unique and curious the world of amphibians is can be seen in the "oral birth" of gastric breeding frogs in Australia; their fully developed young crawl out of the parent's mouth—a phenomenon that has no equal in the entire animal kingdom. Other frog and toad species carry larvae in their gular pouch. Impressive, too, is the behavior of European midwife toads; the males carry the eggs on their backs until the tadpoles emerge. The "kangaroos"

The North American species Pseudotriton ruber *(Plethodontidae) is a member of the most diverse Urodela family, with 280 species. Some representatives of lungless salamanders in South America are the only Urodela in the Southern Hemisphere.*

among frogs, marsupial (pouched) frogs, have a breeding pouch on their backs in which they carry first the eggs and later the tadpoles. Many species carry their young to unusual water sources, such as water-filled bromeliad cups high up in the treetops of tropical forests.

In each animal group, each division, class or order, there are examples of fascinating adaptations. Amphibians are no exception. What is unusual, however, is the "double life" of amphibians—on water and land—and the metamorphosis that accompanies it, like a quick-motion replay of vertebrate evolution. This characteristic is what earned them the name amphibians, derived from the Greek and loosely translated as "living a double life" or "living on two sides." With life on land and the need for mobility while carrying the full burden of their weight under the influence of gravity, the four extremities gradually evolved. Amphibians are the first tetrapods or "quadrupeds" among verte-

*Alpine newt (*Triturus alpestris, *Salamandridae) male in spawning colors. In low-lying regions, the newts migrate to spawning grounds as early as mid-February to mid-March; in higher alpine regions, migration may occur as late as the end of May.*

brates. However, this is only the most noticeable external trait that separates them from fish. They have numerous other unusual adaptations with respect to anatomy and physiology that are connected with their life in water and on land, respectively. The transition from water to land is also inextricably linked to human life, since the step onto land was one of the most significant and portentous events in evolution. Today most amphibian species live in the boundary area between land and water that has always been one of the most interesting environments and the scene of many great leaps in evolution; humans, incidentally, prefer the same environment, possibly a sign of a shared fundamental inclination.

Man has always been aware of amphibians' unique qualities, and these have enriched and fed our imagination since ancient times. Frogs' astonishing reproduction rate has made them into fertility symbols, an association that has been reinforced by their connection to water and rain, both ancient symbols of life and fertility.

Their way of life often seemed mysterious—for example, the ritual of disappearing each fall or during dry seasons,

only to suddenly reappear, often in large numbers, in spring or after heavy rainfalls; other cycles of "coming and going," such as disappearing below water and suddenly resurfacing; the ability to inflate their throats; and, more than anything else, metamorphosis. These characteristics in amphibian biology have engendered numerous myths, legends, traditions, superstitions and fairy-tales. This book contains a separate chapter on the history and culture that surround amphibians, documenting how human perception of them has changed over time, leading to our using images of amphibians as a kind of goodwill symbol in contemporary media.

Amphibians were always considered the smallest class of vertebrates. In 1986 Duellman and Trueb's *Biology of Amphibians*, the standard work on the subject, listed 3,900 living amphibian species. By 1994, the number of amphibian species surpassed the total number of all described species of mammals. And by the end of 1997, 4,371 frog and toad species, 436 salamander species and 163 caecilian species were known—altogether 4,982 species were identified. Thus, Linnaeus' opinion of these animals as ones "whose creator

failed to try to make more of them" has finally been refuted. Today, more species have been described for these "disgusting" animals than for the "highest" vertebrates, the mammals. To provide an overview of this abundance, this book also contains a systematic summary in which readers can see the complicated "genealogy" of amphibians, including the names of (nearly) all currently known species.

Many experts have contributed to this book to provide readers with the latest information on amphibians. Yet even experts find it difficult to keep abreast of the vast amount of research that is undertaken in the many branches of biology. Worldwide research is under way on the physiology, ecology, behavior, reproduction, systematics and genetics of amphibians, and countless works have been published on the subject. Hundreds of new species have been described in the last few years alone, but the biology of many amphibians is still insufficiently researched or even obscure. Despite its 264 pages, this book could not contain descriptions of all species (it would leave us about $1/600$ of a page for each description). We have instead chosen to present a selection, and every effort was made to compile it in a manner that would give readers an informative and exciting overview of the most diverse aspects of amphibian life.

In other words, we make no claim to completeness, since that is hardly possible in so few pages. Yet we do feel confident that this richly illustrated volume represents an important contribution to a better understanding of amphibians and their way of life. At the same time, it is our wish that this work alert the public to the importance and the endangerment of this animal group. If only a few readers who previously regarded amphibians as unattractive or even "disgusting" should feel inspired to revise their opinion, then we have succeeded.

Most amphibians inhabit tropical rain forests, an environment that is perhaps more threatened than any other. Unregulated clear-cutting of rain forests—without exaggeration decried as a crime against future generations—and out-of-control forest fires have become important topics. The forests are a major habitat for many wonderful life-forms

who perish in fires before we have a chance to study and know them. Environmental problems such as climate change and the hole in the ozone layer are sure to increase, as will contributing factors for which we do not even have names yet. For over two decades, amphibian populations have decreased at a terrifying rate, a phenomenon that has occurred worldwide and for which there seems to be no satisfactory explanation. More importantly, the same drop has been noted in regions that are, at first glance, largely untouched by man. The need to study amphibians could not be underscored more dramatically.

Some of the ideas on species protection and trade may appear too provocative or even "ideological" to certain readers. While every attempt was made to remain objective in our discussion, the conditions for amphibian survival have reached a stage where half-hearted or unfeeling approaches to their protection would be not only inefficient, but foolish. Amphibian species are becoming extinct literally before our eyes and this cannot help but evoke an emotional response. We hope that the chapter titled "Endangerment and Protection of Amphibians" will draw much-needed attention to the urgency of the problem.

Eleutherodactylus martiae *pair (Leptodactylidae) in amplexus position. The New World genus* Eleutherodactylus *is by far the most diverse amphibian genus, with a total of 599 species, Leptodactylidae (southern frogs) are currently categorized into 50 genera and 972 species.*

While Linnaeus' achievements were numerous and great, his pronouncement on amphibians, quoted at the outset, cannot be allowed to stand: amphibians have never required their "creator to make more of them." Fully adapted to their various habitats, these are wonderful creatures who have proven their ability to survive across millennia. The first frogs appeared more than 200 million years ago in nearly the same form as today, as is amply documented in fossils, at approximately the same time that the first dinosaurs appeared.

For many amphibian species, there is a very real danger that, having survived for so long, they will be condemned to extinction within one more human generation. It is (still) in our hands to do all that is humanly possible to prevent this from happening.

In the
Devonian
period—some
360 million
years ago—the first
amphibians, that is, the
first land vertebrates,
tetrapods or "quadrupeds," stepped
onto land and began to evolve into the
diversity that would characterize them in
times to come. But many stages of their evolution remain unknown. For a long time, amphibians
were regarded as the least diverse vertebrate group, but
some years ago the number of described species—now
more than 5,000—surpassed that of mammals. The
systematics of amphibians, especially that of Anura
(frogs and toads) as the most diverse order, with
more than 4,370 species, is still subject to change
and has not reached a definitive stage.

Evolution, Systematics and Biogeography

Alfred Goldschmid

What Distinguishes Amphibians from Other Vertebrates?

Frogs and toads, salamanders and newts, form the two most diverse orders of modern amphibians and most people can readily tell them apart. What is more difficult, however, is listing the criteria used to distinguish them from other tetrapods. Limbless caecilians, known mainly to zoologists, are not included here, since their body shape is the result of secondary evolutionary adaptations and reductions.

Bufo asper (Bufonidae) in a rain forest in northern Sumatra. These toads often climb onto trees, where they perch on branches up to 9.6 feet (3 m) above flowing bodies of water.

In systematics, amphibians are in the middle of the vertebrate system but also at the beginning of a development that led to land colonization, to the evolution of large land tetrapods, and ultimately to primates and humans.
[1] *number of species is approximate;* [2] *with protective embryonic membrane;* [3] *quadruped;* [4] *The number of species is fully known;* [5] *secondary colonization of water through numerous groups of these classes.*

The Larval Phase

As the name "amphibians" suggests, these animals live partly in water and partly on land. One should emphasize that most zoological models of amphibians are limited to the many European species, such as the common frog, the "edible" frog and the common toad. Salamanders, frogs and toads are indigenous to Europe and most live—at least during the spawning season—in or near water. Larvae develop from the eggs laid in water and, in the case of frogs and toads, the larvae look different and occupy a very different position in the ecosystem than do the adult animals. The larvae live similarly to fish, breathe through gills, and propel themselves forward with the help of a strong tail. Like fish they possess a lateral line organ. Their inner organs, too, still resemble fish organs to a great degree. At the beginning of the larval phase, tadpoles are internal filter feeders, using a powerful gill basket; later on, they feed on algae with tiny keratinous teeth or graze just below the water surface. This is, incidentally, the only case of keratinous teeth in jaw-bearing vertebrates, because their teeth always consist of adamantine and dentine. Due to their vegetarian diet, tadpoles have the long, winding intestine characteristic of herbivores.

Metamorphosis

Metamorphosis follows the larval phase and is the transformation of the larva into an adult. In a very simplified and visible manner, it mirrors the changes that took place in the evolution of land vertebrates: instead of swimming by means of sweeping movements with the tail, it gradually develops front and hind extremities; we notice a shift from gill respiration to pulmonary respiration; and instead of a mucous membrane, there is a slightly keratinized skin with deeply embedded glands.

Salamander larvae look very much like adult salamanders, only smaller in scale, but they are readily identifiable as larvae by their three pairs of external gills. The diet of the larvae is similar to that of adult salamanders, as well. Their metamorphosis, too, is much less dramatic. A great number of the approximately 5,000 known amphibian species, however, do not live or reproduce according to the standard model of amphibian life described here, because this model—as we have mentioned—is largely based on the observation of European species. Many amphibians no longer depend on larger bodies of water and have a variety of reproduction strategies involving direct development that evolved in at least twelve Anura families; some

comparison of individual vertebrate classes								
	habitat	anamnia[1]	amniota[2]	tetrapoda[3]	poikilo-thermic	homoio-thermic	number of known species[4]	
1. Agnatha		+	-	-	+	-	approx.	75 species
2. Chondrichthyes	WATER	+	-	-	+	-	approx.	710 species
3. Osteichthyes		+	-	-	+	-	approx.	24,000 species
4. Amphibia	WATER + LAND	+	-	+	+	-	approx.	5,000 species
5. Reptilia		-	+	+	+	-	approx.	6,600 species
6. Birds (Aves)	LAND[5]	-	+	+	-	+	approx.	8,800 species
7. Mammals (Mammalia)		-	+	+	-	+	approx.	4,700 species
						Total	approx.	49,900 species

of them (Ranidae) exhibit multiple, independent ways of direct development. Direct development means that the free-swimming larval phase is simply "omitted," thus avoiding a phase when the species is most vulnerable to a drying up of its aquatic habitat and to predators.

The Embryonic Membranes

In summary, once amphibians have spawned, they dwell as larvae in water, at least according to the standard scheme of their biology, and it is in water that they feed and grow into the adult stage. At the end of their aquatic life as larvae, they transform or metamorphose rapidly into young, terrestrial adults. The embryos of fish and amphibians do not develop embryonic membranes or protective structures in the egg. Due to this absence of the embryonic membrane, or "amnion," they are categorized as "amamniota" to distinguish them from other vertebrates, reptiles, birds and mammals, who are all gathered into one classification under the name "amniota." The last three vertebrate classes are "true" terrestrial creatures: in other words, they develop outside of water and no longer go through a free larval phase. At the end of a long embryonic phase, they hatch (or are born) as more or less fully independent young animals.

The amnion present in true terrestrials, but not in amphibians or fish, is therefore the key factor that makes them distinct. The amnion is a protective membrane formed early on in the development of the embryo, surrounding it and enclosing it in an embryonic cavity that is filled with a protective fluid. The embryos of reptiles, birds and mammals thus grow within a "pond" of their own because the amniotic fluid can be compared with the water in which amphibian and fish larvae develop. As they grow, amniotes must feed, breathe and metabolize inside the egg. This problem, too, has been solved by evolution. The energy required for an embryo to fully develop and hatch is provided by the nourishing yolk of the yolk sac, constantly consumed in the process of the embryo's development. The amount of yolk can be considerable; one need only think of an ostrich egg. Amphibian eggs, too, have yolk material, but it is not concentrated in a yolk sac; instead, it is distributed in individual cells, and for amphibians with a free larval phase it provides precisely the nourishment needed to develop a larva capable of feeding itself. Even amphibian eggs of species that do not produce free-living larvae reach a maximum diameter of $7/16$ inch (10 mm).

The amniote embryo therefore resides in a self-made "pond." Gas exchange takes place via the allantois, a protrusion of the embryonic intes-

Representatives of the five vertebrate classes in evolutionary sequence: **River perch** *(Perca fluviatilis, Osteichthyes),* **Marsh frog** *(Rana ridibunda, Amphibia),* **Ring-snake** *(Natrix natrix, Reptilia),* **Mute swan** *(Cygnus olor, Aves),* **Red fox** *(Vulpes vulpes, Mammalia). The five classes are differentiated by distinct differences in the skin: for fish, a mucous membrane with bony scales in the corium; for amphibians, slightly keratinized, naked skin with many glands; for reptiles, skin with keratinous scales (in some cases, for example, crocodiles, subdermal bone plates in the corium); for birds, feathers; and for mammals, hair.*

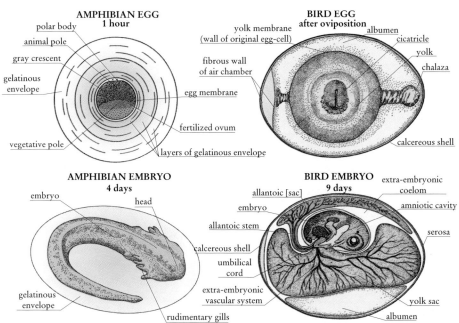

AMPHIBIAN EGG
1 hour
polar body
animal pole
gray crescent
gelatinous envelope
vegetative pole
fertilized ovum
layers of gelatinous envelope

BIRD EGG
after oviposition
yolk membrane (wall of original egg-cell)
fibrous wall of air chamber
egg membrane
albumen
cicatricle
yolk
chalaza
calcereous shell

AMPHIBIAN EMBRYO
4 days
embryo
head
gelatinous envelope
rudimentary gills

BIRD EMBRYO
9 days
allantoic [sac]
embryo
allantoic stem
calcereous shell
umbilical cord
extra-embryonic vascular system
extra-embryonic coelom
amniotic cavity
serosa
yolk sac
albumen

Comparison of amphibian egg and embryo with bird egg and embryo. As basal vertebrates, amphibians and fishes have not developed an amnion (innermost embryonic membrane) and are therefore called Anamnia. In all higher vertebrates, the so-called Amniotes, extra-embryonic structures have evolved for the protection and nourishment of the embryo and also for embryonic respiration.

tine. The allantois also absorbs metabolic toxins from the embryonic cell (the "urine"), which it deposits far away from the embryo. Hence, in reptiles and birds, the allantois is also known as the "embryonic urinary bladder." It is connected to the body of the embryo by a long tube, similar to the yolk sack stem that links the yolk sack and the embryo. Together, these string-like structures are called the "body stalk" (as opposed to the umbilical cord in mammals). Hence, amniota are also called "umbilical animals."

The Skeleton

The four extremities (whose absence in caecilians is secondary, from an evolutionary standpoint) is what distinguishes amphibians most from fish and also provides the greatest link to amniotes. The four vertebrate classifications—amphibians, reptiles, birds and mammals—are therefore called quadrupeds or tetrapods (from Greek: tetra = four; pods = feet). The structure of the amphibian eye, on the other hand, betrays their fish heritage, which clearly separates them from amniotes. As are those of fish, amphibians' eyes are spherical; their curvature and refractive index cannot change. In amniotes, as in humans, the curvature of the lens changes through indirect muscle reflexes when images are brought into focus on the retina. In amphibians and fish, the lens moves forward or backward, much like a telephoto lens. Pulmonary respiration after metamorphosis once again links amphibians to amniotes, although it is also present in some fish, such as Dipnoi and Polypteriformes.

In contrast to fish, amphibians have an occipital joint with two articulating surfaces. In fish, the head acts as a "bow," the torso and tail musculature are the "motor," and the tail fin is the

"propeller." This means that the body is solidly connected to the spine, with no range of motion. Even the pectoral girdle, to which the pectoral fins are attached, is connected to the skull by a chain of bones. In tetrapods, muscles join the pectoral girdle to the axial skeleton and the skull. Amphibians have only two vertebrae between skull and trunk; the mobility of the head at the juncture to the trunk is therefore quite limited. Amniotes, on the other hand, developed a long, highly mobile neck with many vertebrae.

The amphibian skeleton also differs from that of other tetrapods—i.e., amniotes—in the structure of the pelvic girdle. Amphibians have one sacral vertebra linked to the pelvis. Recent salamander species still display sacral ribs. Reptiles always have at least two sacral ribs and no unattached sacral ribs—an important distinction in fossil classification. The number of bones in the fingers and toes plays an important role as well. In true reptiles, the so-called phalangial formula is 2-3-4-5-3, starting with the thumb and ending with the small digit. In different amphibian families, the phalangial formula can vary enormously. The forelimb in all recent salamanders and frogs no longer features a thumb—it is reduced to four digits. The three skeleton characteristics mentioned thus far—that is, the lateral pair of occipital condyles, a single sacral vertebra and the variable phalangial formula—were used to distinguish early amphibians from the first reptiles.

Today's amphibians do not have the closed rib cage that is typical of humans and all amniotes, and thus their respiration differs from that of reptiles, birds and mammals. Amphibians must inhale air through their nostrils into the mouth cavity by lowering the floor, or fundus, of the mouth and then pressing air into their lungs through swallowing motions while keeping nostrils and mouth firmly shut. Amniotes ventilate the lung with the help of the rib cage. Finally, the body covering or skin should be mentioned. While the outer skin layer has evolved into a slimy skin in fish, the outermost cell layer in amphibians tends to keratinize. Powerful bubble-shaped glands with narrow expulsion channels lie beneath the outermost skin layer within a loose connective tissue. The glands ensure that the skin stays moist, an important prerequisite for cutaneous respiration. In contrast to amphibian skin, the skin of reptiles, birds and mammals is protected by scales, feathers or hair, respectively. Amphibians are ectotherms (i.e., their body temperature depends on ambient temperature), as are Agnatha, fish and reptiles. They are also poikilothermic, or cold-blooded, meaning their body temperature varies.

Franz Tiedemann and Heinz Grillitsch

The work of zoological museums and the contribution they make to our knowledge of amphibians is very valuable since knowledge about any life-form can be gained and properly assigned only when the different species have been clearly identified and differentiated. In museum work, the disciplines of comparative morphology and anatomy have played a most important role in making systematic classification possible. Only much later did physiology, ecology, ethology, microbiology, genetics and chemistry begin to contribute to what we have come to call systematics. It is the task of zoological museums to conduct a comparative examination of the multitude of organisms, finding various natural groups to which extant as well as extinct forms can be assigned, based on shared characteristics. Furthermore, systematics describes these organisms and groups and, taking their distribution into account, places them within a system that attempts to reflect their phylogeny, or evolutionary history. From this perspective, systematics is dedicated to researching biological diversity. The fact that several hundred newly described species join the more than 49,000 recorded living vertebrates each year indicates the breadth of this scientific field that deals with the discovery and description of the global species diversity.

The concept of systematics is closely linked to that of taxonomy. The latter involves the classification of the biolog-ical diversity of organisms resulting in the assignment of scientific names (nomenclature) in taxa. Only when a species has been clearly and unequivocally distinguished worldwide by a unique (Latin) name is it possible to organize the various research results and assign specific taxa.

Natural history museums, with their extensive archives, provide most of the information needed to recognize and describe taxa. Their scientific collections, which extend far beyond the public exhibition area, form the necessary foundation for the systematic analysis of species and species groups. The International Code of Zoological Nomenclature, which regulates and standardizes scientific name assignment, also stipulates that specimens of newly described taxa must be deposited in museums or similar facilities in the form of "type specimens," where they can receive appropriate curatorial care and are made accessible to the scientific community. Since all of the type material (holo-, para-, syn-, lecto-, para-lecto- and neotypes) should be viewed as common scientific property, one of the main aspects of the work performed by museums is to identify and catalogue the types contained in a collection and to publish them in the form of catalogues. For example, the Herpetological Collection at the Vienna Natural History Museum currently contains types from 196 nominal taxa (15 caecilians, 31 Urodela, 150 Anura) out of a total of 462 amphibian species. In connection

Detail of specimen cabinet in the Herpetological Collection of the Vienna Natural History Museum, circa 1970. Today, this type of material is kept in a fire-proof metal cabinet in the underground storage facility of the museum.

with a variety of systematic questions, knowledge of the distribution of taxa, and thus the exact geographical origin of each specimen, is vital, and this is why museum material is usually accompanied by detailed information on the location where it was found. Currently, what we know of the geographical distribution of individual species is largely derived from this inventory of locality records. Only with the introduction of the computer-supported management of the large amounts of data will it be possible to link and analyze this information in order to assess changes by comparing former and current distribution patterns. Over the years, these collections are growing in depth and scope, and are increasingly vital depositories of information on biological diversity. Biogeographical changes, species decline and extinction can be charted with the help of these collections. Species extinction has reached a rate and range that has propelled individuals and groups worldwide to take action. A charter for the preservation of biodiversity was approved at the UN conference in Rio de Janeiro in 1992. In order to preserve the world's biological heritage, we must work even harder to research the multitude of species with the help of natural history collections.

Zbyněk Roček

Phylogeny and Evolution

Paleontological findings dating back to the Devonian period (350 to 370 million years ago) prove that amphibian ancestors were fish-like vertebrates with elongated body and a tail fin that allowed them to move forward, much as newts still do today. They also had a number of ventral and dorsal fins; the unpaired of these fins are of no interest in this context. What does interest us, however, are two pairs of fins on the ventral side of the body, the pectoral and abdominal fins, which represent the raw material for a great evolutionary future. These fins, originally used as balancing organs (to maintain the body in a vertical position), evolved into the extremities of terrestrial vertebrates.

The search for amphibian ancestors leads to Crossopterygii (or lobe-fin fishes), more specifically to Osteoleptidae or Panderichthyidae, both families of Rhipidistae. Right: Devonian Eusthenopteron *(after Jarvik, 1980).*

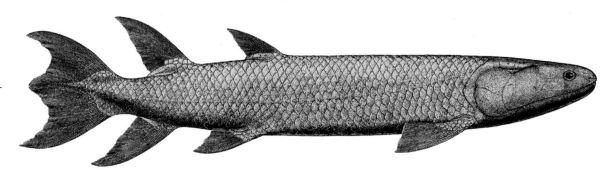

Amphibian Ancestors

In the Devonian, that is, in the period of time when vertebrates began to colonize dry land, oceans abounded with various groups of aquatic vertebrates. Leaving so-called jaw-less fishes (Agnatha) aside (excluded from the list of potential amphibian ancestors because they did not have jaws), the following groups remain as potential forerunners: acanthodians, placoderms, Chondrichthyes (sharks and their relatives), bony fishes (Osteichthyes), lungfishes (Dipnoi), and lobe-fin fishes (Crossopterygii).

At first glance, the Dipnoi seem the most likely ancestors. In their living representatives— *Neoceratodus* in Australia, *Protopterus* in Africa, and *Lepidosiren* in South America—the swim-bladder performs the function of a primitive lung. The swim-bladder develops in the embryo as an evagination of the anterior section of the digestive tract. Since the connection between the digestive tract and swim-bladder is preserved in adults as the "ductus pneumaticus," the air in the swim-bladder can permanently be replenished from the atmosphere by swallowing,

and oxygen can be absorbed into the blood through the walls of capillaries in the walls of the swim-bladder. This is a simple form of air breathing. Despite this fact, Dipnoi, too, do not meet all the criteria necessary to make them ancestors of land vertebrates.

The reasons are found in the anatomy of their Devonian representatives. Some of their structural features clearly separate them both from other fish-like vertebrates and amphibians. For instance, while the skull roof in the majority of vertebrates is formed from a pair of frontal bones and a pair of parietal bones, there is only an asymmetric mosaic of bones in lungfishes. Besides, Devonian "lungfishes" did not breathe atmospheric air; this is an ability they reached only in the Tertiary. Only then did Dipnoi have underdeveloped branchial arches, like in modern Dipnoi, indicating that besides vestigial gill respiration there was some sort of additional (i.e., lung) respiration. Devonian dipnoans, that is, dipnoans contemporary with amphibian evolution, all had fully developed branchial arches and no trace of reduction. This means that they still relied on gill respiration and depended fully on being in an aquatic environment.

In the first half of the nineteenth century, when only fossil Dipnoi were known, no one would have thought to consider them as amphibian ancestors. The view on relationships between

Dipterus, a lungfish (Dipnoi), can be excluded from the possible circle of amphibian ancestors. Dipnoi lack the teeth-carrying premaxilla, maxilla and dentary found in the majority of vertebrates where they form the characteristic tooth-bearing jaws. Instead, Dipnoi have so-called dental plates (after Forster-Cooper, 1937).

amphibians and Dipnoi was first expressed when living lungfishes were discovered in the middle of the last century. The discovery that they are capable of breathing atmospheric oxygen caused a sensation. However, a trivial mistake caused made in comparing living, instead of Devonian, dipnoans with amphibians. Therefore, Dipnoi can be eliminated from the list of potential amphibian ancestors.

The Lobe-Fin Fish Eusthenopteron

In the 1920s the paleontological excavations in Escouminac Bay, Canada, also known by its Native name, Miguasha, yielded a series of well-preserved three-dimensional fish-like vertebrate fossils, among them several specimens of the lobe-fin fish *Eusthenopteron* from the family Osteolepidae. One of these fossils was acquired

mammals. Stensiö's sensational discovery was this: *Eusthenopteron* had been almost "amphibian" but still in the "mantle" of a fish. Since then, a number of osteological matches have proven that crossopterygians were indeed amphibian ancestors. Although *Eusthenopteron* cannot be counted as a direct ancestor, it helped to document the anatomical characteristics that stood at the beginning of the evolutionary changes that led to the birth of amphibians. *Eusthenopteron* cannot be a direct ancestor because it was found in Greenland in the same geological layers as another vertebrate, called *Ichthyostega*; the latter already had the ability to move on land and must therefore be regarded as a creature halfway between fish and amphibian.

The anatomy of Devonian lobe-fin fishes pro-

The skull of Crossopterygian fish Eusthenopteron *with branches of the lateral line system. This superficial duct system contains groups of neuromasts, mechanical receptors that register movement in the water that penetrates into the duct via the pores.* Ichthyostega *and many other early amphibians have this lateral line organ in common and its structure strongly resembles that found in Crossopterygii. It is also present in amphibian larvae and in some aquatic amphibians (after Jarvik, 1980).*

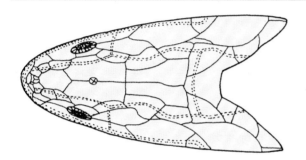
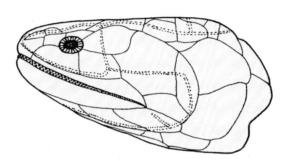

by Swedish paleontologist Erik Stensiö, whose studies at that time concentrated on the inner structure of the skull in primitive jaw-less fishes Agnatha. Stensiö realized that the outer appearance of the fish-like vertebrates was a result of their permanent life in water, and that the answer to the question whether lobe-fin fishes (Crossopterygii) were somehow related to amphibians lay in their internal anatomy. To this end, he decided to make the grinding sections of one of the valuable skulls of the *Eusthenopteron* specimens mentioned above, using Sollas' method to completely reconstruct the internal skull structure even if this process meant the destruction of the specimen. The method requires that an object be cut into extremely thin sections, much like slicing salami. The skull, approximately 5 inches (12 cm) long, was cut in 200 sections, each 60 micrometers thick, and each cut surface was photographed and enlarged. Then, discernible cranial structures were reconstructed as a model in wax. The entire process took 25 years and was completed in 1952.

But the effort had been well worth it. In the end, it proved that the inner structure of the crossopterygian skull displayed a number of similarities with corresponding structures in amphibians and higher vertebrates, including

vides some clues with respect to the ecological conditions in the time when vertebrates first colonized dry land. *Eusthenopteron*, for example, had a characteristically large tail fin and unpaired fins shifted to the end of its body. It was a predator who lay in wait for its prey, like a present-day pike, attacking with a rapid forward thrust. This kind of hunting strategy required the ability to remain motionless in one position. Maybe that is why *Eusthenopteron* and other Devonian crossopterygian fishes developed internal nostrils (choanae), that were an important evolutionary preadaptation for the

The question why choanae evolved in only one of the two phylogenetic lines of Crossopterygii remains unanswered. In one line, Rhipidistia, choanae are present, while in the other, Actinistia, of which the recent species Latimeria chalumnae *is a member, they are not only absent but never evolved in the first place ("Haus der Natur," Salzburg).*

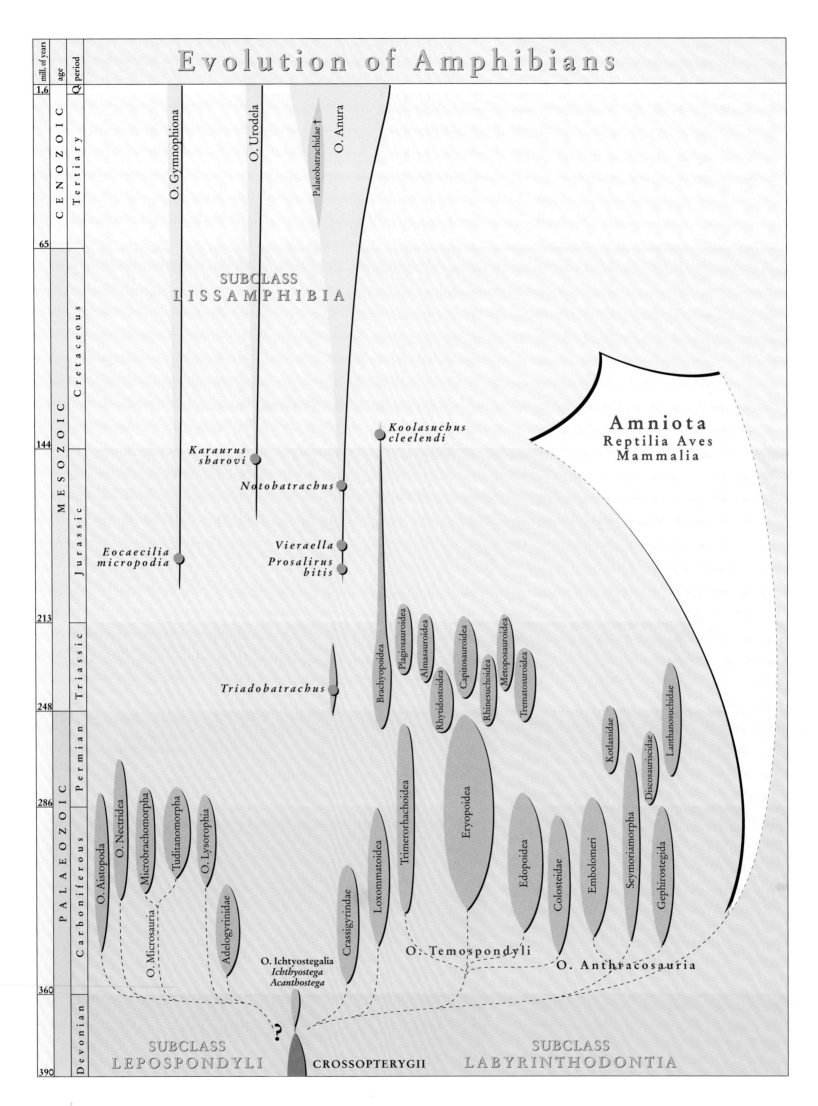

Evolution of Amphibians

mill. of years	age	Q period		
1,6		Q		

SUBCLASS
LISSAMPHIBIA

O. Gymnophiona

O. Urodela

Palaeobatrachidae †

O. Anura

Amniota
Reptilia Aves
Mammalia

Koolasuchus cleelendi

Karaurus sharovi

Notobatrachus

Eocaecilia micropodia

Vieraella
Prosalirus bitis

Brachyopoidea

Plagiosauroidea

Almasauroidea

Rhytidostoidea

Capitosauroidea

Rhinesuchoidea

Metoposauroidea

Trematosuroidea

Lanthanosuchidae

Triadobatrachus

Kotlassidae

Discosauriscidae

O. Aistopoda

O. Nectridea

Microbrachomorpha

Tuditanomorpha

O. Lysorophia

Trimerorhachoidea

Eryopoidea

Seymoriamorpha

Gephirostegida

Adelogyrinidae

Loxommatoidea

Edopoidea

Colosteidae

Embolomeri

O. Microsauria

Crassigyrinidae

O. Ichtyostegalia
Ichthyostega
Acanthostega

O. Temospondyli

O. Anthracosauria

?

SUBCLASS
LEPOSPONDYLI

CROSSOPTERYGII

SUBCLASS
LABYRINTHODONTIA

transition to life on land. Most fishes have two pairs of external nostrils, with no communication between the nasal cavity and the mouth cavity. Water enters into the anterior pair of them, flows along the olfactory epithelium of the nasal sac and then exits again through the posterior pair. But in Devonian crossopterygians the anterior opening of each side lies close to the edge of the upper jaw, and the posterior opening is connected to the mouth cavity. The alternating motion of the jaws and gill slits generates a flow of water that supplies oxygen to the gills; as a by-product in the choanate fishes, the same motion also forces a stream of water through the channel connecting the external nostrils with the internal nostrils (choanae) in the mouth palate. These internal nostrils or choanae are the basic prerequisite for subsequent "nose breathing" in dry-land vertebrates and thus for vertebrate land colonization.

But we should also ask whether internal nostrils—as seen in *Eusthenopteron* and in other Devonian Crossopterygii—are homologous to the external rear nostrils in fishes. There is neither paleontological nor embryological proof for an evolutionary shift of these nostrils from the outside of the skull to the internal roof of the mouth cavity. The argument has been made, however, that this shift not only is possible in theory, but did in fact occur, because the choanae in the oral cavity of the Devonian crossopterygian fishes are directly adjacent to the suture between the maxilla and praemaxilla (two bones of the upper jaw); this is the only position where such a shift could possibly take place. The search for amphibian ancestors should therefore concentrate on the group of Devonian crossopterygian fishes that possessed the choanae, the Rhipidistia.

Devonian crossopterygian fishes included some forms that had adapted to life in extremely shallow water. *Panderichthys*, found in the Devonian strata of Lithuania and Canada, was one. Similar to *Eusthenopteron*, this, too, was a cosmopolite, a fact that is of great importance for early amphibian evolution. *Panderichthys* had a dorsoventrally flattened head, with only the eyes peaking above its dorsal surface. This might be a clue that it lived in very shallow water with fluctuating water levels. One cannot fully exclude that it may already have been able to leave water for short periods of time.

Between Fish and Amphibian

Among those forms that can be considered transitional between lobe-fin fishes and amphibians, *Ichthyostega* has been studied in more detail than any other. The story of its discovery is a fascinating one and represents one of the most significant discoveries in paleontol-

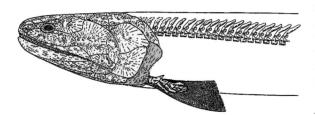

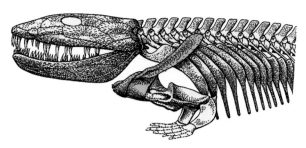

The separation of the pectoral girdle from the skull in the evolution of amphibians: the development of a neck region was an important step in the evolution of tetrapods.
Top: Eusthenopteron *(after Jarvik, 1980);*
Bottom: Ichthyostega *(after Jarvik, 1996).*

ogy and evolutionary research. From the early twentieth century onwards, numerous geological expeditions were undertaken to Greenland with the goal of charting the region and evaluating its mineral resources. At the beginning of the 1930s, Danish expeditions were led to the same area by young Swedish paleontologist Gunnar Säve-Söderbergh.

In 1931 a section of vertebrate tail was discovered: it was fish-like in character with scales and fin rays, but also exhibited some traits of a land-dweller—the lower fin rays were mechanically worn. Professor Stensiö, to whom this specimen was given, identified it as the "fragment of a fish-like vertebrate covered with scales." Further specimens, discovered at the same site the following summer, would turn out to be one of the greatest paleontological sensations of the century.

One should remember that in the 1930s the oldest amphibians known were all from the Lower Carboniferous. Hence it was a true sensation when a similar but far more complete finding surfaced the following year: a seven-toed hind extremity with pelvic girdle. It was soon evident that this animal had moved on land, which explained the worn lower part of the tail fin. As more findings followed, the entire body of the sensational animal was gradually assembled and reconstructed, with the exception of the fore legs. Säve-Söderbergh published his finding as soon as he was able to and named it *Ichthyostega*. The name translates loosely as "fish roof," because the roof of the skull was strongly reminiscent of that found in fossil fishes.

It is remarkable that the same region yielded further fossil vertebrates of approximately the same age, which were no longer fish nor yet typical land tetrapods. Erik Jarvik, another participant in the Greenland expeditions, described this form in 1952 under the name *Acanthostega*.

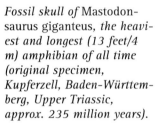

Fossil skull of Mastodon-saurus giganteus, *the heaviest and longest (13 feet/4 m) amphibian of all time (original specimen, Kupferzell, Baden-Württemberg, Upper Triassic, approx. 235 million years).*

Right: Reconstructed Mastodonsaurus. *Its huge mouth could open up to a 90 degree angle. The two fangs in the lower jaw projected upward through two openings located in front of the nostrils in the upper jaw ("Haus der Natur," Salzburg).*

Recently, English paleontologist Jennifer Clack studied extensive material all gathered on British expeditions to the same region of Greenland. She was able to fully reconstruct *Acanthostega. Ichthyostega* and *Acanthostega* are now the best-studied Devonian vertebrates and point the way to amphibians along a path whose evolutionary beginnings were already characterized by a surprisingly high degree of taxonomic diversification. Further Devonian findings in other regions have documented this clearly.

At the beginning of the 1980s fossil vertebrates were discovered in the Devonian strata near the town of Tula, approximately 180 miles (300 km) south of Moscow. The extremities of these vertebrates showed distinct digits, six on both anterior and posterior legs. The animal was named *Tulerpeton* after the site, but was too fragmentary for a full reconstruction. The evolutionary status of this species is therefore not fully understood; the same is the case for *Elginerpeton* from Scotland (Upper Devonian, near Scat Craig), which is documented mostly by the jaw-bones. Details of dentition indicate, however, that this animal had some fish-like features. Another form, described as *Obruchevichthys*, was discovered near Velna-Ala in Lithuania, as was yet another specimen near Novgorod, Russia, and originally classified into the family Panderichthyidae.

But the existence of fish–amphibian transitional forms is not only based on fossil skeletons. There are also fossil trackways preserved in Devonian deposits, which do not resemble the type of imprint one might expect from a fin, for example, footprints and small bone fragments in southern Australia (*Metaxygnathus*). Judging by these findings, there was a range of animal

forms worldwide in the Middle and Late Devonian (370 to 350 million years ago) with characteristics of both fish and amphibians. In any further consideration of the origin and early evolution of amphibians, the astonishingly high diversity of these forms and their widespread geographic distribution from Australia to Greenland are of utmost importance.

The Transition from Water to Dry Land

Which changes were necessary in the anatomy of fish to transform them into amphibians? Some of them emerge from comparative anatomy, such as respiration (gill to pulmonary respiration) and features linked to circulation. Others are proven through paleontological findings. On the basis of data now available, we are able to reconstruct quite precisely a sequence of anatomical changes that led from fish to amphibian, and see how these changes influenced their physiology, ecology and ethology. We are dealing with so-called mosaic evolution, where characteristics evolve at a different rate, some faster, others slower. This results in a pattern or "mosaic" of characters at different stages of evolution.

One of the primary changes is undoubtedly the transition from gill to pulmonary respiration. Surely this was not a sudden but a gradual change; present-day Dipnoi provide a quasi model view of this change even though, as we have noted, they are not linked to amphibian evolution. The lungs evolved from the swim-bladder, which originally performed a hydrostatic function. Since the walls of the swim-bladder are heavily vascularized with small capillaries and since the air in it is separated from the bloodstream only by an extremely thin cellular layer, the blood was enriched with oxygen and this led to respiration. In these early phases, air was swallowed and reached the swim-bladder via the intestine-swim-bladder tract (ductus pneumaticus). Air reached the oral cavity mostly through the external nares and internal choanae. Gradually changes followed in the circulatory system—namely, the separation of body and pulmonary circuits, and subdivision of the heart.

Numerous changes occurred in the skeleton. For instance, *Ichthyostega*'s ribcage was solid, in contrast to fish, whose ribs are thin. This was caused by the fact that the body of *Ichthyostega* was subject to gravity, whereas the body weight of fish is supported by the buoyancy of water and pressure is distributed evenly across the body's surface.

The transformation of the extremities is an excellent example of gradual evolution. Paired fins can be regarded as a polydactyl extremity in which the number of digits gradually diminished. *Ichthyostega* still featured seven toes on the hind limb, *Tulerpeton* six, and only true amphibians had the pentadactyl, a five-toe extremity typical of land tetrapods, diminished even further to four in the fore extremities of frogs. Upon looking at the timeline of this evolution, we find that the transformation of the fish fin into the extremity of a land tetrapod required approximately 9 million years. The weight-bearing and locomotory function of the extremities was made possible by the fact that they were joined to the axial skeleton (i.e., the spine), with fundamental differences between fore and hind limbs.

In the lobe-fin fishes the anterior extremities are still directly attached to the skull, more specifically to the rear margin of its dermal part (dermocranium). The joint is formed through a bone called the scapulocoracoid (which ossifies from the cartilage) fused to the inner surface of the dermal bone, called the cleithrum; the articular fossa that accommodates the head of the short and robust humerus is on the posterior surface of the scapulocoracoid. The pectoral fin projects from the ventral section of the posterior margin of the skull, as it does in other fish. This fin position would have been impractical for movement on land, for which the mobility of the head also needed to increase. For these two reasons the complex that included anterior extremities (pectoral fins) separated from the skull and gradually shifted along the spine to the rear. This resulted in the development of the pectoral girdle and of the anterior movable section of the vertebral column, the neck. During the first phase of adaptation to life on land, the supracleithra gradually diminished as well; one need only look at *Ichthyostega* and *Acanthostega*, although both still featured a

cleithrum. The most important dermal elements of the pectoral girdle in amphibians are the clavicula and the cleithrum, but the entire pectoral girdle is now—in contrast to fish—connected to the skull and the axial skeleton only by muscles.

Entirely different is the situation with the abdominal fins. In fish, they are anchored to a small pelvic girdle that is not connected to the spine, but instead imbedded in the trunk musculature. This has also been well documented in *Eusthenopteron*. *Ichthyostega* already had a well-formed triangular pelvic girdle with a fully formed articular fossa (acetabulum) to receive the head of the femur. Dorsally, this girdle was already syndesmotically joined to the ribs of the sacral vertebrae. In all tetrapods the pelvic girdle is readily divided into three sections: the dorsal bone fixed to the spine is called the ilium, the fore ventral bone is called the pubis and the rear ventral bone is called the ischium. The acetabulum is always between all these three bones. Thus the pelvis evolved into a horizontal, half-cylindric structure that is closed on the ventral side and whose dorsal ends are joined on the outside to the sacral vertebrae.

Noticeable changes occurred in the formation of the vertebrae. In fish, the intervertebral articula-

Upper jaw (middle) and lower jaw of Mastodonsaurus giganteus *("Haus der Natur," Salzburg).*

In contrast to modern amphibians, Ichthyostega *had an impressive array of teeth. The sometimes long and pointed teeth were arranged in two rows (after Jarvik, 1996).*

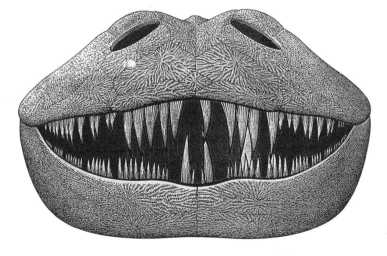

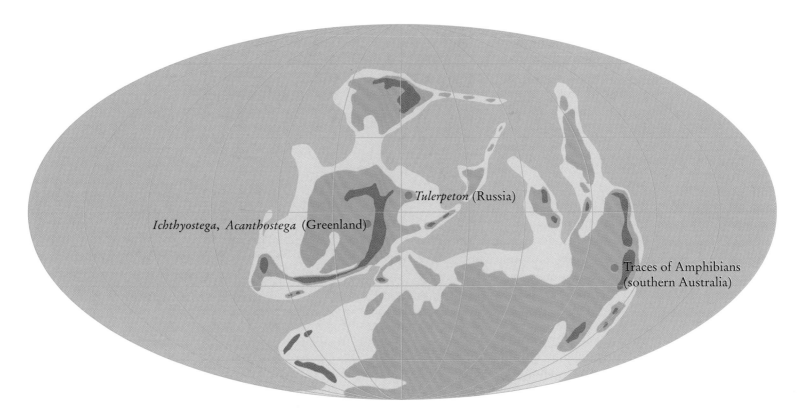

Ichthyostega, Acanthostega (Greenland)

Tulerpeton (Russia)

Traces of Amphibians
(southern Australia)

tion is very simply constructed because the neighboring vertebrae are in contact with one another by the entire surface of the vertebral body. While this structure limits the mobility and flexibility of the skeleton, it is fully sufficient for fish. For life on land, however, away from water's buoyancy, the spine must cope with completely different stresses and loads. Two powerful articular surfaces developed between the neural arches (which enclose the spinal cord) of neighboring vertebrae; those pointing anteriorly are called the praezygapophyses, whereas those on the hind surface of vertebra are the postzygapophyses. These joints improved mobility in the spine.

Other Changes Associated with Land Colonization

The origin of pulmonary respiration was accompanied by a transformation or reduction of the branchial arches, also noticeable in the simplification of the pattern of the dermal bones of the skull. Clearly the bones of the gill cover—the opercular, praeopercular and subopercular—became less important and receded over time. *Ichthyostega* still featured tiny vestigial praeoperculars and suboperculars while, in *Acanthostega,* they had already disappeared completely. The skull remained otherwise unchanged, at least as far as its roof was concerned.

Considerable changes took place, however, in the inner parts of the skull, that is, in the parts that are formed from cartilage (chondrocranium). As we have already mentioned, the first major change to take place was in the branchial or gill arch elements. As in all fish, Crossopterygii, too, had a hyoid arch behind the jaws. Its robust dorsal element, the hyomandibular, was located near the capsule of the inner ear. Ventrally, the hyoid arch continued in the large ceratohyal and small hypohyal, which were originally located on the ventral side of the gill basket. From the amphibian onwards, the hyomandibular is no longer connected to the ventral elements of the hyoid arch. In *Ichthyostega,* and even in amphibians from the Carboniferous, the hyomandibular had approximately the same size and shape as in crossopterygian fishes. As tetrapods evolved, it changed gradually into a small rod-like element, called the columella auris, which is capable of transmitting sound from the outer environment to the inner ear. It is the single element in amphibians, reptiles and birds, while mammals have two additional auditory ossicles.

From the ceratohyal, that is, from the element of the lower section of the hyoid arch to which remnants of the subsequent branchial arch were joined, the main part of the hyoid (i.e., the skeleton that supports muscles of the tongue) evolved in tetrapods. The movable tongue is an organ that appeared for the first time in amphibians, playing an important role in feeding. When land vertebrates take in food, it rests on the floor of the mouth cavity because of the earth's gravity. The food must somehow be transported from the mouth down the gullet and this function is performed by the tongue, a mobile muscular organ attached to the hyoid and in part to the inner surfaces of the lower jaw. The development of the lingual skeleton and the mobile tongue are yet another illustration of the changes necessary as vertebrates shifted from aquatic life to life on land.

Another important change occurred in the internal anatomy of vertebrates. This process is called the blockage of ossification and is best demonstrated by comparing the skull of a fish to the skull of an amphibian. The inner parts of a fish skull are formed by bone that arises from cartilage, and this, in turn, arises from soft connective tissue. In amphibians the sequence tissue –> cartilage –> bone tends to arrest at the stage of cartilage. Only few sections of this inner part of the skull (called the chondrocranium or endocranium) actually ossify, for example, the sphenethmoid, prooticum and the occipital. The other structures, including a major part of the palatoquadrate, remain in the cartilaginous stage.

Surprisingly, no changes touched vertebrae. There are many similarities in the structure of vertebrae in Devonian amphibians and lobe-fin fishes. A well-developed notochord is present in both; it is surrounded ventrally by the intercentrum and dorsally by a pair of the pleurocentra. Hence each body of vertebra is composed of several elements.

Ecological Aspects of Amphibian Origin

Let's look at the transition of vertebrates onto dry land in terms of the environment in which it took place. One important event was the appearance of the first terrestrial plants at the end of the Silurian more or less concurrently with the time when the first invertebrates colonized land (end of the Silurian/beginning of the Devonian). The plants, which soon covered the land surfaces during that age, enriched the earth's atmosphere with oxygen. Geochemical investigations have shown that the oxygen content in the Devonian was as high as 35 percent, much higher than today's 21 percent. This was probably why the Early Devonian was marked by unusual incidents of adaptive radiation. Within nearly all animal groups new lineages emerged—including Crossopterygii and Dipnoi. Adaptive radiation was therefore not limited to the terrestrial environment.

Today, we can only guess at what prompted fishes to move onto land. Was it the abundance of invertebrates (the main diet of present-day amphibians) who covered the land in the wake of the adaptive radiation mentioned above? This hypothesis fails to convince because *Ichthyostega* and *Acanthostega* were mostly fish eaters. American paleontologist Romer convincingly presented another hypothesis on why vertebrates colonized land. He argued that frequent droughts forced the crossopterygians to abandon desiccated ponds in search of other water sources. This led—at least according to Romer's hypothesis—to an evolutionary paradox: lobe-fin fishes adapted to life on land as a result of

their efforts to remain in water. The interpretation is also supported by current observations of fish behavior (not only recent lungfishes) in bodies of water that are drying out. There is an evidence that a long period of aridity occurred in the Devonian. Still, one shouldn't imagine heavy, one-meter-long fish trying to move on land. This behavior probably evolved first in juveniles, who are more adaptable than the adults. Paedomorphosis may have been another factor in land colonization. It is generally understood as a shift of capability to reproduce into the earlier stages of ontogeny (individual development). This phenomenon is well documented, for example, in recent salamanders.

Lessons from Paleogeography

It is very interesting to look at the origin of amphibians in context of paleogeography. For a long time, it was assumed that amphibians evolved in the Northern Hemisphere, or Laurasia, the northern *Ur*-continent, which has been the most prolific region for paleontological discoveries: the crossopterygian fishes *Eusthenopteron* and *Panderichthys*, the so-called transitional forms *Ichthyostega* and *Acanthostega*, and the findings of primitive amphibians from the Early Carboniferous were all found in this region. This, in combination with knowledge gained from comparative anatomy and developmental biology, led scientists to the conclusion that amphibians evolved from a single group of crossopterygian fishes. However, subsequent discoveries have modified this assumption because amphibian trackways from the Middle and Late Devonian were found in Australia, which was then part of the southern supercontinent called Gondwanaland, separated from Laurasia by sea. More recently still, new findings point to an unexpectedly diversified amphibian fauna from the Lower Carboniferous of Australia. This means that the process of anatomical transformation of fish to amphibians took place across a huge area of the entire tropic circle of that age, which stretched from present-day Greenland to eastern Europe, Southeast Asia, Australia, and back to the Northern Hemisphere. The position of this prehistoric tropic circle can be determined by reconstructing the position of the magnetic poles of that time with the help of geophysical methods; the results confirm what we already know from paleontological evidence on the distribution of early amphibians and their crossopterygian ancestors.

What conclusions can we draw from these observations, especially from the fact that transitional forms and early amphibians were so diversified in the geographically distant tropical zones of that age? They evolved from the freshwater crossopterygian fishes whose vast range

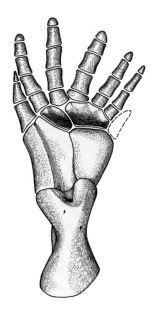

The Devonian tetrapod
Ichthyostega *combined fish and amphibian characteristics. It has been one of the most important palaeontological discoveries.* Ichthyostega's *extremities were already differentiated and corresponded to the basic structure found in tetrapod extremities (from Benton, 1990, after Jarvik).*

of distribution, from present-day Greenland to Australia, separated by sea at that time, suggest that they could hardly have been taxonomically identical everywhere. Therefore it seems reasonable to assume that amphibians evolved from several phylogenetically different groups of crossopterygian fishes living in distant geographical regions.

In fossils the precise boundary between fish and amphibian is extremely vague and it is difficult to say whether *Ichthyostega* was "more amphibian" than its contemporary *Acanthostega*. What is probable is that the evolution of early amphibians was a product of diversity in their ancestors—the crossopterygian fishes of the subgroup Rhipidistia—preceding the actual evolution of amphibians *per se*.

Early Amphibians

As has been noted, it is difficult to draw a clear line between fish and amphibians in the Devonian. The situation changes drastically, however, when we compare fish with the amphibians of the Carboniferous. The latter already had unique adaptations which enabled them to live on land, and reached a high degree of morphological diversity. These early amphibians already included the group that later evolved into reptiles.

The fact remains, however, that there is a considerable time gap between the Devonian transitional forms and Early Carboniferous definitive amphibians with no paleontological record. At the end of this period the amphibians emerged in an evolutionary stage in which they existed for a staggering 200 million years, until the Early Cretaceous.

In the Northern Hemisphere, numerous sites with amphibian fossils have been discovered in Euramerica, a large continent in which present-day Europe and North America were united at that time. Especially well documented are amphibians from the Early Carboniferous. Even then, amphibians had splintered into two distinct phylogenetic lineages: Labyrinthodontia and Lepospondyli. Labyrinthodontia—as their name indicates—have specially formed teeth (a superficial layer of tooth, dentin, is folded like a labyrinth) and include a distinct group called Temnospondyli ("with divided body of vertebra"). In the region of present-day Europe, the Temnospondyli were represented by the genus *Pholidogaster* and in North America by *Greerpeton*. *Caerorhachis*, too, belonged to the Temnospondyli, although its exact taxonomic position within this group is still not quite clear. In addition to Temnospondyli, Labyrinthodontia in the Early Carboniferous included also other forms whose distinguishing feature were orbits

strangely shaped like keyholes; these amphibians are classified into the family Loxommatidae.

In addition to these readily classifiable forms, there were others with unusual features, which made them more difficult to classify. One of them is *Crassigyrinus*, with tiny legs and a snakelike body elongated to 50 inches (130 cm). The head—especially the preorbital section of the skull—was noticeably shortened. This amphibian was a permanent water dweller and a predator that fed exclusively on fish. Its phylogenetic position and relations to other amphibians are still hotly debated. Some argue that this was an advanced amphibian that returned to permanent life in water, while others maintain that it represents a primitive form that had not yet reached the evolutionary stage of life on land. As to its phylogenetic relations to other amphibians, it is generally regarded as a phylogenetic lineage that died out without descendants.

Besides labyrinthodont amphibians classified as Temnospondyli and Loxommatidae, another well-defined amphibian group existed in the Early Carboniferous, the Anthracosauria. Later, by the end of the Carboniferous, reptiles evolved from this group of amphibians; that is, the vertebrates completely independent on water. The main representatives of the Anthracosauria were *Eoherpeton*, *Westlothiana*, *Whatcheeria* and *Proterogyrinus* from Scotland, Iowa and West Virginia. *Westlothiana* shared so many features with reptiles that it was even classified among the reptiles for a certain time. Lepospondyli—after Labyrinthodontia the second largest group of Carboniferous amphibians described so far—displayed an evolutionary innovation in the form of a compact, undivided body of vertebra. The Early Carboniferous Lepospondyli are represented by the genera *Lethiscus*, *Adelogyrinus*, *Adelospondylus*, *Dolychopareias*, *Palaeomorgophys* and *Acherontiscus*.

All fossils mentioned up to this point were found in the Northern Hemisphere. This was a decisive factor to the wide-spread view that early amphibian evolution was limited to this hemisphere. However, Early Carboniferous amphibians recently discovered in northeast Australia point to the existence of highly diversified amphibian assemblages in geographically remote areas of the Southern Hemisphere; they are classified into the temnospondyl (i.e., labyrinthodont) family Colosteidae and the Anthracosauria.

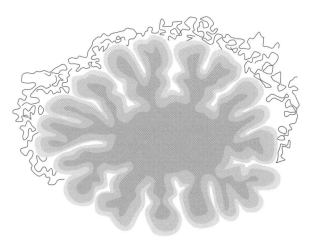

Extinction of Lepospondyli

The first major crisis to hit amphibians occurred in the Early Permian. This was the extinction of the Lepospondyli—one of the major lineages in amphibian evolution. They included bizarre forms, and some authors believe that they stood in no phylogenetic relation to the lobe-fin fishes grouped in the Rhipidistia. Many of them had an extremely elongated, snakelike body with up to 230 vertebrae and vestigial extremities. Others had no legs whatsoever. Many features indicate that most of them were permanent water dwellers. Lepospondyli seem to have evolved into a highly specialized group of amphibians within a very short span of time, only to become extinct soon after. Some paleoherpetologists argue that they survive in present-day limbless caecilians. However, this argument cannot be proven since the period between the Early Permian and the Early Jurassic (to which the earliest caecilian fossils have been dated) was a long stretch for which no fossils have been found that might document such a relationship.

Successful Labyrinthodontia

Labyrinthodontia, on the other hand, survived the mass extinction at the end of the Permian, brought on by deterioration of climate in terrestrial ecosystems, without any visible damage. During this crisis, the most severe in the history of vertebrates, numerous invertebrates and vertebrates died out, including groups that were widely distributed and very successful during the Paleozoic.

Labyrinthodont amphibians of the group Temnospondyli were among successful survivors. As early as the Carboniferous, some temnospondyl phylogenetic lineages became dominant, for example, those represented by the genera *Edops* and *Eryops* with a body length of up to 59 inches (150 cm). These were primitive forms, which is proven by their large columella, the only auditory ossicle in amphibians. On the other hand, another group of temnospondyls, previously called Rhachitomi, produced several progressive forms, many of them described from the Late Carboniferous and Early Permian deposits of the Czech Republic (e.g., *Cochleosaurus, Chelyderpeton*).

Rhachitomi, like other Triassic temnospondyls, inclined to paedomorphosis (abbreviated development), probably caused by climate deterioration toward the end of the Permian. Their larvae did not mature into fully developed adults, and in some the adult stage was eliminated altogether if their larvae became capable of reproduction (a phenomenon called neoteny). This has been proven in many findings of larval but fully ossified skeletons. A completely ossified skeleton is a sign of sexual maturity. Among these findings are *Doleserpeton* from North America, and European forms gathered under the name *Branchiosaurus*, as well as the Triassic amphibians *Capitosaurus* and *Dvinosaurus*. All have short skull, large orbits (eyeholes), and reduced mouth palate that are characteristic for temnospondyl larvae. Recent Anura exhibit a similar skull structure, which has led some to argue that they evolved from Permian and Early Triassic paedomorphic Temnospondyli.

A special group among Paleozoic temnospondyl amphibians are Plagiosauria. Although their vertebrae consisted of two parts as in other Labyrinthodontia, they are different in the position of the boundary between them. Plagisaurs had a short, wide skull, and impressions of their

One important factor in the argument for Crossopterygii as ancestors of early amphibians is their internal tooth structure. In Rhipidistia, as well as in all known Labyrinthodontia (but not in Lepospondiyli), teeth display a characteristic plication in the wall. This is called a "labyrinthodontine" structure. To the left, section of an Eusthenopteron *tooth (after Benton, 1990).*

The massive ribs of Ichthyostega *indicate the need for protecting the thoracic cage or chest and the body cavity against the compression that results from crawling across land. The largest ribs were located immediately behind the heavy skull, decreasing in size until they terminated just in front of the pelvic girdle.*
Below: Greerpeton *from the North American Carboniferous is a representative of the Colosteidae. It had a well-developed lateral line organ and was aquatic (after Carroll, 1988, from Jarvik, 1975, and Godfrey, 1986).*

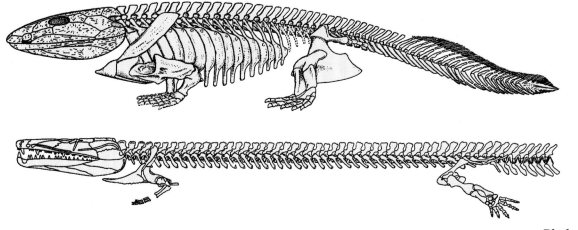

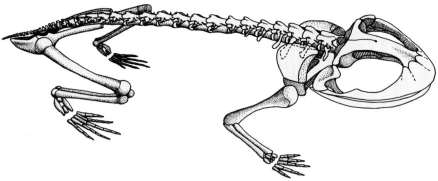

Triadobatrachus massinoti *from the Triassic is the oldest finding of a frog-like amphibian. It probably belonged to an extinct sister group of recent Anura (after RAGE & ROCEK, 1989).*

Right: Eocecilia micropodia *from the Jurassic is the oldest fossil discovery of a Caecilian. These creatures still had tiny extremities; in recent Caecilians neither extremities nor pelvic girdles remain (after JENKINS & WALSH, 1993).*

*The South American tongueless frog (*Pipa arrabali*) is a member of the family Pipidae, of which many fossil findings exist. Many findings date from the Cretaceous.*

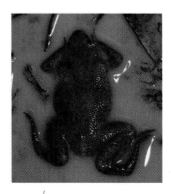

external gills have often been found, which indicates their neoteny.

Besides Temnospondyli, Anthracosauria were also successful amphibians from the Early Carboniferous onwards, and in the Late Carboniferous they gave rise to reptiles. Embolomeri were among the dominant anthracosaur groups. Their intercentrum surrounded the chorda like a ring, and both pleurocentra fused into the ring. These were predominantly aquatic predators (e.g., *Diplovertebron*), while others were adapted to life on land and resembled lizards. One of the latter, *Gephyrostegus*, corresponds to reptile ancestors. Seymouriamorpha, too, were advanced labyrinthodonts—their skeleton was so similar to a reptile skeleton that they were thought of as primitive reptiles for a long time. Only discoveries of their larvae with well-developed external gills proved that they had been amphibians. Numerous representatives of the anthracosaur family Discosauriscidae are known from the Late Carboniferous and Early Permian deposits of Central Europe.

Labyrinthodontia survived the crisis at the end of the Triassic and are documented in Jurassic sediments of Asia and Australia. They survived into the Cretaceous, which is evidenced by findings in Australia. The last survivor was described as *Koolasuchus cleelandi* (Brachiopoidea, Temnospondyli). In summary, Labyrinthodontia can be regarded as an unusually successful group: they lived from the Late Devonian (if we include *Ichthyostega* and *Acanthostega*) until the Early Cretaceous, that is, altogether 230 million years. All present-day amphibians and reptiles evolved from them.

The Origin of Modern Amphibians

At the end of the Permian, a worldwide climate shift occurred in whose wake 75 percent of existing amphibian families and 80 percent of reptile families became extinct. The climate shift had its greatest impact on ectotherms because it involved dramatic drops in temperatures. These resulted in greater seasonal differences, which meant shortened periods of activity and prolonged periods of hibernation for amphibians. The shortening of the breeding season

influenced larval development, because lower temperatures—possibly accompanied by frequent dry spells—meant that the larval phase lasted longer. When cooler weather began before metamorphosis, larvae were forced to hibernate. And when these climatic conditions persisted over long periods of time, the gonads may well have been fully developed even before the metamorphosis was completed. In other words, sexual maturity was reached as early as in larvae. In some forms the adult stage was eliminated altogether. This phenomenon is called neoteny and is quite frequent in various groups, especially among amphibians. As we have already mentioned, these mechanisms played a very important role, especially in the origin of Anura. That Anura evolved from labyrinthodont ancestors is easily proven in a comparison with larval Labyrinthodontia. One of the diagnostic features of frogs and other modern amphibian groups is noticeable underdevelopment of the skeleton. Such reductions are evident in the temnospondyl larvae. We can readily imagine how the skull of a temnospondyl larva transformed into the skull of a frog, as a number of fossils offer paleontological proof of this process.

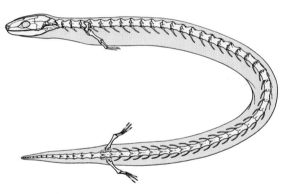

Anurans have yet another feature that distinguishes them from all other amphibians: their frontals and parietals are merged into one single element called the frontoparietal. This advanced stage in the evolution of the Anura is documented by *Triadobatrachus* from the Lower Triassic of Madagascar. Its skeleton represents an intermediate stage demonstrating the transition from the labyrinthodonts to anurans. Its skull is difficult to tell apart from a frog's or toad's skull; its postcranial skeleton, on the other hand, is reminiscent of labyrinthodont ancestors. As anurans evolved, the spine shortened and the number of presacral vertebrae decreased. At the same time, the ilium lengthened toward the posterior, which ensured a certain minimum distance between anterior and posterior extremities. There seems to exist some biomechanical reasons why this minimum distance must be maintained. The skeleton of *Triadobatrachus* shows that it was not yet capable of jumping; instead, it moved forward by means of crawling.

After *Triadobatrachus* comes a gap of more than 30 million years for which we have no fossil evidence of the Anura, although this period was vitally important: it was during this time that the definitive shape and anatomy of Anura were established and they spread across the world. The oldest representative of a "true" anuran is *Prosalirus bitis* from the Early Jurassic. Its pelvis indicates that these frogs already performed saltatory movements. Other anurans from the Jurassic can be classified into the families Leiopelmatidae (*Vieraella*, *Notobatrachus*) and Discoglossidae (*Eodiscoglossus*); both families have survived up to the present time. The family Pipidae is also an ancient group of the Anura, although its contemporary representatives (*Pipa*, *Xenopus*) derive from the original anuran scheme.

When we assess the evolution of Anura, it is obvious that they were particularly successful amphibians despite their "conservative" nature. One needs only consider the fact that their definitive anatomy was established 200 million years ago, that is, or at the time the first dinosaurs appeared. Although Anura, and especially their larvae, are sensitive to environmental changes, they survived the mass extinction at the end of the Cretaceous. The only group of Anura to die out were the Palaeobatrachidae. The uniform anatomy and morphology of the anurans are rooted in their mode of life. Therefore, evolutionary diversification is expressed, above all, in their ecology and reproduction strategies.

Caudata ("tailed amphibians") have an underdeveloped skeleton too. However, their frontal and parietal have remained as independent bones, and they have a tail, which is also an original feature of their ancestors. Moreover, the larvae of Caudata have teeth (teeth are lacking in anuran tadpoles). Like in the Anura, in the tailed amphibians, too, neoteny was the most important mechanism of their evolution and, among their contemporary representatives, neoteny is still quite common. Neoteny, as an evolutionary factor, can be traced in the European Tertiary salamandrids, when from fully developed adult forms (e.g., *Chelotriton*) living in Eocene tropical climate evolved, as a result of the Oligocene drop of temperature, neotenic larvae (*Brachycormus*). From *Brachycormus* evolved the recent genus *Triturus*. Among well-known Oligocene neotenic larvae also belongs *Andrias* (hellbender), which has survived until the present. It is obvious that Caudata are a highly adaptable group that survived the extinction at the end of the Mesozoic, as did Anura. All representatives of recent and fossil Caudata originate in Laurasia and have amphicoelous and opisthocoelous vertebrae. Only a short time ago, a possible representative of Caudata (but with

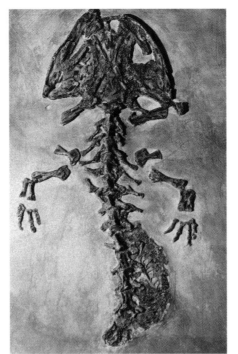 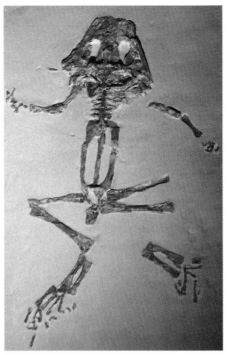

procoelous vertebrae) was discovered from the Cretaceous of Gondwanaland, in Bolivia.

Caecilians (Gymnophiona) are the third group of present-day amphibians. Their recent representatives are limbless and do not have the shoulder and pelvic girdles, while fossil caecilians (e.g., *Eocaecilia micropodia*) still display tiny extremities. The aforementioned genus *Eocaecilia* from the Early Jurassic in Arizona is the earliest known caecilian and it is remarkable that the earliest known anuran *Prosalirus* was also found in the same site. Gymnophiona are therefore at least as old as are Anura. With their small legs, fossil caecilians resemble some salamanders, although they are readily distinguishable from them by their complete skull roof. Findings of fossil caecilians are extremely rare. A new, as yet unnamed, finding from the Lower Cretaceous of Bolivia has been reported, and fossil evidence also exists for the genus *Apodops* from the Paleocene of South America.

Left: The giant salamander Andrias scheuchzeri. In 1726, Swiss doctor and natural scientist Johann Jakob SCHEUCHZER (1672-1733) interpreted a fossil of this kind from the Öhningen quarries as a human remnant from the time before the Flood ("Homo diluvii testis: skeletal remains of human drowned in the Flood.")

Top right: Skeleton of giant frog Latonia seyfriedi. (Both reconstructions; "Haus der Natur," Salzburg. Öhningen in Baden-Württemberg, approx. 13 million years ago).

The oldest amphibian fossils

The oldest known amphibian fossils are *Ichthyostega stensioei* Säve-Söderbergh, 1932 and *Acanthostega gunnari* Jarvik, 1952. Both are from Greenland (Mount Celsius) and date back to the same age (Upper Famennian, Upper Devonian, circa 350 million years). *Ichthyostega* was approximately 1 yard (1 m) long and still had some fish characteristics (fishtail, remnants of opercular bones), but obviously moved on land. *Acanthostega* was somewhat smaller and lived in water.

The oldest known Anura is *Prosalirus bitis* Shubin and Jenkins, 1995 from the Lower Jurassic in North America (Pliensbachian, circa 180–185 million years), Gold Spring Quarry, Arizona, USA. Isolated skeleton fragments were discovered.

The oldest known Urodela is *Karaurus sharovi* Ivakhnenko, 1978 from the Upper Jurassic (circa 150 million years) in southern Kazakhstan.

The oldest known caecilian is *Eocaecilia micropodia* Jenkins and Walsh, 1993 from the Lower Jurassic (Pliensbachian, circa 180-185 million years) in North America, Gold Spring Quarry, Arizona, USA. The skull and parts of the postcranial skeleton with rudimentary extremities were discovered.

Diversity in Amphibians

Jörn Köhler,
Frank Glaw and
Wolfgang Böhme

The term "biodiversity" is often confused with "species diversity." Biodiversity is far more inclusive and describes diversity in all aspects of biology—that is, the morphological, physiological, ethological, ecological and genetic diversity in populations, species or higher taxonomic categories.

The Significance of Research on Diversity

Research on systematics and taxonomy, largely ignored in an era of genetics and biochemistry, is experiencing a comeback under the modern designation "research in biodiversity." This resurgence answers an urgent need, for a few years ago it became apparent that only a small percentage of the earth's species diversity was scientifically known. Since 1758, the official beginning of zoological nomenclature, some 1.7 million species have been described. Today, the actual species pool has been estimated to include anywhere from 10 to 100 million species. At the same time, it is becoming increasingly evident that the near future will bring species extinction on a scale that has occurred only a handful of times in the earth's history. In other words, innumerable species will become extinct before we will have had the opportunity to study and know them.

The species that remain hidden from scientific and general knowledge are by no means inconspicuous insects or worms. Major groups of vertebrates are still unknown. Today, more than 5,000 amphibian species have been described, and the number increases on a yearly basis by approximately 70 to 100 newly discovered species. Never before has the rate of discovering new amphibian species been as great. Since 1994 the number of known recent amphibian species is larger than that of mammals (approximately 4,700 species). With some 4,370 species (as at the end of 1997), frogs and toads (Anura) are by far the most diverse group; only one-tenth (436 species) are salamanders (Urodela), and a mere 163 species are counted among the caecilians (Gymnophiona).

With the exception of oceans, amphibians inhabit a variety of zones, from deserts to the subpolar region, from sea level to snow line, every imaginable type of fresh water, from the ground right up to the highest treetop. Amphibians seem to have once again reached a level of diversity comparable to their first "golden age," the Carboniferous and the Permian. Equipped with lungs and limbs, they were the first vertebrates to leave water in the Devonian, some 350 to 360 million years ago, and to occupy the land masses previously uncolonized by vertebrates. In the process they developed an enormous diversity in form and species, including representatives that were several yards/meters in length and had very little resemblance to present-day amphibians. The fossil evidence of Paleozoic amphibians ends with the Triassic, but amphibians did not become entirely extinct. The first frog-like creature appears in the Triassic in Madagascar, still sporting a short tail, but already displaying the first signs of a saltatory mode of life. In the Jurassic, many recent frog families already existed, such as tongueless frogs (Pipidae) and disk-tongued frogs (Discoglossidae). Salamanders and caecilians followed in the Cretaceous. From that time forward, amphibians experienced a second golden age that has lasted into the present.

Differences in Diversity

Amphibians need water. It comes as no surprise then that the moist environment of the tropics is home to their greatest diversity. High temperatures and constant access to water (precipitation) create ideal conditions, and the number of amphibian species increases the nearer one gets to the equator. But in reality the situation is far more complex and should be examined not only against the background of current climatic conditions. Instead, past climatic changes must also be considered, since they often created environments that were hostile to amphibian survival and caused the extinction of many species.

Climatic change has the least impact on mountain slopes, where flora and fauna simply wander uphill when temperatures increase, or downhill when they decrease. In other words, mountain slopes act as climatic buffer zones that offer a refuge and help curb species extinction in times of climatic change. This is why we can still observe the greatest diversity of amphibians on humid mountain slopes, such as the Andes in South America or in eastern Madagascar. The gigantic rain forests in South America's Amazon basin or Africa's Congo basin, on the other hand, are inhabited by comparatively fewer species.

Of all zoogeographic regions, the Neotropics—that is, the tropical and subtropical region in Central and South America—display by far the widest amphibian diversity. Over two-thirds of

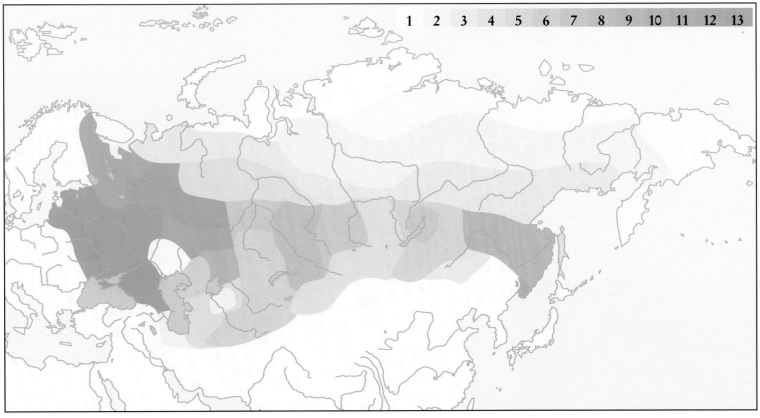

all newly described amphibian species in the last 10 years originate from that region. Of course, current species descriptions do not necessarily reflect the true status of existing species diversity, because different levels in research intensity should also be considered. Research may be more intensely focused in Latin America than in Africa and Asia. Nevertheless, current studies show that there still is no end in sight to the discovery of new species in tropical South America. It is therefore probable that amphibian diversity is most concentrated in the Neotropics. Many areas in South America present a high degree of diversity: 84 species near Santa Cecilia (Ecuador), 67 species near Panguana (Peru), 72 species near Cocha Cashu (Peru). By contrast the diversity falls drastically as we move toward more temperate latitudes. Across Europe, from Portugal to the Ural Mountains, there are only 35 Anura species, and Germany is home to a mere 14 anuran and 6 urodele species.

Comparison of amphibian species diversity in the United States and the former Soviet Union. Large areas of the states of the Soviet Republic have a very low diversity in species, which is understood as a result of the predominantly cold climate in those regions where 47 percent of land surface is subject to permafrost. Altogether only 41 amphibian species occur across an area that covers more than 8.4 million square miles (22 million square kilometers). In the southeastern United States the diversity in species is much higher. The increase in species to the southeast is especially noticeable: these are regions with a warm climate and high levels of precipitation. On the southern tip of Florida the number of species declines again, a result of the so-called peninsula effect. This hypothesis postulates that the diversity in species declines on the tips of large peninsulas (after Kuzmin, 1996, and Duellman and Trueb, 1986).

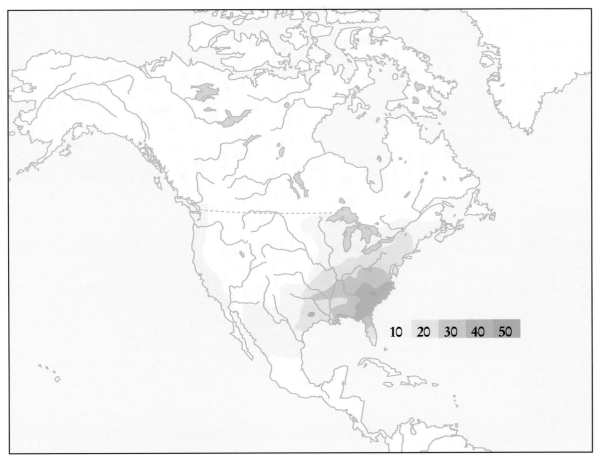

CAECILIA (GYMNOPHIONA)		
FAMILY	NUMBER OF	
	GENERA	SPECIES
1 Caeciliidae RAFINESQUE-SCHMALTZ, 1814	21	88
2 Ichthyophiidae TAYLOR, 1968	2	37
3 Rhinatrematidae NUSSBAUM, 1977	2	9
4 Scolecomorphidae TAYLOR, 1969	2	5
5 Typhlonectidae TAYLOR, 1968	5	20
6 Uraeotyphlidae NUSSBAUM, 1979	1	4
TOTAL (status: end of 1997)33	163	

Hypogeophis rostratus *(Caeciliidae).*

Distribution of Caecilians

URODELA		
FAMILY	NUMBER OF	
	GENERA	SPECIES
1 Ambystomatidae HALLOWELL, 1856	2	32
2 Amphiumidae GRAY, 1825	1	3
3 Cryptobranchidae FITZINGER, 1826	2	3
4 Dicamptodontidae TIHEN, 1958	2	7
5 Hynobiidae COPE, 1859	8	41
6 Plethodontidae GRAY, 1850	29	280
7 Proteidae GRAY, 1825	2	6
8 Salamandridae GOLDFUSS, 1820	16	61
9 Sirenidae GRAY, 1825	2	3
TOTAL (status: end of 1997)	64	436

Plethodon jordani *(Plethodontidae).*

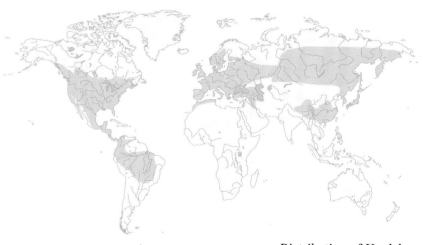

Distribution of Urodela

Siphonops annulatus (Caeciliidae) lives in the tropical regions of South America.

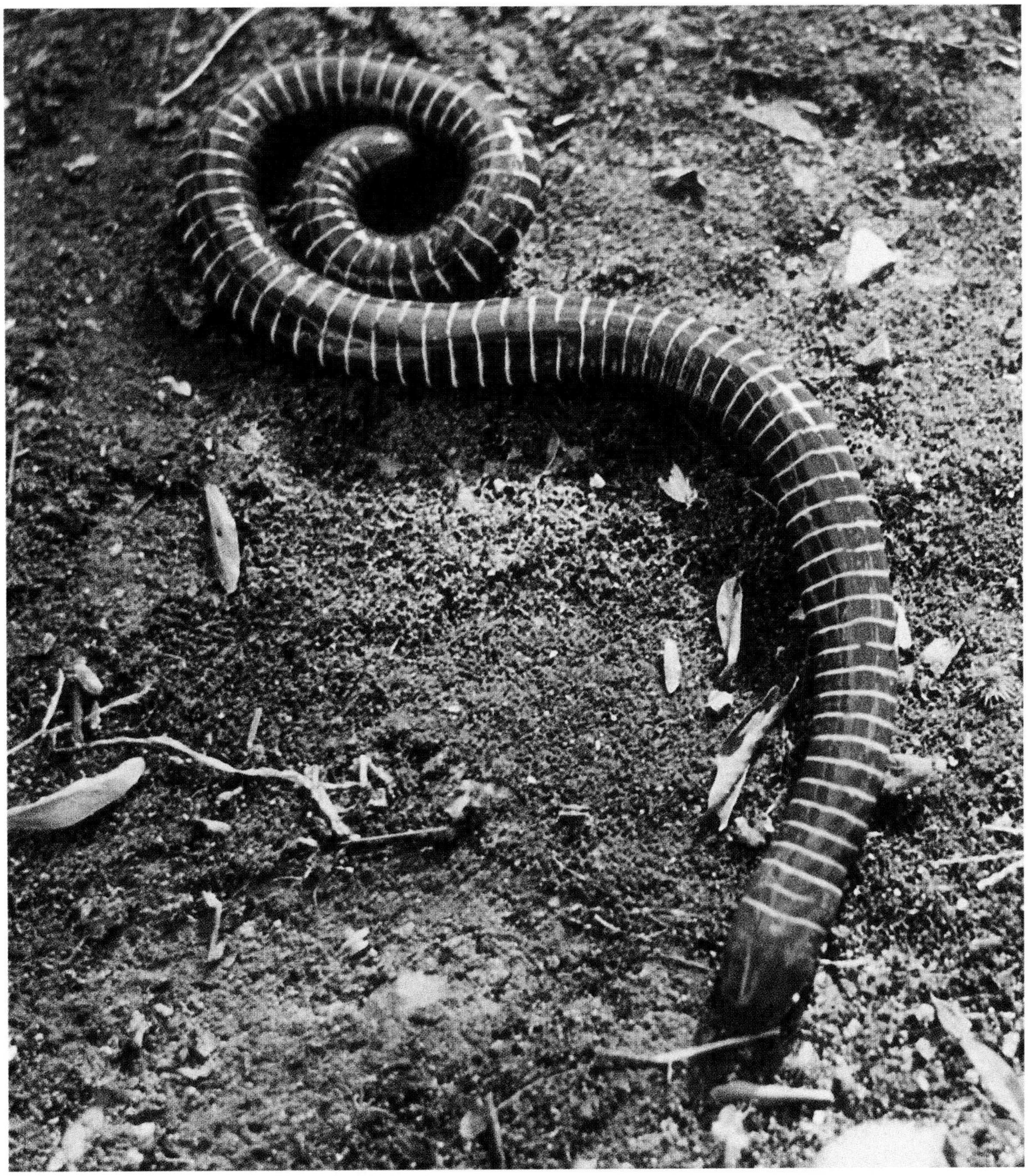

tail; there is, however, a terminal scale. The eyes are relatively large; the distance between eye and tentacles varies, but the tentacles are never positioned right in front of the eye.

The recently described caecilian *Atretochoana eiselti* does not have a lung, a unique phenomenon among caecilians. In salamanders, on the other hand, all species of the family Plethodontidae are lungless. Aquatic caecilians are—as far as is known—viviparous; they are born as fully metamorphosed young. The large external gills are absorbed prior to birth. The larvae are nourished in the paramesonephric tract with so-called uterine milk (thick secretions from the ovarian epithelia). In males, the anal region is modified like a suction disk for the purpose of holding fast during copulation.

6. Family Uraeotyphlidae Nussbaum, 1979

This small Indian family has only one genus (*Uraeotyphlus*) with four species. Uraeotyphlidae have many characteristics in common with Ichthyophiidae, although they are cladistically more closely related to the higher Caeciliidae. A short tail is one of the primitive characteristics; scales in the skin and a high number of cranial bones are others. On the other hand, some derived or secondary characteristics are also present: an inferior mouth opening, large distance between eyes and tentacles, and no tertiary annuli. The premaxillae are not fused to the nasal bones.

Representatives of this family stay relatively small, growing to a maximum length of 12 inches (30 cm). They are predominantly dark gray to brown in color. Very little is known about the mode of life and reproduction of the four species in the genus *Uraeotyphlus*. Evidence of a larval phase has not been found. They are probably oviparous like Ichthyophiidae and Rhinatrematidae, with direct development. There is no fossil evidence of this family.

Salamanders (Caudata, Urodela)

This order has the most primitive body shape of all amphibians and tetrapods. Their characteristics are founded in retrogression and multiple adaptations to various modes of life. The long bodies, tails and snaking movements are most strongly reminiscent of the original amphibians that colonized land. They lead a fairly cryptic life in a variety of habitats. Salamanders are most common in the moderate latitudes of Eurasia and North America, reaching their greatest diversity in species in the United States. In Central and South America the most diverse of all urodele families, the lungless salamanders, are the only salamanders to inhabit the tropical zones of the Southern Hemisphere. Urodela have adapted surprisingly well to extreme habitats—one need only think of the mysterious blind olms who spend their lives in eternal darkness, of the neotonous axolotls, of sirens, amphiumas (or congo eels), or the various tree-climbing newts and salamanders. In contrast to the Anura (frogs and toads), Urodela reproduce mainly by means of internal fertilization with the sperm being carried into the female in spermatophores.

Urodela blend into their natural environment. On the whole, they are small, although this order also includes the largest living amphibian, which grows to 31 inches (180 cm). They often go unnoticed and live a hidden life in their various habitats. No "salamander chorus" draws attention to them. Newts and salamanders differ from the much more numerous frogs and toads in a number of ways. The features by which they are most easily differentiated and that have also given them their name are the tail and an elongated body, with the length of the tail sometimes greater than the length of the body. Like lizards, some species can cast off their tail in moments of danger and grow a new one. With a few exceptions (*Siren, Amphiuma*), all Urodela have two pairs of short limbs, with front and hind limbs approximately identical in length (making the leaps and bounds that are typical of Anura

impossible in this order). The number of fingers is usually four, the toes five. Their eyes are small, and in some species (*Proteus*) even reduced. Tympanum and middle ear are absent.

Urodela do, however, have ribs, and the costal grooves are clearly visible. Their skin is moist and glandular, with some species producing powerful toxins. They regularly shed their skin. In recent Urodela, the skeleton, especially the skull, is less ossified than in their fossil ancestors; sections of the supporting structure consist of ossicles. In some species the lungs may be reduced (*Ranodon, Onychodactylus*, Hynobiidae) or altogether lacking (Plethodontidae). The phenomenon of lung reduction is present mostly in species that inhabit fast-flowing bodies of water as a means of reducing buoyancy and thus the risk of being swept away.

With the exception of the primitive forms, Urodela reproduce by internal fertilization (spermatophores). The large cloacal gland in males plays a role in the production of spermatophores. Urodela often exhibit complex mating behavior. Most species are oviparous and some are ovoviviparous. The larvae have external gills, gill slits and true teeth, but their body shape is not very different from the adult's. Many Urodela have a tendency toward paedomorphosis. During this process the frontal limbs develop and are the first to be visible.

1. Family Ambystomatidae Gray, 1856 (Mole salamanders)

This family, best known by its representative the axolotl (*Ambystoma mexicanum*), currently contains 32 recent species classified into two genera (*Ambystoma, Rhyacosiredon*). Their habitat is restricted to North America. The position of the family in the systematics of the order is still uncertain because of a lack, thus far, of clearly defined derived characteristics. There are some similarities with the Plethodontidae, although most characteristics match the primitive state of the Salamandroidea. The majority of species

The salamander-like Ambystoma tigrinum *(Ambystomatidae) is a member of the same species-rich genus as the paedomorphic axolotl (*Ambystoma mexicanum*). The 32* Ambystoma *species are spread across North America.*

(with the exception of paedomorphic forms) spend most of the year on land, buried in the soil, moving to water only for mating and spawning. The body is robust and stocky, the head broad. The maximum body length is approximately 13 inches (35 cm) (*Ambystoma tigrinum*). The eyes are relatively small. The name derives from the palatine teeth, arranged in lateral rows in the roof of the mouth. The costal grooves are very noticeable. Males tend to have longer tails and swollen cloaca. The limbs are strongly formed with four fingers and five toes. The vertebrae are amphicoelous. Most species have lungs, although some species feature lungs that are strongly reduced in size. Larvae have four gill slits and long gills, adults usually no gills. Obligatory and facultative neoteny is fairly common in this family (in 10 of the 30 species). *Ambystoma taylori* inhabit brackish water. Some species wander during the spawning period, usually in spring, although some species do so in fall. Two species are triploid (gynogenetic); some practice brood care and larval hibernation. The current area of distribution has yielded fossil mole salamanders from the Oligocene and Pleistocene (*Amphitriton* Rogers, 1976, and the recent genus *Ambystoma*).

2. Family Amphiumidae Gray, 1825 (Congo eels)

This highly specialized North American family, represented by a single genus (*Amphiuma*) with three species, exhibits numerous unusual characteristics. One of these is the elongated, eel-like body with tiny limbs and one, two or three fingers and toes in different species (*A. pholeter, A. means, A. tridactylum*). Congo eels are nocturnal and predominantly aquatic, inhabiting both stagnant and flowing waters; they rarely venture onto land. Their position within the systematics order is uncertain, as is the case for other paedomorphic groups. Metamorphosis in congo eels is incomplete with different organs developmentally arrested to varying degrees. Adults have a fully metamorphosed skin—very smooth as a result of the secretions from numerous skin glands—but they lack eyelids (as all larvae do); they have four branchial arches, with a gill slit between the third and fourth branchial arch, but no external gills. A very long windpipe leads to the lung. Their Erythrocytes are among the largest of all vertebrates (75 x 40 μm). The pectoral and pelvic girdles are greatly reduced, the vertebrae amphicoelous. Eggs are usually laid close to water into a depression on land, with a maximum of 150 to 200 eggs per nest and the female guarding the nest. The larvae hatch at 1.75 to 2.5 inches (45 to 64 mm) length; they have external gills and are apparently swept from the nest either by rainwater or by rising water levels. Fossils dating back to the Cretaceous, the Palaeocene, Miocene and Pleistocene have been discovered in North America (*Proamphiuma* Estes, 1969, and the recent genus *Amphiuma*).

Important morphological and morphometric characteristics of Urodela *(after Nöllert and Nöllert, 1992)*

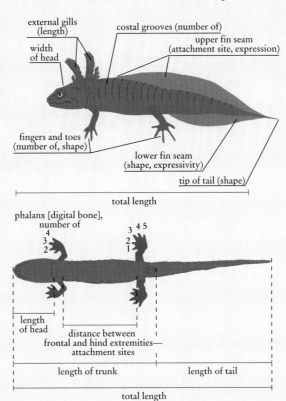

Trunk length: *from tip of snout to rear end of cloaca.*
Tail length: *from rear end of cloaca to tip of tail.*
Total length: *sum of first two lengths.*
Head width: *measured at broadest section of head.*
Length of frontal and hind extremity.
Length of longest finger/toe.
Length of cloacal region.
Length of parotide gland: *length of this gland.*
Width of parotide gland: *greatest length measured vertically to previous dimension.*

Larvae
Gill clefts: *slit-shaped opening from forearm to external wall on both sides of posterior skull section. Between the gill clefts lie branchial arches which support the gill filaments as respiration organs.*
Length of gills: *Urodela larvae have up to three pairs of external gills.*

Adults
Costal grooves: *grooves found in many Urodela between the ribs on the lateral sides of the trunk (number of; in larvae and adults).*

Fin seam: *position of front appendage, shape of upper and lower fin seam, shape of tail end (in larvae and adults).*
Parotides: *presence, size, shape.*
Spur: *some Urodela species have a spur between the dorsal crest and the tail fin seam.*
Rib protuberance: *number of.*
Nasolabial groove: *small groove on both sides of the head from nostril to upper lip. Very distinct in some Plethodontidae and protruding past the lip in a cirrus.*
Cloaca: *joint exit of*

hind-gut (anus) and urinary and genital ducts and the cloacal gland typical of Urodela males. It produces the gelatinous material for the creation of spermatophores, pheromenes, which play a role in sexual behavior and other scents important for territory marking. Urodela with internal fertilization have especially complex and (in males) large cloaca. The cloaca of the female is smaller and its function is different.
Dorsal gland crest: *distinctive row of skin glands on the backs of some species.*
Indenture between dorsal crest and upper tail fin seam.
Shape of tail in cross-section: *in aquatic species, laterally flattened; in terrestrial species often rounded.*
Webs and fringes: *expressivity.*

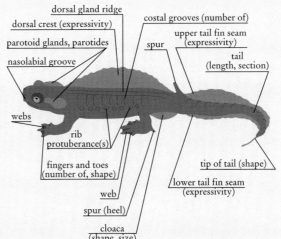

The congo eel Amphiuma means *(Amphiumidae) occurs in the southeastern United States and is predominantly aquatic. Its extremities are severely reduced and in this species terminate in two fingers and two toes.*

Distribution of Amphiumidae (after Duellman and Trueb, 1986).

Right: Distribution of Dicamptodontidae in North America and Proteidae in southern Europe (after Duellman and Trueb, 1986).

Distribution of Cryptobranchidae in North America and South East Asia (after Duellman and Trueb, 1986).

3. Family Cryptobranchidae Fitzinger, 1826 (Giant salamanders)

Giant salamanders are permanent larvae; their total maximum length of 5.9 feet (1.8 m) makes them the largest extant amphibians. Today they appear only disjunctively in the eastern United States and in East Asia, represented by two genera (*Andrias*, *Cryptobranchus*) and three species. The gill slits are closed externally; internally two branchial arches are present, one on each side. Giant salamanders are aquatic in oxygen-rich moving waters. Their metamorphosis is incomplete: while the gills regress, other larval characteristics remain. Some cranial bones are missing. Adults, like other salamander larvae, have no eyelids and retain their larval teeth. They have a very large mouth and tiny eyes. *Andrias davidianus* is the largest and heaviest extant amphib-

Cryptobranchus alleganiensis *(Cryptobranchidae) from the eastern United States.*

ian, said to reach up to 6 feet (1.8 m) in length. One 45-inch (115-cm) specimen weighed in at 23 pounds (10.5 kg). The paired egg-strings are laid in spaces between rocks and are externally fertilized; *Andrias* practices brood care. In captivity, they can reach an advanced age (50 to 60 years). Their meat is considered a delicacy, one of the reasons why this is an endangered species. Fossils of recent genera dating back to the Palaeocene, Miocene and Pleistocene have been discovered in North America, Asia and Europe. Fossil representatives of the genus *Andrias* reached up to 90 inches (230 cm) total length.

4. Family Dicamptodontidae Tihen, 1958 (Giant salamanders)

This small family with seven species divided into two genera (*Dicamptodon*, *Rhyacotriton*) occurs exclusively in western North America. Two subfamilies are distinguished: Dicamptodontinae (*Dicamptodon*) and Rhyacotritoninae (*Rhyacotriton*), whereby the two lines are (probably) polyphyletic in origin. Good and Wake (1992) have elevated Rhyacotritoninae to the rank of family. The position of this family in amphibian systematics was debated for a long time; giant salamanders were usually classified as a subfamily of the Ambystomatidae. *Rhyacotriton* was also linked to the Plethodontidae. In the latter case, the similarities are, however, more likely related to convergences caused by paedomorphosis. Giant salamanders are aquatic, occurring in cold flowing water up

to 5,900 feet (1,800 m) above sea level. They are predominantly nocturnal and reach a maximum body length of 13.7 inches (35 cm) (*Dicamptodon*). The body is robust with strong limbs; the eyes are lidded. The number of costal grooves ranges from 12 to 14. The vertebrae are amphicoelous; the columella is unattached. The premaxillae are paired; septomaxillae and lacrimalae are also present. Nasal bones, pterygoid and the lung are reduced in *Rhyacotriton* and well developed in other species (*Dicamptodon*).

The eggs are laid in cold, fast-flowing water on top of or beneath rocks. The embryonic phase can last up to nine months and two to four and a half years may pass until metamorphosis. The larvae have four pairs of gill slits and short gills. Five genera are documented by fossil findings (*Ambystomichnus* Peabody, 1954; *Bargmannia* Herre, 1955; *Chrysotriton* Estes, 1981; *Geyeriella* Herre, 1950; *Wolterstorffiella* Herre, 1950) from

the North American Palaeocene (Eocene, Pliocene) and in Europe (Palaeocene and Upper Miocene).

5. Family Hynobiidae Cope, 1859 (Asian salamanders)

This primitive salamander family with 8 genera and 41 species is distributed across Central and East Asia. *Salamandrella keyserlingii*, or Siberian salamander, is the only species that has reached Europe (in a small area near the town of Gorki).

In appearance, these salamanders are similar to European newts. They are relatively small (4 inches/10 cm), although some species grow to 8 inches (20 cm). Keratinization is often present on fingers and toes (so-called amphibian claws). The larvae have external gills and four gill slits. The palatine teeth are arranged in a V-shape. Most species have lungs, which can be reduced in mountain species (a frequent phenomenon in these species). Adult representatives of most Asian salamanders live on land or are partially amphibic, and this may be the reason why their lungs are well developed. Other species live in flowing water (e.g., the genus *Onychodactylus* with two species) and are lungless.

Asian salamanders are mostly nocturnal. They

have external fertilization; the eggs are laid in two gelatinous egg-sacs that are attached to rocks or plants in stagnant water, or in moving water for some species. While *Ranodon* does form spermatophores, the females do not absorb them, but lay their eggs onto the spermatophores. In some species the males guard the eggs. To date, no fossil Asian salamanders have been discovered.

6. Family Plethodontidae Gray, 1850 (Lungless salamanders)

The largest and most diverse salamander family, with 280 species in 29 genera, is distributed across the New World with one exception: seven species of the genus *Speleomantes* (cave salamanders) survive as a Tertiary relict in southern Europe. The most important and name-giving characteristic of the family is the absence of a lung. All gas exchange in lungless salamanders is effected by means of skin and mouth-cavity respiration. Hence there are few problems with respect to systematics. Some species (e.g., *Desmognathus fuscus*) have rudimentary lungs. Externally, adults (i.e., metamorphosed) representatives of the Plethodontidae can be recognized by a groove with glands between the nostril and the upper lip (nasal-labial groove), which is sometimes elongate and cirrate in the male. Two subfamilies are recognized: Desmognathinae (related to dusky salamanders, *Desmognathus*, *Leurognathus*, *Phaeognathus*) and Plethodontinae (woodland salamander relatives, all other genera). The high species diversity corresponds to the wide ecological tolerance and the range and diversity in habitats that can reach up to 11,980 feet (3,500 m) above sea level. Lungless salamanders live in and near stagnant and flowing bodies of water; some cultivate more terrestrial habitats either in the ground or in caves. Other species climb onto vegetation and colonize hollowed-out

Distribution of Hynobiidae in Asia and Ambystomatidae in North America and Mexico (after Duellman and Trueb, 1986).

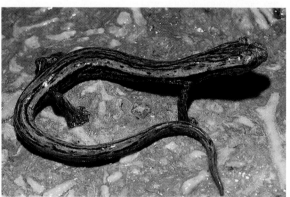

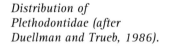

tree trunks or bromeliad cups. Body size varies from about 1 inch (2.5 cm) (*Thorius*) to more than 10 inches (25 cm) (*Pseudoeurycea bellii*). The body shape tends to be elongate, and the limbs are relatively small, even thin and weak in some species. Many species have a long tail that can be shed and regrown. Maxilla and premaxilla are present; in some genera they display secondary reduction. There are no lachrymal sacs or pterygoids. Some species have protrudible tongues. The vertebrae are amphicoelous or opisthocoelous. The Desmognathinae are characterized by a unique mouth-opening mechanism.

Eggs are generally laid in water (Desmognathinae and eight other plethodontine genera); these forms also have aquatic larvae. Other genera have direct development without aquatic larvae; the eggs are often deposited on land. In many such species the female (or the male, although this is rare) practices brood care. Paedomorphosis is more frequent, and in *Haideotriton* and *Typhlomolge* it is obligatory. For some recent genera (*Aneides, Batrachoseps, Desmognathus, Gyrinophilus* and *Stereochilus*) fossils have been discovered from the North American Miocene and Pleistocene.

7. Family Proteidae Gray, 1825 (Olms)

Olms are aquatic, elongate neotenes represented by two genera (*Proteus, Necturus*) and six species. For intrafamilial systematics, some authors have suggested separating *Proteus* and *Necturus* into separate families. But numerous similarities indicate that they are closely related. *Proteus* lives exclusively in parts of southeastern Europe; the only range of *Necturus* is restricted to North America.

Proteus has a very elongate body. The *Necturus maculosus* reaches a total length of 16 inches (40 cm) with very small limbs. In five species of the genus *Necturus* toes are reduced to four. As neotonous forms, olms also have external gills and very simple lungs. The skull consists mostly of ossicles and displays some bone reduction. Uniquely, this family has no maxillae, nasal bones and prefrontals. The vertebrae are amphicoelous. In *Proteus*, the eyes have regressed in

An unusually elongated body with tiny extremities is the special characteristic of Oedipina sp. (Plethodontidae) from Central and South America. Some species of this genus can grow to 9.8 inches (25 cm) in length and are among the largest lungless salamanders.

adaptation to life below ground in caves. *Necturus* live in above-ground bodies of water; they have small, lidless, but functional eyes and are predominantly nocturnal. Olms live and reproduce in water; eggs are laid on stones and water plants. Fossils of recent Paleozoic and Pleistocene genera have been found in North America, and two additional fossil genera: *Mioproteus* Estes and Darevsky, 1978, from the Caucasian Miocene, and *Orthophyia* Meyer, 1865, from the German Miocene.

Distribution of Salamandridae (after Duellman and Trueb, 1986).

8. Family Salamandridae Goldfuss, 1820 (Gold-striped salamanders and newts)

Sixteen genera and 61 species comprise this family, which has a wide distribution across North America, Eurasia and Northern Africa. Gold-striped salamanders and newts can be recognized by the arrangement of their palatine teeth in an undulating row along the roof of the mouth. This clearly establishes their position within salamander systematics. Gold-striped salamanders and newts have a very diverse biology. They are predominantly terrestrial, although some are amphibian or even permanent water dwellers who are active at dusk or are nocturnal.

Their body shapes are quite varied: long and slender to stunted, with the total length varying from 2 inches (5 cm) to more than 12 inches (30 cm); the limbs are well developed. The vertebrae are opisthocoelous. Lungs and eyelids are fully developed. In terrestrial species the tail is rounded, in aquatic species slightly flattened on the sides. Costal grooves are only moderately visible. The skin secretions in some species are poisonous.

Most species are oviparous (e.g., *Triturus*); some are also ovoviviparous. The eggs are laid in stagnant or flowing waters. *Salamandra salamandra* (European, or spotted salamander) is ovoviviparous and the larvae are deposited into small creeks. *S. atra* (Alpine salamander) as well as

Mertensiella luschani antalyana are viviparous in adaptation to life in the mountains. Neoteny is rare in this family. The larvae have four gill arches and large, external gills. Numerous fossil forms are known from the Eocene to Pleistocene across the range in those ages (*Archeotriton* Meyer, 1860; *Brachycormus* Meyer, 1860; *Chelotriton* Pomel, 1853; *Koalliella* Herre, 1950; *Megalotriton* Zittel, 1890; *Oligosemia* Navas, 1922; *Palaeopleurodeles* Herre, 1941; *Procynops* Young, 1965 and others).

Impressive "wedding attire" of a Triturus vittatus ophryticus male (Salamandridae).

Male of alpine newt (Triturus alpestris, Salamandridae) in spawning pigmentation.

9. Family Sirenidae Gray, 1825 (Sirens)

This exclusively New World family currently has two genera (*Pseudobranchus*, *Siren*) with three species. Their position in salamander systematics is uncertain because a number of primitive characteristics relate them to Cryptobranchoidea and some derived characteristics link them to the more highly evolved Caudata. Moreover, they display a number of paedomorphic and some primitive and derived characteristics. Some systematists have even suggested classifying them in an order of their own (Trachystomata). These elongated, eel-shaped neotenes with a maximum body length of 37 inches (95 cm) have tiny forelimbs located just behind the external gills. The hind limbs (including the pelvic girdle) are

absent. The tail is short, the eyes small and lidless. Adults have gill openings, external gills and lungs. In *Pseudobranchus* only one pair of gill openings and three fingers are present, in *Siren* three paired gill openings and four fingers. Maxillae are absent, as are premaxillary teeth, and the maxillary ridges are covered in a horny sheath. The vertebrae are amphicoelous. The males have no cloacal glands and are therefore unable to produce spermatophores; sperm pouches are accordingly absent in the females. Hence, it is unclear what the method of fertilization is. The eggs are attached individually or in small clumps to submerged vegetation in water. Sirens can survive periods of aridity buried in mud.

Some fossils have been found, among them representatives of the recent genus *Siren* beginning in the North American Eocene, through to the Pleistocene, and *Pseudobranchus* from the Pliocene and Pleistocene in Florida. The fossil genus *Habrosaurus* Gilmore, 1928 has also been described; fossil remnants of this genus are already known to date back as far as the Cretaceous period (approx. 130 million years ago).

Distribution of Sirenidae (after Duellman and Trueb, 1986).

Frogs and Toads (Anura)

Anura—simply known as "frogs" to most people—are the most successful of the three recent amphibian orders. They have produced the greatest diversity not only in number of species (nearly nine-tenths of all known amphibian species are frogs and toads), but also in geographic distribution, which is far greater than that of either salamanders or caecilians. They populate all continents with the exception of Antarctica. Anura are found in nearly all habitats from seacoast to high mountains, dry steppes and desert. Their greatest number of species, however, occurs in tropical rain forests. This is where 80 percent of all anuran species live and where new species are regularly described. The Anura were the first vertebrates, filling nature with calls and "song" long before birds.

Anura display a number of strong differences from newts and salamanders—among others, the absence of a tail, the saltatory mode of movement, and their loud vocalizations. Of these, the first two (no tail and leaping motion) are based in their evolutionary context: for most basal vertebrates the tail plays an important role in movement, while it would be rather more of a hindrance for jumping.

The ability to jump as the typical movement in Anura has in some families regressed in the "toad typus." The tail is present only during the larval phase, regresses during metamorphosis, and is completely absent in adults. The tail vertebrae are fused into a urostyle. Further details on the anatomy of Anura are contained in the chapter "Biology and Physiology."

Frogs and toads are very different in appearance from salamanders and caecilians. Their body is far stouter and shorter, reflected in the number of vertebrae. Only five to nine presacral vertebrae are present—in most cases eight. By comparison, salamanders have up to 100 and Gymnophiona up to 300 vertebrae. The hind limbs of frogs and toads are generally longer and more muscular to facilitate jumping.

Most anuran species reproduce through external fertilization; only *Ascaphus truei* has a copulation organ for internal fertilization, while *Mertensophryne micranotis* and some species of *Nectophrynoides* and *Eleutherodactylus* effect internal fertilization by means of pressing the cloacal together. The impressive diversity in modes of life and reproductive strategies of Anura are presented in the chapter "Ecology and Ethology."

1. Family Allophrynidae Goin, Goin and Zug, 1978

The South American monotypic genus *Allophryne* (the only monotypic family in the systematics presented here, aside from Rhinophrynidae) are classified with the tree frogs (Hylidae, subfamily Hylinae) by many authors, including Duellman and Trueb (1986). The *Allophryne* differs from the Hylidae because of the toothless maxilla and premaxilla, and the absence of a cartilage omosternum in the pectoral girdle that is present in the Hylidae. Savage described the family as early as 1973 but did not establish a clear diagnostic difference from the Hylidae; therefore the name Allophrynidae remained invalid at the time. Dubois (1986) classified *Allophryne ruthveni* among the Bufonidae (as the subfamily Allophryninae).

Distribution of Allophrynidae in South America and Arthroleptidae in Africa.

2. Family Arthroleptidae Mivart, 1869 (African tropical frogs)

This purely African family with 74 species and 7 genera was introduced as a family by Dubois (1981). Most of their anatomical characteristics correspond with those of the Ranidae. Duellman and Trueb (1986) classify them as two subfamilies (Arthroleptinae with three genera and Astylosterninae with five genera) of the true frogs (Ranidae). Laurent (1979) refers the two subfamilies to the family Hyperoliidae. According to Poynton and Broadley (1985) the genus *Schoutedenella* Witte, 1921, is synonymous to *Arthroleptis*. *Arthroleptis* and *Cardioglossa* (classified into one subfamily, the Arthlopetinae) have horizontal pupils; the other genera (subfamily Astylosterninae) have vertical pupils. The males in several *Arthroleptis* and *Cardioglossa* species have a noticeably elongated third finger ("bush squeakers"), a secondary sex characteristic unique among the Anura.

The Smallest and the Largest Anura

At ¹⁄₃ inch (1 cm) the Cuban *Eleutherodactylus limbatus* is probably the smallest Anura. The adults of this species are smaller than European grass frogs or common toads after metamorphosis.

The goliath frog *Conraua goliath* of the family true frogs (Ranidae), which dwells in West African rivers, is the largest Anura. It grows to a body length of 15.7 inches (40 cm) (without extended hind legs) and a weight of 7.2 pounds (3.3 kg). This makes it approximately the same size as a newborn baby. Its thighs are about the same size as a human wrist.

Important Morphological and Morphometric Characteristics in Anura

Larvae

Spiracle: *paired or unpaired tubular opening of the gill region in tadpoles. Water taken in with respiration is ejected through this opening (position, distance to front and end of larva).*

Peristome: *totality of structures in the peristome of tadpoles with different keratinous bills or maxilla; upper and lower lip, rows of labial teeth and papilla on the margins of the mouth or taste buds (number, placement and shape of rows to teeth, also important indicators of larval feeding habits).*

Eye: *position and size.*

Anal tube: *position.*

Fin seam: *position of frontal protuberance, shape of upper and lower fin seam and shape of tail end.*

Adults

Tympanum: *three-layered membrane covering the middle ear and serving to receive sound waves. In most Anura, the tympanum can be seen as a round surface behind the eye. In others (e.g., Pelobates, Bombina, Rhinoderma) it has undergone a secondary reduction (position, diameter, distance to eye).*

Laryngeal sacs: *laryngeal sacs are protrusions of the oral fundus in varying shapes. In principle the following laryngeal sacs are differentiated: 1. singular, median, jugular; 2. bilobate, median, jugular; 3. paired, jugular; 4. paired, lateral (position, shape, number, size).*

Parotides (Parotis-, Parotoid- or ear glands): *large, usually bulging gland complexes behind the eyes and above the tympanum region. They differ from species to species and are especially large in toads, salamanders and some leaf frogs. When stimulated or in danger, they produce a milky, defensive or even poisonous secretion (size, form, position).*

Claspers: *claspers are dark, rough skin callouses in the males of many Anura and Urodela. They are especially noticeable before and during the spawning season. They serve to facilitate the amplexus when the male holds the female. In Anura they are particularly common on the first finger (thumb callouses or claspers), on the inner and—less often—the outer sides of the other fingers, on toes, lower arm, foot, chest or, rarely, abdomen. Some species may even develop claspers on the lower jaw (expressivity, position, shape, size, degree of pigmentation).*

Heel tubercle: *also called metatarsal tubercle. Inner tubercle on the tarsus of some Anura, characteristic used for species identification. Shape, size, relation to first toe. Some metatarsal tubercles may grow quite large.*

Dorsal gland crest: *also called subdorsal crest, distinctive row of skin glands on the backs of many Anura species. Often distinguished by different coloring (expressivity; distance to shoulder area).*

Shape of pupil: *the pupil is the central opening in the iris. It can be round, a vertical or horizontal slit, or elliptical, triangular or Y-shaped (heart-shaped as in Bombina).*

Webs: *webs are stretchable pieces of skin between the fingers and toes. They can be full, i.e., reaching to the terminal phalanx, or partial.*

Tips of fingers and toes: *shape, expressivity, fixation disks.*

Lateral row of warts.

upper row of teeth · labial teeth · keratinous maxilla · peristome · lower row of teeth · papilla at edge of mouth

eye (position, size) · upper tail fin seam (attachment site, expressivity) · tip of tail (shape) · spiracle (position) · anal tube (position) · lower tail fin seam (shape, expressivity)

total length

length of lower thigh

length of trunk

external heel tubercle

a — length of 1st toe
b — length of inner heel tubercle
1–5 — number of fingers and toes

a – distance tip of mouth — nostril
b – distance nostril — front ridge of eye
c – nostril — diameter
d – eye diameter
e – distance rear ridge of eye — tympanum
f – tympanum — diameter
g – length of head
h – length of mouth (a+b+c)

a – distance between nostrils
b – distance nostril — front ridge of eye
c – distance between eyes
d – eye diameter
e – width of head

eye (shape of pupil) · mouth (shape) · laryngeal sac (shape, position) · shape of fingertips · claspers · upper arm, gland complex · shape of tip of toes · tympanum (size, position) · parotides (size, expressivity) · dorsal gland crest (distance) · row of warts · heel turbercle · webs

3. Family Brachycephalidae Günther, 1858
(Brachycephalid toads)

This small South American family contains two genera (*Brachycephalus*, *Psyllophryne*) and three species. These small anurans, with a maximum body length of 3/4 inch (2 cm), are predominantly soil dwellers in the humid southeastern coastal region of Brazil. Their biology has not

been studied in detail. Amplexus is axillary. They lay only a few large, terrestrial eggs, from which small toads hatch directly. The pupil is horizontal; the tympanum is not visible. The maxillae and premaxillae bear teeth. The pectoral girdle is arciferal; the vertebrae are procoelous. The sacral vertebra has expanded transverse processes and are connected to the urostyle by two sacral diapophyses. The number of digits is reduced to two functioning fingers and three toes. The name Brachycephalid toads (in German: "saddle" toads) derives from a leathery membrane (corium) that stretches across a dorsal bony plate fused to the processes of the second and seventh vertebra. They are distinguished from true toads (Bufonidae) by the absence of a Bidder's organ (a rudimentary ovary of unknown function present in all Bufonidae with the exception of

Dendrophryniscus). Fossil Brachycephalid toads have not been discovered.

4. Family Bufonidae Gray, 1825
(True toads)

With 410 species classified into 34 genera, true toads are the most widely distributed anuran family worldwide, marking the southernmost occurrence of amphibians at the southern tip of Tierra del Fuego (e.g., *Bufo variegatus*). Dubois (1987) names five subfamilies (Bufoninae, Atelopinae, Torniereobatinae, Adenominae and Allophryninae) that are, however, insufficiently defined. The last of these subfamilies is treated herein as an independent family (Allophrynidae). True toads do not occur naturally in Australia, New Zealand, Papua New Guinea and Madagascar. With 225 species the genus *Bufo*, from which the name of the family derives, is the most variable of all genera of true toads. Numerous toads are generalists that populate different, even anthropologically influenced habitats, primary forests, or deserts, and even mountains up to 16,400 feet (5,000 m) above sea level.

One significant and exclusive characteristic found in all true toads with the exception of *Dendrophryniscus* is the so-called Bidder's organ, a rudimentary ovary in the males that develops into a functioning ovary following surgical removal of the testes. The body of most toads is short and stocky with a broad head and short limbs. The body length varies from 3/4 inch (2 cm) (*Oreophrynella*) and 9.8 inches (25 cm) (*Bufo blombergi*). The large parotoid gland is particularly noticeable; this gland and the entire skin of toads produce different toxins. The pupil is

Distribution of Brachycephalidae (a) and Rhinodermatidae (b) in South America (after Duellman and Trueb, 1986).

Bufo typhonius margaritifer *(Bufonidae, left in image) encounters a horned frog (*Ceratophrys cornuta, Leptodactylidae*) on the ground in the rain forest in French Guyana. Horned frogs have massive heads and large mouths. They cover themselves partly with earth and leaves and lay in wait for prey, which may sometimes be as large as they are.*

horizontal. The maxillae and premaxillae are without teeth. The pectoral girdle is arciferal; in some genera (*Atelopus, Osornophryne*) it is pseudofirmisternal. The sacral vertebra has expanded transverse processes and is attached to the urostyle by two sacral diapophyses. The vertebrae are procoelous. The number of presacral vertebrae can be less than eight (even reduced to five).

The amplexus is axillary in most species, and inguinal in a few (*Osornophryne, Nectophrynoides*). Most species lay their eggs in water in long strings; for *Bufo marinus* up to 35,000 eggs have been counted on one string. *Ansonia* and *Atelopus* larvae live in flowing waters; the oral region has developed into a suction disk. Some species of *Nectophrynoides* and *Mertensophryne micranotis* have internal fertilization; some species also exhibit direct development and are ovoviviparous or viviparous. True toads are often traditional spawners and return yearly to the same breeding ponds. Fossil documentation exists for the recent genus *Bufo* in numerous findings from the Upper Paleozoic in South America, as well as the Upper Tertiary in South and North America, Africa and Europe.

5. Family Centrolenidae Taylor, 1951 (Glass frogs)

Glass frogs are similar to tree frogs. They are

tree-dwelling anurans currently divided into 3 genera and 125 species. The ventral part of the body is often translucent (hence the name). The maxillae and premaxillae have teeth; the shoulder girdle is arciferal. The vertebrae are procoelous (eight presacral vertebrae). The sacral vertebra has expanded transverse processes and is connected to the urostyle via two sacral diapophyses. The astragalus and the calcaneus are completely fused (in contrast to those of tree frogs, which are only proximally and distally fused). The terminal phalanges are expanded into a T-shape; the phalangial formula is increased by one element. Amplexus is axillary; the eggs are deposited onto vegetation in a gelatinous covering (*Centrolene*) or onto rocks above water; the larvae then drop directly into the water. There have been no discoveries of fossil glass frogs.

6. Family Dendrobatidae Cope, 1865 (Poison-dart frogs)

This exclusively New World family (Central and South America) comprises 10 genera and 186 species. The systematic position of the family (sometimes also classified as a subfamily of Ranidae or Leptodactylidae) and the intrafamiliar classification on the genus level have not been discussed. They inhabit tropical rain forests but also adjacent habitats, and many species dwell on the ground or in ground cover. Others are tree

dwellers (larvae in bromeliad cups). Their often spectacular coloring and their fascinating biology (pronounced territorial behavior, reproductive strategies with mating ritual, in some species feeding of larvae with special fodder eggs) make them favorites of terrarium hobbyists. The skin produces toxins. The most poisonous amphibian (*Phyllobates terribilis*) is a member of this family.

Poison-dart frogs tend to be small, ranging from 1/3 inch (1 cm) to a maximum of 2 inches (5

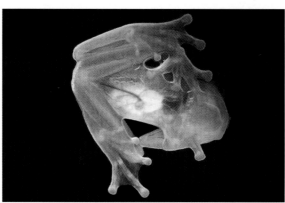

cm). Their fingers and toes end in suction pads. Males have an unpaired vocal sac at the throat. The vertebrae are procoelous; the number of pre-sacral vertebrae is eight, with the eighth vertebra fused to the sacral vertebra, which in turn contacts the urostyle by two sacral diapophyses. The pectoral girdle is firmisternal; maxilla and premaxilla are without teeth in some species. The astragalus and calcaneus are only proximally and distally fused.

Amplexus is either completely absent or formed as a head amplexus. The eggs—a mere 2 to 40 at a time—are laid on the ground among leaves and rocks. Some species exhibit highly developed brood care, which includes humidifying and guarding the nest; the larvae are transported on the back of the males, sometimes also the females, to small bodies of water (bromeliads). The females of some *Dendrobates* species return regularly to the larvae and lay special unfertilized eggs to feed the larvae. There is no fossil documentation of this family.

7. Family Discoglossidae Günther, 1858 (Disk-tongued frogs)

The primitive group of disk-tongued frogs with four genera (*Alytes, Bombina, Barbourula,*

Discoglossus) and 18 recent species are distributed exclusively in the Old World. These anurans have a disk-shaped tongue whose ventral side is fused partly or completely with the bottom of the oral cavity. The eyelids are mobile, the pupil often heart-shaped or triangular, the tympanum small. The presence of ribs in adults is a primitive characteristic. The pectoral girdle is arciferal, the vertebrae opisthocoelous. The sacral vertebra has expanded diapophyses; the urostyle has remnants of transverse processes. The maxillae and premaxillae bear teeth. Disk-tongued frogs inhabit a great variety of habitats, from plains (*Bombina bombina*) to high mountains (*Bombina maxima* up 9,840 feet/3,000 m above sea level). They reproduce up to three times a year. All males in this family clasp the female around the waist (amplexus lumbalis). Most disk-tongued frogs are semi-aquatic, with the exception of the Midwife toad, which is a land dweller. The unusual reproductive strategy of the midwife toads (*Alytes*) is well known. The systematics of the family have often been subject to debate and subsequent revisions. *Bombina* and *Alytes* have been classified as a separate family (Bombinidae). An individual genus was originally created for the Majorca midwife toad (*Baleaphryne*), but it was subsequently included in *Alytes*.

With eight fossil genera, this family is very well documented. Two genera originate in North America (*Paradiscoglossus* Estes and Sachiz, 1982, and *Scotiophryne* Estes, 1969), the other genera (*Eodiscoglossus* Villada, 1957; *Latonia* Meyer, 1843; *Pelophillus* Tschudi, 1838; *Prodiscoglossus* Friant, 1944; *Spondylophryne*

Left: Dendrobates auratus (Dendrobatidae). Like most species in this family, this representative has vivid aposematic pigmentation that draws attention to its toxic skin secretions, a defense mechanism against potential predators.

Distribution of Discoglossidae in Eurasia and Africa, Leiopelmatidae in North America and New Zealand and Rhinophrynidae in North and Central America (after Duellman and Trueb, 1986).

*Chinese fire-bellied toad (*Bombina orientalis, Discoglossidae*).*

Distribution of Hylidae (after Duellman and Trueb, 1986).

Facing page:
*This European tree frog (*Hyla arborea*) and the Mediterranean tree frog (*Hyla meridionalis*) are the only European representatives of Hylidae, whose 770 species make it the second-largest Anura family. Most tree frogs occur in Central and South America.*

Kretzoi, 1956, and *Baranophrys* Kretzoi, 1956) originate in Europe.

8. Family Heleophrynidae Noble, 1931 (Ghost frogs)

This small family with only one genus (*Heleophryne*) and five species occurs in South Africa. It was once classified as a subfamily of the southern frogs (Leptodactylidae) or the Australian frogs (Myobatrachidae). Ghost frogs are predominantly aquatic and are frequently found near flowing water.

The body is slender, partially flattened, the limbs relatively long. The maximum length is 2.5 inches (6.4 cm). The eyes are large and prominent with a vertical pupil. The tympanum is clearly visible. The maxillae and premaxillae bear teeth; the vertebrae are procoelous. The sacral vertebra has expanded processes and is attached to the urostyle by two sacral diapophyses. The astragalus and calcaneus are proximally and distally fused. The fingers and toes are expanded into a T-shape at the tip with an adhesive pad. Amplexus is inguinal. Eggs are laid on top of or beneath rocks in fast-flowing mountain streams or on moist ground. The tadpoles have a unique suction mouth. They are predominantly nocturnal or crepuscular. Thus far no fossil ghost frogs have been discovered.

9. Family Hemisotidae Cope, 1867 (Shovel-nosed frogs)

This family has only one genus, *Hemisus*, and eight species, previously classified as the subfamily Hemisinae of the common frogs (Ranidae) or Hyperoliidae. They differ from the Ranidae in some anatomical characters (presacral vertebrae I and II are fused). The pupil is vertical. The eight species of the genus all inhabit Africa south of the Sahara and are marked by a pointed snout and plump body shape. They lead a cryptic, predominantly subterranean life and feed on ants and termites. *Hemisus marmoratus* spawns in subterranean brood chambers near still waters. The females stay with the nest, and it is assumed that they transport their larvae to nearby water.

Distribution of Hemisotidae.

10. Family Hylidae Rafinesque, 1815 (Tree frogs)

With 773 described species in 40 genera, the common tree frogs are the second largest anuran and amphibian family. The most diverse genus is *Hyla* with 304 species. Usually four subfamilies

are distinguished (Hemiphractinae, Hylinae, Pelodryadinae, Phyllomedusinae). Pellodryadinae have sometimes also been classified as a separate family. *Allophryne*—here listed as a separate family—was previously classified as belonging to the tree frogs, but Savage (1973) has already defined them as a unique family. Tree frogs are widely distributed, and with the exception of Africa (where there are rare occurrences north of the Sahara) they inhabit all continents and many islands. Their greatest diversity occurs, however, in the New World; only four genera populate other continents (*Cyclorana, Litoria, Nyctimystes* and *Hyla*). Tree frogs are predominantly tree dwellers, but some also dig into the soil or are predominantly aquatic. They are mostly nocturnal or crepuscular. The body size varies between 3/4 inch and 5.5 inches (2 and 14 cm).

In most species the skin is smooth. The eyes are large and prominent; the pupil tends to be horizontal (exception: *Phyllomedusa* and *Nyctimystes*). The tympanum is clearly visible. The pectoral girdle is arciferal, the vertebrae procoelous. The sacral vertebra typically have expanded transverse processes and are connected to the urostyle by two sacral diapophyses. The maxillae and premaxillae bear teeth. Between the last and the next-to-last phalangial elements most species have an additional cartilage on both fingers and toes. These create flexibility for the last phalangial element, a feature necessary for climbing. Suction disks are present at the end of the phalanges. Both features are adaptations to an arboricolous mode of life. Additional cartilage also occurs in other tree-dwelling families (e.g., Pseudidae, Centrolenidae).

The reproductive biology of this family is highly diversified. Amplexus is axillary. Most species lay their eggs in water, some in mud nests on the ground or on top of vegetation, in small tree hollows or into bromeliad cups. In some genera (e.g., *Gastrotheca, Flectonotus*), the females have special brooding pouches and exhibit unusual brood care behavior.

Numerous fossil findings document this large anuran family (*Australobatrachus* Tyler, 1976, from the Australian Miocene, *Proacris* Holman, 1961, from the Miocene in Florida, as well as fossil representatives of the recent genera *Litoria, Pseudacris* and *Hyla*).

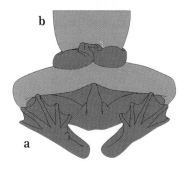

The tailed frog (Ascaphus truei, Leiopelmatidae) from the northwestern United States is the only Anura species that exercises internal fertilization with the help of a copulation organ. The protrusible extension of the cloaca is inserted into the cloaca of the female for insemination. In this species the amplexus is inguinal (Amplexus lumbalis), i.e., just above the hind extremities, as in the majority of the more original taxa.
a–male
b–female
(Sketch after Duellman and Trueb, 1986).

11. Family Hyperoliidae Laurent, 1943 (Reed and lily frogs, sedge frogs)

The African family of reed frogs currently comprises 233 species in 19 genera. Reed frogs are morphologically and ecologically very diverse: they live near still and flowing water, in swampy areas, rain forests, but also in relatively dry savanna regions. Many species are tree dwellers and are similar to the tree frogs; others are ground dwellers (*Chrysobatrachus*, many *Kassina* species). *Heterixalus* occurs in Madagascar and *Tachycnemis* on the Seychelles islands. Usually four subfamilies are recognized (Hyperoliinae, Kassininae, Leptopelinae, Tachycneminae).

Laurent (1943) described the Hyperoliidae as a family, also adding the Astylosternidae and the Artholeptidae as subfamilies. Some authors classify reed frogs as a subfamily of the Rhacophoridae.

Reed frogs are relatively small frogs with a body length of 1/2 inch to 3.5 inches (1.5 to 9 cm). They have eight procoelous presacral vertebrae. The sacral vertebra has cylindrical diapophyses and is in contact with the urostyle via two sacral diapophyses. The pectoral girdle is firmisternal. The maxillae and premaxillae bear teeth. The pupil is usually vertically elliptical, in some species also horizontal or round (*Acanthixalus*, *Chrysobatrachus*, *Hyperolius*). The astragalus and calcaneus are proximally and distally fused. Between the last and the next to last phalanges there is an intermediate cartilage; the terminal phalange carries an adhesive pad.

Amplexus is mostly axillary, inguinal in *Chrysobatrachus*. Acoustic communication plays an important role. Eggs are laid either in water— usually on top of submersed vegetation—or on

Distribution of Hyperoliidae (after Duellman and Trueb, 1986).

floating vegetation (*Afrixalus*, *Hyperolius*). Larvae then fall into the water. Thus far no fossil reed frogs have been discovered.

12. Family Leiopelmatidae Mivart, 1869 (Tailed frogs and New Zealand frogs)

Two fairly different and geographically distant genera (*Ascaphus*, *Leiopelma*) and four species are placed in this probably artificial family. Both genera are marked by several primitive characteristics, one being a spine with nine presacral, amphicoelous vertebrae, the greatest number of vertebrae in extant Anura (all others have at most eight), an arciferal pectoral girdle, free ribs

on the second to fourth vertebrae (sometimes also on the fifth and sixth) and remnants of muscles connecting to the tail (musculus caudaliopuboischiotibialis).

The tailed frog (*Ascaphus truei*) occurs in the northwestern United States and in extreme southwestern Canada. Its name is not derived from a "tail" but from a copulatory organ that is unique among the Anura. This tube-like extension of the cloaca is used for internal fertilization—paradoxically the only instance of such fertilization in Anura and occurring in one of the most primitive families. It is likely an adaptation to life in fast-flowing waters. Internal fertilization prevents the spermata or eggs from being swept away before fertilization can take place. Tailed frogs prefer clean, fast-flowing mountain streams up to 7,218 feet (2,200 m) above sea level and therefore a rather cool climate. In this characteristic, the tailed frog is very similar to the New Zealand frog. The larval phase of two to three years is unusually long. Some authors (Fejérváry, 1923; Savage, 1973) have suggested a separate family for *Ascaphus* (Ascaphidae).

The three species of the genus *Leiopelma* are the only Anura indigenous to New Zealand. They lead a cryptic life and differ from *Ascaphus* in that they are predominantly land dwellers. Fossil documentation for the family includes two occurrences (*Notobatrachus* Reig, 1957, and *Vieraella* Reig, 1961) from the Jurassic in Patagonia.

13. Family Leptodactylidae Werner, 1896 (Southern frogs)

Southern frogs occur in the New World. With 972 species in 50 genera, they are the largest and most diverse amphibian family, including the

most diverse amphibian genus of all (*Eleutherodactylus* with approximately 600 species).

Many authors (e.g., Duellman and Trueb, 1986) prefer to divide the group into four subfamilies (Ceratophryinae, Telmatobiinae, Hylodinae and Leptodactylinae), and some have even suggested assigning the status of family to Ceratophryinae. Body size ranges from 3/8 inch to 9.8 inches (1.2 to 25 cm) with great variety in body shapes (*Ceratophrys* is stocky, toad-like, *Leptodactylus* are shaped like bullfrogs, *Eleutherodactylus* like tree frogs). The pupil is generally horizontal, although in some genera it is vertical. The maxillae and premaxillae bear teeth in most species. The pectoral girdle is arciferal, sometimes pseudofirmisternal. The vertebrae are procoelous; the sacral vertebra has narrow or slightly broadened transverse processes and contacts the urostyle via two sacral diapophyses. The astragalus and the calcaneus are proximally and distally fused; in *Geobatrachus* they are completely fused. Southern frogs have developed a number of survival and reproductive strategies: amphibious, purely aquatic (*Batrachophrynus*, *Telmatobius*), terrestrial, and subterranean. The predatory carnivorous horned frogs (*Ceratophrys*) are the best-known southern frogs.

Eggs are usually laid in water. Some species also build foam nests in water, on plants above water or in ground nests. In *Thoropa*, eggs are laid in soil, and the larvae crawl to water, while other larvae complete their development on land. Other species exhibit brood care in the form of guarding the nest, while others have direct development. *Eleutherodactylus jasperi* has internal fertilization (as does *E. coqui*) and is viviparous.

The family is well documented in fossils through findings of the genus *Wawelia* Casamiquela, 1963 (Argentinian Miocene), *Neoprocoela* Schaeffer, 1949 (Patagonian Oligocene) and other discoveries of recent genera.

14. Family Microhylidae Günther, 1858 (Narrow-mouthed toads)

The diverse and heterogeneous family of narrow-mouthed toads currently comprises 66 genera and 321 species. Narrow-mouthed toads occur across Africa, America, South East Asia and northern Australia. The members of the family are morphologically and ecologically diverse, and often highly specialized. Some are soil

dwellers and are similar to true frogs or true toads in appearance, but many are tree dwellers and therefore more similar to tree frogs. The intrafamilial taxonomy is still unclear; frequently as many as 10 subfamilies are recognized (Asterophryinae, Brevicipinae, Cophylinae, Dyscophinae, Genyophryninae, Melanobatrachinae, Microhylinae, Otophryninae, Phrynomerinae, Scaphiophryninae), although they are treated differently by many authors. The body length ranges from 1/3 inch to 4.3 inches (1 to 11 cm), but most species are very small (3/4 inch to 2 inches/2 to 5 cm). Many species have short, pointed heads and narrow mouths (hence the name). The pupil is horizontal or round, and in some species vertical. The maxillae and premaxillae bear teeth in most species (toothless examples are *Calluella* and *Dyscophus*). There are eight presacral vertebrae; the vertebrae are procoelous with only the eighth being biconcave. The sacral vertebra has slightly expanded transverse processes and contacts the urostyle by two sacral diapophyses. The astragalus and calcaneus are proximally and distally fused. The pectoral girdle is firmisternal. A unique feature is the presence of two or three folds (transverse epidermal ridges) in the roof of the mouth. The reproductive strategies are diverse and incompletely known. Many species have small, aquatic eggs and free-swimming tadpoles; others have terrestrial eggs and direct development.

*The ornate Argentine horned frog (*Ceratophrys ornata*, Leptodactylidae) has impressive coloring; the different patterns blend the outline of the frog with the surrounding forest floor.*

Left top: Distribution of Leptodactylidae in the New World and Myobatrachidae in Australia and New Guinea (after Duellman and Trueb, 1986).

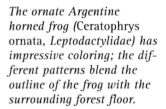

Distribution of Microhylidae (after Duellman and Trueb, 1986).

Thus far only one fossil representative of narrow-mouthed toads has been discovered. It belongs to the extant genus *Gastrophryne* Fitzinger, 1843 (Miocene in Florida, USA).

15. Family Myobatrachidae Schlegel, 1850 (Australian frogs)

This family, with 23 genera and 119 species, occurs in Australia, Tasmania and New Guinea. Its relationship to other families and within the family was and still is largely undefined. They have been recognized as related to the Leptodactylidae; for *Rheobatrachus* some authors have suggested a separate subfamily or even a family. Generally two subfamilies are recognized (Limnodynastinae, Myobatrachinae). Australian frogs inhabit a variety of arid and humid habitats; some dwell in rapidly flowing rivers or mountain regions above the tree line. As a consequence they have developed a number of survival and reproductive strategies. One of the most unusual species, and unique in the animal kingdom, is the gastric brooding frog, *Rheobatrachus*, discovered in 1973 and possibly already extinct.

The body shape varies considerably: small and toad-like for the burrowing species, while others are large and stocky with powerful limbs. Body size ranges from 3/4 inch (2 cm) (*Assa darlingtoni*) to 5 inches (12 cm) (*Mixophies iteratus*). The pupil is horizontal in most genera, but vertical in *Heleioporus*, *Megistolotis*, *Mixophys* and *Neobatrachus*. The maxillae and premaxillae bear teeth in most species (except *Myobatrachus*, *Notaden*, *Pseudophryne* and some *Uperoleia*). The pectoral girdle is arciferal; intervertebral disks are present in subadults (except *Lechriodus* and *Mixophys*). The sacral vertebra has broad transverse processes and is in contact with the urostyle via two sacral diapophyses. The astragalus and the calcaneus are proximally and distally fused.

Amplexus is inguinal. Reproductive strategies are numerous. The majority of species lay their eggs in water and have free-swimming tadpoles; some build foam nests. Land dwellers have direct development, and frequently specialized forms of brood care. Fossil documentation exists in *Indobatrachus* Noble, 1930, from the Eocene in India as well as several findings of the recent genus *Limnodynastes* Fitzinger, 1843 (Australian Pleistocene).

16. Pelobatidae Bonaparte, 1850 (Spadefoot toads)

Spadefoot toads inhabit the Old and New World and are currently divided into 10 genera and 109 species. Usually two subfamilies are recognized: Megophryinae and Pelobatinae. The Megophryinae are sometimes recognized as a separate family. Some authors classify Pelodytidae (mud divers) as a subfamily of the spadefoot toads. Most spadefoot toads are adapted to arid locations and dig beneath the soil during the day (some species, such as *Scaphiopus*, dig up to 2 yards/2 m deep). Their bodies are stocky, from 3/4 inch to 6 inches (2 to 17 cm) long. The pupil is vertical. The tympanum is barely visible or completely hidden. The maxillae and premaxillae bear teeth. The pectoral girdle is arciferal; the vertebrae procoelous (subfamily Pelobatinae) or amphicoelous (sub-

Right: Distribution of Pelobatidae (after Duellman and Trueb, 1986).

*Spadefoots (*Pelobates fuscus*, Pelobatidae) are a steppe species that prefers sparsely vegetated and relatively arid ground. As an anthropophilous species it does, however, also occur near human habitation, in pastureland, gardens and parks.*

family Megophryinae, with intervertebral disks). The sacral vertebra has noticeably expanded transverse processes, and is either fused to the urostyle or contacts it via a single sacral diapophysis. The astragalus and the calcaneus are proximally and distally fused. Often a spade-like structure is present on the foot—hence the name spadefoot toads. Amplexus is inguinal. All spadefoot toads have aquatic eggs and larvae. Gigantism has been observed in larvae (e.g., the common spadefoot toad *Pelobates fuscus*). Larval hibernation may occur. The eggs are laid in short, thick strings. The larvae of many species have adapted to life in fast-flowing waters (*Leptobrachium*, *Leptolalax*, *Scutiger*); others feed on particles at the water surface and have a funnel-shaped mouth (*Megophrys*). Spadefoot toads are documented by numerous fossil find-ings (*Aralobatrachus* Nessov, 1981; *Eopelobates* Parker, 1929; *Kizylkuma* Nessov, 1981; *Macropelobates* Noble, 1924); fossils have also been discovered of the recent genus *Pelobates* (*Protopelobates* Bieber, 1880).

17. Family Pelodytidae Bonaparte, 1850 (Mud divers)

This small Eurasian family has only one genus (*Pelodytes*) and two species. It was frequently classified as a subfamily, Pelodytinae, in the fam-ily Pelobatidae. Mud divers differ from the latter in that presacral vertebrae I and II are completely fused, as are the astragalus and the calcaneus. They also have some other distinguishing fea-tures. Mud divers are small, delicate frogs; their body length does not exceed 2 inches (5.5 cm). The eyes are large and prominent, the pupil ver-tical. The dorsal skin is warty. The parotoid gland is narrow and the tympanum small. The hind legs are relatively long with short webbed feet (no spade). The pectoral girdle is arciferal, the vertebrae procoelous. The sacral vertebra has broad processes and is in contact with the urostyle via two sacral diapophyses. Males have internal vocal sacs and obvious nuptial excres-cences (chest, upper and lower arm, fingers, toes). Amplexus is inguinal; eggs are laid in short, thick strings. After the spawning period, the adults live on land but tend to stay near water. Fossil mud divers have been discovered dating back to the Miocene, Eocene and Pleistocene in Europe and in North America (*Miopelodytes* Taylor, 1942; *Propelodytes* Weitzel, 1938 and the extant genus *Pelodytes*).

18. Family Pipidae Gray, 1825 (Tongueless frogs)

This primitive anuran family with five recent genera and 29 species occurs in Africa south of the Sahara and in South America. Many authors recognize three subfamilies (Pipinae, Siluraninae, Xenopodinae). They are predominantly, and in some cases exclusively, aquatic. The (African) clawed toad (*Xenopus laevis*) is an important lab-oratory species. Mating behavior is sometimes expressed in an acrobatic "water ballet." Amplexus is inguinal; the eggs are laid in the

Distribution of Pelodytidae in western Europe and South West Asia and Pipidae in Africa and South America (after Duellman and Trueb, 1986).

water (*Xenopus*) or onto the back of the female (*Pipa*). Some species have free-swimming larvae; others (*Pipa pipa*) remain in the embryonic state until they metamorphose into small frogs (approximately 100 to 150 days) in the pits on their mother's back.

Body size attains a maximum of 7.8 inches (20 cm). Tongueless frogs are generally broad and flattened. The eyes are small, the pupils round. As the name indicates, this family of frogs does not have tongues—a unique phenomenon among all anuran families. The sacrum girdle has broad diapophyses and is fused to the coccyx. Free ribs are present only in larvae. In some species, adults retain a lateral line organ. Two or three inner toes have calloused claws that are shed with the skin. In *Pipa* the fingertips are formed into multi-branched tactile organs (a species charac-teristic). Fossil tongueless frogs are well docu-mented (*Cordicephalus* Nevo, 1968; *Eoxenopoides* Haughton, 1931; *Saltenia* Reig, 1959; *Shomronella* Estes, Spinar and Nevo, 1978, and *Thoraciliacus* Nevo, 1968). These discoveries were made in Africa, Israel and South America.

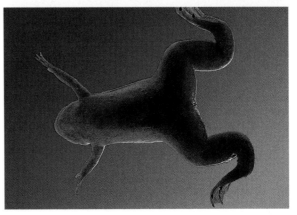

South American tongueless frogs (Pipa pipa, *top*) and African clawed toads (Xenopus laevis) are repre-sentatives of the primitive family of tongueless frogs (Pipidae). They are predom-inantly or exclusively aquatic. The lower image clearly shows the three claws on the hind extremi-ties of Xenopus.

19. Family Pseudidae Fitzinger, 1843 (Paradox frogs)

Paradox frogs are exclusive to South America with three species and two genera (*Lysapsus*, *Pseudis*). These diurnal, shy frogs are primarily aquatic and inhabit tropical and subtropical, still, heavily vegetated bodies of water. Amplexus is axillary; eggs are laid in water among vegetation. Gigantism in the tadpoles is an unusual characteristic and can be extreme in some species (e.g., *Pseudis paradoxa*): the 9.8-inch (25 cm) larva metamorphoses into a frog whose adult size is no more than 2.7 inches (7 cm). The eyes are large and prominent, the pupil horizontal. The tympanum is clearly visible. The pectoral girdle is arciferal, the vertebrae procoelous. The sacral vertebra has broad transverse processes and contacts the urostyle via two sacral diapophyses. The maxillae and premaxillae bear teeth. Thus far there have been no discoveries of fossil paradox frogs.

20. Family Ranidae Rafinesque-Schmaltz, 1814 (True frogs)

With few exceptions (Australia, New Zealand) true frogs are distributed worldwide in a total of 746 species and 44 genera, making them the third-largest anuran family. The nominate genus *Rana* currently contains 242 species. True frogs are most diverse in Africa. Systematic relationships between the Ranidae and other taxa (e.g., Rhacophoridae, Hyperoliidae, Mantellidae) and the intrafamilial definitions are frequently revised and cannot be regarded as final. Duellman (1993) recognizes seven subfamilies (Dicroglossinae, Petropedetinae, Ptychadeninae, Pyxicephalinae, Raninae, Ranixalinae, and Tomopterninae), with Arthroleptidae and Astylosternidae—here classified as separate families—frequently defined as subfamilies of the Ranidae (Duellman and Trueb, 1986). The Rhacophoridae are currently defined as a subfamily (Rhacophorinae) of true frogs (e.g.,

Below right: Spawning Grass frogs (Rana temporaria, Ranidae) on the bottom of a pond. The female (middle) is grasped in an embrace by a second male (bottom). As females are usually less numerous, they are often mobbed by several males.

Worldwide distribution of Ranidae (after Duellman and Trueb, 1986).

Dubois, 1992). For practical reasons they are listed here as a separate family.

Body length ranges from 2 to 15 inches (5 to 40 cm) (*Conraua goliath*, the largest frog species in the world). The pupil is usually horizontal. Males frequently have paired, lateral vocal sacs. The number of presacral vertebrae is eight; seven of these are procoelous, and the eighth presacral vertebra is biconcave in most taxa. The sacral vertebra has cylindrical transverse processes and contacts the urostyle by two sacral diapophyses. There are no ribs. The pectoral girdle is usually firmisternal; the maxillae and premaxillae bear teeth in most species. The astragalus and the calcaneus are proximally and distally fused.

True frogs are often loyal to their spawning sites, returning every year to the same breeding ponds. The amplexus tends to be axillary, absent in Mantellinae or cephalad. Most species lay their eggs into open water, frequently in large clots, and have free-swimming larvae; in some species development is direct (various Petropedetinae and representatives of the general *Ceratobatrachus*, *Discodeles*, *Palmatorappia* and *Platymantis*). *Amolops* tadpoles are adapted to running waters.

Many fossil discoveries (Tertiary, Quartiary) of representatives of the genera *Rana* and *Ptychadena* have been found in Europe, North America and Morocco.

21. Family Rhacophoridae Hoffman, 1932 (Old World Tree Frogs)

The Rhacophoridae are divided into 236 species and 10 genera. They occur in Africa, Madagascar, Southeast Asia and Japan. Many common characteristics link them to African reed frogs. Many systematists currently classify them as a subfamily (Rhacophorinae) of the Ranidae. Usually two subfamilies are identified (Buergeriinae, Rhacophorinae). The Rhacophoridae exhibit adaptations and live in a wide range of habitats, even in disturbed habitats such as rice fields, plantations and even urban environments. Many species resemble tree frogs and are arboricolous;

some are ground dwellers (e.g., *Aglyptodactylus*). The gliding frogs of the genus *Rhacophorus* are widely known. Body size ranges from 1/2 inch to 5 inches (1.5 to 12 cm). There are eight presacral vertebrae; the vertebrae are procoelous; the eighth vertebra biconcave. The sacral vertebra has cylindrical transverse processes and is in contact with the urostyle via two sacral diapophyses. The pectoral girdle is firmisternal. The maxillae and premaxillae bear teeth. The pupil is horizontal. The astragalus and the calcaneus are proximally and distally fused. There is an intermediate cartilage between the last and the next to last phalangia; the terminal phalange often carries an adhesive pad. In some *Rhacophorus* species (gliding frogs) there is extensive toe webbing. The eggs are laid in water, on the ground, in foam nests on vegetation above water or in tree hollows. Some species also have direct development without a free larval phase, others exhibit a variety of brood care behaviors. Thus far no fossils of Rhacophoridae have been found.

22. Family Rhinodermatidae Bonaparte, 1850 (Mouth-breeding frogs)

This small South American family has only one genus (*Rhinoderma*) and two species. The mouth-breeding frog *R. darwinii* discovered by Charles Darwin is especially famous due to the unusual mouth-breeding reproductive strategy in males. These small frogs grow to a mere 1.2 inches (3 cm) and live mostly in humid forests, often near water. Amplexus is axillary. *R. rufum* deposits its tadpoles into small bodies of water, whereas *R. darwinii* carries them in a gular pouch until metamorphosis. The name of this family is taken from the mouth which is elongated into a triangular, nose-shaped lip. The maxillae and premaxillae are toothless, the tympanum clearly visible, the pupil horizontal. The pectoral girdle is pseudofirmisternal, the vertebrae procoelous. The sacral vertebra has broad transverse processes and contacts the urostyle via two sacral diapophyses. Thus far no fossils of mouth-breeding frogs have been found.

23. Family Rhinophrynidae Günther, 1858 (Burrowing toads)

This New World family consists of only one monotypic genus (*Rhinophrynus dorsalis*). Burrowing toads live in a variety of habitats, including arid to semi-desert grasslands. These nocturnal toads, which can be up to 2.7 inches (7

cm) long, are excellent burrowers, morphologically well equipped for this mode of life with shovel-shaped feet. Males have paired, internal vocal sacs. Amplexus is inguinal; spawning usually takes place in open bodies of water, with the tadpoles free-living. The body is robust, egg-shaped, with a pointed snout and short limbs. The eyes are small, the pupil vertical. The tympanum is not visible. The maxillae and premaxillae are toothless. Among the Anura, burrowing toads are unique in that they possess a very long, projectile tongue. The vertebrae are opisthocoelous and modified; the pectoral girdle is arciferal. The sacral vertebra has very slightly broadened transverse processes and is in contact with the urostyle via two sacral diapophyses. The exact position of burrowing frogs in the phylogeny of the Amphibia is still being debated. Several authors place them with the Pipidae, Rhinophrynidae or Leiopelmatidae. Fossil documentation of burrowing frogs is found in the genus *Eorhinophrynus* from the American Paleozoic and Eocene. The recent genus *Rhinophrynus* is also documented in fossils.

24. Family Sooglossidae Noble, 1931 (Seychelles frogs)

This small anuran family with three species and two genera (*Nesomantis*, *Sooglossus*), whose systematic position hasn't been fully determined, occurs only on the islands Mahé and Silouette, which are part of the Seychelles islands in the Indian Ocean. Some have suggested classifying them as a subfamily of the true frogs (Ranidae) or as a sister group of the Australian frogs (Myobatrachidae). These frogs are small soil dwellers with a terrestrial mode of life. Even the embryonic development occurs away from water. Amplexus is inguinal; eggs are laid in gelatinous clumps. In *Sooglossus sechellensis*, the female carries the larvae on its back until metamorphosis sets in. The body is slender to stout. Body length can reach up to 1.7 inches (4.5 cm). The maxillae and premaxillae bear teeth. The pectoral girdle is arciferal. The sacral vertebra has broad transverse processes and contacts the urostyle via a single sacral diapophysis. The astragalus and the calcaneus are proximally and distally fused. Fingers and toes terminate in very small disks. The pupil is horizontal. Thus far no fossils have been found of these frogs.

Distribution of Rhacophoridae in Asia and Africa (after Duellman and Trueb, 1986).

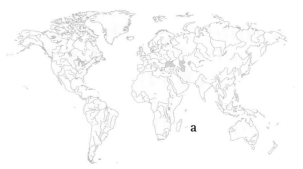

a

Distribution of Heleophrynidae in South Africa and Sooglossidae (a) on the Seychelles Islands (after Duellman and Trueb, 1986).

Amphibians still share characteristics with their fish ancestors. Of all the "innovations" that developed in amphibians, the four limbs are the most important. The evolution of extremities enabled vertebrates to colonize land on a massive scale and to develop a new method of mobility: the frog leap. But the shift onto land also brought with it drastic changes in anatomy and morphology. These and the numerous unusual characteristics in amphibian physiology, respiration, skin, toxic secretions, vivid coloring, the mysterious processes of metamorphosis and paedamorphosis, hybridization, sex determination and many other topics make this chapter an exciting excursion into the world of biology.

Biology
and
Physiology

Anatomy

Modern amphibians have many anatomical features in common, such as similarities in skull structure, dentition, brain structure, skin and glands, the histological structure of internal organs, and many other characteristics. These are in turn related to many physiological similarities. All recent amphibians breathe through their skin, and all undergo a metamorphosis as they pass from the larval into the adult phase. Yet the morphological differences between a newt, a caecilian and a frog are obvious even at first glance. This chapter explores the main characteristics of amphibian anatomy and investigates how these characteristics relate to the various modes of amphibian life.

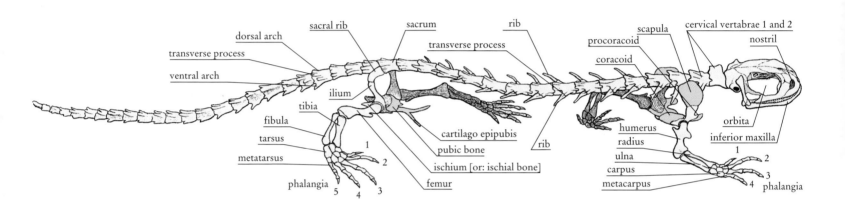

Urodela skeleton (Salamandra salamandra). Cartilage is shown in blue, bone in pale green.

Skeleton and Musculature
(Alfred Goldschmid)

As in all vertebrates, the skeleton in amphibians is constructed of cartilage and bone, both of which are forms of connective tissue. The two materials differ in structure and in cellular composition. In cartilage, cells are isolated from one another and suspended in a cartilage matrix. A cartilage cell can "feed" from this only by diffusion; cartilage itself does not contain blood vessels. Cartilage is resistant to pressure; it contains large amounts of bound water, small and short fibers of connective tissue; it is rarely mineralized. In adult land vertebrates and in humans, cartilage is usually present only in joint structures. Cartilage is "cheap" material and can be quickly constructed. As a result, large sections of the skeleton consist of cartilage during the embryonic phase and often even into the adolescent phase.

Bone cells form many fine cell processes that link cells to each other within the bone and also connect them to the nurturing blood vessels. Strong connective fibers permeate the basic bone matter in an alternating arrangement, in which deposits of minerals such as calcium phosphate and calcium carbonate are stored.

Bone is therefore a very hard substance because of the alternating orientation of fibers in layers

of connective tissue. Bone elements are formed in two ways: either directly in the connective tissue or in place of an existing cartilage element that is fully deconstructed and replaced with the newly formed bone. In the latter case, it is referred to as a "replacement bone." In layman's terms, the process is generally called "hardening." Which of the skeletal elements are prefabricated from cartilage? The so-called axial organs, the vertebrae of the spine and the ribs connected to them, the inner or primary girdle elements, the scapula (shoulder blade) and coracoid in the pectoral girdle, as well as the three elements of the pelvic girdle, ventrally the pubic bone, followed by the ischium, and dorsally the ilium. We should mention that the Latin terminology common in human anatomy describes the function only in humans and in mammals. However, since these are homologous structures, these designations are generally applicable to all quadrupeds.

The skeleton of the limbs is also formed from cartilage. The following basic pattern is present in all tetrapods: one element each joined to the girdle—at the shoulder joint, the upper arm (humerus), and at the hip joint the thigh (femur). The joint at the shoulder and hip is always formed by a combination of the elements of the girdle skeleton. In both elbow and knee joints, two elements contact the humerus and the femur: in the arm these are the internal radius and, externally, the ulna; in the leg, the tibia internally, and the fibula externally. The hand and foot bones absorb the actual contact with the ground and force a transfer in motion. The forearm and the lower leg are followed by the carpal bone (hand) and the tarsal bone (foot), next come the metacarpus (hand) and metatarsus (foot) and the radial arrangement of the finger and toe bones. The terminal elements in fingers and toes are the actual ground-gripping agents, subject to high mechanical stresses. In some amphibians, keratinous claws evolved from the epidermis at the end of the digits.

While up to seven fingers and toes were present in early fossil amphibians, various palaeozoic amphibian groups had already evolved five-igit extremities—i.e., the basic pattern for all subsequent tetrapods. Different degrees of use and varying functional stresses can lead to considerable changes in the individual elements that make up the three sections of the arm and leg skeleton. Thus all recent amphibians have only four fingers and it is assumed that the outermost fifth finger has regressed. The number of individual segments in fingers and toes is relatively stable among vertebrates; the numbers begin with the thumb as the first and continue on to the fifth—this is called the "phalangial formula," phalangia being the generic term that includes both toes and fingers. In principle, humans, like all mammals, present the formula 2-3-3-3-3 (one need only look at one's own hand or feet). Reptiles have the phalangial formula 2-3-4-5-3, which is why the fourth finger and, above all, the fourth toe are especially long in lizards. Most sala-

manders have the formula 1-2-3-2 or 2-2-3-3 in their fingers. Aquatic species which swim with a snake-like motion of the trunk and tail often have a reduced number of fingers and toes. The extremities and the girdles may even be absent altogether, as in the American sirens, which have neither pelvic girdle nor hind legs. The typical foot in Urodela has five toes and a phalangial formula of 1-2-3-3-2, with the fifth being reduced in some species from different groups (e.g., *Hynobius, Salamandrina, Necturus*).

In the Anura the most common phalangial formula in the fingers is 2-2-3-3. The *Rhamphophryne* toad has noticeably shortened fingers, and the South American genus Atelopus has a first digit that is no longer visible. Dimorphous sex differences, especially in the thumb segments of the Anura, have also been noted, since males often have claspers underlaid with an additional bone crest. In some groups, above all tree frogs, an additional cartilaginous segment called the intercalary, occurs between the last and the second last finger segment, supporting the toe disk. Anura generally have five toes with a phalangial formula of 2-2-3-4-3, with the exception of two species (*Psyllophryne didactyla*, Brachycephalidae *Didynamipus sjoestedti* and the true toads), which have only four toes.

The saltatory movement in Anura with a synchronized extension of the hind extremity led to characteristic changes in the skeleton of the extremities. In the Urodele, the otherwise paired bones in the cubitus and the lower leg are fused into a single element. Moreover, the hind

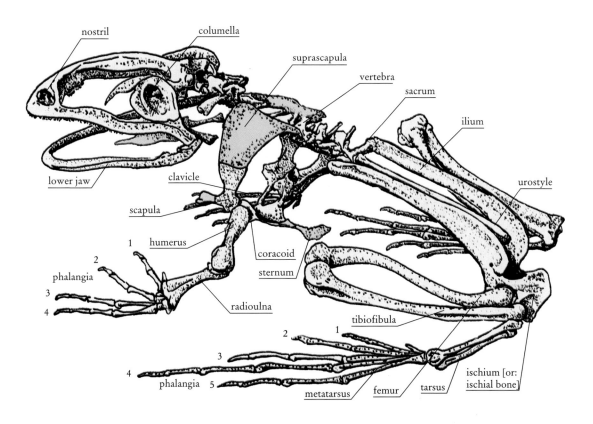

Anura skeleton (Rana sp.). Cartilage is shown in blue, bone in pale green.

extremity, which provides the shear force for leaping, has grown significantly longer than the forelimb; in this process the lower leg bone (evolved from a fused tibia and fibula) grows extremely long. In the foot, a "second" heel joint (called an intertarsal joint because it develops between the tarsals) has evolved between the elongated hind tarsals, and the tarsal bones in front. The motion of jumping has also influenced the elongation of the ilium in the pelvic girdle as well as a keel-like structure of pubis and ischium, which has shifted the hip joint toward the body center. Many Urodela, such as salamanders, have a cartilaginous Y-shaped "prepubic bone" which sticks out at the junction of the left and right pubic bones; it is set between the muscles in the rear abdominal wall. Prebupic bones are also found in some Anura (*Xenopus, Ascaphus*). *Ascaphus* is the only anuran with a tail-like copulation organ supported by two cartilaginous rods originating from the caudal pelvic ridge ("post pubic bone").

In the Urodele, the shoulder girdle consists of two wide, laminate coracoids that cover the heart region ventrally and at whose outer side the upper arm muscles originate. The shoulder blade, projecting dorsally, and the coracoid are bony only near the joint region; the bulk of both elements remains cartilaginous. The coracoid laminates overlap along the ventral median line and can slide above one another when the arms swing as the body is being pushed or pulled. Although Anura have only short ribs as extensions of the transverse processes of the vertebrae and do not develop a closed rib cage, a small, cartilaginous, round to romboid sternum is embedded in the muscles that surround the rear ridge of the shoulder girdle; the shoulder girdle is only connected to the head and to the spine through muscles. Oddly, muscles branch off from the front region of the scapula in the direction of the skull, and also in the direction of the base plate of the columella, the auditory ossicle that covers the oval window. In contrast to the Anura, Urodela do not have an external tympanum.

Anura display a great variety in the construction of shoulder girdle. In true frogs it tends to be relatively inflexible and enlarged by an anterior sternum (omosternum) and a rear sternum. A rod-like element lies in front of the coracoid: this is the clavicle or wishbone, which provides support between the pectoral joint and the ventromedians. This bone is not preformed in cartilage; instead it develops directly out of connective tissue. It derives from a fossil bone carapace, which still contained a non-paired interclavicle between the two clavicles and supported the heavy torso at rest, a factor that was probably important in relieving the heart func-

tion. This kind of inflexible skeletal structure is called firmisternal. When the broad coracoid segments move against each other—as they do in true toads—we speak of an arciferal skeletal structure. In the past, these two structures of the pectoral girdle were viewed as being of great importance. Today, numerous examples of transitory forms between the two types are known even within smaller groups.

When we look at the spine, we find a great diversity in its structure in recent amphibians and in their fossil ancestors. In many amphibians, the chorda dorsalis remains intact throughout the adult phase. The chorda is a typical structural component of the axial skeleton of all vertebrates and is always present during embryonic development. It is a rod made up of large, vacuolate, turgescent cells surrounded by a firm sheath of connective tissue. It originates immediately behind the hypophysis at the base of the skull and stretches to the tail. Outside of the skull, cartilaginous or ossified vertebrae form around the chorda, on which the neural arches sit like roof tiles, forming the hollow channel through which the spinal cord can pass. The neural arches develop strong, paired joint (or articular) processes that ensure the flexibility of the spine. While amphibians do not have true joints between the vertebrae, their embryonic development produces vertebrae that appear to be hollowed out on the front and at the back (amphicoelous as in *Ascaphus*) or hollowed out on one side only: at the front (procoelous) or the back (opisthocoelous). The formation of vertebrae in recent amphibians is known for only a few species. In some species, bony shells grow to surround the chorda without any formulation of cartilage, similar to what has been observed in fossil Lepospondylii.

What is clearly distinguishable, however, is a presacral spine (presacral = located in front of the sacral vertebra) and a postsacral or caudal spine. The first presacral vertebra is called "atlas" because of its double contact with the skull and the absence of any rib element. However, it is surely not homologous with the vertebra of the same name found in Amniotes. The number of vertebrae varies greatly among individual amphibian orders. Depending on body size, caecilians have 95 to 285 vertebrae in addition to the first vertebra. In Urodela, too, the "atlas" is called a neck vertebra. This is followed by 10 to 60 trunk vertebrae, with the single sacral vertebra followed by another 20 to 100 tail or caudal vertebrae that diminish in size toward the tip of the tail. Ventrally, the caudal vertebrae have a haemal arch that surrounds the caudal artery and vein, in addition to the very small dorsal neural arch. The Chinese newt *Echinotriton* and the sharp-ribbed

Vertebrates typically have paired maxillar muscles connected to the lower part of the right and left jaw, respectively. When this adductor mandibulae muscle contracts, as the name of the muscle indicates, the lower jaw is "adducted" or moved toward the upper jaw; in other words, the jaws close (1). Caecilians, too, have this jaw adductor. They also have a second pair of maxillar adductor muscles, unique among vertebrates in this form. The additional muscle is attached to the retroarticulate process (processus retroarticulatus). This inter-

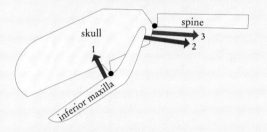

hyoid posterior muscle is part of the hyoid musculature in other amphibians; in caecilians it pulls the maxillar process backwards and downwards, which shifts the part of the jaw that lies in front of the joint upwards, thus effecting an adductive or closing motion. The maxillar process is also the connector for the mandibular depressor muscle. As in other amphibians, this muscle pulls sideways on the cranial cap from the process, which means that a contraction of the depressors will lift the maxillar process, thus lowering the lower jaw and opening the mouth. It is notable that the maxillar process in caecilians is significantly longer than in other amphibians. When this process serves only as a connector for the opener, a shorter lever is evidently sufficient. The comparatively long lever in caecilians indicates that the contractions of the second depressor must be very forcefully transmitted to the teeth-carrying section of the jaw.

The question arises why caecilians have developed a second maxillar musculature, while all other vertebrates, including powerful predators, make do with a single set of maxillar muscles. Anatomists who have studied this question have drawn attention to the fact that this unique mechanism can be

interpreted as an adaptive feature to a burrowing mode of life. The highly specialized apparatus is yet another indicator that the skull of caecilians is anything but primitive.

When comparing the maxillar musculature of several caecilian families, one notices that the additional muscle, the interhyoid posterior muscle (2), is of varying strength. Categories of forms can be created that are more adapted to burrowing than others by virtue of their cranial anatomy and the position of the mouth. The size of the second maxillar muscle increases within this group. The relatively original Rhinatrematidae are fairly inefficient burrowers. Their skull is not as ossified as in other families and the mouth is positioned at the end of the head. In *Epicrionops petersi* the "normal" maxillar muscle, the adductor mandibular muscle, is relatively large and is obviously an important part of the closing apparatus. It lies, as in other vertebrates, stretched dorsally through the temporal foramina and is attached to the cranial roof. The new additional maxillar muscles are present and functioning, but still relatively small.

Ichthyophiidae are already more adapted to a burrowing mode of life than are Rhinatrematidae. Thus in *Ichthyophis* the temporal foramina are closed, which strengthens and stabilizes the cranium. The original maxillar muscles can no longer grow on the upper side of the cranial roof; instead they are attached to its inside, which means that they must remain relatively small. In *Ichthyophis* the new maxillar muscles

are already the larger and more powerful parts of the closing mechanism. This evolutionary tendency is even more noticeable in Caeciliidae and Scolecomorphidae. The illustration below shows *Microcaecilia rabei* and *Crotaphatrema lamottei* as representatives of these two families. The reduced number of cranial bones, the rigidity of the cranium, and the subterminal mouth are all interpreted as adaptations to burrowing, adaptations that are most advanced here by comparison to other Gymnophiona families. In these very efficient burrowing species, the new adductor muscle takes up much more space than in Ichthyophiidae. Obviously, the original maxillar adductor in Caeciliidae and Scolecomorphidae plays a subordinate role. The main labor in biting and closing is presumably the task of the indirectly acting interhyoid.

In addition, biting motions of caecilians can also be supported by muscles that are part of the trunk musculature and which act as cranial flexors. Their position and functions are marked by "3" in the drawing. This is the large musculus longus captitis, which originates from the 12 to 16 frontal vertebrae, connecting to the skull directly beneath the occipital joint. Because of its position and size, this muscle is a powerful flexor for neck and head. And this surely makes it vitally important for burrowing, while at the same time ensuring that the lowering motion of the head can add extra force to the efficiency and power of the bite.

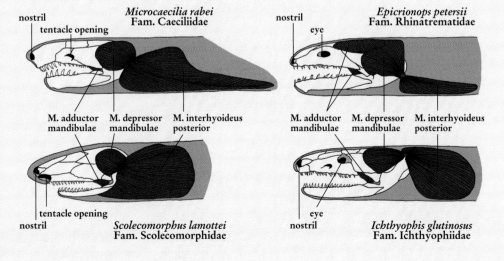

Microcaecilia rabei
Fam. Caeciliidae

nostril
tentacle opening

M. adductor mandibulae / M. depressor mandibulae / M. interhyoideus posterior

Scolecomorphus lamottei
Fam. Scolecomorphidae

tentacle opening
nostril

Epicrionops petersii
Fam. Rhinatrematidae

nostril
eye

M. adductor mandibulae / M. depressor mandibulae / M. interhyoideus posterior

Ichthyophis glutinosus
Fam. Ichthyophiidae

eye
nostril

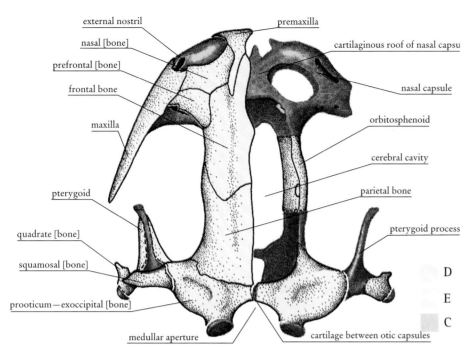

external nostril
nasal [bone]
prefrontal [bone]
frontal bone
maxilla
pterygoid
quadrate [bone]
squamosal [bone]
prooticum—exoccipital [bone]
medullar aperture

premaxilla
cartilaginous roof of nasal capsu
nasal capsule
orbitosphenoid
cerebral cavity
parietal bone
pterygoid process
cartilage between otic capsules

D
E
C

Urodela cranial skeleton (Salamandra salamandra, top) and Anura cranial skeleton (Rana esculenta, bottom). D—dermal bone (dermal bones develop directly out of the embryonic connective tissue); E—endochondral bone (endochondral bones develop as cartilage to begin with and are then replaced with bone tissue); C—cartilage (or chondral tissue) (after Duellman and Trueb, 1986).

salamander *Pleurodeles waltl* feature long ribs that end in sharp points that sometimes penetrate through pores in the skin. They are surrounded by poison glands—an effective defense mechanism. Anura are easily identifiable by their shorter, inflexible spine and the rod-like urostyle (os coccygis) which consists of fused tail vertebrae. The average number of presacral vertebrae is eight; only *Ascaphus* still has nine. In some species the first two and the last two vertebrae are fused to the sacral vertebra, which reduces the total length and leaves only six distinguishable elements (for example, *Hymenochirus* and *Oreophrynella*). In these extreme cases the urostyle fuses completely with the sacral vertebra.

And finally there is the skull, constructed out of several components that form one functional unit. The skull must be regarded as being part

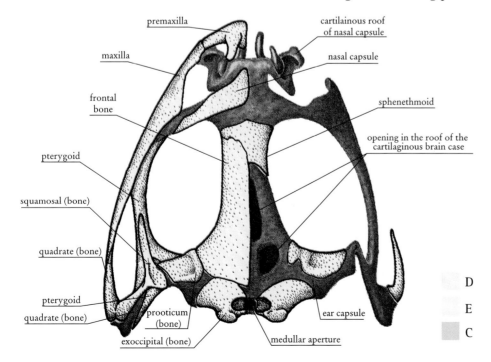

premaxilla
maxilla
frontal bone
pterygoid
squamosal (bone)
quadrate (bone)
pterygoid
quadrate (bone)
exoccipital (bone)
prooticum (bone)
medullar aperture

cartilainous roof of nasal capsule
nasal capsule
sphenethmoid
opening in the roof of the cartilaginous brain case
ear capsule

D
E
C

of the axial skeleton, as it is the foremost mobile element and also the element at which the chorda originates. However, unlike other vertebrates, recent amphibians do not have frontal vertebrae that elongate the skull. That is why the hypoglossus, the twelfth cerebral nerve, lies outside of the cerebral capsule. The foremost cranial locomotion and orientation pole is formed by the cluster of large sensory organs: the nose, the eyes, and the stato-acoustic system, which is, the sense of hearing and of equilibrium with three semicircular canals. Each of these three paired sensory organs is surrounded by a cartilaginous capsule and is thus protected. While the two nasal and ear capsules are firmly fused with the cartilaginous brain capsule, the eye is laterally attached to the skull through six bands of muscle on each side. The brain capsule at the center of the skull is still relatively small in a frog, with the brain being noticeably narrower than the diameter and only a little longer than twice the diameter of the eye.

The primary maxilla is fused to the cerebral capsule near the ear capsule. The whole of the cerebral capsule, including the attached nasal and ear capsules, is called the neurocranium; the cartilaginous primary branches of the upper and lower jaw are called the viscerocranium because they originate in the supportive components of the foregut. Both skull components, the neurocranium and the viscerocranium, are always cartilaginous. In recent amphibians, sections of the cranium remain cartilaginous throughout adulthood.

These two skull components are joined by a third, the dermatocranium. It is a roof plate carapace that forms the jaw ridges, the roof of the palate and the roof of the cranium. The bone elements of the dermatocranium develop directly from within the deeper connective tissue above and on top of the cartilaginous elements with which they fuse more or less into functional units. Sections of the dermatocranium, the jaw ridges and the palate roof may carry true teeth. If the number and composition of the cranial bones in the skull of recent amphibians are compared with fossil specimens, a noticeable reduction in number can be detected. The covering bones are differentiated only in the areas where they carry out a necessary function. The most compact and in some characteristics still primitive skulls are found in Gymnophiona, whereby the compactness is undoubtedly a result of their burrowing mode of life. The majority of Anura have a rather solid skull, although significant amounts of cartilage remains beneath the covering bones. The very large eyes in Anura require that the skull has a laterally closed maxillary ridge and a central fixed brain case. In many Urodela, the lateral covering bone elements are reduced and the eye cavity is open on the lower lateral side, which means that there is no continuous maxillary ridge. Paedomorphic, aquatic Urodela display the most pronounced reductions in the cranial skeleton, the girdles and even in the spine and the extremities.

The tongue or hyobranchial skeleton (tongue-gill-skeleton) develops out of the ventral components of the hyoid arch and the branchial arches (usually two) that lie next to it. Unpaired median elements are joined laterally to the paired remnants of the hyoid arch and the adjoining branchial arches. Especially in aquatic Urodela, where external gills are still often present, this basic structure is usually found in its original form. They also feature a third lateral branchial arch. In air-breathing terrestrial species, the tongue skeleton has points to which the highly differentiated musculature for the usually protrusible tongue can attach. In summary, we can say that in recent amphibians the embryonic skeleton material—the cartilage—is still widely present in the adult phase and is transformed into bone only in some small areas. The covering bones of the skull are also reduced in number and size.

Most information on the structure of the musculature is contained in the chapter on saltatory movement. What is remarkable—especially in the more primitive urodele species—is the noticeable segmentation of the musculature in the trunk, which becomes even more pronounced behind the pelvic girdle in the tail region. When the pectoral and pelvic girdle, with its attached fore and hind legs, is removed in dissecting a urodele specimen one is left with an impression of a bony fish. The musculature itself consists of striated muscle fibers. Dorsally, in the epoxonic section, the segments continue without interruption from tail to head. A triple-layered lateral trunk wall and an abdominal wall are found only in the ventral, hypaxonic section. The musculature in the extremities has evolved from the hypaxial musculature. Here we can differentiate an external dorsal and a ventral inner chain of muscles from the girdle to the upper arm and upper thigh, and from upper thigh to lower thigh and to hand and foot. The external dorsal muscles generally enable the joints they surround to flex and extend; the internal ventral muscles are used for contraction and bending.

The Digestive System
(Alfred Goldschmid)

Most recent amphibians are predators. Hence, their intestinal tract has the characteristics of carnivorous vertebrates, even though they may follow many different feeding habits. They con-sume nearly anything that is not too large and easily grasped. Compared with the gut of other tetrapods and of fishes, that of amphibians shows no specialized characteristics. As in all vertebrates, the oral cavity gives onto a relatively short esophagus through which food is passed quickly into the stomach. As carnivores, their stomachs are voluminous enough to accommodate prey, which is usually swallowed whole.

The stomach acid prevents bacterial growth and assists in breaking down proteins with the help of pepsin, an enzyme produced in the stomach. In all these aspects amphibians do not differ from other vertebrates. Immediately adjoining the contractible pylorus are the pancreas and the large liver. The latter is usually divided into two lobes, and in many Anura the left lobe is again divided in two. Its secretions collect in a spherical, relatively large gall bladder, whence they flow directly into the small intestine where the stomach contents undergo further processing and absorption.

The gall secretion of the liver helps to emulsify fats; in other words, it is not a fermenting agent. Digestive enzymes, on the other hand, are produced by the pancreas, whose duct merges with the gall duct before joining the smaller intestine. Urodela have an additional pancreatic duct that leads into the intestine. As in humans and mammals, the liver is the central metabolic organ that regulates blood sugar and thus is the main source of energy, but it also produces the final metabolic products and transports them through the vascular system to the kidneys and finally to excretion.

The size of the liver is determined by its vital function as the storage organ for glycogen (or animal starch), and, as in fish, for fat. It is subject to seasonal changes in size and content. European amphibians, for example, use large amounts of energy during the winter months to build up their gonads for the next reproductive season; in spring they often undertake a long and arduous trek to spawning grounds where they have to fight for space to mate, then migrate to their summer habitat, followed by a period of rest, as is the case for the common toad. By that time, depending on the distance covered in migration, six months may have passed since they were able to consume their last "full" meal.

In Anura especially, the large intestine is more clearly defined; the feces form in this part of the gut and this is where water is largely reabsorbed. The gut in tadpoles is significantly different from the system described above. Prior to metamorphosis, tadpoles are herbivores, filtering single-cell algae out of the water with the help of a large gill basket and, with tiny keratinous teeth, feeding off the fine algal growth on rocks and water plants. The teeth are arranged in characteristic formations and are often used to classify larvae into species. In all vertebrates, herbivorous modes of life always lead to an enlarged intestinal surface for greater absorption. In tadpoles, however, instead of the formation of small pockets or terminal sacs, the small intestine is simply elongated and wound into a tight spiral. As they grow, this intestinal spiral grows larger on the abdominal side, causing the abdominal wall to bulge outward.

Newly metamorphosed anurans (still bearing tail remnants) are noticeably smaller than the often considerably larger late tadpoles prior to metamorphosis. Typically, the tadpoles of some South American frogs, which develop in the small environment of bromelia cups where they feed on their own eggs or those of other species, have a short intestine characteristic for carnivores. Urodele larvae, too, are carnivorous from the beginning and therefore do not display a spiral elongation of the intestine. Nevertheless, the foregut is histologically and cytologically reconstructed in salamander larvae during metamorphosis and the intestinal wall thickens. In the course of evolution, the young tadpoles—just able to feed—were at a significant disadvantage in their ability to swim and their sensory apparatus (especially the eyes) to the larvae of bony fish competing in their role as plankton hunters. The transition to algae filtering and plant feeding was an evolutionary and advantageous path for them. Many anuran larvae are so adapted to herbivorous feeding that the pharynx is incapable of transporting ingested food to the stomach by means of peristaltic muscle contractions. Instead, food is pushed down into the stomach with the help of the dense ciliation of the esophageal epithelium through cilia movement. Remnants of these cilias are still present in some types, and

in addition to the movement created by gulping, they help transport fine food particles to the stomach. In several tadpole species the stomach may not even have the ability to split proteins (for example, *Pelobates*). This type of stomach merely serves as a storage area ("Manicotto").

By comparison to fossil amphibians—for example, *Ichthyostega*—contemporary representatives have strongly reduced dentition. The teeth are usually very small, hardly perceptible to the naked eye and constructed with few bones. In the upper jaw, teeth are usually present along the ridge of the praemaxilla and the maxilla, yet already in frogs they are completely absent on the lower jaw. True toads (Bufonidae) have no teeth at all. The most frequent location of teeth is vomeronasal in the frontal palate roof, just behind and medial to the choanae, the internal nostrils. In the Urodela, palate dentition is usually better developed than in Anura. Teeth are often present on the paired palatines and on the unpaired parasphenoid, the bone of the lateral and middle palate roof. At the entry to the pharynx, a long slit at the back of the throat opens into the larynx from which it often leads directly to the right and left lung sacs.

How do amphibians, who are hunters, grab their prey since they either have only tiny teeth or no teeth at all? Almost all terrestrial amphibians solve this problem with the help of their tongue. In most frogs and toads, the tongue is attached only at the front of the floor of the oral cavity. Its rear is unattached and fills most of the floor of the oral cavity. Crisscrossed bands of muscles from the tip of the tongue to the tip of the chin and on toward the fleshy, rear section of the tongue allow the tongue to flap outward like a heavy fly-whip when the mouth is open. In this manner, the upper side of the tongue—made sticky by secretions from glands in the tongue—is projected

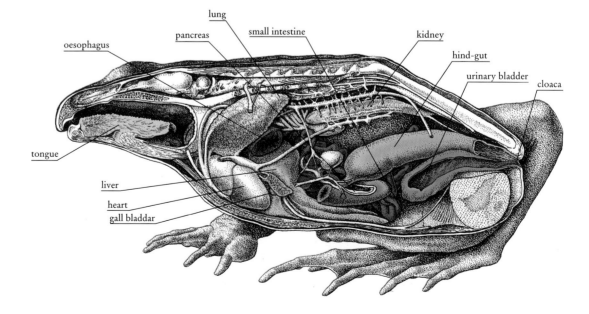

Anatomy of a frog in situ. The stomach, left kidney, left testicle and the fat body have been removed; the third hepatic lobe has been sliced. The organs belonging to the digestive tract are shown in color (original drawing: M. Mizarro-Wimmer).

far outward, hitting the prey from above. Often the upper side of the tongue is molded into the shape of an inverted spoon during this projectile movement. The insect or the worm sticks to the tongue. The rear edge of the tongue is at the greatest distance from the open mouth, its underside pointing up. On average, the entire process takes place within one five-hundredth of a second. Retracting the tongue to which the prey is now attached occurs with even greater speed. It is little wonder that these processes have become known only recently. Technical advances in photography and camera construction in the early 1960s played a vital role in answering many questions about this method of catching prey. The small teeth—provided there are teeth at all—serve only to hold onto the prey during swallowing.

North American lungless salamanders and European cave salamanders (*Speleomantes*, Plethodontidae) have developed protrusible tongues that can stretch even farther, and in which the tongue skeleton too is projected forward like an unfolding pole. In this manner they can "hit" prey at distances that exceed their own body length by 44 to 80 percent. Only a chameleon's projectile tongue can extend farther. The entire process from mouth opening and tongue projection to capturing prey, retraction and jaw closing takes less than a tenth of a second. Swallowing occurs in a mere seven-hundredths of a second. If the tongue cannot be projected, as is the case in the disk-tongued frogs (Discoglossidae), to which the European fire-bellied toads (*Bombina*) and the midwife toad (*Alytes*) belong, the entire body is projected forward in a rapid motion that is synchronized with closing the jaw. Hence, the absence of dentition and the construction of the tongue also influence motion behavior. In aquatic urodele larvae, paedomorphic, aquatic urodele or representatives of the primitive tongueless frogs (Pipidae), all of which have neither tongue nor dentition, prey is captured by means of a sudden rapid thrust forward, creating a small eddy in the water and an equally rapid opening and lowering of the floor of the mouth. This method of catching prey, also described as "suction and gulping," can be viewed as a remnant of primitive fish behavior; today this is still the most common manner of catching prey in fish.

Excretion and Reproductive Organs (Alfred Goldschmid)

In amphibians, the kidneys are located near the roof of the body cavity immediately below the dorsal musculature. They are paired organs, quite large, usually reddish brown due to their abundant vascular supply. As in all vertebrates, the glomerular filtrate voids first into the renal

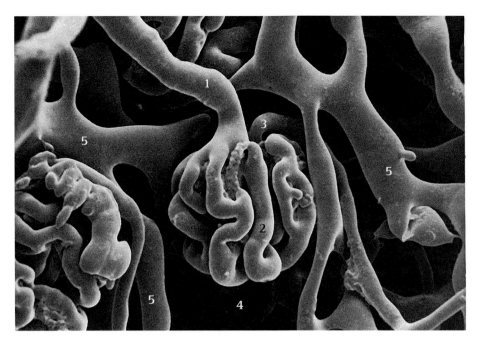

corpuscle (Malpighian body). A small artery leads into this body, leading into a number of capillary loops, the glomerules, which are covered in many-branched cells, the podocytes. Another smaller artery drains blood from the glomerules. Since the pressure in the incoming and outgoing artery is fairly equal, water is voided into the small urinary tract through the filter provided by the podocytes. This water contains ions and low-molecular matter. Nitrogen excretion is usually effected through water-diluted urine and in aquatic species, the urine includes toxic ammonia.

Amphibians generally have plentiful water supplies. Therefore they produce a very dilute, watery urine that is hypotonic relative to the blood—that is, it contains fewer dissolved electrolytes and is therefore less concentrated. This is in significant contrast to mammals, who produce a hypertonic urine that is more highly concentrated than their blood. In all vertebrates the glomerular filtrate is processed and vital substances and ions are reabsorbed and returned to the body's circulatory system prior to excretion. In mammals, large amounts of water are reabsorbed from the globerular filtrate, which causes the urine to be more concentrated. Amphibians are unable to perform this process because they lack the necessary section in the small tubule that leads away from the kidney, the so-called loop of Henle. In contrast to mammals, the renal tubule in amphibians begins with a strongly ciliated "neck section," which rapidly transports the glomerular filtrate away from the kidney. The amphibian system is therefore quite "wasteful" of water, which is the means of transporting and diluting body waste: on a daily basis amphibians evacuate up to one-third of their body weight in the form of urine. In humans, this value is only one-fiftieth. While humans reabsorb approximately 99 percent of the water

Glomerulus of renal corpuscle of a common toad (Bufo bufo).
1—afferent arteriole
2—glomerulus with subunits
3—efferent arteriole
4—cavity containing Bowman's capsule
5—peritubular vessels.
Vascular capacity preparation, SEM image, magnified by 450.

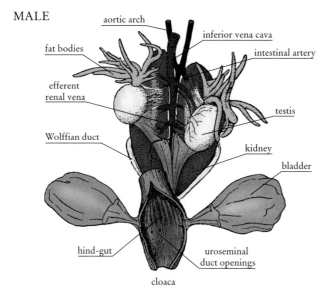

MALE

aortic arch
inferior vena cava
fat bodies
intestinal artery
efferent renal vena
testis
Wolffian duct
kidney
bladder
hind-gut
uroseminal duct openings
cloaca

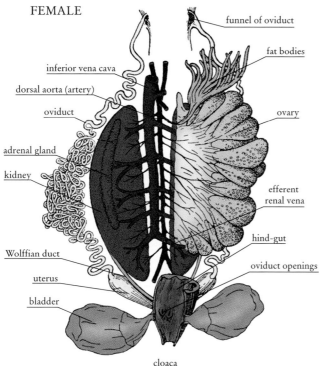

FEMALE

funnel of oviduct
fat bodies
inferior vena cava
dorsal aorta (artery)
oviduct
ovary
adrenal gland
kidney
efferent renal vena
hind-gut
Wolffian duct
oviduct openings
uterus
bladder
cloaca

Urogenital system of a frog (Rana esculenta), ventral view. The cloaca and bladder have been cut open. (modified version after several authors).

contained in glomerular filtrate, the same absorption rate is 10 percent in aquatic amphibians, approximately 30 percent in Urodela and between 20 and 40 percent in most Anura. Only a few species can reabsorb up to 60 percent of the water in the kidney. Yet despite this abundant evacuation of water, up to 96 percent of dissolved salt is reabsorbed from the glomerular filtrate.

In amphibians the number of capillary loops with arteries, the glomeruli, varies from 400 and 2,000. The diameter of these is between 120 and 160 micrometers, which makes them about the same size as they are in humans. In most Urodela the glomeruli degenerate in the pars sexualis of the kidney, so that only the rear section is active for excretion. In some species, such as *Euproctus asper*, the pars sexualis is completely separated from the excretory section of the kidney.

The individual podocytes are much larger in amphibians than in humans. And with 2.5 million glomeruli, humans have approximately three times as many as frogs, relative to body weight. In addition to the arterial system of the glomeruli, amphibian kidneys are fed through a venous venal portal system. Thus the veins draining the body, the hind limbs and the tail, lead into the kidney, where they split into capillaries that surround the renal tubules which are capable of resorption, and then form a large vein that leads to the heart, the inferior vena cava. This venus renal portal system goes back to fish ancestors and is typical for Anamnia. In reptiles it is still partially present in a reduced form, but in mammals it is altogether absent.

Amphibians retain primitive structures not only in the well-developed renal portal system. Even under a magnifying glass, several hundred round to oval openings can be seen in the surface of the kidney. The radius of each of these openings is slightly protuberant and studded with fine hairy cilia. They each lead into an equally densely lashed small tubule that terminates in one of the small rear veins. These open lashed funnels, so-called nephrostomes (or kidney mouths), are present in all vertebrates during development and are, to begin with, an open connection between the body cavity and the deferent renal tubule. Only in amphibians are these kinds of open connections between the kidney and the peritoneal cavity still present in adults. What is new is that these no longer merge with the renal tubule but with the vena, and the function of this structure is still unknown.

The urine is collected in the urinary bladder prior to excretion. This bladder is a ventral sack in the cloacal region. In *Proteus* and *Amphiuma* the urinary bladder is in the shape of a long cylinder, which is divided into two chambers, or even two sacs, in most Salamandridae and frogs. Water can be reabsorbed again through the vascular network in the wall of the bladder. Large volumes of urine are often voided in moments of flight or stress—it often happens when you hold a frog in your hands—and this makes the body noticeably lighter.

The kidneys in male and female amphibians are more or less similar in shape, but their connection to the reproductive glands is very different, as are the various efferent ducts. In amphibians, the testes are attached via small tubules to the frontal and abdominal side of the kidneys. The tubules are linked to the deferent renal tubules. In Anura, the Wolffian duct, or primary urinary duct is located at the edge of the kidney where the efferent ductules that permeate the kidney anastomose. During the reproductive season seminal fluid is transported via the anterior part of the kidney into the urinary duct. For the duration of the mating period this duct has therefore a double function: transport of seminal fluid and transport of urine. Excretion is mainly performed in the caudal part of the kidney at that time. Anurans have a left and right spherical or ovoid testicle. In Urodels the two testicles are elongated, often show two to three lobes in line and lie on both sides of the narrow elongated cranial part of the kidney. This part of the kidney serves only for transport of the seminal fluid to the Wolffian duct which resembles in this case a true seminal duct. The sperm transporting part of the kidney is called "pars sexualis" and may even be separated from the excretory part lying behind. To excrete urine up to 20 separate collecting ducts have developed on both excretory kidneys, each leading to the cloacal region. These secondary developed urinary duct fuse with the seminal duct (the "primary urinary" duct, or "Wolffian" duct or archinephric duct) very late, immediately before entering the cloacal region.

In contrast to anurans, urodele males have an often darkly pigmented duct which lies close to the deferent duct and continues far beyond it in an upward direction, becoming gradually thinner and finally terminating in a dead end. This is a non-functioning oviduct or Müllerian duct. While it is placed in male Urodela, it does not develop fully because an ovary has not evolved. This retention of male and female genital or reproductive elements even in the adult phase has made amphibians into a preferred research subject with regard to sex differentiation and sex determination. The males of true toads have attracted special interest. They possess the so-called Bidder's organ located just in front of the testis, and this organ contains undifferentiated gender cells. When the testis is removed, these cells can differentiate within one to two years into a fully functioning ovary with its hormonal regulation, an oviduct is then formed. In Anura, this kind of sex transformation occurs in nature under certain ecological conditions.

Different Anura, especially the South African clawed frog (*Xenopus laevis*), were often used for pregnancy testing during the first half of the century by injecting urine taken from pregnant women. The hormones contained in the urine caused the corresponding reaction to occur in the test animal—spawning, semen excretion, etc. These labor-intensive tests have today been replaced by more expedient and safer biochemical procedures. Before we turn to the female genitalia, we should take a quick look at the fat bodies in amphibians. While

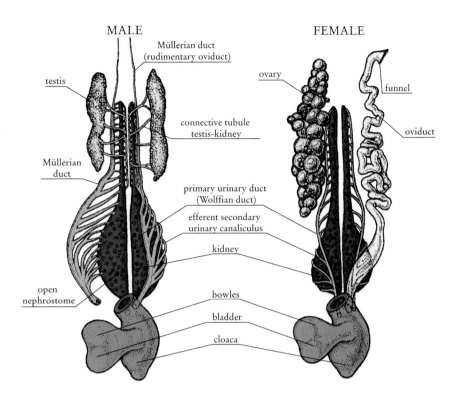

birds and mammals can store considerable amounts of fat in their skin and in the mesenteries of the gut, and even reptiles develop mighty fat bodies in an abdominal fold in the wall of the body cavity, amphibians develop paired long fat bodies (Urodela) to finger-shaped fat lobules (Anura) on the anterior side of the sex organs, i.e., the testes or the ovaries. Like the gonads, the fat body is suspended from the roof of the body cavity and hangs into the cavity. This position becomes understandable when we look at how the fat body develops. It gathers in the anterior section of the paired genital fold of the wall of the body cavity. Only later do the primordial germ cells migrate into the folds and develop corresponding gonads or, in the case of toads, an area with undifferentiated germinal cells, the Bidder's organ mentioned above. The dimension of the fat body is closely related to the maturity of the reproductive glands since it resembles the necessary energy store.

In female amphibians a left and right ovary develops posterior to the fat body. In Urodela it remains elongate, while it is lobulous and voluminous in Anura. The eggs mature in the cell envelopes, the follicles. Even in the ovary, the dark animal pole of the egg can be differentiated from the whitish vegetative pole rich in yolk. The mature eggs are released into the body cavity when the follicle bursts open and are then transported by motion and ciliary straights in the wall of the peritoneum to the openings of the two oviducts. The wide openings of the oviducts, the ostia (or funnels), lie far forward near the region of the heart and close to the base of the lung pouches. Depending on the level of maturity, the oviducts have many loops and are usually con-

*Urogenital system of a salamander (*Salamandra salamandra*), ventral view (modified after several authors).*

siderably wider at the ends. Eggs are stored there before spawning and this part of the oviduct is called a "uterus." The walls of the ovaries are equipped with glands that produce the gelatinous layer that surrounds the eggs, and which—after the eggs have been expelled into water—expands jelly-like into a thickness several times bigger than the egg's diameter. While the Anura display the characteristic clasping position with the smaller male clasping the female from behind, fertilization itself is actually external. Only the American frog species *Ascaphus truei* has internal fertilization, whereby a short, wedge-shaped extension of the cloaca, supported by two internal cartilaginous rods, is inserted into the cloaca of the female as a copulatory organ. The Gymnophiona, too, have internal fertilization by means of a protrusible cloacal tube with keratinous warts, but without cartilaginous rods.

Most unusual among all vertebrates is the indirect method of fertilization in most Urodela. A complex glandular system at the cloaca produces a "semen carrier" (spermatophore) from secretions. This "carrier" is placed on the ground and a stem carries a thick, cap-shaped mass of sperm. The size of this spermatophore varies between 1/16 and 7/16 of an inch (2 and 10 mm), depending on the body size of the species. During the mating dance, the female passes above the spermatophore, and her lip-like cloacal rim picks up the cap on top of the spermatophore. In the roof of the female cloaca, near the entry to the ovaries, lies a bundle of tubular glands, often with a joint duct. The sperm that the female has picked up penetrate into this "sperm bank," where they remain until the mature eggs are released and are then inseminated. In some salamanders the sperm are said to survive up to two and a half years inside the female. The Cryptobranchidae, Hynobiidae, and Sirenidae do not produce spermatophores. *Ranodon sibiricus* exhibits a unique behavior. In contrast to all other

Hynobiidae, it produces a spermatophore. But instead of picking it up, the female places the eggs on top of the spermatophore.

The Vascular System
(Alois Lametschwandtner)

Amphibians have a closed vascular system. Its main function is to transport oxygen, carbon dioxide, nutrients, hormones, metabolites, immune cells and antibodies, with the blood acting as transport agent. Blood consists of solid elements, the blood cells (red blood cells, white blood cells, platelets), and liquid elements, the plasma and the proteins and electrolytes contained in it.

The red blood cells are larger than the disk-shaped, flattened red blood cells in humans (7.5 x 7.5 µm); they are oval in shape and have a nucleus. Red blood cells vary in size in different amphibian species (common toad: 20.5 x 13.3 µm; crested newt: 31.0 x 22.0 µm; European salamander: 43.0 x 25.0 µm; olm: 58.0 x 43.0 µm). The number of red blood cells per microliter also varies (common toad: 2.202 million; crested newt: 164,000; fire salamander: 90,000; olm: 36,000). The circulatory system of amphibians consists of the heart, the large and small arteries, the arterioles, capillaries, venoles, small veins and cava vena. Arteries are blood vessels that transport the blood away from the heart, and veins return the blood to the heart.

The Larval Circulatory System

Most amphibians live in water during the larval phase and have external (external body protrusions) or internal (located in internal gill chambers) gills. The blood flow in the gills is extremely high and in general they serve as respiratory organs; in some species they are also used to filter nutrients from water and are therefore a part of the filter apparatus. This dual role—filtration of nutrient particles versus gas exchange—can lead to functional conflicts.

In larval amphibians (tadpoles) the heart consists of a sinus venosus, two atria, a common ventricle as well as a conus arteriosus, which leads into the arterial stem (truncus arteriosus). The arterial stem splits into the paired ventral aortas, from which the caudal afferent gill arteries as well as the anterior external carotids branch. The efferent gill arteries anastomose with the two lateral dorsal aortas, from which the internal carotids branch anteriorly and merge farther back with the unpaired dorsal aorta. The dorsal aorta splits into a number of main vessels and these supply the internal organs and the hind limbs, before continuing as a tail artery right into the tip of the tadpole's

Diagram of red blood cells, various sizes. Amphibian erythrocytes always have a nucleus, while mammal erythrocytes are non-nucleated.
a—ibex
b—human
c—elephant
d—flounder
e—lizard
f—ostrich
g—tortoise
h—Petromyzontoid
i—ray
j—frog (Rana)
k—olm (Proteus)
l—congo eel (Amphiuma)
(after Waterman et al., 1971).

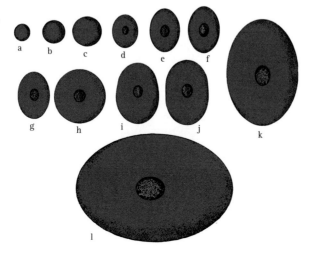

tail. From the tail region, blood is transported to the pelvic region via the tail vein. In the pelvic region the tail vein joins the vein that carries the blood from the pelvis and from the hind limbs and they together form the renal portal veins. The renal portal vena capillarize in the kidneys where they form the peritubular capillaries that surround the renal tubuli. The efferent arterioles of the glomeruli also lead into the peritubular capillaries. The glomeruli are fed via the afferent arterioles that depart from the renal arteries. The renal arteries depart from the dorsal aorta. The renal vein transports blood into the inferior cava vena which leads to the sinus venosus. The blood from the head is transported to the sinus venosus via the superior caval vein.

The Circulatory System in Adult Amphibians

The heart of adult amphibians displays the same sections as the larval heart. It is simply larger and has thicker walls than it does in the larva. In the Urodela, the ventricle has deep clefts caused by sponge-like septums; in the Anura one can observe a balanced arrangement of crypta and septa.

As in other vertebrates, the heart of amphibians is able to contract spontaneously. The heart contraction is caused by the pacemaker, the sinus node, which creates an electrical signal with a specific frequency that reaches the heart muscle cells through the excitatory system of the heart and causes the muscles to contract. Special tight junctions between the individual heart muscle cells, the so-called electrical synapses or gap junctions, ensure that the signal is rapidly passed from one cell to another, which leads to a rapid, coordinated contraction of the heart. This coordination is vital for the effective functioning of the pump that we call a heart. The sequential contractions ensure that the heart chambers are filled with blood in the proper sequence and that the efferent performance of the heart with respect to volume and quality of blood (oxygen deficient, oxygen enriched) is adapted to the immediate needs of the animal.

In adult amphibians blood leaves the heart via the conus arteriosus, a short vascular stem to which the artery stem (truncus arteriosus) is attached. A spiral fold is located inside the lumen of the artery stem; this fold develops during the larval phase and divides the blood leaving the ventricle into the three main vascular stems that branch off on both sides of the artery stem. The uppermost blood in the ventricle, oxygen enriched, is transported into the left and right carotid arteries; the blood from the middle region, less abundant in oxygen, is expelled into the right and left systemic

arteries, and the blood at the bottom, which is most deficient in oxygen, is conducted into the right and left pulmo-cutaneous trunk which bilaterally split into the lung artery and the dermal artery. Regulatory mechanisms in lung and dermal arteries shunt the blood only into the lung, only into the skin or into both, depending on the metabolic demands.

The oxygen-deficient blood from the inferior and superior caval veins enters the right atrium via the venous sinus. The large dermal vein empties into the right atrium and transports oxygen-enriched blood from the skin to the heart. Thus the right atrium contains blended blood. The pulmonary vein that transports blood enriched with oxygen in the lung empties into the left atrium, which contains oxygen-enriched blood only.

In the region of the smallest blood vessels, the capillaries, which connect the arterioles and the venoles and branch out into a complex network that closely embraces body cells, blood velocity is low. Because of their small diameter (5 to 15 micrometers or 5/1000 millimeter to 15/1000 millimeter) and their density, the capillary net-work has a large inner total surface. This makes them an excellent exchange area for oxygen and nutrients for body cells; it also enables them to absorb carbon dioxide and waste products discharged by active body cells. Carbon dioxide is largely released through the skin. Waste products are expelled through the kidneys and the skin.

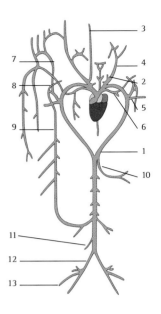

Diagram showing arterial system of a frog (after Waterman et al., 1971):
1–aorta
2–arteria carotis communis
3–arteria carotis interna
4–arteria carotis externa
5–arteria subclavia
6–arteria pulmonalis
7–arteria occipitalis
8–arteria cutanea
9–arteria vertebralis
10–arteria coeliaca
11–arteria mesenterica posterior
12–arteria iliaca communis
13–arteria femoralis

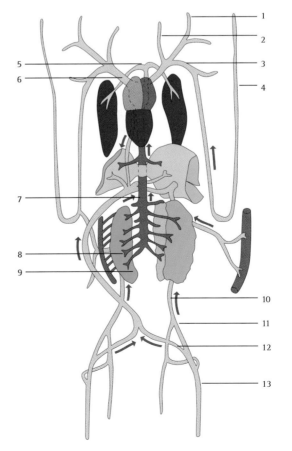

Diagram showing vena system of a frog (after Waterman et al., 1971):
1–vena jugularis interna
2–vena jugularis externa
3–vena subclavia
4–vena cutanea
5–vena pulmonalis
6–vena cava superior
7–vena cava posterior
8–vena renalis
9–kidney
10–vena iliaca communis
11–vena iliaco exterua
12–vena abdominalis
13–vena femoralis

Respiration
(Alois Lametschwandtner)

Amphibians extract the oxygen they require from water and/or air. The former is performed with the help of their gills, the oral epithelium and the skin; the latter by pulmonary respiration. Both types of respiration (in water and in air) are used to varying degrees but usually simultaneously.

Respiration in Larval Amphibians

Tadpoles breathe through the skin with the help of external (Urodela) or internal (Anura) gills and/or with the help of lungs. After metamorphosis only a few (paedomorphic) amphibians continue breathing through gills; the skin and the lung become the primary respiratory organs. During specific developmental periods two or all three respiratory organs may operate simultaneously.

The size, shape and construction of amphibian gills vary greatly. To perform efficiently, they must have a large surface, a very thin epithelium and a dense capillary network. Gill performance can be increased through the counter-current created between the current of water flowing past the gills and the blood flow inside the gill vessels; the counter-current enhances oxygen absorption from water into the bloodstream.

Generally the external or internal gills in tadpoles are supplied with blood from afferent gill arteries. These vessels branch from the ventral aorta, which in turn originates in the artery stem. In the gills themselves, the afferent arteries branch out into a dense network of capillaries that lie directly beneath the thin gill epithelium.

In most tadpoles the skin is the most active respiratory organ. Up to 60 percent of the oxygen intake and up to 50 percent of carbon dioxide exchange occur via the skin. Experiments during which tadpoles were kept for four weeks in water with reduced oxygen content have shown that the capillarization in the skin increases and the capillaries move closer to the surface of the skin.

The pulmonary respiratory system in tadpoles consists of a larynx, a short windpipe that branches into short right and left bronchi, with the bronchial tubes leading directly into the slightly septate sac-shaped lungs. The lung is equipped with a dense network of noticeably broad, flattened capillaries supplied from the pulmonary artery. The pulmonary vein connects to the left atrium of the heart.

The Respiratory System in Adult Amphibians

Skin, lungs and oral epithelium are the respiratory organs in adult amphibians. Gills are rarely present. Amphibian skin is an effective respiratory organ due to its low degree of keratinization, its thinness, its pronounced capillarization and its moist surface. The percentage of skin respiration versus overall respiration varies greatly among amphibian species. The extent of skin respiration depends on the partial pressure of oxygen and carbon dioxide in the ambient environment (air, water). Regulatory mechanisms can increase or decrease blood circulation in the skin in the short term, or can reroute the blood flow directly to the lung with the help of sphincter muscles at the afferent vessels. Long-term adaptations to increased oxygen requirements are effected through an increase in the surface of the skin—for example, by formation of skin folds, ridges, wrinkles, papillae, or through an increase in the number of skin capillaries.

With the exception of lungless salamanders (Plethodontidae) and the genus *Onychodactylus* (Hynobiidae), all other amphibians are equipped with lungs, as are reptiles, birds and mammals. In 1995, the discovery of a lungless caecilian caused a sensation. The lung is constructed as a sac lung with minimal septation—its internal surface is rather small—and its structure greatly resembles the lung in Dipnoi. It performs 20 to 75 percent of the total respiration. The lung is respirated through the larynx, a short windpipe and short bronchial tubes. It is ventilated by means of active gulping of air; expiration (breathing out) occurs through opening the larynx and the positive pressure that exists inside the lung, and while diving through hydrostatic pressure.

The Oral Epithelium

Due to its dense capillarization, the oral epithelium in amphibians contributes from 1 to 10 percent to their overall respiration.

Amphibian skin, bare and only slightly keratinized with strong capillarization, is ideal for skin respiration. The illustration shows the tree frog Hyla minuscula (Hylidae).

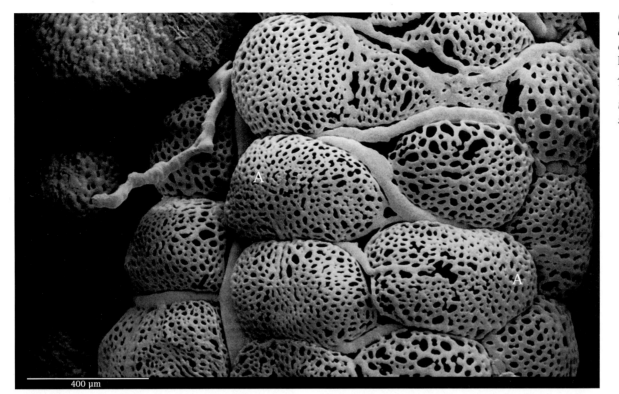

Capillary bed of the lung in a tadpole of the African clawed frog (Xenopus laevis).
A–alveolus.
Vascular secretion preparation, electron-microscopic scanned image.

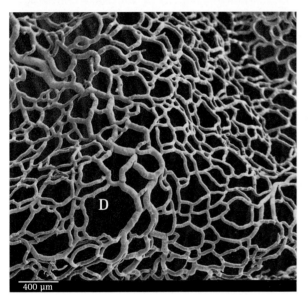

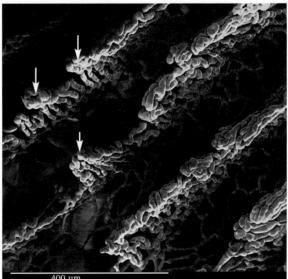

Middle left: Vascular network in the skin of an alpine salamander (Salamandra atra).
D–opening in a skin gland. Vascular secretion preparation, electron microscopic scanned image.
Middle right: Parallel rows of capillaries in the region of the palatine epithelium of the common toad (Bufo bufo). The arrows indicate vascular bundles near taste buds. Vascular secretion preparation, electron-microscopic scanned image.

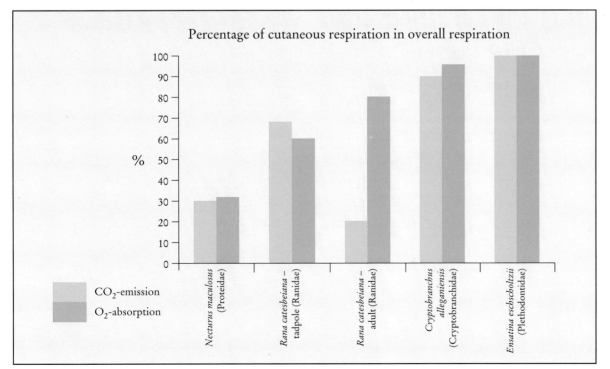

Percentage of skin respiration in total respiration in selected amphibians. Lungless salamanders (Plethodontidae) breathe almost exclusively through the skin (after Feder and Burggren, 1986).

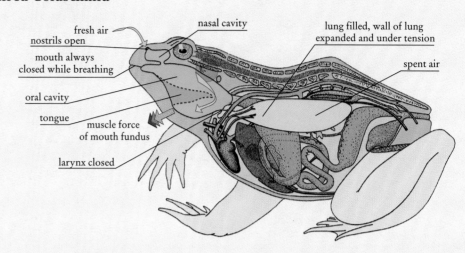

The lungs in modern amphibians are paired sacs that begin immediately behind the larynx and hang down into the visceral cavity. When filled they reach almost all the way to the cloacal region. They are not separated by any walls from the peritoneal cavity, such as the diaphragm in mammals.

Recent amphibians do not have a closed mobile rib cage like reptiles, birds and mammals. Their ribs are noticeably shortened; in most species they are absent altogether. Thus the lung cannot be ventilated by rib movement as it is in amniotes.

Hence, amphibians are the only tetrapods to continue practicing the original deglutition respiration, still present in Dipnoi,

The larynx is also closed and the lung, filled with used-up air, is expanded; the elastic fibers in its wall are stretched taut. Now the fundus is lowered far down and

air out of the mouth and the open nostrils. Next the nose is closed off from the inside, the fundus and tongue are lifted to the roof of the mouth, and the oxygen-enriched air is swallowed down into the lung, which causes the lung once again to expand. In Anura the protuberant eyes can even be pulled back with a special set of retractory muscles to support the act of swallowing air. The oral-laryngeal cavity can accommodate only approximately one-quarter of the capacity for air volume of the expanded lung. Swallowing and pressing air down into the lung is therefore a process that is repeated in rapid succession until the lung capacity has been fully exchanged. Lungless salamanders breathe mostly through a rapid ventilation of the oral-laryngeal cavity, whose mucous membrane is capillarized and carries out the gas exchange; during this process the fundus and, visible from the outside, the larynx may vibrate up to 180 times per minute. The lungs filled with air can be a hydrostatic organ, similar to the swim-bladder in fish, in aquatic species and during time spent in water in all other species, whereby the degree to which it is filled can strongly influence floating to the top or diving under.

a method that has been perfected in their evolution. Several important structural and behavioral physiological characteristics have developed as a result and are today the prerequisites for successful swallowing or deglutition respiration: a large oral cavity with a fundus that can be lowered to a great degree, maxillar rims that close tightly with a fold-like formation between upper and lower maxilla inside the lips, and above all an external nostril that can be closed shut as well as a muscular flexible entrance to the larynx. How does this process of respiration occur, during which air enriched with carbon dioxide is exhaled from the lung and replaced with fresh, oxygen-enriched air?

At first the mouth and the maxillar rims are firmly shut; amphibians cannot ventilate their lungs with an open mouth and would suffocate *in extremis*, should cutaneous respiration fail as well!

the nostrils open, which allows fresh air to flow into the oral-laryngeal space; the muscular fundus of the eye cavities is also lifted and thus enlarges the oral cavity even more. As soon as the laryngeal gap opens, the "old" air is expelled by means of contraction of the stretched and tensed lung sac, supported by its smooth musculature, flowing past and above the fresh

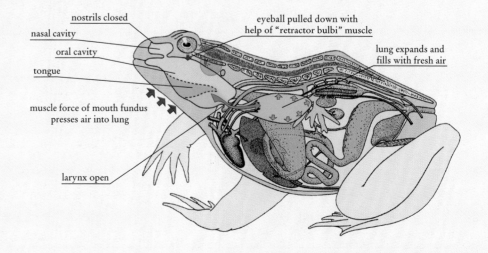

Illustration: modified, based on Storch & Welsch, 1991

Lungless Tetrapods
Werner Himstedt

In addition to extremities and two heart atriums, the lung is another typical characteristic of four-legged terrestrial vertebrates. The transition from life in water to life on land became possible only with the formation of these respiratory organs. In general, amphibians have additional surfaces for gas exchange: the mucous membrane in the oral cavity and the pharynx, as well as the surface of their skin. One of the primary reasons why increased cutaneous respiration led to the reduction of the lungs in the evolution of amphibians is that their bare, scale-less skin is amply supplied with blood. Many frogs and salamanders were thus able to achieve quite efficient cutaneous respiration, which complemented pulmonary respiration or, in some cases, completely replaced it. Among salamanders there is an entire family where the lungs disappeared altogether in the course of phylogeny. All the members of the very successful family of the lungless salamanders (Plethodontidae), which numbers 290 species, are lungless. Members of the genus *Onychodactylus* belonging to the salamanders (Hynobiidae) are also lungless. In the case of the *Salamandrina terdigitata* and *Chioglossa lusitanica* (Salamandriae family), the lungs show only rudimentary development—i.e., they are very small. All other Urodela, however, all Anura and—as it was thought until recently—all caecilians have lungs like all reptiles, birds and mammals.

It has been known since 1995, however, that caecilians without lungs do exist. The discovery of a lungless caecilian by Nussbaum and Wilkinson (1995) was very exciting. Under number NMW 9144, the Natural History Collection at the Vienna Natural History Museum contains a relatively large caecilian specimen, which is a total of 28.5 inches (725 mm) long. The description of its habitat as "South America" is anything but precise. Due to similarities with other South American aquatic caecilians, Taylor (1968) placed this animal in the genus *Typhlonectes* and, in honor of the Viennese herpetologist Josef Eiselt, gave this species the name *eiselti*. Apparently, only one museum collection in the whole world has just one single specimen of *Typhlonectes eiselti*. It lay in alcohol there for many decades until its sensational characteristics were discovered. At first it was noticed that this animal's choana were closed. Choana, the interior nasal openings, are characteristic for all tetrapods and for lungfish (Choanata). Inhaled air travels from the nasal cavities through the choana into the pharynx to be directed from there via the trachea into the lungs. If the choana are closed off, normal pulmonary respiration is impossible. After this unusual discovery, the present zoological custodian at the Vienna Natural History Museum, Franz Tiedemann, donated the valuable holotype NMW 9144 to the American Ronald A. Nussbaum and his English colleague Mark Wilkinson for dissection, in order to find out how this animal might have breathed. Nussbaum and Wilkinson performed the dissection and drew only the left side of the body. With computer graphics, the right side of the animal's body was then added on as a mirror image so that the real right side of the animal still exists as specimen. The dissection only shows that this animal did not have a lung. In the case of *Typhlonectes*, one might have expected a well-developed lung on the left side of the body. There are also no pulmonary arteries or pulmonary veins. Due to the noticeable anatomical characteristics, Nussbaum and Wilkinson allocated these caecilians a genus of their own, which they named *Atretochoana*. The Greek word *atretos* means "closed." The name also refers to the closed choana.

It is possible for animals to exclusively breathe through the surface of the skin only under certain conditions. The following factors are important:

1. The ratio between the surface and the size of the animal; this ratio is more favorable with smaller animals than with larger ones.

2. Low metabolic rate; relatively inactive animals require less energy and have a relatively low need for oxygen, especially in the case of poikilothermic animals that live in cool habitats.

3. High O_2 concentration in the exterior medium.

Most lungless tetrapods are relatively small, slender salamanders with an approximate total length of 1.3 to 6.2 inches (35 to 160 mm). The lungless caecilian in the Vienna Museum is not particularly slender and more than twice the length of the largest known lungless salamander, *Pseudoerycea belli*, which has a total length of 10.8 inches (275 mm). There is no information on the ecology of *A. eiselti* in existence, but if such a large animal obtains all of its required oxygen through the skin, it can be assumed that it lives in relatively cool, fast-flowing mountain rivers. For lunglessness to develop during the course of evolution, the reduction of this organ must be linked to a selective advantage. Plethodontidae probably reduced the size of their lungs in adapting to life at the bottom of bodies of water, where buoyancy caused by air-filled lungs can be a disadvantage. Many Plethodontidae, viewed as primitive because of their anatomy, live in mountain rivers today, and the terrestrial Plethodontidae probably descended from the salamanders occuring in flowing water. Nussbaum and Wilkinson believe that, in the case of aquatic caecilians, the reduction of the lung also occurred to adapt to the reduction of buoyancy and during the colonization of bodies of flowing water, rich in oxygen. It would be desirable to discover more specimens of *Atretochoana* some day to learn more about the ecology and habits of these remarkable caecilians.

Plethodon yonahlossee, *one of 280 species of lungless salamanders.*

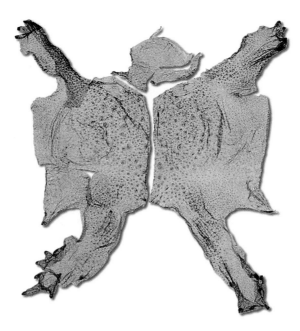

The Skin
(Alois Lametschwandtner and Franz Tiedemann)

The dermis or skin (integument) forms the boundary layer between the organism and its surroundings. It protects against mechanical, physiological and chemical influences of the animate and inanimate environment and also fulfils physiological functions for sensory perception, excretion and respiration. Amphibians have many different modes of life. As tadpoles (larvae) they dwell in water; after metamorphosis most species live on land and often return to water sources only during the spawning season. The skin is correspondingly variable, being equally adaptable to each requirement, and this adaptability is reflected in the structure and function of the skin.

The Skin of the Tadpole

In tadpoles the skin consists mostly of a very thin, multi-layered, non-keratinized epidermis and, in different areas of the body, a thick corium with connective tissue. Depending on the age of the tadpole, some parts of the body may already be equipped with multi-celled glands. Structurally, the epidermis resembles

This Megophrys nasuta (Pelobatidae) from South East Asia tries to alleviate exuviation by opening its mouth, by yawning, and by using swallowing motions.

that of fish, especially in young tadpoles, where it has single-cell glands.

The glandular secretions are defense mechanisms against predators and also a means of communication within a school of tadpoles. But the skin of tadpoles also plays a sensory role by means of unattached nerve endings or sensory receptors (e.g., neuromasts, taste buds).

The Skin of the Adult Amphibian

After the transition from life in water to life on land, the amphibian must protect against desiccation. This is usually accomplished through a thickening of the individual skin layers, relocation of the skin glands from the epidermis to the corium beneath, and keratinization of the outermost epidermal layers.

In adult amphibians, the skin consists of the epidermis, the dermis (or corium) and the subcutis. The latter is well developed in only a few species. In most others, instead of the subcutis there are large lymphatic sacs divided by septae. The epidermis consists of several cell layers whose uppermost layer is keratinized and varies in thickness from one body area to another; the thickness is also influenced by the habitat (*Salamandra salamandra*: dorsal: 64–94 µm; abdomen: 120 µm; *Triturus cristatus*: dorsal 27 µm; *Rana esculenta*: abdomen: 46 µm). Epidermal formations may include warts, tubercules, spines, claws, and in larvae, keratinous teeth. The lowest layer of the epidermis is the stratum germinativum, or Malpighian layer. Cells in this layer divide frequently and produce the cells of the next layer, the stratum spinosum, or prickle-cell layer, which in turn are also capable of division. These are large cells with a polygonal shape. Their name derives from the unusual strong intercellular connections that give them a thorn-like appearance under the microscope. These connections make the prickle-cell layer mechanically very stable. The prickle-cell layer is followed by the stratum granulosom, or granular-cell layer, a layer of flattened cells with perishable nuclei and distinctive granular content. The uppermost layer of the epidermis, the actual keratin layer, is formed by alternating layers of flat, dead, keratinous scales. The keratinous scales consist of the resistant protein keratin.

The mucous and serous granular glands located in the dermis extend into the surface of the epidermis. Secretions from the mucous glands keep the skin moist and slippery; those from the granular glands are scent, defense or toxic secretions. The skin secretion of the South American *Phyllobates terribilis*, used for poison arrows, is the most effective of all such toxins. The dermis consists of two separate dense layers of connective tissue, blood vessels, nerve strands, and pigmentation cells with different pigments. The uppermost layer consists of a loose connective tissue which surrounds the large granular glands and the smaller mucous glands located in this layer. These skin glands excrete their secretions to the skin surface via a tubular duct. They are surrounded by a layer of smooth muscle cells, arranged like baskets, which contract in reaction to hormonal or nervous stimulation and release the gland secretions to the skin surface.

The density of the skin glands varies greatly among amphibian species, but it also depends on body size. For example, the density of mucous glands in the dorsal skin of the common toad (*Bufo bufo*) is 9 per mm^2, in the tree frog (*Hyla arborea*) it is approximately 130, in the grass frog (*Rana temporaria*) approximately 40. The glands are often gathered into dense glandular packages. Since these glands are very active, they are surrounded by a dense capillary network.

The cement gland and the hatching gland in embryos are special glands. The latter aids the embryo in enzymatic degradation of the surrounding gelatinous sac during hatching on its way to becoming a freely swimming larva. The thumb pads (callouses) of males also fill with glands during the mating season.

The lowest layer of the corium consists of many layers of densely packed bundles of connective tissue fibers. Blood vessels and bundles of nerve fibers permeate this layer and extend into the boundary layer between epidermis and corium. Only some caecilian (Gymnophiona) species feature ossification formation in the corium, where smaller bony scales are present.

The pigmentation cells or chromatophores are star-shaped cells with long extensions. Depending on the color of the pigment, they are called melanophores (brown or black pigment), xanthophores (contain yellow pigment) or etrythrophores (red pigment). In addition there are iridophores (guanophores), which contain crystalline platelets in their center that reflect incident light in a variety of ways. The number of pigmentation cells, their placement, interaction and various light refraction effects lead to the often quite beautiful and distinct coloring in amphibians. Colors may change quickly (physiological color change) or gradually (morphological color change). Many amphibians are also able to adapt their coloring to light or dark backgrounds. Prerequisite for this color adaptation is the presence of iridophors, xanthophores and melanophores.

Color adaptation is regulated through the

The Lake Titicaca Frog—a Master of Cutaneous Respiration

Lake Titicaca, once the Incas' holy sea, is the only navigable lake in the world located at such a high altitude; this, however, is not the only reason it warrants superlatives. Lake Titicaca is also the habitat of a remarkable Anura. The water surface of the 3,392-square-mile (8,786-km^2) lake near the Peruvian-Bolivian border is located at a height of 12,507 feet (3,812 m) above sea level. The air is therefore very thin.

In order to increase the effectiveness of cutaneous respiration, the Lake Titicaca frog (*Telmatobius culeus*, Leptodactylidae)—who looks prehistoric, is exclusively aquatic and has a comparatively small lung—developed a special "dermal habit." This dermal habit with special skin flaps and folds makes it appear as if a much larger Anura could fit into its skin. The resulting enlargement of the skin surface contributes to increased oxygen intake. This morphological adaptation is further increased by ethological mechanisms: with push-up movements, the frog pumps water to flow past its body, thereby receiving an additional supply of oxygen-enriched water. The Lake Titicaca frog's blood also displays special adaptation characteristics. The erythrocytes are the smallest among all the amphibians; the so-called P_{50}-value (50 percent oxygen saturation of the erythrocytes) is the lowest known among the Anura; the number of erythrocytes and the hemoglobin content of the blood are the highest known among the Anura. Various other species that only live in South America and belong to the known 46 species of the genus *Telmatobius*, living at higher altitudes, demonstrate enlarged skin surfaces. Other *Telmatobius* species living at low altitudes do not.

Hairy Frogs?

The African hairy frog *Trichobatrachus robustus* (Arthroleptidae) is unique among amphibians because of its hair-like dermal appendages. During mating season, the males of this species, which are up to 8.5 inches (22 cm) long, develop dense, up to half-inch (15 mm) long hair-like dermal appendages or dermal threads on their flanks and legs. They consist of very vascularized epidermis, which enlarge the body's respiration surface. The function of these appendages used to be a mystery and has not been fully explained to this day. There is one seemingly evident explanation for these unique appendages that immediately comes to mind: the "hair" is used for cutaneous respiration. The question arises, however, why only the hairy frog, and only males of this species, have to rely on such an enlargement of the body's surface, given that it lives in bodies of flowing water and frequently also near waterfalls, where it deposits its eggs. There is obviously sufficient oxygen there. According to one hypothesis, the "hair" helps *Trichobatrachus* males stay under water for longer periods of time, allowing them to leave the clutch of eggs, which they guard, less frequently. Due to the flowing water, the "hair" is constantly surrounded by fresh water, rich in oxygen. "Push-ups" like the ones performed by *Telmatobius culeus* are therefore unnecessary. Besides this rational but not sufficiently evidenced explanation, there are many views, which are unlikely. For example, the "hair" is thought to serve as a "spawning brush" to attach the eggs. Or it is believed that it is used for camou-

flage or to imitate cushions of algae. Another opinion states that the "hair" has venom glands, organs of touch or other sensory receptors. Or it is seen as a gender-specific characteristic related to sexual selection used to impress females. And lastly, some say that it does not serve any purpose at all.

The "hair" on the African hairy frog Trichobatrachus robustus *is a unique feature among amphibians. This strong Anura is quite capable of defense in comparison to other Anura species: sharp claws on the second, third and fourth toe ensure that the frog can maintain a good hold on the substrate beneath rapidly flowing waters. The claws can also create deep wounds when people misguidedly attempt to capture these frogs. (from: Boulewger, 1902).*

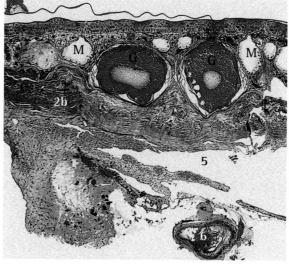

melanophore-stimulating hormone (MSH or intermedine) of the hypophysis (or pituitary gland) which controls the movement of color pigments in the pigmentation cells.

The Subcutis

The subcutis is the innermost skin layer. It contains blood vessels, nerves and large lymph sacs. The lymphatic sacs make it especially remarkable in frogs because these render the skin very flexible on the underlying musculature or the bones. The lymphatic spaces divide the subcutis into outer and inner lamellae. Septa, containing blood vessels and nerves that lead to the skin, connect the two lamella and are located between the lymphatic sacs. In different parts of the body the thickness of the subcutis varies and it contains bundles of collagen and elastic fibers that make it so solid. The subcutis also contains chromatophores. The connection between subcutis and the layer beneath it is effected through a direct skin-muscle link.

Exuviation

Amphibians shed their skin constantly, and during specific periods they exuviate large sections of the corneal membrane. The hormonal exuviation process occurs in several phases. Most amphibians immediately ingest the exuviated skin.

The Skin as a Respiratory Organ

The low degree of keratinization in the epidermis, lobe, wrinkle and papillae formations, as well as extensive capillary networks in the boundary layer to the epidermis, make the skin of larval and adult amphibians an important respiratory organ. Plethodontidae, lungless salamanders, comprising approximately two-thirds of all known urodele species, breathe exclusively through the skin.

The Nervous System

(Wolfgang Walkowiak)

By comparison to other vertebrates, the central nervous system (CNS) of amphibians has a relatively simple structure. Recent discoveries indicate that this is a result of the fact that adult amphibians display numerous pedomorphic (larva-like) characteristics because of a delayed or incomplete development, whereby the degree of pedomorphosis is in direct relation to the species-specific size of the genome. Pedomorphic characteristics are, for example, the ventricular location of neurons, the low degree of lamination in the brain, and the lack of neuronal nuclei. Structures that develop late in the larval phase or even later, during metamorphosis (for example, the auditory pathway or the cerebellum), are especially affected. This simplification in amphibians is seen as a secondary feature in their entogeny because fish brains have a far more complex structure.

Nevertheless, the CNS in amphibians corresponds to a large degree to the general structure present in vertebrates—i.e., the brain is divided into five sections: the segmented spinal cord (medulla spinalis) leads into the hind brain (medulla oblongata), which continues ventrally without visible boundary into the midbrain (mesencephalon). On the dorsal side between the medulla oblongata and the mesencephalon lies the cerebellum (metencephalon). The forebrain is divided into the diencephalon and the telencephalon, which has two separate hemispheres. It should be stressed that the sequential segments represent not only a hierarchy in brain functions. Rather, there are numerous parallel and reciprocal connection between the individual segments, an indication that many brain functions are organized in networks.

The detailed organization of the brain and the function in each segment are best understood by taking a look at the conditions within the spinal cord. The sensory roots of the spinal nerves enter the spinal cord dorsally and terminate in areas that lie above the central canal. The ventral areas of the spinal cord, on the other hand, are motoric. Within the medulla oblongata, the ventricle increases in size and penetrates through to the surface. The overall division into dorsal sensory and ventral motoric areas remains consistent, however, although special sensory nerves (N. VIII, lateral line organ) also enter the medulla oblongata. The ventral part of the spinal cord continues to the floor of the midbrain (mesencephalon), where it forms the tegmentum, where more complex motor functions are located than in the caudal sections of the CNS. The top of the midbrain consists of the optic lobe, the most important visual processing center, and below the torus semicircularis, where complex

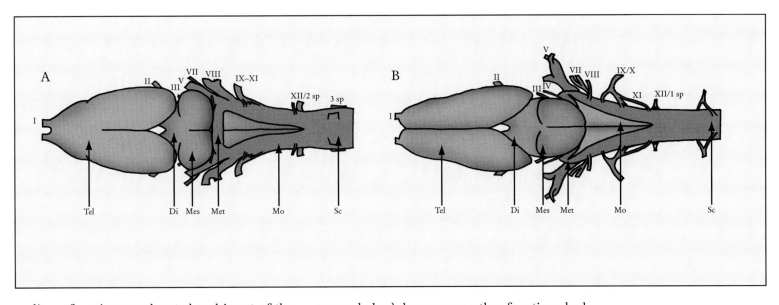

Top view of the brains of an Anura:
A (Bombina orientalis) and a Urodela
B (Speleomantes italicus).
The Roman numerals indicate cranial nerves (see table below).
1 sp, 2 sp, 3 sp = 1.-3. spinal nerve
Di–diencephalon
Mes–mesencephalon
Met–metencephalon (cerebellum)
Mo–medulla oblongata
Sc–spinal cord
Tel–telencephalon

auditory functions are located and input of the lateral line organ and the somatosensory system is processed.

The cerebellum is an important area of integration for various sensory modalities and serves to coordinate movement. The diencephalon is divided into three main compartments in a dorsal to ventral direction. Dorsally is the epithalamus, in which the reproductive functions among others are represented. Moreover, the epiphysis and the parietal organ originate here. The wall of the diencephalon is formed by the thalamus with specific sensory, especially visual, acoustic and somatosensory tasks. It is often regarded as a relay station between midbrain and forebrain. The thalamus projects into the hindbrain in parallel ways, wherein the dorsal projections are usually more prominent. The hypothalamus is at the bottom of the diencephalon; it is an important regulatory center for the physiological functions and at the same time a link between the nervous system and the hormonal system, since this is where the hypophysis is attached. For a long time, the forebrain was called "olfactory brain" (or rhi-

nencephalon), because no other functions had been allocated to it aside from the olfactory sense. This limited interpretation is false, however. Brain damage, modern neuroanatomic techniques and physiological measurements have shown that the forebrain in amphibians does correspond to the basic plan of a vertebrate brain. The ventral forebrain contains areas that correspond to the basal ganglia and parts of the limbic system; in other words, these are areas that have to do with the evaluation of sensory input and the generation of biologically meaningful behavior. The dorsal wall is formed by the lateral, dorsal and medial pallium, structures whose meaningful homologization to corresponding brain areas in other vertebrate groups is currently the subject of lively debate. To reach a final evaluation of this question, a series of more extended comparative studies are necessary.

The cerebral nerves in amphibians with termination and origin and function (N.–nervus; m–motoric, s–sensory).

Name	Modality		Termination / Origin	Function
N. terminalis	N. 0	s	Telencephalon	olfactory sense (reproduction)
N. olfactorius	N. I	s	Telencephalon	olfactory sense
N. olfactorius accessorius		s	Telencephalon	olfactory sense (reproduction)
N. opticus	N. II	s	Diencephalon	visual sense
N. oculomotorius	N. III	m	Mesencephalon	4 eye muscles
N. trochlearis	N. IV	m	Mesencephalon	1 eye muscle
N. trigeminus	N. V	s/m	Medulla oblongata	skull sensitivity, maxillar musculature
N. abducens	N. VI	m	Medulla oblongata	1 eye muscle
N. facialis	N. VII	s/m	Medulla oblongata	skull sensitivity, maxillar musculature
N. lateralis anterior		s	Medulla oblongata	lateral line system
N. statoacusticus	N. VIII	s	Medulla oblongata	sense of equilibrium, hearing
N. lateralis posterior		s	Medulla oblongata	lateral line system
N. glossopharyngeus	N. IX	s/m	Medulla oblongata	sense of tast, throat and tongue musculature
N. vagus	N. X	s/m	Medulla oblongata	innervation in skull, throat, larynx and viscera
N. accessorius	N XI	m	Medulla oblongata	pectoral girdle muscle
N. hypoglossus	N. XII	m	Medulla oblongata	tongue musculature and others.

Wolfgang
Walkowiak

Sensory Systems

The sensory organs receive physical or chemical events from the environment (exteroreceptors) or conditions and processes from the body (interoreceptors) and transform them into signals from which the central nervous system can gain information that is biologically important for the organism. Many sensory organs are composed of the actual sensory or receptor cells and auxiliary structures. This chapter focuses on the first group of sensory systems.

Skin Receptors

The skin is the largest contact surface with the surrounding environment. As in all other vertebrates, in amphibians the skin contains numerous free nerve endings that transmit a variety of sensory modalities. These are the temperature receptors in the upper layers of the skin, tactile receptors as well as pain receptors in the lower layers.

The Lateral Line Organ

In addition to these generalized skin receptors, amphibians also have specialized sensory organs in the skin of their head and body, the lateral line organ. It is found in aquatic larvae, aquatic adult Urodela and frogs (for example, discoglossid frogs and clawed frogs) or in adults that intermittently return to an aquatic mode of life. We can differentiate two types of lateral lines (organs) according to their construction and function: electroreceptors and neuromasts. The actual sensory cells of the former are located in "indentations" below the skin surface from which open pores lead to the surface. Electroreceptors enable animals to locate prey using electrical fields. They are present only in some larval Gymnophiona and in aquatic salamanders, where they are localized in the head region.

Neuromasts, on the other hand, are specialized mechanosensitive receptors located at the skin surface and they perceive movements in the water or in water surface waves. Their pear-shaped sensory cells are surrounded by mantle and supporting cells. Spines of the sensory cells, the stereo- or kinocilia, project into the gelatinous cupula that receives the stimulus. Clawed frogs use this organ to locate prey on the water's surface. It has been proven that fire-bellied toads utilize the lateral line organ during mating to detect waves in the water created by the mating calls of other members of their species. These species-specific signals can thus be used to establish territorial boundaries.

Statoacoustic Organs

The statoacoustic organ in amphibians performs a variety of tasks. It combines the sense of equilibrium and of rotation, as well as the vibratory and auditory senses. The inner ear, or otic labyrinth, contains different sensory epithelia that serve this function. It is a membranous structure filled with endolymphatic liquid and is incorporated into the cranial otic capsule. This membranous labyrinth is surrounded by the perilymph. It is divided into two main compartments, the utriculus and the sacculus. The latter features an additional lobe, the lagena. Three semicircular canals originate in the utriculus in perpendicular arrangement to each other.

The sensory epithelia are constructed of secondary sensory cells with characteristic processes— one kinocilium and several rows of stereocilia each. The processes are in fact the structures that transform a mechanical stimulus into an electrical signal. An adequate stimulus results in a movement of the cilia. The sense of rotation is located in the cupula organs in the semicircular canals, which in turn are located in the ventral parts of the canals, the ampullae. The sensory hairs of the receptor cells project into a gelatinous cap, the cupula. When the head turns more rapidly, the endolymphatic liquid in the semicircular canals follows less rapidly than does the wall of the semicircular canal as a result of its inertia. The relative movement between liquid and wall bends the cupula and stimulates the sensory cell through the bending of its cilia.

The utriculus, lagena and sacculus are statolithic organs and provide equilibrium. Assemblies of small calcareous crystals are localized above the maculae; the crystals are embedded into an organic matrix. The orientation of the maculae determines their function. The macula utriculi is oriented horizontally, the macula lagenae and the macula sacculi vertically on different planes. When the head changes its position, the cilia bundles in the sensory cells of the right and left inner ear are sheared to different degrees which enables the

be allocated to one xanthophore, it is called a xanthoiridosome; several xanthoiridosomes, in turn, are related to one large melanophore and together they form a chromatic organ.

Depending on the orientation of the melanin granulae within the melanophore, different color patterns are created: when melanin granulae are bundled around the nucleus of the melanophore, the coloring brightens and—to take the tree frog as an example—we see a yellow to greenish tint. When the melanin granulae migrate to the place where the cell processes of the melanophores originate, creating a dark "umbrella" of pigmentation beneath the guanophore layer, the blue of the guanophores and the yellow of the xanthophores above result in a green color. If the melanin granulae are also found in the cell processes between the guanophores, then we perceive a darker green coloring. But if the melanin granulae migrate into the cell processes above the xanthophores, this negates the yellow coloring and produces gray.

These pigmentation shifts produce a physiological color change (or often only changes in the intensity of the color): it consists only of an intracellular flow of pigmentation granulae, takes place rapidly and is hormonally regulated in amphibians; direct light influences on chromatophores can also occur.

Coloring and Hormones

When an amphibian is placed on a dark non-reflecting surface beneath a bright (white) source of light, its eyes perceive the difference in brightness, and this information is relayed to the tectum opticum in the mesencephalon or midbrain. This section of the brain contains special centers where the information is processed and compared. Should the comparison recognize a difference in brightness, messages are dispatched to the hypothalamus of the diencephalon or interbrain, activating the melanotropin-releasing hormone (MRH) which initiates melanotropin (melanocyte-stimulating hormone, or MSH) being released from the hypophysis. The hormonal injection causes an expansion in the melanophores and a dispersion of the melanin granula, which then brings about the color changes or darkening of color mentioned above. The hormone adrenocorticotrope (ACTH) from the anterior lobe of the pituitary gland produces the same effect on the melanophores.

However, when a frog is placed in complete darkness, it either turns lighter in color or remains pale, because the basic condition in amphibian melanophores consists of a pigment aggregation producing a lightening of color.

In completely bright surroundings (lit from above and on a light surface as well as background), amphibians react by dumping melanotropin-inhibitor hormone (MIH) from the hypothalamus. This inhibits the MSH release from the pituitary gland, which once again causes the coloring to a lightening of color.

The coloring can also become lighter as a result of hormones from the adrenal medulla (adrenalin and noradrenaline), as well as by melatonin from the epiphysis, that is still equipped with light sensor cells in frogs. The epiphysis also performs other important regulatory functions—for example, the rhythm of daily activity (endogenous rhythms, biological clock) or the coordination of seasonal changes and reproduction.

Other Mechanisms in the Color Change Process

In natural conditions, color changes in amphibians are subject to many influencing factors. Temperature increase, strong light or dry air tends to cause lighter, more brilliant colors; temperature decrease, low light or relatively high humidity causes darker coloring.

In contrast to the above-mentioned color changes, morphological color changes are relatively slow processes whereby the pigments or chromatophores themselves are increased or decreased. Examples of such processes are: adolescent coloring, adult coloring in males and females (sex dichromatism), or mating colors.

Usually inconspicuously brown, moor frog males (Rana arvalis) have a distinct and colorful mating habit that results from a relatively slow morphological color change.

*Example of somatolysis in Amalonian horned frog (*Ceratophrys cornuta*): its dorsal color markings are in no relation to the body contours and create a perfect camouflage. The photograph also documents color variability within one population.*

is another form of concealing habit: an attempt to mimic other animals, plants or inanimate objects. The *Hyla* species are known for their mimesis: their green coloring is often an exact match to surrounding leaves. The brown Malawi horned frog of the genus *Ceratophrys* is another example: this species imitates dried leaves.

Conversely, so-called warning coloration (or sematophylactic habits) invites attention, recognition or, sometimes, misrecognition. Baiting or aggressive habits are those with which prey is actively attracted, as in South American *Ceratophrys* species: the well-camouflaged animal sits motionless, moving only one finger of one hand. This often attracts the attention of other smaller creatures which are then devoured by the horned frog (angler effect).

Fright coloration or intimidating appearance (or caenophylactic habits) is used to frighten or startle enemies through unusual behavior, often in combination with warning colors. One typical example is the "fire-belly reflex," during which amphibians roll over abruptly in moments of danger, presenting the enemy with their less familiar, often yellow or yellow-red-black abdomen. This reflex is by no means limited to fire-bellied toads; in modified versions it is also found in several urodele species in North America—for example, in *Taricha granulosa* (roughskin newt) or in *T. rivularis* (red-bellied newt).

Here we should also mention the phenomenon of so-called eye spots—for example, in the South American toad species *Pleurodema bibroni*: when in danger, the toad assumes the characteristic warning position with arms and legs pressed closely against an inflated body. This causes two large, contrastingly colored gland complexes in the hindquarter to take on the appearance of eyes, making the rear aspect of the animal appear like the head of a much larger animal with threatening eyes.

Aposomatic or warning appearances employ distinct signaling colors that communicate unequivocally that the creature is "not for consumption" and capable of defending itself. Predators quickly learn that this poisonous prey should be avoided. Strong colors such as red, yellow and black seem to become more quickly embedded in predators' memories than other hues. These warning colors may cover the entire body or concentrate on specific body areas (for example, throat, abdomen, below the tail); color patterns may also serve as a signal of recognition for members of the same species.

One typical example is the black and yellow (sometimes also red) warning coloring of the poisonous fire-bellied salamander. Newts often

Different Colors and Their Functions

The variety in pigmentation produces different color and pattern characteristics that are utilized by the animals in many ways, such as defense colorings and patterns that support and complement the standard protective mechanisms of attack or defense.

Concealing coloration makes it difficult to see the animal in a natural environment. Sympathetic appearances try to emulate the colors and patterns in the surrounding environment as much as possible. This is the case in many European species—for example, *Rana temporaria*, *R. arvalis*, *Triturus vulgaris* or *T. alpestris*. Extreme variations of this principle may lead to an effect whereby the outline of the amphibian appears to blend into the surroundings through stripes and/or spots in their appearance; this is called somatolysis. Mimesis

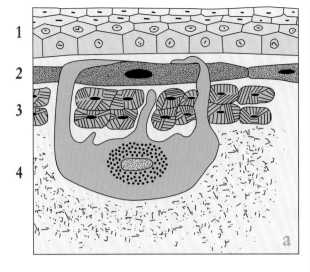

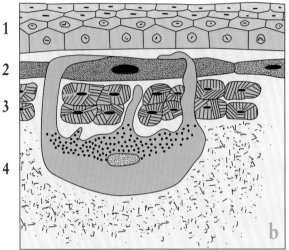

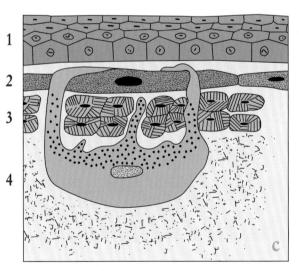

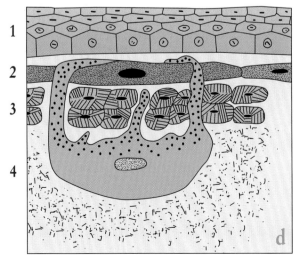

display extremely bright coloring on throat and abdomen. In the extremely poisonous North American mud salamander *Pseudotriton montanus*, red covers the entire body as a warning color.

The most distinct warning colors are present in many highly poisonous tropical frogs—for example, the golden mantella species (*Mantella*) in Madagascar and the Argentine harlequin frog (*Atelopus*) with its highly visible red-black-yellow coloring. The most extreme signaling colors are found in the poison-dart frogs of South America (*Dendrobatidae*) whose color palette has a wide range, from yellow, red, green to dark blue and black. The most poisonous, but not most colorful, representative of this brightly hued frog family is *Phyllobates terribilis*.

Yet defenseless, edible species also capitalize on the frightening effect that colors can produce by imitating the coloring of a poisonous or aggressive species (simulated warning habit, pseudapososomatic habit or mimicry). The harmless, edible North American mountain salamander (*Desmognathus imitator*) almost perfectly mimics the highly poisonous forest salamander *Plethodon jordani*, whose habitat it shares.

Thus amphibian coloring fulfills many purposes and is vitally important to the survival of these animals.

*Blueish male common tree frog (*Hyla arborea*).*

*Left: Pigmentation cells in the integument of a common tree frog (*Hyla arborea*).*
1 epidermis
2 xanthophore
3 guanophore
4 melanophore
and distribution of melanin granula in
a) yellow pigmenation
b) green pigmentation
c) dark green pigmentation
d) gray pigmentation

Miloš Kaležič

Ontogeny and Metamorphosis

In spite of the similarities in the basic egg structure and the pattern of development among major groups, living amphibians vary tremendously in reproductive modes, more than any vertebrate classes. There is much variation in different aspects of reproduction, ranging from gamete transmission to oviposition to modes of parental care. Thus, fertilization can be external or internal. Also, most amphibian species lay eggs (oviparity), but others retain developing embryos through metamorphosis in the maternal oviducts with nutrition provided by the female (viviparity), or embryos may be carried by females (or males) with nutrition provided only by its own yolk (ovoviviparity). Further, the developing young may be released at any stage of development, or retained through metamorphosis (direct development). Viviparity has developed independently in all three amphibian orders. However, only a few cases of viviparity are known among the 4,370 described Anura species and only two among Urodela species have been documented. On the other hand, approximately 75 percent of Caecilian species are viviparous. Ovoviviparity exists in numerous Urodela and Anura, but is absent in Gymnophiona. The most impressive phenomenon in the life cycle of amphibians is undoubtedly their metamorphosis. Aside from insects, amphibians offer the best examples of this type of biological transformation.

Advanced larval stage of Crested (warty) newt (Triturus cristatus).

Two Stages in Amphibian Life

The life cycle with two distinctly different stages is one of the most typical characteristics in amphibians. The aquatic, larval stage is usually followed by a short transition phase into the terrestrial or semi-terrestrial stage of the metamorphosed individuals. In Urodela, the larvae are more or less the aquatic equivalent of the subsequent adult. They are morphologically similar and feed on the same material. Anura larvae, on the other hand, are fundamentally different from Anura adults in appearance and in mode of life.

The phenotypical characteristics and the growth

Right: Adult male Common newt (Triturus vulgaris). Larval and metamorphosed Urodela are more or less identical in shape with the exception of the external gills.

of amphibian larvae are to a larger degree, and perhaps decisively so, subject to environmental influences. The size of the individuals during metamorphosis and the duration of larval development can vary within each species and also from one species to another. Thus larval development can require several days or several years, also dependent on the aquatic habitat of the species.

Metamorphosis is of great interest to biologists because of the dramatic changes that occur within a relatively short period of time. Amphibians are the only tetrapods to display this kind of transformation, familiar even to the lay person. The radical changes in anatomy, structure, and the organism's physiological, bio-chemical and ethological characteristics are related to the transition to a new, terrestrial habitat. Metamorphosis affects nearly all body tissues and causes a number of transformations. We distinguish three types of cells and organs that behave differently during the transforma-tion: cells and organs specific to larvae; cells and organs during the transition from larva to adult; and adult-specific cells and organs. The development of the latter is often accompanied by the formation of completely new structures and the development of new functions. External gills and dorsal tailfin, for example, are typical larval characteristics; they are absent in adults (with the exception of paedomorphic species). Keratinous teeth in tadpoles are another exam-ple: dentition regresses in the adult, where it is replaced by adult maxilla.

Metamorphosis in Anura

In non-tailed Anura, metamorphosis is much more dramatic than in Urodela due to the fun-damental differences in mode of life (between larva and adult). Almost all organs are affected by the metamorphosis: the resorption of the tail, the development of the extremities, the loss of gills and the development of the lung as well as the related changes in the circulatory system, the replacement of larval haemoglobin with adult haemoglobin, the shift from ammonia excretion (typical for aquatic species) to urine, the shift from a predominantly herbivorous to nearly exclusive carnivorous nutrition and the related regression of the keratinous jaw, the expansion of the mouth opening and the short-ening of the intestine, as well as numerous other changes. The lateral line organ in tadpoles regresses and it is replaced by the middle ear and a tympanum. The nervous system and the skin also undergo fundamental restructuring processes. In the European grass frog (*Rana temporaria*) the optical pigment in the tadpole in the retina (porphyropsin) is replaced by rhodopsin in the adult. While Urodela continue in their feeding practices throughout their con-tinuous metamorphosis, Anura must cease feed-ing altogether during the most dramatic phase of the transformation, when the larval oral region is transformed and the adult maxilla develop. The resorption of the tail provides the energy necessary for survival during this phase. Nevertheless, the phase of being "no longer a tadpole and not yet a frog" is a critical stage in the life of each Anura individual. Tadpoles with legs are clumsy swimmers and the tail remnants make jumping difficult. Anura are easy prey during this phase. Rapid transformation and synchronization during metamorphosis in large numbers of larvae are the mechanisms intended to help defend against these dangers.

Metamorphosis in Urodela

In Urodela, metamorphosis is less dramatic; it involves the reduction of the dorsal caudal fin, the disintegration of the external gills and the closure of the gill clefts. The cranial skeleton and musculature are completely reconstructed and other changes occur in the body skeleton. The least dramatic metamorphosis occurs in Caecilians, where it is characterized mostly by regression of gills and dorsal tail fin, as well as changes in the skin and the eyes.

The Role of Hormones in Metamorphosis

Even today, the complexity of metamorphosis as a hormone-regulated process is not fully understood. A major role falls to the degree of sensibility in various tissues to the participating thyroid hormones. Experiments have shown that thyroxine and triiodothyronine, hormones produced in the thyroid, are indeed responsible for metamorphosis. When the thyroid is removed in a tadpole or its function is chemi-cally inhibited, metamorphosis does not take place and they grow into gigantic tadpoles. Conversely, if the thyroid and its hormones are fed to tadpoles, premature metamorphosis occurs. The transformation is coordinated by means of a steady rise to hormone levels during which each tissue responds differently to the increased hormone concentration. Extremities begin to develop, for example, when concentra-tions are quite low, i.e., prior to the resorption of the tail. The release of thyroid hormones is regulated by the thyroid-stimulating hormone (TSH) of the hypophysis (or pituitary gland), which in turn is dependent on the thyrotropin-releasing hormone (factor) (TRH) of the hypo-thalamus. Prolactin, a protein hormone of the anterior lobe of the pituitary gland, is the antag-onist and regulator of the thyroid hormones. Other endocrine glands are also involved in the complex process of regulating the metamorpho-sis, such as interrenals, pineal and ultimo-branchial bodies and endocrine pancreas.

1

2

3

4

5

Developmental cycle and metamorphosis of a common toad
(Bufo bufo):
1/2 spawn
3 embryonic stage after four
days
4 embryo at five days
5 larvae at one week
6 tadpoles at ten days
7 at three weeks
8 tadpole at two months
9 tadpole in metamorphosis

6

7

8

9

Metamorphosis is commonly understood as the dramatic transformation from larval to post-larval life. Yet, some amphibians undergo other, less dramatic changes in morphology during other ontogenetic stages. For example, the return to water for reproduction after reaching sexual maturity can be viewed as a "second" or "secondary" metamorphosis. In adult newts, above all, in the males, the dorsal and caudal fins increase in size during this stage. Gonadal steroids are the driving factors behind these types of changes.

"Shrinkage"

In some Anura species, gigantism occurs in the tadpole. Generally speaking, larval size increases with the length of the developmental period. The South African frog *Kassina maculata* grows to 2.4 inches (6 cm) as an adult, but its larvae reach a length of up to 5 inches (13 cm) during the ten-month larval phase. The larvae of the harlequin frog *Pseudis paradoxa* grow as long as 10 inches (25 cm) and require four months for their development, while the adult measures only slightly more than 2.8 inches (7 cm). The extreme reduction in body length from tadpole to newly metamorphosed frog is called "shrinkage." The largest tadpoles among European species are found in the spadefoots (*Pelobates fuscus*) whose larvae are between 3.0 and 3.9 inches (8 and 10 cm) long, but can grow up to 6.0 or 7.9 inches (15 or 20 cm) long. After metamorphosis the young toads measure a mere 0.75 to 1.6 inches (2 to 4 cm).

Litoria infrafrenata *(Hylidae) tadpole in final stage of metamorphosis. In Anura, a skin fold in the gill region covers the frontal extremities that are forming underneath and are visible only at the end of metamorphosis.*

Miloš Kalezič

Paedomorphosis

*Heterochronism is understood as a deviation from the normal sequence of organ formation. Paedomorphosis in amphibians is one example of heterochronic development. (This phenomenon has various names, but in recent years, especially in English, "paedomorphosis" has become the most commonly used term.) It refers to sexual maturation in individuals where embryonic, larval or juvenile characteristics are still present. In 1861, zoologist De Filippi discovered sexually mature representatives with characteristics that were clearly larval among metamorphosed alpine newt (*Triturus alpestris*). Since then, paedomorphosis has been observed in numerous Urodela species, but never in Anura or Caecilians.*

*The external gills are the most distinctive larval characteristic, remaining intact throughout the adult phase in paedomorphic species. The axolotl (*Ambystoma mexicanum, Ambystomadiae*) is the best-known paedomorphic amphibian.*

Below: In a natural setting Gyrinophilus palleucus (Plethodontidae) from North America is obligatorily paedomorphous.

"Juvenile" Adults

Although paedomorphosis has been studied for a full century—more than 3,500 scientific articles and books have been published on the axolotl (*Ambystoma mexicana*) alone, perhaps the most familiar of all known paedomorphic amphibians—many genetic, ontological and ecological aspects of paedomorphosis remain unknown. Paedomorphic Urodela of different species often exhibit similar external (phenotypical) characteristics, although the manner in which they arrive at paedomorphosis may vary. In some species development is delayed to such a degree that sexual maturity is reached before physical transformation is complete; this is known as neoteny. Other instance of paedomorphosis occur when gonads mature prematurely or in an accelerated fashion even before the somatic development is complete; this is called progenesis. While most Urodela with this phenomenon are in fact neotenous, (true) progenesis does also occur. In both cases a similar, nearly or fully identical phenotype develops and recognizing whether neoteny or progenesis occurred is often impossible through observation alone. It is therefore best to apply the more general, and inclusive, term "paedomorphosis."

In Urodela, paedomorphosis has many faces and a variety of sometimes subtle forms. Morphologically, the main paedomorphic characteristics are a functional lateral line organ, the absence of eyelids, the retention of external gills and gill clefts, as well as a tail fin. One or several of these characteristics may occur within all Urodela families either in all members of a species, or in certain populations or even in single individuals. In four Urodela families, Cryptobranchidae, Sirenidae, Amphiumidae, and Proteidae, all representatives are obligatorily paedomorphic. Distinct changes in the external morphology need not go hand in hand with anatomical or biochemical changes. Although paedomorphic species may not experience a morphological metamorphosis, biochemical changes such as the replacement of larval by adult haemoglobin may occur. For some morphological characteristics it is difficult to establish a clear boundary between paedomorphosis and metamorphosis. In Urodela, different stages of partial metamorphoses lead to a range of adult morphologies, from purely larval through to a mosaic of mixed larval and adult characteristics, and finally purely adult (i.e., metamorphosing) characteristics. It may result in low genetic diversity, in a shift of the sex distribution, in a simplification of the nervous system or an

increase in phenotypical variations among populations. In some Urodela species, paedomorphic individuals are albinos as a result of a malfunction of the hypophysis (or pituitary gland), since the production of the pigment melatonin is controlled by this gland.

Obligatory paedomorphic forms never transform under natural conditions, and forced metamorphosis may be lethal to these species. They are characterized by low thyroid activity, low tissue sensitivity, large cells with high DNA content (second-highest content among all vertebrates after the Dipnoi) and to a lesser degree also a low metabolic rate. Facultative paedomorphic forms, such as Hynobiidae, Dicamptodontidae, Ambystomatidae, Salamandridae, and Plethodontidae, are marked by a high responsivity of the tissues to thyroid hormones and low thyroid activity. Failure to metamorphose in these families is usually related to a hypophysis or hypothalamus blockage; low temperatures and increased prolactin production are other contributing factors. Yet even in this group there are obligatory paedomorphic species, for example, *Haideotriton wallacei, Typhlomolge rathbuni, T. robusta*, and various species of the genus *Eurycea* (all representative of the lungless salamanders or Plethodontidae).

Three different ontogenetic patterns are distinguishable in Urodela. The most common pattern is the metamorphosis of the larva into immature juvenile newt with a predominantly terrestrial mode of life prior to sexual maturity (obligatory metamorphosis). The second pattern is a prolonged developmental phase in the larva and thus sexual maturity, followed by metamorphosis. The third pattern is permanent paedomorphosis: the larva experiences a prolonged growth and reaches sexual maturity without ever undergoing metamorphosis.

How Does Paedomorphosis Occur?

Experiments have shown that the ability to paedomorphose is hereditary, probably with the involvement of several genes, but also under the influence of environmental factors. Thus paedomorphosis is a phenomenon that depends on (species) density, occurring frequently when larva density is low. In the majority of populations, genetic variability is present in one or several genes that are involved in paedomorphosis. Experimental factors regulate their occurrence through natural selection. Some paedomorphic taxa differentiate relatively quickly on a molecular as well as a morphological level. Their genetic isolation from other populations that undergo standard transformation seems to lead to an increased probability of speciation and significant ecological divergency by comparison to metamorphosing relatives.

Several extreme environmental conditions contribute to an increase in the occurrence of paedomorphosis, for example, frigid water in subterranean cave systems in karst regions or permanent aquatic locations without fish stock surrounded by cold or arid land and subject to frequent temperature changes and food shortage. In habitats of this type paedomorphosis is more frequent in *Hynobius lichenatus* or in different *Triturus* and *Ambystoma* species than is the case when environmental conditions are favorable, when the same species tend to metamorphose as usual. The aquatic habitat may offer more constant conditions for survival and sufficient nutrition. It has also been shown that the absence of sympathetic fish fauna is related to an increase in paedomorphosis in some species. Thus facultative paedomorphosis is more frequent in *Ambystoma* and *Notophthalmus* in bodies of water without fish stock than it is in well-stocked waters.

In American lungless salamanders we can observe a relationship between mode of life, subterranean bodies of water and paedomorphosis: species that dwell almost exclusively in subterranean water—such as *Haideotriton wallacei* or *Typhlomolge rathbuni* and *T. robusta*—are obligatorily paedomorphic, while others whose habitats range from both surface and subterranean bodies of water are predominantly facultatively paedomorphic, such as *Eurycea neotenes* or *Typhlotriton spelaeus*. Other Eurycea species in surface waters undergo a standard metamorphosis. Despite all these observations, no definite ecological or geographical factors have been identified that would deliver qualitative or quantitative causes for paedomorphosis.

Extreme environmental conditions can increase the frequency of paedomorphosis. The North American Typhlomolge rathbuni *(Plethodontidae), a cave dweller, and the olm (*Proteus anguinus*) share many features such as reduced eyes and an absence of pigmentation.*

Sex Determination

Robert
Schabetsberger

All hereditary information on the structure of an organism and hence the information on gender is contained in the genes. Genes are elements of chromosomes, which can be made visible under the microscope by means of special dyeing methods. When certain dyes are used, banding patterns also become visible on the chromosomes. When all chromosomes are sorted according to size and numbered, pairs of chromosomes that are identical in size and banding patterns (diploid chromosome set) match up. One chromosome of such a pair is paternal in origin, the other is maternal. When size or banding patterns differ in a single chromosome pair, it is, with few exceptions, usually a pair of both sex chromosomes. But how is sex determined?

How Is Sex Determined?

The total number of chromosomes varies from species to species, ranging from 14 to 62 in the amphibians studied thus far. Yet only two of all these chromosomes are responsible for sex determination: the sex chromosomes X and Y. During fertilization of the egg cell, the chromosomes decide the future sex of the growing embryo. Males have a heteromorphic sex chromosome pair, both the X and Y chromosomes. In females, the Y chromosome is replaced by a second X chromosome. Hence the Y chromosome carries the genes responsible for starting the development of male sex characteristics in the embryo.

To avoid a constant increase in chromosomes when egg and sperm cells merge, the pairs are divided in the parental gender cells, a process called meiosis, at the time when eggs and sperm mature. They now contain one single chromosome set (haploid chromosome set). Males produce semen cells with either one parental Y chromosome or one maternal X chromosome; females, on the other hand, produce only egg cells with X chromosomes that can be either maternal or paternal. If a sperm with a Y chromosome fertilizes the egg cell, a male develops (XY), and if the sperm contains an X chromosome, a female develops (XX). Since the sex of the next generation depends on whether the father passes on a Y or an X chromosome, the males are called "heterogametic." In amphibians, however, the opposite system also occurs: the ZW system. If the female carries two different sex chromosomes, these are not designated as X and Y but as Z and W. Females then have a Z and a W chromosome; males have two Z chromosomes. In amphibians the sex chromosomes are still in an early stage of evolutionary development. Most are identical in size and differ, if at all, only in their banding patterns. But how is sex determined when even the banding patterns are identical (homomorphous sex chromosomes)? There may well be differences in the ultrastructure of chromosomes that cannot be made visible with the dyes currently in use. At present, only a fraction of all amphibian species have been cytogenetically studied. In approximately 40 species, the sex chromosomes have been described, and of these some 20 percent are species where the female is heterogametic (ZW).

An interesting phenomenon was discovered in reptiles as recently as the 1960s: in many species sex determination is controlled not by sex chromosomes but by egg-brooding temperature. In lizards and alligators, more females hatch when brooding temperatures are below 82.4°F (28°C), while temperatures above 86°F (30°C) result in more males. The reverse is the case in turtles; high temperatures (86 to 91.4°F/30 to 33°C) create females and lower temperatures (73.4 to 80.6°F/23 to 27°C) create males. In the narrow temperature range between the highs and lows, both males and females hatch in equal numbers. In some turtle species, females hatch when temperatures are low (68 to 73.4°F/20 to 23°C) or higher than 82.4°F (28°C), while males hatch in the moderate temperature range. Gonad development is dependent on temperature only during a period of 10 to 15 days toward the end of the first third of an embryo's development.

All land vertebrates descended from a primitive group of amphibian-like creatures that colonized land some 360 million years ago. Is it possible that temperature also plays a role in sex determination in amphibians? Renowned embryologist Emil Witschi was able to demonstrate in 1929 that in the North American wood frog (*Rana sylvatica*) sex changes could be brought about by increasing the temperature during embryonic development. Increased temperatures surrounding tadpoles in their fifth

developmental phase from 68 to 89.6°F (20 to 32°C), resulted in ovaries formations changing into testes.

Many studies followed and showed that amphibian species can be sexually differentiated, undifferentiated or partially differentiated. In sexually differentiated species, the gonads develop according to the sexual genotype (XY-XX or ZW-ZZ), as is the case in the common toad (*Bufo bufo*). In sexually undifferentiated species, like the grass frog (*Rana temporaria*), even genotypical males develop ovaries to begin with. At the time of metamorphosis, both males and females have ovaries. For several weeks or even months after metamorphosis, these ovaries are transformed in the males into a hermaphroditic stage. In species that are partially sexually differentiated, some individuals have ovaries at the time of metamorphosis and others have hermaphroditic gonads. Shortly after metamorphosis, the hermaphroditic gonads

and some ovaries change into testes. The transformation occurs more rapidly than it does in undifferentiated species (for example, *Hynobius retardatus*).

Does Environment Influence Sex Differentiation?

Complex brood experiments are necessary to understand the reciprocity between these complicated forms of sex differentiation and the environment. To this day the impact of temperature and other potential factors, such as pH-value, are not well known. French scientists carried out an astonishing experiment in the mid-eighties. In two closely related sharp-ribbed salamanders (*Pleurodeles waltl* and *Pleurodeles poireti*), an increase in brooding temperatures from 68° to 88 or 89°F (20 to 31 or 32°C) resulted in a complete reversal of both sexes, although sex chromosomes (ZW system) had been discovered in both species. While the sex chromosomes do not differ in form or in banding patterns, their presence could be proven as a result of experiments in crossbreeding and biochemical studies. The paradox, however, was that in these two species, which are closely related, the increase in temperature had opposite effects. While *Pleurodeles waltl* ZW females changed into fertile males, *P. poireti* ZZ-males changed into fertile females, called thermoneofemales. Subsequent generations of these specimens were able to reproduce normally. By crossing a ZW thermoneomale with normal ZW-females in *P. waltl*, fertile females of a WW genotype could be created, a type that does not occur naturally. Until now, scientists have been unable to prove whether temperature also influences sex determination in amphibians in their natural environment. This area of research will undoubtedly yield fascinating results in the future.

*Left: The grass frog (*Rana temporaria*) is a sexually undifferentiated species. Males also develop ovaries during reproduction.*

*Right: Common toads (*Bufo bufo*) are sexually differentiated: depending on sexual genotype they develop testes or ovaries.*

Caryogram of Triturus marmoratus *(marbled newt). In addition to the pair of sex chromosomes (XY, No. 4) in this species pair 1 is also heteromorphous (1A and 1B) in males and females. When chromosome 1A or 1B is homocygotic (genotype 1A 1A or 1B 1B) the embryos die in the tail-formation stage (when heterocygotic individuals are crossed, the next generation is always split into 25 percent individuals with genotype 1A 1A, 25 percent with 1B 1B, and 50 percent with genotype 1A 1B). In* Triturus cristatus *50 percent of descendants die as a result of this genetic peculiarity. So far, there is no explanation of how such a "wasteful" system could evolve (Fig.: Pilar Herrero, University of Madrid).*

Heinz Tunner

Clonal Reproduction in Amphibians

The evolution from bacteria to highly differentiated organisms is closely related to sexuality. Sexual reproduction has been and continues to be the "engine" behind structural evolution in all living organisms. Differentiation into two sexes made the exchange of hereditary characteristics between individuals possible, creating the potential for combining these characteristics in new ways. The cytogenetic mechanism that leads to new combinations of hereditary information is termed "recombination," and it is the key element of cell division or meiosis. From a strictly genetic point of view, recombination is synonymous with sexuality. Aside from spontaneous changes (mutations) to genetic information, recombination is the only source of genetic variation.

Sexual Parasitism in Newts and Frogs

Asexual reproduction, which occurs in bacteria, as well as many plants and lower life forms, but also in genetic engineering, leads to clones. We know today that asexual (clonal) reproduction occurs also in natural vertebrate hybrids. Some of these hybrids have, however, been traced back to gametes from sexual species. When hybrids appropriate the reproductive potential of sexual species it is called sexual parasitism. Here is an example: the hybrid edible frog (*Rana esculenta*) can reproduce only when it mates with a pool frog or a marsh frog. In 1932 American scientists published an article in the journal *Science* in which they reported for the first time existence of a fish species consisting exclusively of females and reproducing asexually (clonally). Several experts found this a thrilling find, while others, especially geneticists and anatomists, viewed the report with

skepticism. They held that vertebrates could not develop without the participation of male hereditary material.

The critics were proven wrong, however, and today we know that natural cloning exists not only among fishes but also among amphibians and even reptiles. In accordance with the fundamental biological and cytogenetic mechanisms, three forms of clonal reproduction are distinguished:

Parthogenesis: Development occurs without the participation of male sperm.

Gynogenesis: While male sperm cells instigate development, they are not incorporated into the egg cell—i.e., fertilization does not take place.

Hybridogenesis: The nuclei of the male and female cells merge—i.e., fertilization does take place, but one parental genome is later "eliminated" from the germ line of the hybrids.

It is notable that parthogenesis is limited among vertebrates to reptiles (seven families); whereas gynogenesis and hybridogenesis occur exclusively in fishes (four families) and amphibians (two families). Clonal reproduction has been documented for amphibians in American mole salamanders (Ambystomatidae) and in European water frogs (Ranidae).

Gynogenetic and hybridogenetic research in vertebrates has led to the following discoveries that are applicable to both clonal reproduction modes: 1. Development requires species hybridization. This means that gynogenetic and hybridogenetic taxa evolved spontaneously and not, as in other animals, as a result of adaptation processes that span millennia; 2. Gynogenetic and hybridogenetic taxa utilize the gametes of sexual species for their own

Known Ambystoma hybrids, parent species as well as number of chromosome sets (ploidy). The numbers refer to the parent species from which the polyploid hybrids have 2, 3 or 4 chromosome sets (modified after Vriejenhoek et al., 1989).

Genus / hybrid taxon	Parent species	Ploidy
Ambystoma	laterale–jeffersonianum (= tremblayi) –– lat. x jeff.	2n
Ambystoma	2 laterale–jeffersonianum (= platineum) –– lat. x jeff.	3n
Ambystoma	laterale–2 jeffersonianum –– lat. x jeff.	3n
Ambystoma	3 laterale–jeffersonianum –– lat. x jeff.	4n
Ambystoma	4 laterale–jeffersonianum –– lat. x jeff.	5n
Ambystoma	laterale–3 jeffersonianum –– lat. x jeff.	4n
Ambystoma	2 laterale–2 jeffersonianum –– lat. x jeff.	4n
Ambystoma	laterale–texanum –– lat. x tex.	2n
Ambystoma	2 laterale–texanum –– lat. x tex.	3n
Ambystoma	laterale–2 texanum –– lat. x tex.	3n
Ambystoma	3 laterale–texanum –– lat. x tex.	4n
Ambystoma	laterale–3 texanum –– lat. x tex.	4n
Ambystoma	2 laterale–2 texanum –– lat. x tex.	4n
Ambystoma	laterale-jeffersoniamun-texanum –– lat. x jeff. x tig.	3n
Ambystoma	laterale-texanum-tigrinum(= nothagenes) –– lat. x tex. x tig.	3n
Ambystoma	laterale-2 texanum-tigrinum –– lat. x jeff. x tig.	4n
Ambystoma	laterale-2 jeffersonianum-tigrinum –– lat. x jeff. x tig.	4n
Ambystoma	laterale-2 jeffersonianum-texanum –– lat. x jeff. x tex.	4n

reproduction; and 3. Clonal taxa have a strong tendency toward polyploidy.

The major difference between gynogenesis and hybridogenesis is that during gynogenesis the development of egg cells is initiated merely by sperm, while in hybridogenesis true fertilization occurs. Since one complete parental chromosome pair (genome) is "eliminated" from the germ line of the hybrids in hybridogenesis (i.e., only one genome is clonally transmitted to the next generation), hybridogenesis is also referred to as hemiclonal reproduction. Two cytological mechanisms guarantee the constancy of the somatic chromosome number in clonal taxa: endoreduplication (doubling of chromosomes without subsequent cell or core division) or bypassing of the meiotic chromosome number reduction.

Gynogenesis in Mole Salamanders

The genus *Ambystoma* contains some 30 sexual species that are widely distributed across North America. Four species—namely, *Ambystoma laterale*, *A. jeffersonianum*, *A. texanum*, and *A. tigrinum*—have hybridized and produced 18 hybrids with fascinating chromosomal diversity. In *Ambystoma* we also find so-called trihybrids—i.e., hybrids with chromosome sets from three different sexual species.

All *Ambystoma* hybrids are predominantly female, and the genome of *A. laterale* is present in the genotype of all hybrids. While these hybrid females were thought to reproduce exclusively by gynogenesis, recent studies have shown that hybridogenesis also occurs among Ambystomatidae.

Hybridogenesis in Edible Frogs

Over the last 15 years the number of known water frog species in the western Palearctic has risen from five to ten or twelve. The following four gave rise to three morphologically and genetically distinguishable hybridogenetic hybrids of both sexes: *Rana ridibunda* (marsh frog), *R. lessonae* (pool water frog), *R. perezi* (Spanish or Iberian water frog) and the Italian edible frog (*Rana sp.*) which hasn't yet been assigned a scientific name. It is notable that *R. ridibunda* is involved in the genotype of all known hybridogenetic edible frogs. The hereditary material of some marsh frogs appears to contain a "molecular factor" which modifies normal sexual reproduction during hybridization in such a manner that hybridogenesis results. In the Balkan region one can find "typical"—i.e., non-hybridogenetic—hybrids which can be traced back to hybridization between *R. ridibunda* and *R. epeirotica* (Epirus frog) and between *R. ridibunda* and *R. shqiperica* (Balkan

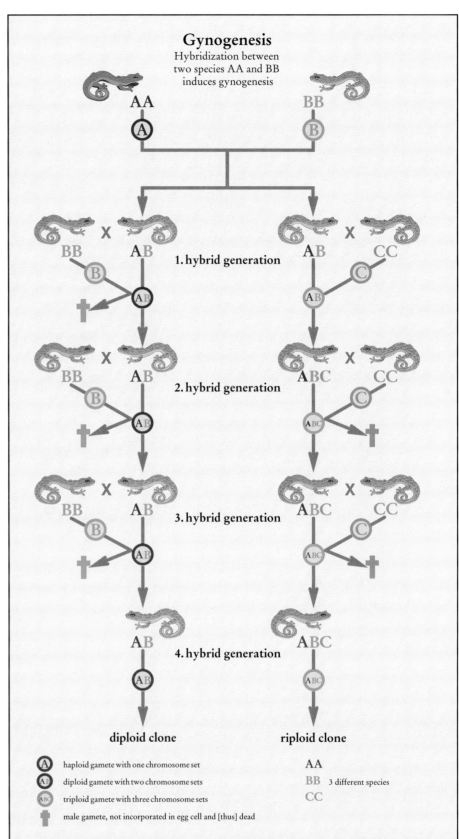

Reconstruction of the development of a diploid and triploid (trihybrid) clone by means of gynogenetic reproduction.

Left: the egg-cell of a gynogenetic hybrid female (AB) is fertilized for development with the semen cell of a male with parental BB heritage; however, no true fertilization (cell fusion) takes place. All descendants are genetically identical and with the parents of the first hybrid generation; they represent a clone.

Right: the male of a different but related species (CC) fertilized a hybrid diploid egg-cell (AB) and induced a renewed gynogenesis. The result is a triploid gynogenetic female with chromosome sets from three different species (ABC). The trihybrid descendants are genetically identical and with the parents from the third hybrid generation onwards and represent a clone.

water frog). The ability of marsh frogs to induce hybridogenesis in a hybrid genotype seems to vary according to geographical location.

The only well-studied representative among hybridogenetic amphibians is the European edible frog *Rana esculenta*. The hereditary scheme below documents its parasitic reproduction and the phenomenon of hybridogenesis.

Evolutionary Consequences of Clonal Reproduction

A convergence of variability and selection enables species with sexual reproduction to cope with changes in the environment. Clones, on the other hand, have only a limited ability to adapt because they are genetically invariant as a result of the loss of recombination. When recombination does not occur, there is no possibility of eliminating harmful mutants from the population. This means that all clones inevitably produce an increased number of unfavorable mutants (Müller's hypothesis of the ratchet-mechanism—ratchets can be turned in only one direction). The negative consequences of clonal reproduction are therefore closely linked to the absence of recombination.

This heavy genetic burden can be compensated for in clonal taxa to some degree by means of the following processes:

Polyploidization: Additional chromosome sets may diminish the effect of the Müller's ratchet. In all known vertebrates with clonal reproduction, a strong tendency toward polyploidization has been shown to exist.

Heterosis: In highly heterozygotic (of mixed heritage) hybrids, a positive heterosis effect (supremacy of heterozygotes) may result in an increased plasticity of characters. For example: hybrid edible frog has better survival odds when oxygen levels are low than do either of its parental species.

Clone Selection: Multiple and frequent primary hybridization processes enable numerous clones to coexist in a heterogeneous habitat. Each individual clone has its own, narrowly defined ecological niche (frozen niche hypothesis). When conditions change, entire clones are wiped out, along with their niches. New niches form; clones adapted to the new niches can be

"supplied" by the hybridizing sexual species. Here, selection doesn't target the individual, it targets the entire clone. The hybrid taxon remains intact, because clones are "interchangeable." The spatial and temporal coexistence of clones whose morphology and life history are clearly different is a well-known phenomenon.

Unisexuality: Gynogenetic populations are always unisexual; whereas hybridogenetic populations are sometimes unisexual. Unisexual hybrid populations can reproduce rapidly because each individual can participate in reproduction. But this applies only when the reproductive potential of the sexual host allows it; reproduction in the parasitic hybrid is inextricably linked to the host species. These "strategies" that help compensate for the loss of recombination should not detract from the fact that amphibians with clonal reproduction are most likely evolutionary "dead ends." Does this

Known hybridogenetic hybrids in European water frogs, their parent species as well as the number of chromosome sets (ploidy). The number 2 preceding the species name indicates the parent species from which the polyploid hybrids have inherited an additional chromosome set.

Genus / hybrid taxon	Parent species	Ploidy
Rana	ridibunda–lessonae (= esculenta) –– ridibunda x lessonae	2n
Rana	ridibunda–2 lessonae (= esculenta) –– ridibunda x lessonae	3n
Rana	2 ridibunda–lessonae (= esculenta) –– ridibunda x lessonae	3n
Rana	ridibunda–perezi –– ridibunda x perezi	2n
Rana	ridibunda–Ital. water frog ––ridibunda x Ital. water frog	2n

make a study of gynogenesis or hybridogenesis less interesting? Surely not, for associations of species and hybrids enable us to study problems that reach far beyond the world of amphibians and which are of fundamental importance in the study of evolutionary biology.

How Should Gynogenetic and Hybridogenetic Taxa Be Named?

While clones are taxonomic units (a taxon is defined as a formal unit of individuals without reference to a specific systematic category), they are not reproductive communities in the sense of the biological concept of species. This creates some difficulties with respect to naming the individual morphologically and/or genetically defined hybrid taxa with clonal reproduction. Below, two options for a uniform nomenclature are presented:

In 1969, A. Schultz applied a nomenclature that identifies the hybrid origin as well as the ploidy (the tables in this chapter adhere to this system). The scientific name of the hybrid and polyploid salamander *Ambystoma platineum* would therefore be *Ambystoma 2 laterale-jeffersonianum*. This name provides information on:
1. the genus (*Ambystoma*),
2. the hybrid status (*laterale-jeffersonianum*),
3. the parent species (*A. laterale* and *A. jeffersonianum*) and
4. the ploidial degree (two chromosomal sets from *A. laterale* + one from *A. jeffersonianum*).

The only disadvantage of this otherwise clear nomenclature is that some established species names such as *platineum*, *tremblayi* or *esculenta* would have to be replaced. They were formulated before anything was known about the hybrid status.

In 1982 B. Dubois and Günther created new systematic categories for two gynogenetic and hybridogenetic taxa with the name "klepton" (from the Greek word for "thief"—because cells are "stolen" from another species) and "synklepton." Accordingly, the hybrid edible frog would be assigned the scientific name *Rana* (synkl. *esculenta*) kl. *esculenta*, or, in abbreviation, *Rana* kl. *esculenta*. The synklepton (kl.) refers to the fact that the klepton (hybrid) belongs to a group consisting of several species and hybrids. The marsh frog, as parental species to the edible frog, would be *Rana* (synkl. *esculenta*) *ridibunda*, or, in abbreviation, simply *Rana ridibunda*.

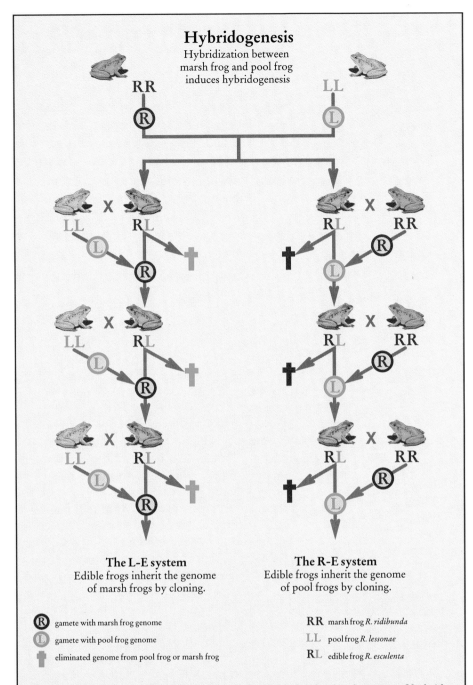

Hybridogenesis
Hybridization between marsh frog and pool frog induces hybridogenesis

The L-E system
Edible frogs inherit the genome of marsh frogs by cloning.

The R-E system
Edible frogs inherit the genome of pool frogs by cloning.

Ⓡ gamete with marsh frog genome
Ⓛ gamete with pool frog genome
✝ eliminated genome from pool frog or marsh frog

RR marsh frog *R. ridibunda*
LL pool frog *R. lessonae*
RL edible frog *R. esculenta*

Hybridization between marsh frog and pool frog induces the development of hybridogenesis. In nature one distinguishes between two main types of mixed or hybrid populations: 1. pool frogs + edible frog (L-E system; edible frogs inherit the genome, i.e., the chromosomes of the marsh frog). 2 Marsh frogs + edible frogs (the R-E system; edible frogs inherit the genom of the pool frog). The first hybridogenetic edible frogs evolved from a cross of marsh frog and pool frog. Today, edible frogs no longer result from such primary hybrid cross-breeding, but—in the L-E system—from reversible cross-breeding of hybrids with pool frogs or—in the R-E system—from reversible cross-breeding with the marsh frog. According to the laws of heredity such reversible cross-breedings should quickly lead to a fusion between the hybrids and the corresponding parent species. However, this is not the case; edible frogs remain typical edible frogs (F1-hybrids), i.e., they correspond genotypically and phenotypically to the descendants of hybrids between marsh frog and pool frog. One explanation for this unusual hereditary pattern can be found in the hybridogenetic gametogenesis during which the germ line chromosomes of that parent species are eliminated and can be delivered instead by the syntopic parent. During hybridogenesis only one parental genome is passed on to the descendants, unlike gynogenesis, whereby genomes from both parents are passed on. Therefore hybridogenesis is also called hemiclonal reproduction. The occurrence of polyploid hybrids and disorders in gender realization can be additional variables in the relationships in the L-E and R-E system. In summary, hybrid edible frogs in the L-E system are quasi marsh frogs (they inherit only the genetic material of the marsh frog) while in the R-E system they are quasi pool frogs (inheriting the genome of the pool frog).

Ulrich Sinsch

Thermoregulation

Temperature is an important environmental factor for all living creatures because nearly all metabolic reactions, physiological processes and behavior are influenced by it. Therefore some form of regulation of body temperature is essential to survival. In contrast to mammals and birds, amphibians are unable to produce thermal energy through their metabolic activity, which would allow them to regulate their body temperature independently of surrounding or ambient temperature. They are poikilothermic. Since their heat sources (sun, geothermal heat, etc.) lie outside of their bodies, amphibians are sometimes also called ectothermic.

Even Amphibians Control Their Body Temperature

The idea that amphibians have no control whatsoever over their body temperature has been proven false because their body temperature does not always correspond to the surrounding temperature. While amphibians are poor thermoregulators, they do exercise control over their body temperature to a limited degree. Physiological adaptations such as increased tolerance for low or high temperatures assist them in colonizing even habitats where extreme conditions prevail. Some species have a form of neural control via secretions from the mucous glands that enable them to decrease their temperature through evaporative cooling on the skin. Morphological adaptations as well as a modified reflective reaction in the skin are also used in thermoregulation. However, behavior is by far the most important factor in thermoregulation: when migration to microhabitats with preferred temperatures occurs, body temperature is not only maintained within vital species-specific boundaries, but may remain constant for many hours each day.

Temperature Tolerance

The tolerance range in body temperature represents the range of temperatures within which a species can survive. The North American urodele *Hydromantes platycephalus* is still active when temperatures drop to 28°F (−2°C), while the South American frog *Phyllomedusa sauvagei* feels comfortable even when temperatures rise to 105.8°F (41°C) (highest body temperature measured in a free-ranging amphibian). Recently it has been shown that some North American anuran species, among them the wood frog *Rana sylvatica*, can survive up to five days with a body temperature of 21°F (−6°C) with approximately one-third of their body fluids frozen. The other tissues are protected because they contain the frost-protective agents glycerin or glucose. In many species the tolerance boundaries are flexible and can change as a result of acclimatization (long-term exposure to a specific temperature). Thus the upper and lower critical temperature for the North American leopard frog *Rana pipiens* can shift upward or downward by approximately 7 degrees F (4°C) as a result of acclimatization.

The European natterjack (Bufo calamita) is a eurythermous species that tolerates temperatures ranging from 39.2 to 110.4°F (4 to 38°C) without specific temperature preferences.

Morphological Adaptations

Frog species that remain exposed to the sun despite high diurnal temperatures exhibit some fascinating modifications in the skin structure that function as morphological adaptations. Most amphibian skin is fully water permeable and is therefore not a barrier against evaporation or solar radiation. The African savanna frog *Hyperolius viridiflavus* stores guanine crystals in the iridophores of its skin, which enable it to better reflect solar radiation, thus providing protection against overheating. The tree frog *Phyllomedusa sauvagei* responds to evaporative losses with secretions from lipid glands that have thus far been demonstrated to be present only in the skin of this hylid genus. The fore and hind limbs are used to spread a greasy film over the entire body, much like a sun lotion. This allows for heliothermal behavior without risk of desiccation.

Behavioral Thermoregulation

The principal elements in behavioral thermoregulation are basking (heliothermy), heat exchange with substrates such as rock or earth (thigmothermy), diurnal and annual avoidance behaviors such as moving to shelter during the day for cooling and estivation and hibernation, respectively, to avoid lethal temperature extremes. Heliothermy is especially common among Anura: it allows even ectothermal creatures to increase their body temperature by more than 28 degrees F (10°C). The Andean toad *Bufo spinulosus* exposes itself immediately after sunrise on moist ground and attains its preferred body temperature by this means, long before either ground or air is correspondingly warmed. However, in this case basking is not a means of achieving a more or less constant body temperature; instead, it optimizes the diurnal temperature. A positive side effect of this approach is that it accelerates the digestion of the prey consumed overnight, thus also accelerating growth. Thigmothermy is a behavior present in most amphibians, although pressing against the ground serves a dual purpose: heat absorption by conductivity and water absorption through the skin. The effect of thigmothermy is especially evident in the Andean toad during rainfall: its body temperature corresponds to the temperature of the warm earth and not to the much cooler air.

Avoidance behavior occurs whenever physiological and morphological adaptations are insufficient to maintain body temperature within the vital range. Nocturnal activity in amphibians with low tolerance for high ambient temperatures is a typical thermoregulatory behavior of avoidance. This behavior is common in the European toad *Bufo bufo* and the

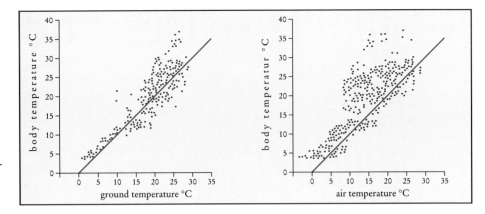

grass frog *Rana temporaria*. Seasonal avoidance behavior is an extremely important factor in many amphibians. Species whose habitat lies in the temperate latitudes are confronted by lethal low temperatures in winter, while species dwelling in arid and semi-arid regions are exposed to long dry, hot periods in summer.

Hibernation

In amphibians hibernation occurs in mud or deep holes away from frost. North of the Pyrenees mountains, the natterjack (*Bufo calamita*) offers a good example of hibernation, passing the winter dug deep into sandy ground (as deep as 2 yards/2 m). Conversely, natterjacks in southern Spain remain active during the mild winters common to the region and are instead forced into inactivity during the dry, hot summer season. Summer estivation also occurs by burrowing into the ground or hiding in cool, deep rock crevasses to avoid desiccation and lethal ambient temperatures. During the estivation of the North American *Scaphiopus couchii*, metabolism is reduced by approximately 20 percent. Amphibians are therefore hardly at the mercy of ambient temperatures. By means of the mechanisms described above, they are more than able to exercise some control over their body temperature and to optimize their metabolism.

*The body temperature of natterjacks (*Bufo calamita*) in natural surroundings compared to ground temperature (left) and air temperature (right). The straight line represents the isothermal line; each dot represents a measured value (after Sinsch, 1998).*

*Diurnal curve of radiotelemetrically measured body temperature of *Bufo spinulosus* in different weather conditions (after Sinsch, 1989).*

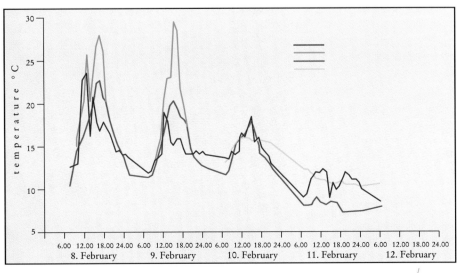

Andreas Hassl

Diseases and Immunology

Like other creatures, amphibians are integrated into their environment, interacting with each other and with the environment. As a result of internal factors such as aging or external influences such as infections, individual body cells, tissues or organs may fail or mutate; regulatory functions may collapse, tissue may die or be attacked by foreign organisms such as protozoa or bacteria that use it as a substrate. As vertebrates, amphibians are in principle exposed to the same pathogenic mechanisms as humans or domestic animals, although some peculiarities exist due to their mode of life and phylogeny.

Diseases in Amphibians

Not much is known about systematic diseases, infectious diseases, immunology and disease defense in all amphibians with the exception of the clawed frog (*Xenopus laevis*), which is often used as a laboratory specimen, as few case histories have been recorded in each field. Above all, the relevance of individual factors which are expected to be pathogenic by themselves or to modulate the immune system—for example, increased UV radiation or the resorption of industrial toxins—in disease manifestation is unknown altogether. This is why it is currently impossible to predict the survival of amphibian populations or even the worldwide well-being of this class in the context of the global amphibian decline. However, precise studies in pathology and immunology in special laboratories can reveal the cause of disease or death in an individual.

Before attempting to organize amphibian diseases into logical and systematic categories, we should take a closer look at amphibians' living conditions. Veterinary studies on amphibians in their natural environment yield findings that are considerably different from those obtained from terrarium specimens. In nature creatures that are weakened by disease are the preferred prey of predators. This means that, in comparison to specimens kept in captivity, chronic infections, diseases that result from aging processes and benign tumors are less frequently diagnosed. Furthermore, the range of diagnosed infectious or viral diseases is considerably different.

In captivity the vectors necessary to the life cycle of some germs are almost always absent, but unnaturally high population densities create epidemic conditions that are specific to captivity. In nature, however, limited germ coloniza-

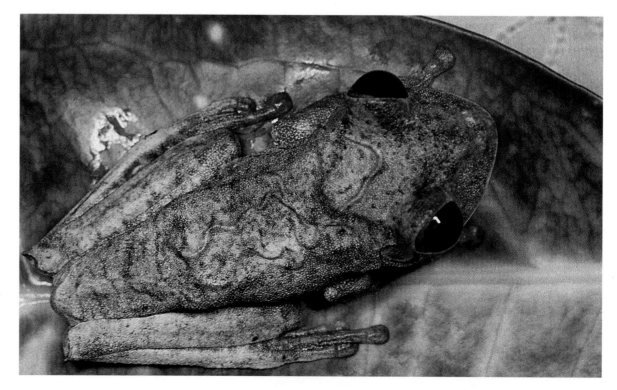

*Filaria-infection in a tree frog (*Hyla geographica*) from Trinidad. Although the 1.5-inch (4-cm) long nematodes could be seen shifting and moving beneath the skin, the host animal did not seem to be handicapped.*

tion is normal and sometimes even conducive to the health of the host. This relates to a broad spectrum of usually hardy or non-pathogenic germs that are slowly propagating; among them are many opportunists. Only when considerable stress occurs—for example, during an increase of toxin exposition or constant uneasiness with the connected immunosuppression—do these germs multiply in an uncontrollable way and begin to develop pathogenic characteristics.

The colonization of free-living amphibians by opportunistic germs is clinically barely noticeable and it is thus rarely documented; nevertheless, it is the main factor for a lasting regulation of population density. In captivity, however, we see a preponderance of infections caused by a small number of usually highly pathogenic species of germs that multiply rapidly and have a tendency to autoinfection. Diseases in amphibians can be classified into the following groups:

Cancer (Tumors): Benign tumors are difficult to recognize because there is an even transition to encystation of foreign tissue. Malign tumors in amphibians are almost invariably epithelial in origin. They may be striking because they can reach unbelievable dimensions. The transplantable, renal adenocancer of *Rana pipiens* (Lucké tumor) is a long-known and relatively well-researched cancer whose herpes virus–induced genesis is, however, still in question.

Metabolic Diseases and Regulatory Malfunctions: This category includes ontogenetic abnormalities and malformations that are unusually frequent among amphibians and are caused by abnormal genes or abnormal gene combinations. Abnormalities are well researched because they are easy to induce in a laboratory setting and are well documented in the genetic literature. Amphibian larvae with thyroid hypofunction do not metamorphose, but continue to grow and sometimes even reach sexual maturity.

Deficiency Diseases manifest themselves clinically almost exclusively as a result of poor nutrition in captivity. Skeletal damage has been described for the clawed frog as a result of insufficient calcium intake. The standard values of required vitamin and mineral intake for individual amphibian species have not been determined until now.

Infectious Diseases are caused by transmitable germs that harm the host by robbing it of its energy, but which are not lethal to it, at least at the initial contact. Amphibians are susceptible to viruses, bacteria, fungi, protozoa and metazoa. Although infectious diseases may threaten the life of the host, they are the driving

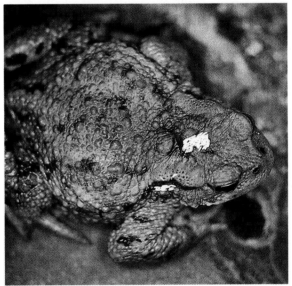

*Nostrils in a common toad (*Bufo bufo*) ravaged by* Lucilia bufonivora *larvae.*

Left: Freshly laid Lucilia *eggs on the head of a common toad. The maggots hatch after two to three days and penetrate the nostrils of the toad. Adult toads are most frequently affected by this infestation.*

force behind the immunological and—to a smaller degree—the biological evolution.

In recent years certain germs have received a lot of attention for different reasons: virus identification and detection continue to present a diagnostic and technical challenge. Specific viruses (for example, iridovirus-like particles) can now be identified quite easily and efficiently with the help of electron microscopy, so they are now frequently detected in amphibians. The clinically conspicuous and epidemic-causing "red-leg" disease in frogs has excited interest across the world; the germ *Aeromonas hydrophila* is a ubiquitous, mobile, gram-negative bacterium regularly found in the intestine of amphibians. The cold-water mycobacteria, which cause tuberculosis in amphibians, are similarly ubiquitous opportunists; they colonize the skin of the host. Protozoa from the phylum Microsporida create completely different

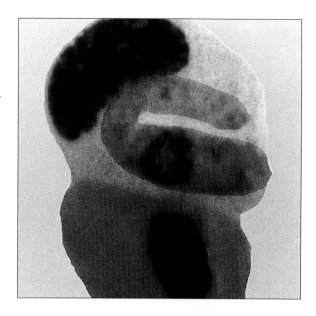

Lankesterella sp. *or Dactylosoma sp.-infection of a Rana ridibunda in Thagit oasis in Algeria (Giemsa staining). The protozoa penetrate the erythrocytes, where they modify and displace the host cell nucleus. The probable vector, a leech from the genus Placobdella, is common to the same body of water.*

Amphibians as Vectors

When thinking about a possible link between human health and amphibians, cases in which people were harmed by poison excreted through these animals' skin, by touching or coming into contact with a wound, immediately come to mind. There is, however, another frequently overlooked aspect of amphibian impact on the health of human beings: certain taxa of this group of animals can serve as intermediate hosts for pathogenic germs, and can transport these germs or cause contact between man and infectious foci.

Amphibians as Intermediate Hosts

The most severe and most dangerous illness that humans can contract from a germ transmitted by amphibians is an infection caused by the larvae of the tapeworm genus *Spirometra*. These parasites are located in the muscles of frogs as outwardly undifferentiated worm larvae. They can actively move into human tissue if direct contact occurs, stay there permanently, perhaps even metastasize, move, and increase in size to several cubic inches or centimeters. Especially in South East Asia, where direct contact with frog meat is quite common, since compresses containing amphibian meat are used as an antibiotic remedy and placed on patients' eyes or on festering wounds. Particularly serious cases of these sparganoses [infestations with plerocercoids of the genus Spirometra] may lead to the loss of one's eyes; in minor cases, surgery is required to remove the worm. The development of a mature tapeworm in human beings is impossible.

Amphibians as Carriers of Potentially Pathogenic Germs

Several potentially pathogenic bacteria have such a low host specificity and are so widespread that they can be found in sick amphibians as well as in sick humans. These include *Aeromonas hydrophila* (red leg, sepsis), *Pseuolomonas sp.*, and *Salmonella* (diarrhea, sepsis). Contrary to the situation with reptiles, an actual transmission of these germs from amphibians to humans has not been proven until now. Nevertheless, caution is advised when dealing with excrement or in treating wounds.

Amphibian Cultivation as the Source of Infections

In cases where human beings keep amphibians, it is inevitable that the caretakers come into contact with a special flora of germs, specific to aquaterrariums. The human pathogenic germs of this flora include *Mycobacterium marinum* (but not *M. ranae*!), free-living, potentially pathogenic amoeba *Acanthamoeba spp.* *Naegleria fowleri*; a germ that produces brain abcesses) and the pathogen that causes a subcutaenous mycosis in Africa, *Basidiobolus ranarum*.
So far, there are no basic scientific studies in existence concerning the health risk to humans in handling amphibians. Also, the risk to the animals during their first contact with humans, when germ exchange and "germ adaptation" occurs, has not been examined, although this phenomenon has a significant impact on physiological studies and on their chances of survival in captivity.

scenarios: In recent years they led to catastrophic mortality among non-adapted hosts (*Bufo bufo*) in southern England. This was caused by intensified commercial fish breeding and the introduction of fishes foreign to the local fauna.

Immunology

Immunology is a basic and vital function of any union of cells. In all higher animals it maintains individual integrity or, put very simply, maintains health. The key function of immunology is to distinguish reliably between the body's own working cells and foreign and/or mutated cells. In amphibians, self-recognition is realized with the help of complex and multi-structured protein molecules at the cell surface (MHC complex). Protein structures that do not carry these recognition signals are captured by means of a complicated mechanism by phagocytic cells that are part of the body (macrophages); divided through digestion, the parts are then kept at the macrophages surface and are utilized by other immune cells as a starting point to control their own activity. This "presentation" sets in motion a cascade of several reactions that ultimately lead to a complete destruction of the foreign structure. Unique characteristics of the amphibian immune system are a strong seasonal activity cycle and a partial functioning at temperatures that would lead to paralysis of the immune functions in other poikilothermic animals.

Another immune function is the production of proteins (antibodies) floating in bodily fluids that attach to foreign proteins according to the "keyhole" principle. Its task is to clot and thus immobilize the foreign structure and to mark the surface for the purpose of targeted attack by phagocytes. These antibodies are divided into several classes according to their specialized tasks. In Anura we find the so-called IgX (dimension: probably 170 kD), during an infection early arising IgM (900 kD) and IgY (170 kD); in the phylogenetic older Urodela only IgM and in some species IgY are present. Antibodies are produced during the active stage of an infection and are still present in small amounts months later. Hence, identifying and documenting antibodies that target a specific germ provides conclusive proof of an infection without having to isolate the germ itself. Such immunological-diagnostic procedures are currently becoming rapidly more significant in amphibian research.

Biologically Active Peptides in Amphibian Skin
Günter Kreil

Round and round the cauldron go;
In the poison'd entrails throw.
Toad, that under cold stone
Days and nights has thirty-one
Swelt'd venom sleeping got,
Boil thou first i' the charmed pot....
Fillet of fenny snake
In the cauldron boil and bake;
Eye of newt and toe of frog,
Wool of bat and tongue of dog,
....For a charm of powerful trouble,
Like a hell-broth boil and bubble.
—from William Shakespeare's
Macbeth, Act IV, Scene 1

Since antiquity, the skin secretions of amphibians have been invested with special properties. Numerous documents tell about the use of such secretions in home remedies, for the hunting rituals of Amazon natives or, as in the quotation above, for magic, in the seventeenth century. The familiar "ch'an su" of Chinese apothecaries is made from dried toad skin.

From about 1930 onward, the ingredients of these skin secretions have also been studied with the help of modern methods. At first, several biogenic amines were discovered, such as the well-known serotonin and its derivatives. In the past 30 years, biochemists, pharmacologists and molecular biologists have focused their studies on the peptides formed in the skin of amphibians.

The high concentrations of these peptides in amphibian skin stirred scientists' interest and facilitated their research. To begin with, they focused on those peptides related to or even identical with peptide hormones and neurotransmitters found in mammals. This similarity applies to both the structure and the biological activity. One example is caerulein, a peptide first discovered in the Australian tree frog *Pelodryas caerulea*, later in *Xenopus laevis* and in other frogs; this peptide is closely related to the mammalian hormone gastrin and to cholecystokinin. The same applies to a number of amphibian kinines and the mammalian peptide bradykinine.

Thyrotropin-releasing-hormone (TRH) is an especially interesting case. "Releasing" hormones are hormones that promote hormonal release; the opposite are "inhibiting" hormones, which inhibit the release of hormones. The peptide hormone TRH was isolated through a labor-intensive and arduous process by two research teams from several hundred thousand pig and sheep hypothalami, an achievement for which they received the Nobel Prize. The hypothalamus (located below the thalamus) is a small hormone-producing section of the diencephalon, which plays an important role in vertebrates in regulating the internal balance of the organism. A few years later, TRH was shown to be present in high concentrations in amphibian skin. It would have been possible to obtain the same amount of this hormone from a few dozen frogs of the species *Xenopus laevis* as from the huge number of mammal hypothalami.

A peptide of initially unknown function was isolated from the skin of the South American tree frog P*hyllomedusa sauvagei*, for which it was named sauvagin. When the corticotropic-releasing hormone (CRH) was successfully isolated from the mammal hypothalamus after nearly 20 years of work, it proved to be closely related to sauvagin. The skin of this frog and other species from the subfamily Phyllomedusinae also yielded a number of peptides—for example, dermorphines—that bind with high affinity and selectivity to opiatereceptors. These peptides are up to 1,000 times more active than morphine, and in test animals an injection into the brain has produced long-lasting and profound loss of consciousness. The second group, deltorphines, bind selectively with delta-opiatereceptors. These peptides are also of great interest to the biochemist as they contain one D-amino acid each, whose formation from the corresponding bilateral L-amino acid is currently under investigation.

In addition to these peptides with structural and functional similarities to mammal hormones, the skin secretions of amphibians contain a high number of peptides with antibacterial or fungicidal properties. Among others, the magainine /PGS peptides from *Xenopus laevis*, bombinine from the *Bombina* species, dermaseptine from Phyllomedusinae, brevinine and esculentin from the *Rana* species and many more. These are all chemicals closely related to peptides which are present to varying degrees and in varying concentrations in the skin secretion. Thus more than a dozen bombines were identified. Each seems to have a slightly different effect on bacteria; the whole "peptide cocktail" effectively protects the animals against infections by microorganisms.

Recently isolated peptides which are related to snake venoms have been discovered in the skin secretions, although they do not seem to be toxic in themselves. Three peptides have been isolated from the skin secretion of *Xenopus laevis* whose structure is similar to a group of neurotoxins contained in the poison of different snakes. The function of these peptides is still unclear. These findings do demonstrate, however, that even after three decades of intensive research into the peptides contained in the skin secretions of amphibians, many questions still remain unanswered.

To biochemists, amphibian skin and its many secretions are a fascinating research object. One the most important amphibian species for research is the South African clawed frog Xenopus laevis.

Alfred
Goldschmid

The Frog Leap

Who hasn't stood at a pond and been startled by the sudden leap of a frog disappearing into the water? This "escape" makes it nearly impossible for a potential enemy to find the creature. In witnessing a frog leap, we are experiencing, in just a few seconds, the result of millennia of selection. We take a frog's body shape for granted, and yet it could evolve only as a result of the development of a saltatory mode of movement.

Record Jumps among Anura

The performance of a frog's leap would warrant an entry in the *Guinness Book of Records* if duplicated by a human. After all, the small American cricket frog (*Acris gryllus*) exceeds its own body length by 62 times in the high jump! To reach a comparative peak performance, a person of average height 5 feet, 3 inches (1.6 m) would have to jump approximately 330 feet (100 m) high, which corresponds to a 38-floor building. The distance crossed in the jump is impressive too: the New Guinean tree frog *Litoria nasuta* jumps 7.5 feet (2.3 m), 46 times its body length. The powerfully built American bullfrog (*Rana catesbeiana*) leaps 17 feet (5.2 m) or approximately 38 times its body length. And in the triple jump, frogs hold an unbeaten record: the African *Ptychadena oxyrhynchus* can span 33 feet (10 m) in three sequential leaps.

These staggering statistics are taken from one of the comprehensive studies carried out by American amphibian researcher George R. Zug on leap performance in Anura through tests on 80 species from 11 families. Results revealed that smaller frogs—in size and weight—delivered the best performance. While large frogs jump farther in absolute distance, the distance relative to body length and the leap height relative to body weight decreases with larger species. Poor jumpers, such as toads, deliver consistent performance: even after many leaps, the distance remains the same.

This is in contrast to "high-performance jumpers," who seem to tire quickly and whose performance deteriorates in sequential jumps. Generally speaking, ground-dwelling or burrowing anurans inhabiting arid regions—for example, many Bufonidae or Pelobatidae—are less capable jumpers than are semi-aquatic non-burrowing ground dwellers—for example, European true frogs (Ranidae), whose performance levels are much higher. The best jumpers of all are found among the tree frogs (Hylidae), especially those species inhabiting moist meadows, and reedy and marshy areas.

Locomotion in Vertebrates

To understand the body shape and construction of Anura and the sequence of movements performed during a leap, it is best to begin by looking at locomotion in amphibians with a "normal" tetrapod structure, the Urodela, and even to some degree at fish. The skeletal musculature in vertebrates in the trunk and tail

region is proportionate in size and differentiation. From head to toe there is a sequence of muscular compartments—so-called muscle segments. The segments are separated from each other by walls of connective tissue, the muscle septa, and the muscle fibers run between these septa parallel to the longitudinal axis. The spine, too, originates from this compartmentalized material, and the number of vertebrae tends to correspond to the number of muscle segments. However, the vertebrae are always shifted by half a segment along the longitudinal axis so that the muscle septa originate from the vertebrae and not between vertebrae. This means muscle power is indirectly transferred via the septa onto the spine as the central body axis. The segmentation of the muscle and axial apparatus also has an impact on the nervous system: each segment has its own supply of sensory and motor nerves.

This basic plan of the locomotory apparatus is present in all vertebrates, and the basal locomotion in all vertebrates, the undulating swimming motion that first evolved in fish-like vertebrates, is a result of this structure. When some trunk segments contract on one side of the body, the corresponding segments on the opposite sides are stretched and the axis of the spine is bent. Waves of muscle activity running from head to tail are transferred to the tail fin and, where present, the median dorsal and anal fins. The result is a propulsion, or forward motion, through water. The paired pectoral and abdominal fins in fish are of little consequence for locomotion, but they contribute to steering or in slow precision movement.

These paired pectoral and abdominal fins gave rise to the front and hind limbs in tetrapods. Without water as a supporting medium, the body had to be supported and lifted against the pull of gravity. Strong muscle systems extend

During the leap (Rana sp.) the frontal limbs are pressed close to the underside and are brought forward into a landing position again only after the culmination point of the jump has passed.

from the girdle skeleton to the upper arm and upper thigh, which project laterally in early tetrapods and in Urodela, and move forward and backward by means of a shallow, long rotation. It is important to note that in fish the muscle segments are divided into a dorsal and a ventral section, easily seen every time we are served a fish on a platter. When you remove the skin from a cooked fish there is a distinct cleft running from head to tail separating the dorsal and ventral parts of each muscle segment. In living fish this separation is made by a connective tissue sheet that is destroyed in the cooking process, leaving a cleft.

The division into muscle segments leads to a separate reverse supply and thus creates the potential for differentiated control in the dorsal and ventral section of a muscle segment. Moreover, in fish the paired fins are already controlled in alternating movements so that the corresponding opposite extremity is moved in the opposite direction. When the left forelimb moves forward, the right forelimb moves backward. Only the diagonally opposite fore and hind limbs move in the same direction. This is especially evident when salamanders crawl and is still visible among reptiles (in lizards). To support the body during this slow movement, three limbs are always in contact with the ground. For faster forward motion only the diagonally opposite fore and hind limbs maintain ground contact. As a result of inertia, the part of the body attached to the limb that is lifted off the ground does not collapse onto the ground.

Movement on four limbs, such as we have just described, is supported by a powerful, lateral bending of the spine. The tail moves sideways, as it did in the undulating motion of fish, yet now it serves only to maintain balance and not to propel the body forward. In water, newts still move in an undulating motion and the narrow, flattened tail is used much in the same way as in fish. The legs are held close to the trunk and are not used in swimming. Frog tadpoles also swim in a fish-like manner through pronounced undulations of their tail.

How and Why Did Leaping Evolve?

This was the basis from which the saltatory mode in Anura evolved. The first, and most decisive step was probably a transfer of the propulsive force to the hind limbs. This was the most important change from the primitive alternating movement of limbs. All other changes must have been subject to strong selection forces to improve the efficiency of the new mode of moving. Urodela sometimes exhibit a sudden short forward movement in which hind limbs move simultaneously. However, this movement is jerky and not very effective.

The ability to leap powerfully and quickly is most helpful in the hunt for moving prey and in most cases the evolution of this motion was accompanied by the development of an extendable tongue. Another important advantage in jumping is more efficient escape behavior. An olfactorily oriented predator—such as many snakes—suddenly loses track of the frog immediately after the jump. The same happens to the visually oriented predator, which is confused by the rapid change in position and the sudden increase in size of his prey. Even in water, the simultaneous propulsive force improves speed. Among all mammals, humans are unique in being able to swim more effectively in the breaststroke by moving all four limbs simultaneously. The crawl, alternating swimming movements of the arms is much more energy-consuming for humans. Quadrupeds such as dogs or horses, and even young children prior to taking swimming lessons, move in water and on land only through the alternating motion of the extremities.

The "Frog Shape"

The characteristic frog shape is the result of a logical evolution in jumping: the shortening of

Stages of motion in a frog leap.
a–sacral joint
1–extreme stretch phase immediately after lift-off; pelvic girdle, upper and lower thigh and elongated tarsus form almost a straight line
2, 3, 4–change in spinal bend in the sacral region during each phase of the jump, made possible by the moveable connection between pelvic girdle and sacral vertebra (after Rogers, 1989).

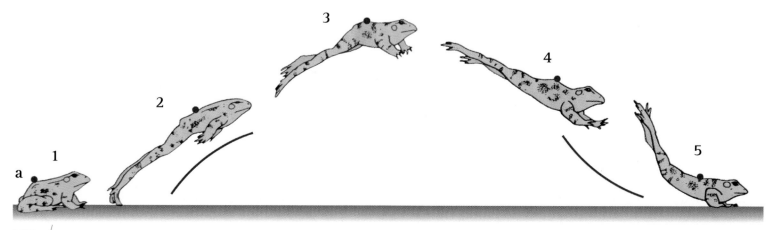

the spine to a mean of nine vertebrae; the simultaneous broadening of the trunk and the concentration of the internal organs, resulting in a drop-shaped trunk; the shortening of the caudal section of the spine and the fusion of its vertebrae into a rod-like "urostyle" or "coccygial bone," in the pelvis region; the rod-like elongation of the ilium which provides the link to the sacral vertebra and which has shifted the hip joint far behind the actual sacrum and thus far behind the gravitational center of the trunk and body cavity. Whenever a powerful simultaneous propulsive force is present in quadrupeds, the force is shifted to the hind limbs. In some cases, this led to rapid bipedal forward movement (bipedal dinosaurs) or to bipedal hopping (kangaroo, gerbil). Humans too shift the propulsive force to the rear tires in high-performance, rapidly accelerating vehicles (race cars, monster trucks).

The forelimb must absorb the shock at landing. Powerful forward and backward movements to "drag" the body along are no longer necessary. The hands point inward and the two bones of the lower arm (ulna and radius), separate in

other tetrapods, are fused into one robust shock-absorbing, supportive element between hand and upper arm.

The skeleton of the hind limb exhibits two interesting and unusual adaptations: the tibia and the fibula are fused into one long element, tibio-fibula (also "os cruris"). In the tarsus, the skeletal elements that connect with the tibia have evolved into an elongated, rod-like tibial (astragalus) and those following the fibula into equally rod-like fibular (calcaneus). This creates an additional joint in the foot, absent in Urodela and most other quadrupeds: near the middle of the foot is a "second heel joint." Such additional joints are present in groups of mammals that have evolved synchronized bipedal jumping. However, every taxonomic group has developed unique structures within the foot. In the kangaroo, for example, the middle foot is elongated while the toes are bent, and gerbils (Dipodidae) show similar specializations as do Macroscelidae. Some monkeys, such as bushbabies or makis, exhibit high performance in bipedal jumping. In all these jumpers, the position of the hind legs at rest is

*The female common toad above (*Bufo bufo*) demonstrates the typical alternating motion of the extremities characteristic of tetrapodes. The ability to jump is less pronounced in toads.*

similar to that of the Anura. The entire hind limb is tightly folded, with the individual bones set at acute angles to each other at each joint. The thigh lies horizontally, pointing forward and slightly sideways so that the knee, which is not covered by a kneecap in amphibians, is positioned at approximately the same height as the joint between the sacral vertebra and the pelvic girdle.

The Sequence of a Jump

Strong muscles, especially in the thigh, serve to extend this tightly folded chain of bones. From the pelvic girdle, short but powerful muscles extend to the head of the femur and support the broad muscles on the lower and inner sides of the thigh that also lead to the pelvic girdle and can pull the thigh downward with great force and speed. The muscles on the upper and outer sides of the thigh extend the knee joint, and the lower thigh muscles extend the heel joint. For take-off, hip, knee and heel joints are extended in sequence. Only the "second" heel joint is at an obtuse angle to the front section of the foot at rest. During the first phase, this is shifted into a 90-degree angle position, so that the proximal section of the foot (fibular and tibial) adds extra height, and the full force is now shifted to the distal part of the foot, which is still in contact with the ground and is the last to be extended. One could visualize the sequence in a jumping motion much like a wheel whose spokes grow longer during rotation as each of the joints,

mentioned above, is extended, and thus begins to roll faster. Lift-off takes only about 70 milliseconds with a starting velocity of 5.9 feet (1.8 m) per second; the average starting angle is 55 degrees. The longest jumps have a starting angle of 34 degrees.

During the jump, the forelimbs point backwards and are pressed close to the body; they move forward only after the culmination point has passed. At first, the spine is stretched so that it is slightly concave to the horizontal ground beneath, nearly straightening the bend in the sacral vertebra. Only at the culmination point of the leap the axis bends downward, becoming convex. In a predatory leap, the prey is usually caught at the culmination point or just after. It is interesting to note that Anura close their eyes when leaping, or even retract the eyeball so that the eyes disappear into the contour of the head. The resulting streamline aerodynamic effect is probably less important than the protection of the eye. This is emphasized by the amphibian's nictitating membrane, present only in Anura and apparently evolved together with leaping. The nictitating membrane is a translucent, colorless, whitish connective tissue membrane inside the lower eyelid. When the eyeball is retracted, this membrane is pushed passively over the eyeball from the bottom, enabling the frogs to maintain limited visual orientation despite this "curtain." This is evidenced by adjustments in the flight path, visible in a sideways spreading of a hind limb, lateral motions of the trunk, or

Movement and position of limbs during forward motion of a newt.
The left frontal limb begins in a forward motion in A, nearly completed in C. During this phase the left hand is placed on the ground, level with the head; the left hind limb has almost completed the forward motion in A and points backwards. In B and C the left hind limb is freely swerved forward without ground contact; in D a new forward pushing phase begins. The diagonally opposite pattern in extremity position is notable, supported by the lateral bending of the spine. (after Schaeffer, 1941).

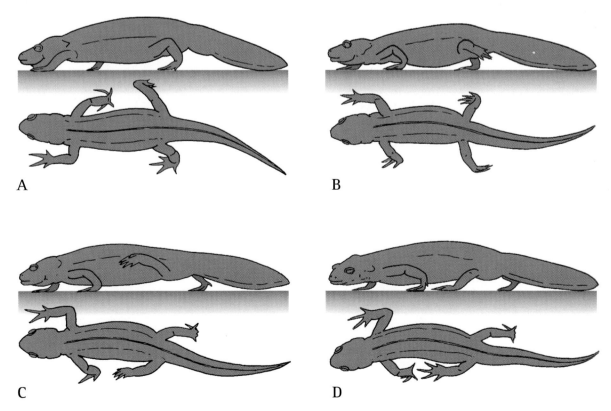

A

B

C

D

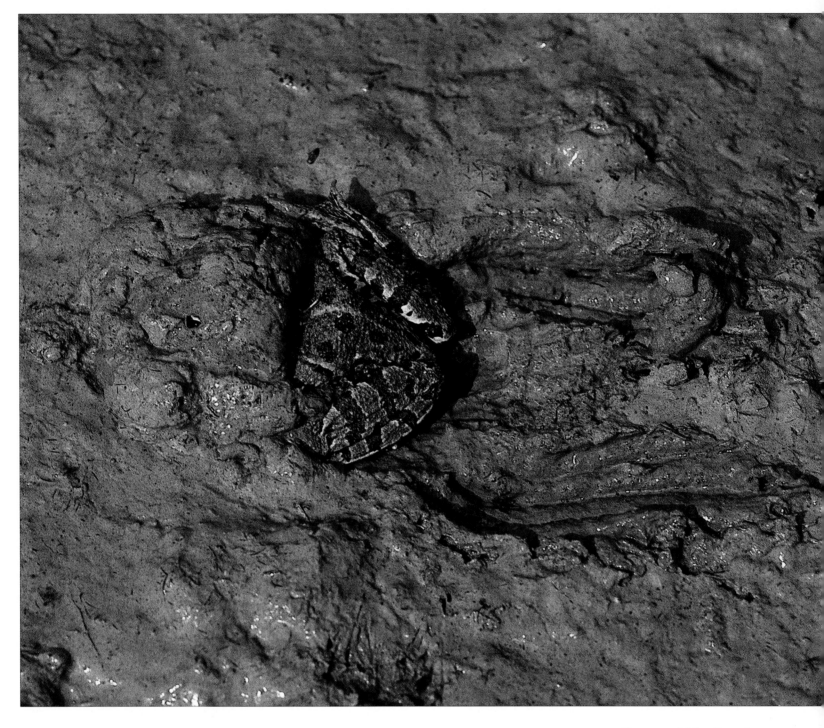

slight raising of the head, especially in predatory leaps. In leaps to escape from predators, no attempts to adjust the path are made. Here all that matters is to "get up and away," as far as possible. In addition, most frogs can also resort to a slower, walking motion; this is quite common, for example, in toads or in leaf frogs when climbing through dense branches.

What Makes a Good Jumper?

The proportions of single bones in the hindlimb and between arms and legs provides some clues about the laws that govern jumping abilities. Good jumpers always have smaller arms than poor jumpers. In distance jumpers, the hind leg may be twice as long as the head-body length, and their shauks are always longer than the tights, with the elongated tarsus longest of all. This creates a significant

distance between the two heel joints. The powerful musculature—especially in larger frogs—has unfortunately gained these creatures a preferred place at the table of some connoisseurs. This is a rather sad chapter in the history of the human-frog relationship, with devastating ecological consequences in all regions where people began to capture masses of frogs as a gastronomic treat. Hence, the very factor that has made frogs so successful in their evolution—and the reason why there are so many more frogs than other amphibian species—is also the reason why they have become so attractive to connoisseurs; for some species, their powerful thigh muscle may become the cause of their extinction.

Unsuccessful landing of a marsh frog (Rana ridibunda) in the muddy shore of a small pool. He's just able to watch out for potential danger with one eye peeking through the mud. Effective escape from predators is one of the greatest evolutionary advantages of the frog leap.

On hearing the word amphibian, most people think of frogs who migrate to ponds in the spring to lay their eggs and then wander off again into the surrounding landscape. Or they think of edible frogs sitting at the edge of a pond croaking loudly. The truth is that only a fraction of all amphibians live according to this pattern. Many species have developed astonishing survival strategies and have grown independent from large bodies of water. They colonize subterranean cave systems, alpine regions, rapidly flowing mountain streams, human settlements, tundra and desert areas. They can withstand aridity and frost; they carry their young in their mouths, on their backs and in their stomachs; some even lay their eggs in foam nests on trees.

Amphibians surpass all other vertebrate groups in the diversity of their survival and reproductive strategies. These impressive modes of life, rarely known to the non-expert, are the subject of this fascinating section.

Ecology and Ethology

Milan Kminiak

Amphibian Habitats

Today, amphibians are found in nearly all habitats around the world. Many return to water and lead an amphibious or aquatic life, while others have become independent of large water bodies. Some species have even adapted to extreme environments such as deserts, the tundra or high mountains, habitats that seem unlikely environments for amphibians. Today, the greatest impact on amphibian life has come with the expansion of human populations, which often occupy the few remaining amphibian habitats. With these last pockets disappearing, many amphibian species have no chance of survival. Loss of habitat is undoubtedly a contributing factor in the dramatic drop in amphibian populations in recent decades.

Previous page:
Male and female leaf frog
Hyla brevifrons *(Hylidae)*
from Peru during spawning.

Amphibian Habitats

Since amphibians populate nearly all regions of the globe, we cannot present each habitat in detail. Europe alone is home to countless biotopes; riverbanks, still and flowing waters, landing areas, fens, moors, swamps, wetlands, alpine meadows, gorges, beaches and coastal dunes, deciduous forests, broad-leaved and mixed forests, karst landscapes with cave systems, and other types of environments too numerous to list. The selection of typical and extreme habitats presented here bears witness to the enormous ecological plasticity of these vertebrates.

Amphibians need favorable ambient temperatures to use their muscles and organs to their full ability. The dependence on fluctuating temperatures is especially important in land-locked habitats, because water can buffer temperature changes. Hence, most amphibians are caught in a dilemma: on the one hand, the sun's heat promotes their mobility and activity; on the other hand, they must compensate for the sun-induced loss of water by taking in more water. This happens almost exclusively through the skin, because amphibians do not "drink." Therefore most amphibians prefer moist habitats, and even species in arid regions must develop different strategies to ensure sufficient water supply. Water accounts for approximately 70 to 80 percent of the body mass in amphibians, the upper limit of this range occurring in aquatic species.

The diversity of amphibian species declines the closer one gets to the poles. This has to do with their basic requirements for life and survival—favorable temperatures and water sources. Species that have become largely independent of open water have had to develop nocturnal modes of life when humidity is high. Others have developed special physiological and behavioral mechanisms to counter unfavorable factors.

Endangered Amphibian Habitats

Primary and (nearly) untouched amphibian habitats are today found only in tropical rain forests; in large wetlands and swamps; in the tundra and taiga; in high mountains, steppes, deserts and semi-deserts. Many forest areas have shrunk to small oases surrounded by cultivated land. Steppes, too, have given way to grazing lands and grain fields. Large savannas and swamps have been transformed into arable land.

Habitats that are still uncompromised are also threatened by global environmental change. Millennia ago human changes had a positive impact on amphibians. Clearings created open biotopes that absorb and store heat and offer greater diversity. All this had a positive effect on species diversity. However, the sustainable level of environmental change and destruction through human habitation reached its peak at the end of the nineteenth century and has become unsustainable in the twentieth century.

Relatively few amphibian species can be counted among the so-called hemerophilous or synanthropic species. Members of these species are able to adapt to areas cultivated by humans. Of the European species, the green toad (*Bufo viridis*) is synanthropic. Abandoned quarries with small bodies of water and artificial bodies of water such as garden ponds, fountains and reservoirs are examples of beneficial human activity utilized, for example, by the natterjack (*Bufo calamita*), common grass frog (*Rana temporaria*), and some other species. Even military training areas with water-filled tracks can be an important amphibian refuge in many areas of Europe. Most amphibians, however, are dependent on

natural habitats within which they colonize specific microhabitats, defined as specific sites frequently used by individuals.

Aquatic Habitats

The structure, form and size of the water body, its depth, and fluctuating water level, the seasonal consistency of the habitat, the composition of the underwater soil, water movement, temperature, food supply, shading, flora, fauna, and many other factors, give an aquatic habitat its unique character and define its biotic and abiotic conditions for life. Hydrobiological surveys also differentiate between lentic areas (slow-moving or still waters in rivers, lakes, ponds, swamps, etc.) and lotic areas (swiftly moving waters in rivers, creeks, sources, etc.). Numerous amphibian species—caecilian, Anura, and urodele species—lead a more or less fully aquatic life.

Running Waters and Riverbanks

Many Urodela inhabit running waters, among them veritable amphibian giants from the paedomorphic Cryptobranchidae family. The East Asian giant salamander (*Andrias davidianus*) inhabits some Chinese rivers. Giant salamanders hide in hollowed-out spaces in riverbanks; prefer clear, cold, water high in oxygen content; and are predominantly nocturnal. The related North American hellbender (*Cryptobranchus alleganiensis*), a mere 12 to 27.5 inches (30 to 70 cm) long, has a similar mode of life. It is most frequently found in shallow, swiftly moving waters.

East Asian mountain streams are inhabited by the Chinese frog species *Amolops chunganensis*. During the spawning season they live exclusively in water or in immediate proximity to water. When in danger, they jump into the water and let themselves be swept along to pools downstream. In Northern Cameroun the toad *Bufo preussi* is known as an inhabitant of fast waters. These toads hibernate during the dry season. As a transition area between land and water, the banks of running rivers are populated by many amphibian

European tree frogs (Hyla arborea) are predominantly active at dusk and at night in Central Europe. During the day they like to sunbathe, preferring to rest on large-leafed plants, bushes, trees and reeds. Tree frogs are very sensitive to changes in their habitat and are endangered throughout Europe.

species. Caecilians (Gymnophiona) are frequent riverbank dwellers. Especially in the tropics, land and water habitats merge along the riverbanks. During the rainy season, when lowland rivers have high water levels and when deltas flood, amphibians are exposed to constant changes and fluctuation in water levels. In many amphibian species the reproductive season and the rainy season with subsequent flooding are directly related to one another, and several species have developed a strong seasonal dynamic.

The riverbanks of small, mountain streams in New Guinea are home to *Sphenophryne palmipes* (Microhylidae) with fingers and toes that terminate in large suction disks to hold onto the rocky riverbanks. *Microhyla heymonsi* is a mountain species of the same family from Vietnam and Thailand, whose tadpoles have also adapted to life in mountain streams. The North American frog *Ascaphus truei* (Leiopelmatidae), too, prefers clean, fast mountain streams and their immediate vicinity. Its larvae have a suction mouth that enables them to survive the two to three years necessary for their development in water. Many other amphibian species or larvae are well-equipped for life in running waters through morphological and behavioral adaptations.

Still Waters

While rivers are natural transportation systems, still waters are important reservoirs in any type of landscape. They offer an enormous range of microhabitats that are colonized by amphibians year round or during the reproductive season. Various eutrophic, oligotrophic and dystrophic lakes of different sizes are amphibian habitats of great diversity depending on their food supply, water chemistry and flora. In Europe, examples of amphibians typically found in eutrophic lakes are representatives of the family Ranidae, such as the Edible frog (*Rana ridibunda*) and salamanders, among them newts from different *Triturus* species. Nutrient-poor oligotrophic lakes, often found in subalpine and alpine regions in the Carpathian mountains and Alps, are the spawning grounds for the Alpine newt (*Triturus alpestris*) and the Grass frog (*Rana temporaria*). In Central and South America several representative of the genus *Telmatobius* are fully aquatic, while others, such as the "Titicaca" toad, penetrate alpine regions as high as 1,312 feet (4,000 m) above sea level, where they inhabit extremely frigid oligotrophic lakes.

Natural and artificial ponds, a variety of natural pools and small bodies of water in wetlands and moors are other types of still waters of great importance to the amphibian fauna. Although smaller pools may dry up when precipitation diminishes over several years, this is easily compensated for in years with good precipitation. Even the smallest, temporary bodies of water can be of vital importance to the survival of amphibian populations.

*Alluvial forests provide the habitats with the greatest species diversity in Europe. For many amphibians they offer valuable sanctuary. The bodies of water ensure successful reproduction and repopulation of the surrounding landscape. Weed thickets in river meadows offer ideal habitat conditions for the Moor frog (*Rana arvalis*).*

Alluvial Forests

Alluvial forests count among the most diverse habitats in the moderate latitudes. At one time they occurred along all larger rivers in lowland areas. On stepping into an alluvial forest, one is overwhelmed by an impression of wilderness and the abundance of co-existing biotopes. We discover a mosaic of humidity- and nutrient-rich forest, meadow and swamp ecosystems: on higher-sediment deposits, so-called hot-air lands have developed. The deciduous forest near the rivers with willows and poplars is still subject to regular flooding in alluvial forests; the hardwood forests farther away from the rivers feature elms, ash, oak and many other hardwood species. The abundance in alluvial forests is a result of the rich supply of water and nutrients—resulting from regular floods—and of the habitat dynamic characterized by a constant cycle of new habitats being created and existing ones being destroyed. Finally, alluvial forests also feature structural diversity because of an abundant and varied flora.

In Europe, alluvial forests boast the highest amphibian populations. In summer, amphibians migrate from these forests into surrounding areas. The great number of descendants—eggs, tadpole, adolescent or adult—plays a crucial role in the overall food chain of an alluvial forest.

Tropical Rain Forests

In contrast to the evergreen monsoon forest, which can survive even in a long dry spell, tropical rain forests are characterized by constant warmth and humidity. This is the most natural environment for anurans. More than 80 anuran species may inhabit a single hectare of rain forest. By comparison, all of Europe is home to no more than 62 amphibian species. Rain falls throughout the year and temperatures never drop below 64°F (18°C)—annual precipitation ranges from 78 to 157 inches (2,000 to 4,000 mm). Conditions of this kind prevail across large areas of South East Asia, in the Congo and Amazon-Basin, on the east coast of Madagascar and on some islands. The diversity of the rain forest is a result of the great structural diversity in these forests; habitats are divided into several "stories," from the forest floor to the treetops. One hectare is often home to 200, even up to 600 different species of tree, accompanied by countless other plants, epiphytes (air plants), liana and stranglers. A single rain forest tree can offer habitats and nutrients for 50 ant species, more than 500 insect species and countless other organisms. The tree is thus a microcosm on its own. Many species have specialized in specific ecological niches in one single type of tree. No one knows how many species exist in the rain forests of the world, but estimates indicate that the number surely lies in the millions. Rain forests bordering mountains—such as the Andes in South America or in Madagascar—are especially rich in species. Here, vertical zoning of climate parameters seems to have a positive effect on species diversity.

Of the rain forest regions in Africa, South East Asia and South America, the latter are home to the greatest diversity of amphibian species. However, the ancient rain forests that covered vast areas have been destroyed in many locations through deforestation, slash burning and nomadic agriculture. Every year, millions of hectares fall prey to these destructive campaigns intended to produce farm and cropland, although these clearings provide only short-term solutions for economic problems because the soil of deforested rain forest areas is nutrient-poor and extremely prone to erosion.

A unique amphibian habitat in rain forests is found in isolated, aerial water, the so-called phytotelma. These arise in the hollows of trees, in the leaf axils of Bromeliaceae, in banana trees, in the aerial bulbs of epiphytic orchids or the flowers of other plants and are fed mainly by rainwater. Some contain plant secretions. Phytotelma are home to a characteristic symbiotic ecosystem of bacteria, algae, ciliates, rotifers ("wheel animals"), insect larvae and numerous other small organisms. Many tree-dwelling and ground-dwelling amphibian species in tropical rain forests have discovered this niche and use it for reproduction. Most Anura in the rain forest are active at dusk and at night, while the brightly colored and poisonous Dendrobatidae are diurnal.

The rain forests in Central and South America are unique because of the diversity of some 1,700 species of Bromeliads, between whose leaf rosettes a miniature world unfolds high up in the rain forest. These plants, part of the pineapple family, are predominantly epiphytic. Their seeds are dispersed by wind. The initially minuscule seedlings on branches of jungle trees can grow into impressive plants of more than 2 feet (60 cm) in diameter in a matter of years, and the leaf rosettes can store up to 10 quarts (10 liters) of water. Although most habitats are generally much smaller than that and may contain less than a pint (a few deciliters) of water, they may be home to as many as 250 different animal species, as one study has shown.

Surprisingly, Urodela are generally not represented in most tropical rain forest regions of the world; their distribution is more or less limited to the temperate zones in the Northern

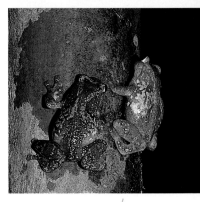

The small Platypelis pollicaris (Microhylidae) *from Madagascar squeezes through a narrow hole into the trunk of a bamboo tree to mate and lay its eggs.*

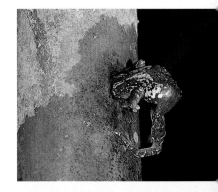

Tropical rain forests are one of the habitats with the greatest species diversity worldwide. Rain forests in the New World may feature as many as 80 amphibian species in a small habitat range.

Hemisphere. Only representatives of some genera of the species-rich lungless salamander family (Plethodontidae), such as *Bolitoglossa* and *Oedipina*, have spread to South America and are found in tropical rain forests. This was a secondary colonization from North and Central America.

Deserts and Semi-deserts

Small water deposits in the fork of a Bromeliad leaf in South American rain forests are vital as reproduction sites. The illustration shows an Epipedobates tricolor *(Dendrobatidae).*

Deserts and semi-deserts are characterized by irregular precipitation with a maximum of two humid months per year, low air and soil humidity, strong temperature fluctuations, sparse or no vegetation, and solid or sandy ground. The daily temperature differences may be as high as 90 degrees Fahrenheit (50 degrees Celsius). All these are conditions that are hardly compatible with the needs of amphibians.

Nevertheless they have conquered even this environment with the help of impressive strategies. Amphibians in extreme habitats such as deserts or high mountains have adapted to the unfavorable climatic conditions in a variety of ways. Many, such as the North

American toad species *Bufo debilis, B. punctatus* and *B. kelloggi* are so-called occasional (or opportunistic) breeders whose spawning cycles adapt to rainfall. Almost all species in arid regions are nocturnal to escape the life-threatening daytime heat; however, species in high alpine regions are frequently diurnal, provided there is sufficient humidity. Amphibians in arid regions tend to be closely tied to permanent water, if such bodies of water exist. The Colorado river toad (*Bufo alvarius*), for example, which inhabits the Sonora desert, is usually found either in or near water, a circumstance that has earned it the contradictory designation "aquatic desert species."

Adaptations similar to the toads are found in some Australian Anura. *Cyclorana platycephala* (Hylidae) are masters in surviving dry seasons. Representatives of *Notaden nichollsii* (Myobatrachidae) have been dug out from depths of more than 4 feet (120 cm) where temperatures were still above 86˚F (30˚C). The obvious conclusion is that such species require additional physiological adaptations to prevent desiccation. Another frog species in the Australian arid zone is the frog species *Neobatrachus pelobatoides*. In appearance and mode of life, it resembles the European Garlic toad (*Pelobates fuscus*).

The most significant adaptive behavior of amphibians in arid and semiarid habitats is cocooning. The cocoon prevents excessive loss of water, has a parchment-like consistency, and surrounds the entire animal, leaving only the nostrils free; in some species the mouth is left uncovered as well. The cocoon structure of several species has been studied under the microscope. It does not consist of desiccated mucus but rather the cell layers of the epidermal stratum corneum. In *Lepidobatrachus llanensis* (Leptodactylidae) up to 60 cell layers were counted in the cocoon wall, in *Pternohyla fodiens* (Hylidae) 43 layers. The thicker the cocoon the less water is lost through the skin. In addition to the species mentioned above, *Ceratophrys ornata* (Leptodactylidae), *Pyxicephalus adspersus* (Ranidae), *Leptopelis bocagei* (Hyperoliidae), *Limnodynastes spenceri*, *Neobatrachus pictus* (Myobatrachidae) and numerous *Cyclorana* species have been found to build cocoons. Among the Urodela, *Siren intermedia* forms similarly constructed cocoons, using the mud in desiccated pools to protect itself against loss of water.

Many Anura have specialized skin areas on the abdomen and on the upper thighs through which they can absorb large volumes of water. The permeability of amphibian skin is controlled by the hypophyseal hormone arginine vasotocin (AVT).

Breviceps adspersus (South African short-head or common or bushveld rain frog, Microhylidae) is one of most extreme desert-dwelling anuran species. They even occur in dry sand deserts on South Africa's Atlantic coast where there is practically no precipitation. They never encounter a water-filled puddle. Their water requirements are met by extracting water from the humidity brought inland in frequent, cool ocean winds and fog from the Atlantic. Condensation drips from the sparse vegetation into the sand, where the frogs absorb it through their skin. Only a fraction of the life-sustaining water is absorbed through nutrient intake. Since there are no opportunities for spawning, this species lay their eggs into the sand and the female provides an additional moisture "blanket": a layer of unfertilized eggs is laid on top of the large fertilized eggs from which the small frogs hatch by direct development.

Savannas and Steppes

Savannas are dry grass habitats above deep groundwater in subtropical or tropical regions. The relative plainness of the landscape is somewhat relieved by scattered trees, stands of trees, and bushes. Savannas and steppes develop in regions where annual precipitation is between 24 and 70 inches (600 and 1,800 mm) and where the climate follows a distinct pattern of dry and rainy seasons. Dry savannas are another example of an environment that seems to have little to offer amphibians. Yet quite a few amphibian species have managed to adapt to the conditions prevailing there. Among the Anura in African savannas, we find representatives of the true frogs, true toads, and above all Hyperoliidae. Savanna landscapes do not receive the same attention as tropical rain forests do. Yet they too are threatened by the ever-continuing expansion of human populations and by transformation into arable land.

There are some similarities between savannas and steppes in non-tropical regions. The latter are dry landscapes with little or no trees and with a more or less full ground cover consisting mainly of grasses and shrubs. The eastern European and Asian steppes that stretch from the Ukraine to Mongolia, the North American prairies, and the east Argentine pampas are typical steppe regions. Hot, dry summers and cold, windy winters are hardly ideal living conditions for amphibians. In deserts, savannas and steppes we find predominantly burrowing, nocturnal amphibian species that have become independent of large water bodies. The key factor in their life cycle is the duration of the rainy season. The Common (Garlic) spadefoot is an unusual European steppe species (*Pelobates fuscus*). Its habitat stretches from Central to Eastern Europe, and it is sometimes known for its huge tadpoles (10–18 cm). When the pools dry out, they crawl into deep, moist cracks in the mud where they await the next rainy season.

Cannibalistic Tadpoles in the Desert

Given their fundamental biological characteristics, it seems strange that frogs can also live in the desert. American spadefoots (genus *Scaphiopus* and *Spea*, Pelobatidae), inhabit the Sonora desert in Arizona.

After more than 11 months without rain, the "internal clock" begins to tick in innumerable spadefoots buried in the ground one yard (a meter) below the surface. Rain is near; but the amphibians do not begin to dig themselves out because of large raindrops falling from the sky. Instead, nearly imperceptible tremors in the ground, caused by raindrops falling, suffice as a signal for them to emerge. On less than half a square mile (one square kilometer), thousands of mud-covered frogs break to the surface and gather in newly formed pools. These frogs are intent on only two things: fast reproduction and getting as much food as possible. A loud frog chorus resounds during that single night, once a year. This marks the beginning of a race— not just against time, but also against the sun, the high temperatures, and a dwindling water supply. *Scaphiopus couchii* sets a new development record during this period: from the deposited egg, a metamorphosed juvenile spadefoot develops in only 7 to 10 days. The spadefoots lay their eggs during the first night following the rain. The tadpoles hatch 24 hours later and complete their metamorphosis in just 6 to 9 days. High water temperatures and an abundance of food play an important role in this accelerated development. Not only amphibians, but a whole variety of crustaceans and other animals, as well as several algae, thrive at this time, experiencing record reproduction. One *Scaphiopus* female alone can lay up to 4,000 eggs. Statistically, only two of them will survive to reach sexual maturity.

The shrinking water supply quickly becomes a source of stress in crowded pools. Amphibian larvae must now fight for their survival. *Spea bombifrons* tadpoles turn into predators and devour *S. couchii* larvae. What happens to the *S. hammondi* tadpoles, however, is even more bizarre. When water is scarce, some of the larvae turn into predatory, all-consuming "sharks." Within a period of just one to two days, they grow to five times their original size. Their jaws change: instead of the typical labial teeth and keratinous maxilla, tadpoles develop strong jaws with teeth. The predatory larvae devour anything smaller in size, including their own species. Even one- to two-year-old metamorphosed specimens that have not yet reached sexual maturity yet and accidentally wander into the pools are consumed. At times, several hungry larvae literally tear these animals to shreds. The great increase of energy boosts the predatory larvae's chances to complete their developments and to ensure successful reproduction for another season at the cost of their own kind.

Open, Cold Landscapes—the Tundra

The tundra, like the desert, seems another unlikely amphibian habitat. The cold climate typical of this type of landscape, with extremely low air and ground temperatures—in summer the ground thaws only to a depth of an inch or two (a few centimeters)—combined with a very short summer season, clearly limits the distribution of poikilothermic species. Despite this, amphibians have also penetrated into this region, although distribution and numbers of species are low. In a huge area of the former Soviet Union covering 8.6 million square miles (22.4 million square kilometers), we can find only 41 amphibian species, representing 0.8 percent of all known amphibian species; of these, two occur north of the arctic circle. By comparison, South American rain forests contain more than 80 different amphibian species per hectare!

The arctic tundra, with dwarf shrubs, lichen and mosses, encompasses the Eurasian and North American regions above the tree line. This truly extreme environment has constant daylight in summer and constant darkness in winter. The photoperiod effect inevitably influences the animals who live in this environment, and population densities vary greatly. In most poikilothermic animals active life is restricted to one to three months out of the year as a result of the extreme climate conditions. In summer, temperatures lie between 28 and 50°F (2 and 10°C), in winter they fall to –40 and –60°F (–40 and –50°C). Among those species who can cope with these temperatures are the Siberian (or Manchurian) salamander (*Salamandrella keyserlingii*), the North American wood frog (*Rana sylvatica*) and the Spring peeper (*Pseudacris crucifer*). Even the European Grass frog (*Rana temporaria*), the Moor frog (*Rana arvalis*), *Rana amurensis* and sometimes the Common toad (*Bufo bufo*) cross the boundary into the arctic tundra regions at times. Similar ecological conditions are found in the northern mountain ranges above the tree line, the so-called alpine tundra. Toward the south, the tundra meets the boreal coniferous forest, where climate conditions are somewhat milder and a more varied fauna is present.

Habitats in Urban and Agrarian Landscapes

In urban environments, amphibians are exposed to many human factors in addition to the usual biotic and abiotic factors. Increasing human activity tends to translate into a decrease in amphibian species diversity. Some species may disappear altogether when the aquatic environments they require for repro-

duction are destroyed or when new, man-made environments do not meet their requirements. Negative factors in urban environments are the gradual temperature increase in cities, decrease in heat transfer to the ground surface, diurnal temperature fluctuations, intensive fog formation, decrease in average wind velocity, noise, vibration and pollution stresses.

The areas surrounding large cities tend to exhibit a decrease in groundwater levels. This is the result of drainage for construction projects as well as the regulated and rapid removal of rainwater due to canalization and diversion of water into neighboring arable land. Aquatic habitats near cities are therefore quite rare, if present at all, and often are compromised by negative influences. Nevertheless, urban environments can be a refuge for some amphibian species. Although these environments are severely compromised and even threatened, they do provide the basics for the continued existence of some amphibians. Several studies have shown that the number of amphibian species need not necessarily be smaller than that in nearby natural habitats. However, the species we find in such man-made habitats are predominantly synanthropic and therefore mostly allochthonic, displacing the natural, autochthonic species typical for the area. In many areas of the world the giant (marine) toad (*Bufo marinus*) is a typical synanthropic

species. Synanthropic species in the European fauna are the green toad (*Bufo viridis*), the common toad (*Bufo bufo*), and in some urban areas also the common (garlic) spadefoot (*Pelobates fuscus*) and the fire-bellied toad (*Bombina bombina*). Agricultural areas can also provide habitats to some amphibian species as long as the minimal requirements of the species are met. More sensitive species such as the tree frog (*Hyla arborea*), however, have very little chance of survival in such areas.

Loss of Habitat and Its Impact on Population Size

We have listed only a few types of amphibian habitats. Most are threatened by human destruction. Tropical rain forests receive the passionate interest of the public, yet 50 to 75 million acres (20 to 30 million hectares) are still destroyed every year through deforestation. In the past 50 years more than 50 percent of rain forests have been destroyed. But the loss of each small pool, water-filled trench, every wetland or low moor is often catastrophic for local amphibian populations even though it may not have a global impact. Populations affected by such local destruction cannot simply move to other habitats that are still intact. Habitat protection must therefore be as much a focus in species protection as is atmospheric protection.

*This common toad (*Bufo bufo*) was discovered in the Hohe Tauern mountain range in Austria near the Grossglockner peak at an elevation of 6,562 feet (2,000 m) above sea level, close to the vertical distribution range of this species. In the Alps, Grass frogs (*Rana temporaria*), Alpine newts (*Triturus alpestris*) and Alpine salamanders (*Salamandra atra*) are quite common at these elevations.*

New Zealand was originally home to only three Anura species of the genus Leiopelma *(Leiopelmatidae)*. Over the past hundred years many foreign species have been imported and have encountered virtually ideal habitat conditions with almost no interspecies competition, which has led to their rapid distribution. Litoria raniformis *(Hylidae)* originates from Australia.

"One of the rarest and most remarkable amphibians I found on Borneo was a large tree frog... which he [a Chinese worker] saw gliding down from a tall tree on a diagonal path, almost as if in flight.... Upon closer inspection, I discovered that its toes were very large and were covered with skin extending to the very tips. Thus, when spread apart they formed a surface much larger than the body.... To my knowledge, this is the first example of a flying frog, and it deserves general attention...." Alfred Russel Wallace, renowned naturalist and competitor to Darwin, used these words to describe the first time he saw a gliding frog.

Several reptile and frog species have in fact acquired the remarkable ability to perform "parachute flights," which can be viewed as a precursor to gliding. This, however, is less applicable to frogs than it is to reptiles. Of course, they are not actively flying, but rather falling slowly at a 45-degree angle as opposed to a vertical drop. Usually, only specific morphological adaptation can make such "flights" possible. The small South American common tree frog *Phrynohyas venulosa* and several other species can drop from a great height. To reduce their speed when falling, they soften the fall by flattening their bodies and spreading apart their extremities.

Real "gliders" can be found among the Southeast Asian genus *Rhacophorus* (*Rhacophoridae*) which contains many species. The Borneo gliding frog (*Rhacophorus pardalis*) and several other members of this genus (*R. nigropalmatus, R. reinwardtii*) have developed webbing, which extends to the tips of fingers and toes. They may also have membranous flaps on feet and forearms.

It is remarkable that, at least in a rudimentary fashion, almost all classes of vertebrate have developed the ability to "glide." Besides active "flyers" among reptiles (Pterosauria), birds and flying mammals (bats), there are several examples among fish, amphibians, reptiles and mammals that evolved passive gliding or parachute flight. The following animals belong to this group: flying fish among fish; the gliding frogs, mentioned above, among amphibians; lizards and snakes that glide between trees among reptiles; and various gliding marsupials, the squirrel family (Sciuridae) and Dermoptera among mammals. Many of them are able to glide for a distance of 98 to 164 feet (30 to 50 m), although flying fish can "fly" much farther.

*This Gliding frog (*Rhacophorus malabaricus*) from India, one of 63 known species of the genus* Rhacophorus, *has large webs between fingers (left) and toes (middle). Underneath the upper and lower arm there are additional membranous seams.*

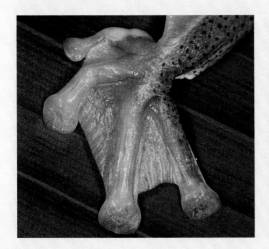

Whether in tropical rain forests or in deserts, all life requires water for survival. When humidity levels fall below the saturation point, amphibians, whose skin is highly water-permeable, are in danger of dehydration. The respiratory surfaces of the lungs and the oral epithelium also contribute to the loss of water during respiration. Osmoregulation is also closely related to the water balance. It encompasses water absorption or intake and excretion, as well as maintaining levels of dissolved substances—i.e., ions—which play a key role in the regulation of all vital processes. The illustration (right) shows how amphibians absorb water and what are the main causes of water loss. This helps us to understand the habitat requirements of amphibians and their mode of life.

1. Metabolic water plays a relatively minor role in the total water balance of amphibians.

2. Adult amphibians do not drink, and their digestive tract is relatively unimportant for water absorption. A portion of the water absorbed with food is excreted via the intestine.

3. The skin is the most important organ for water absorption in aquatic, semi-aquatic and terrestrial amphibians.

4. Aquatic amphibians and their larvae excrete urine that is very diluted, thus eliminating the excess water absorbed through the skin. Terrestrial amphibians excrete urine that is more concentrated with urea and thus limit the amount of water lost. Some anurans in arid regions such as *Chiromantis xerampelina* (Rhacophoridae) or *Phyllomedus sauvagii* (Hylidae) even excrete relatively insoluble uric acid, similar to reptiles or birds. This enables them to execute nitrogen with only very little water.

5. Terrestrial amphibians lose water mostly through the skin. Amphibians have therefore developed different physiological and behavioral mechanisms to limit this loss.

6. In areas with low humidity, exhaled air also causes water loss. In humid habitats, such as tropic rain forests, this is a negligible factor.

7. Next to the skin, the bladder is the second most important organ for regulating the water and ion balance in amphibians.

8. Lymph sacs provide protection against evaporation and also serve as water reservoirs. They are located directly beneath the skin or sometimes deeper in cavities created by expanded lymph vessels. The lymphatic system of the Urodela consists of four longitudinal divisions, smaller lymph vessels, and a network of lymph capillaries.

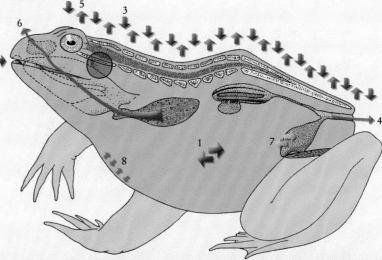

Why Are There No Amphibians in the Sea?
Robert Hofrichter

Amphibians are almost exclusively freshwater creatures, and even a few hours in seawater would be fatal for almost any frog or toad. But once again there are some exceptions to the rule: green toads (*Bufo viridis*) are steppe animals with a tolerance for heat, cold, aridity and salinity. Their tadpoles can endure saline concentrations equivalent to approximately 15 percent of that found in seawater. Other representatives of the true toads (Bufonidae) also sometimes spawn in brackish water—for example, *Bufo calamita, B. danatensis, B. melanostictus, B. marinus* and *B. mauritanicus*. The paedomorphic mole salamander *Ambystoma taylori* inhabits the saline waters of Lake Alchichica in Mexico. And in South East Asia the inconspicuous *Limnonectes cancrivorus* is known to inhabit brackish water in mangrove swamps; it can even survive in seawater, where it hunts for its favorite staple, crabs. Its larvae, too, are saline tolerant.

Amphibian skin is thin and naked, unprotected by hair, keratinous plates or scales. It is much more permeable than is the skin of other vertebrates. After metamorphosis, the epidermis is shed at regular intervals, and the skin can thus perform its function as a respiratory organ while remaining very permeable to ions and water. In fresh water, water enters the body of amphibians through the skin and is evacuated again in the form of strongly dilute urine. A loss of ions results from this exchange, compensated for by active ion intake from the surrounding water. Amphibians are able to extract NaCl even from highly diluted solutions (up to 10^{-5} mol/L). The Na^+ ions are actively transported and the Cl^- ions are drawn in passively by the resulting potential.

Should a frog or toad end up in a hyperosmotic solution such as seawater, it could lose too much water, on the one hand, and absorb too many ions through the skin, on the other hand. Sea-dwelling vertebrates use two different strategies to cope with this problem: Teleostei possess hypotonic body fluids relative to seawater and are at risk of losing too much water to their environment. To compensate for this loss of water, they drink seawater, absorbing between 70 and 80 percent of the water into their bloodstream through their intestine and excreting excess ions

through their digestive tract. The ions absorbed into body fluids are eliminated actively through the gills. Marine Chondrichthyes (Elasmobranchii) and the crossoperygiean *Latimeria* follow a different strategy. Their blood is isotonic to seawater. This balance is only partially achieved through electrolytes—inorganic ions—while the difference is compensated for through organic osmolytes such as urea and trimethylamine oxide. Because the body fluids are in osmotic balance with seawater, osmotic water loss is prevented. Marine Chondrichthyes also have a special rectal gland for the excretion of excess ions.

Limnonectes cancrivorus, too, follows the strategy of the Elasmobranchii. Urea is not simply a metabolic, nitrogen by-product, but an important factor in osmoregulation. Urea is retained through a reduction of urine excretion in the body and reaches a concentration of 480 mmol urea per liter of blood. Nevertheless, the blood does not become wholly isomotic with the surrounding saltwater, but remains slightly hyperosmotic, which results in a slight water intake through the skin. This intake is important for urine production in *L. cancrivorus*. Urea also plays an important role for muscle contraction in these frogs and when concentrations are too low, contractility is compromised. It is notable that the larvae of *L. cancrivorus* are even more saline tolerant than the adults, although their osmoregulation is different

than that of adults, following instead the pattern adopted by the Teleostei.

Amphibians whose habitats are distant from water or in arid regions often have difficulties with osmoregulation. They tend to have very large bladders for water storage; enlarged lymph spaces beneath the skin serve the same purpose. Urine concentration in amphibians is strongly hypotonic in comparison to their blood. When the water supply in the environment is insufficient, water is moved osmotically from the bladder into the dehydrated body fluids and into the bloodstream. When the water supply in the environment is abundant or even excessive—i.e., when the body fluids are "diluted"—Na^+ and Cl^- ions are actively transported from the bladder into the blood. Thus the bladder performs two vital functions: it is a water reservoir when water is scarce, and a saline reservoir when water is overabundant.

In conclusion, amphibians cannot inhabit the sea because their skin is too thin and permeable and because ion concentrations are too high in seawater. In other words, they do not live in oceans for osmotic reasons. The first amphibians, which were at the same time the first land vertebrates, colonized land from fresh water. However, we should also mention some giant amphibians that moved from swamps and marshes to oceans as a secondary wave of colonization during the Triassic. (This amphibian belonged to the Trematosauria group, which also included the largest known amphibians—among them *Mastodonsaurus*, which grew to more than 13 feet [4 m] in length.) One can only assume that the larvae of sea-dwelling amphibians were equally unable to develop in seawater as are today's amphibians, for even *Limnonectes cancrivorus* needs fresh water or at least very diluted brackish water for successful fertilization and metamorphosis. The frequent tropical rainfalls in its habitat create small pools of water on a regular basis in the littoral zone; at the very least, the existing flood pools are diluted with rainwater. This dilution enables the tadpoles in these pools to reach metamorphosis. It is assumed that the Trematosauria, too, moved to fresh water for reproduction and inhabited oceans only as adults.

Phenology and Migration

Ulrich Sinsch

Most amphibian species have a complex life cycle. The first phase often takes place in water and the second on land. The timing of reproductive behavior in individual ontogenesis must be finely tuned to the seasonal cycles to make optimal use of them. The species-specific seasonal activity pattern depends on the ontogenetic stage as well as on the geographic location of the habitat. In many species whose specific activities take place in spatially separate temporary habitats, the seasonal component of the life cycle must be matched to the spatial component of migrations. Phenology is the study of the issues relating to the temporal sequences in life cycles.

Seasonal Activity Patterns

In tropical rain forests, the important abiotic factors such as temperature and precipitation are so favorable throughout the year that nearly all activities can take place at any time. Therefore most amphibian species can reproduce all year long, and all stages of a life cycle can occur congruently. However, there can be intensive competition between species—in some rain forests up to 80 species have been recorded in one hectare—and thus diurnal or annual periodic niche formation within habitats may occur. Some species are exclusively nocturnal, others exclusively diurnal, and a third group are crepuscular (active at dusk). Some reproduce immediately after heavy rainfalls in temporary water, others utilize permanent bodies of water such as lakes and streams. It is impossible to do justice to the variety of life cycles of tropical rain forest amphibians in a generalized text, but rest periods such as estivation (summer dormancy) and hibernation are absent from their activity patterns.

In the temperate zone, alpine regions and arid habitats, behavior must adapt to the seasonal changes in temperature and precipitation. The reproductive period of cold-stenothermal species such as the common toad (*Bufo bufo*), the grass frog (*Rana temporaria*) and the agile frog (*Rana dalmatina*) begins immediately after winter and is restricted to a few days or weeks (explosive breeders). Therefore the embryonic and larval phases can be observed only in spring, and newly metamorphosed adolescents only during the early summer period, while subadults and adults are found throughout the entire activity period. Migrations linking the various temporary habitats (breeding ponds, summer habitat, winter habitat) are as much a part of the activity patterns as are the migration of the metamorphs, individuals from breeding ponds, and their dispersal across the terrestrial habitat. In fall, the annual activity period ends with hibernation, which may last from one to eight months, depending on latitude.

Eurythermal species such as the natterjack (*Bufo calamita*) deviate from this activity pattern, especially in their long reproductive period which may last up to four months in central Europe (prolonged breeders). During the summer months, most aquatic and terrestrial ontogenetic stages can therefore be observed at the same time. Natterjacks are unique in the plasticity of their annual activity pattern, which differs greatly in the northern part of the range (Sweden) and the southernmost part (Spain). In Northern Europe, the natterjack's active period is rarely longer than four months and hibernation is the only period of rest. In Central Europe the active period lasts approximately six months; in a hot and dry summer it may be shortened by facultative periods of inactivity. Here the activity pattern includes hibernation as well as estivation. And finally, in Southern Europe, an obligatory estivation period replaces hibernation altogether and the reproductive period moves from spring to December and January.

Amphibians in extreme habitats such as deserts and alpine regions have adapted to their hostile environments in a number of ways. The activity period of the Couch's spadefoot (*Scaphiopus couchii*), which inhabits the Californian desert, is limited to a maximum of one month per year. The toads leave their subterranean hiding places for a short period of time after the rare but heavy rainfalls, reproduce in puddles and feed as much as they can in order to survive the following long period of inactivity. The aquatic development in the larval period (egg to metamorphosis) of this species lasts only seven to ten days, a world record among amphibians. Similar adaptations can be observed in the Australian desert frog (*Cyclorana platycephala*). In alpine regions shorter activity periods are also common, in this case as a result of the long winter season.

The alpine salamander (*Salamandra atra*) has become completely independent of water thanks to viviparity. A tendency to shorten the aquatic stages is also prevalent in Andean marsupial frogs of the genus *Gastrotheca*. Other species such as the giant frog *Batrachophrynus macrostomus* have switched to a fully aquatic mode of life in the high-altitude lakes at the center of Peru (9,843 to 14,108 feet/3,000 to 4,300 m above sea level), where sufficiently high temperatures prevail even during the cool dry season to ensure an active period without dormancy. These few examples demonstrate how varied activity patterns are, and how this has enabled amphibians to successfully colonize almost all environments (except for salt water and the Arctic).

Migrations

Geographic displacement among amphibians may serve one or more purposes: (1) to change from one temporary habitat to another; (2) to search for food; (3) dispersal. While vagility varies greatly from species to species and during each ontogenetic phase, it is a prerequisite for the colonization of new habitats. The active radius of amphibians is still frequently underestimated, even though we have known for 30 years that the small North American urodele species *Taricha rivularis* may traverse distances up to 8 miles (13 km). Similar distances (6 to 9

Some spawning waters are visited within a short period of one to two days by thousands of grass frogs (Rana temporaria). The spawning period of these explosive spawners is very short, with most of the population spawning in three to four nights.

miles/10 to 15 km) have also been documented in the European tree frog (*Hyla arborea*), the small water frog (*Rana lessonae*) and the leopard frog (*Rana pipiens*). The migratory distances covered by adults are often exceeded by juveniles. The marine toad (*Bufo marinus*) is spreading across Australia at a rate of almost 29 miles (35 km) per year as a result of juvenile migration. By comparison to the other vertebrate classes, a range of 29 miles (35 km) seems relatively small. However, it demonstrates a remarkable level of mobility in these ectothermal, earthbound animals.

Breeding Migration

The mass migration of explosive breeders such as the common toad (*Bufo bufo*) to their breeding ponds is one of the most extraordinary migratory phenomena among amphibians. Although the distances are relatively small, the synchronized arrival of many thousands of conspecifics is impressive even to non-herpetologists. For some species (e.g., *Bufo bufo, Rana temporaria*), the destination of the migration is the pond of birth, while others migrate opportunistically toward any body of water that offers the right conditions for reproduction (e.g., *Bombina variegata, Rana lessonae*). We should note that even among those species known for their fidelity to the original breeding ponds, a small percentage of the population is not programmed to return to the breeding ponds; this ensures the genetic exchange between neighboring populations and the colonization of new bodies of water. The spawning migration of the common toad is the exception rather than the rule, in that it begins in fall prior to the start of the reproductive period, is then interrupted by hibernation near the breeding ponds, and is

Grass frogs are explosive spring breeders. In mild winters they may begin migration to their spawning grounds as early as mid-February in Central Europe, especially in lowlands, following paths that take them across large snow-covered fields. In the Alps–grass frogs spawn even at elevations of 7,218 feet (2,200 m) above sea level–migration begins much later, depending on temperature, sometimes as late as the end of May or the beginning of June.

concluded within a few days in spring.

Migration to Summer Habitats

Some species spend their entire active period (outside of the reproductive period) within the relatively narrow boundaries of a summer habitat, called home range. When we take the common toad (*Bufo bufo*) as an example, we realize that a home range may cover no more than 120 square yards (100 square meters) and that the extended activity range during periods of foraging may not exceed 1,200 square yards (1,000 square meters). Naturally, these numbers differ greatly from species to species. Within any one species the quality of the home range (e.g., density of prey) defines the size of the home range.

Many different behaviors lie between these two extremes—fidelity to a lifelong home range and complete absence of fidelity to a specific summer habitat. The natterjack (*Bufo calamita*), for example, changes its home range every two to four weeks, and we can therefore say that it has only temporary home ranges.

Dispersal

A "deluge of frogs"—that is, the mass appearance of newly metamorphosed frogs near breeding ponds—is the result of dispersal away from the spawning water. Most metamorphs leave the breeding ponds a few days or weeks after metamorphosis and disperse across a wide range. Juveniles (e.g., *Rana pipiens*) who are barely an inch or two (a few centimeters) long in body size may often cover up to 2,600 feet (800 m) in one day. Young toads (*Bufo woodhousii, B. calamita*) have an activity radius that is up to six times greater than the adult range. The spa-

tial map acquired by the juveniles during the dispersal enables sexually mature adults to find their way back to the breeding ponds or to target new waters for spawning.

Orientation Mechanisms

Orientation behavior of amphibians is well studied, especially in those species that show site fidelity—i.e., species that return voluntarily to temporary habitats after passive or active displacement (homing phenomenon). Return migrations to breeding ponds (e.g., many *Bufo* and *Triturus* species), summer habitats (e.g., *Bufo bufo*, *B. woodhousii*, *Eurycea lucifuga*), or winter habitats (e.g., *Salamandra salamandra*, *Bufo hemiophrys*) are quite frequent.

The sense of orientation in amphibians is based on four types of environmental cues: acoustic, magnetic, olfactory and visual. These orientation cues fulfill specific tasks in the multisensory orientation system of amphibians, and some hereditary species-specific differences as to how each sense is used are known. Amphibians exhibit the following behaviors for spatial orientation: 1. direct orientation—following an environmental parameter to the destination—is called piloting; 2. reference to fixed or predictably moving landmarks is called compass orientation; and 3. defining their own position in a cognitive map is considered navigation.

Acoustic Cues

In Anura acoustic communication plays an important role in reproductive biology. The mating calls of the males permit the phonotactic approach of the female, in the southern chorus frog (*Pseudacris triseriata*) and the natterjack (*Bufo calamita*) (calls are audible over distances of 600 to 1,200 yards (500 to 1,000 m). Migration toward the source of the sound is a typical example of pilotage. Whether and to which degree environmental sounds—for example, the gurgling of a stream—are used for orientation remains unknown.

Magnetic Cues

Phillips's research in 1977 established that the North American salamander species *Eurycega lucifuga*, and several other amphibians, can utilize the Earth's magnetic field for orientation. In the meantime it has been proven that other salamanders and frog species (*Notophthalmus viridescens*, *Bufo bufo*, *B. calamita*, *B. spinulosus*) share this ability. It is commonly accepted that, like birds, amphibians utilize the inclination (vertical component) of the Earth's magnetic field as a compass. The role of Earth's magnetic field as a map in navigation is still controversial.

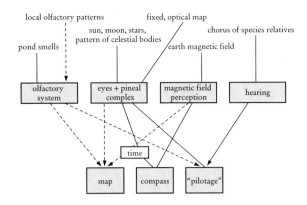

Olfactory Cues

We have known for many years that olfactory cues are important orientation factors for amphibians. They are an essential component in the orientation system of toads (*Bufo americanus*, *B. boreas*, *B. bufo*, *B. valliceps*) as well as in newts (*Triturus vulgaris*). The significance of odors for initial orientation has been proven and this points to the possibility of site recognition by means of a kind of "olfactory map." Odors emanating from the breeding ponds can, however, also be used in piloting.

Visual Cues

Visual cues are either fixed such as silhouettes, or mobile like the sun, moon and stars. The utilization of celestial cues requires the existence of an internal clock to compensate the diurnal, pseudo-movement. Perception of visual stimuli does not occur through the eyes alone, but also with the help of the pineal organ.

Forest silhouettes serve as an orientation marker for pilotage in common toads. Nevertheless, a blinded common toad is still able, without any problems, to replace visual markers with other orientation markers and to reach its spawning site. The same applies to *Bufo americanus* and *B. valliceps*, but not to the Andean toad *B. spinulosus*. The utilization within the framework of a visual map is possible in some species.

Celestial bodies and the polarization pattern in the sky are used, for example, by *Acris gryllus* for orientation. In this case visual stimuli serve as orientation markers for a time-compensated compass system.

The information available to us today with respect to migratory and orientation behaviors in amphibians shows that they move by means of a multisensory, redundant orientation system and can migrate toward specific destinations within a familiar range. When one orientation marker is absent, its function can be taken over by another. This is why disabling one orientation marker does not prevent amphibians from homing.

Migratory path of a reproductive male common toad (Bufo bufo) from April 20, 1985, to April 10, 1986 (after Sinsch, 1990).

Top right: Directional cues, sensory systems and function of directional indicators in the orientation system of amphibians. Hypothetic links are indicated by a broken line (after Sinsch, 1990).

Karl-Heinz
Jungfer and
Peter Weygoldt

Amphibians as Caring Parents

Amphibians not only take care that their eggs are placed in a favorable spot, they also practice many types of brood care, which can be manifested in surprising ways in some species. In fact, no other vertebrate group has developed a comparable variety of reproductive strategies. Nearly all anuran eggs are fertilized outside of the parental body—that is, after the eggs have been laid. Most salamanders, on the other hand, have internal fertilization: the female takes the male spermatophore into her cloaca and lays fertilized eggs or gives birth to larvae. In only a few cases do amphibians retain fertilized eggs or larvae in the body for further development.

Anurans (Frogs and Toads)

*Tadpoles of the common toad (*Bufo bufo*) demonstrate typical schooling behavior. Most North American and European amphibian species do not practice brood care. The number of eggs is high—large common toad females may lay as many as 8,000. The eggs are laid into water, after which no further parental care is given.*

The apparently most ancestral reproductive strategy among frogs and toads is exhibited by those species that place a large number of eggs into a body of still water, such as a pond or pool. This is where the larval feeding stage of frogs and toads occurs and the larvae (tadpoles) find plentiful food sources in these environments. Predator pressure and competition from other species may be the most important causes that have led anurans to adapt to new spawning grounds. Such new environments may be different types of water bodies—e.g., rain puddles in arid and semiarid zones that exist only for days

before they dry out again, or the cascading waters of mountain streams. There seems to be a trend to move away from water altogether: more than 20 percent of the anurans lay their eggs on land. In general, an increased effort in parental brood care goes hand in hand with fewer eggs being laid. Laying eggs on land with larvae hatching into environments where they cannot find food leads to the development of larger eggs with increased yolk content. Small eggs in relatively low numbers, however, are laid by species that feed their larvae with nutritive eggs. Smaller eggs are easier to ingest and a low number of eggs per egg clutch and the ability to produce more eggs within a short

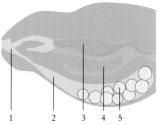

The gular pouch is used for transportation by mouth-breeding frogs (Rhinoderma) in Chile and Argentina. As soon as the larvae start to move inside the terrestrial eggs, the male gulps and takes them into his mouth without swallowing them. Five to fifteen larvae are thus deposited inside the gular pouch, which extends greatly to accommodate them. R. rufum simply carries the larvae to a body of water, while the entire development of the larvae takes place inside the gular pouch in R. darwinii, with the larvae possibly even ingesting nutrition while inside the pouch. The fully developed small frogs hatch from the male by way of the mouth. Top: longitudinal section of the trunk of a Rhinoderma darwinii: 1. oral cavity; 2. gular pouch with eggs (5); 3. stomach; 4. lung (after Blüm, 1985).

period of time enable the female to feed the larvae on a regular basis.

Suitable spawning sites are very often at the same time the territories from which the males call to attract females, and which they defend against other males. Yet there are also species where the sex roles are reversed. The males of two poison-dart species (*Dendrobates auratus* and *D. tinctorius*) care for and transport the larvae to tree hollows and other small water bodies. In both species, the females are territorial and aggressive, playing the active role in mating and, in a manner of speaking, guarding their sexual partner. This ensures that their male will not extend his care to the larvae of other females and will not transport them to water bodies that may be available only in limited numbers.

Brood Care

European grass frogs (*Rana temporaria*) are among the species with an ancestral reproductive strategy. They lay up to 4,000 eggs in pools and ponds. They, too, exhibit adaptations to their specific habitat and have evolved reproductive behaviors to ensure favorable conditions for their offspring. Grass frogs spawn in early spring when many bodies of water are still covered with ice. They choose shallow areas where the sun warms the water by 20 degrees Fahrenheit (10 degrees C) and more in daytime, which favors rapid development of the temperature-dependent embryo.

Adaptations to prevailing temperatures have also been observed in tropical zones. In tropical regions, the bodies of water are often so warm that the larvae are able to develop quickly and hatch in less than 24 hours. The disadvantage of such small puddles exposed to the sun is that warm water contains little dissolved oxygen,

which the embryos require for respiration. To adapt to this situation, many frogs do not lay their eggs in clumps, but rather in a thin layer that floats like a film on the water's surface. This allows atmospheric oxygen to diffuse directly into the gelatinous layer of the egg.

Many aquatic organisms, such as fish and tadpoles, appreciate frog eggs as a source of food.

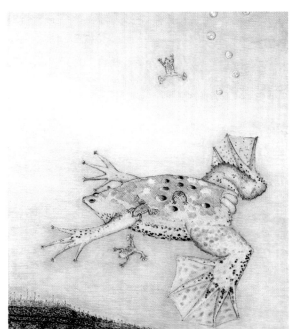

South American Pipa carry their young on the back. Males and females simultaneously execute somersaults, with the female dropping the eggs at the highest point of the jump. When she lands on the ground again, the eggs land on her back. There they sink into the swollen skin on the back and develop into tadpoles inside breeding pockets or pouches, in some species even into fully developed young frogs. Middle: section of breeding pouch of Pipa sp.: 1. epidermis; 2. "lid" (after Blüm, 1985; drawing by: T. Podlesny). 3. larva with yolk sack (5); 4. gelatinous material; 6 & 7. blood vessels with capillaries.

Gastric-brooding Frogs of the Genus Rheobatrachus

In 1973 a small and, at first glance, inconspicuous frog was discovered in Queensland in Australia and described as *Rheobatrachus silus* (Myobatrachidae). The 2-inch (5-cm) Anura were an aquatic species, inhabiting flowing waters north of Brisbane. Only the following year did scientists realize what an extraordinary find this had been: *R. silus* had a reproduction strategy unique not only among amphibians but among all vertebrates. A female in captivity had been behaving strangely for some time and suddenly "retched" up several young. Subsequent observation showed an abnormally enlarged and stretched stomach: it had obviously served as a "uterus."

The fertilized eggs were swallowed by the female and developed in the stomach. The eggs are rich in yolk, and the development from fertilized egg to young takes approximately six to seven weeks. During this time the mother does not eat and the production of digestive juices is prohibited through the hormones in the egg sac and the skin secretions of the larvae. The fully metamorphosed young are passed through an enlarged esophagus and are born by mouth.

In 1979, only six years after their discovery, a dramatic decline in *Rheobatrachus* populations became obvious, and the last specimen in a natural environment was sighted in 1981.

Scientists and terrarium owners exhibited great interest in this frog once its unique reproduction strategy became known, and many individuals were taken from their natural habitat, but the real reason for their rapid disappearance is not known. They have also disappeared from managed forest areas and national parks, where neither habitat destruction nor excessive removal from nature could have played a role.

In 1984, just two months after the death of the last living *R. silus* specimen in captivity, a second *Rheobatrachus* species was discovered and described as *R. vitellinus*. It seems to have the same gastric-brooding reproduction strategy and is also listed as missing.

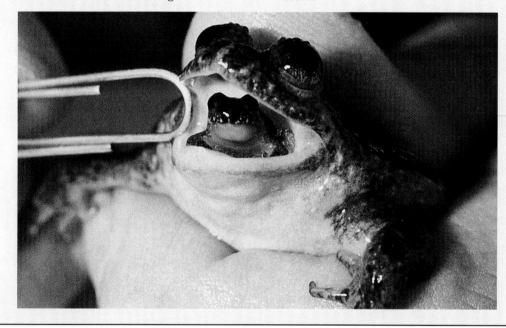

"Oral birth" of Australia's Rheobatrachus silus, *unique among all vertebrates: the young develop in the stomach (gastric-brooding) and hatch from the mother's mouth.*

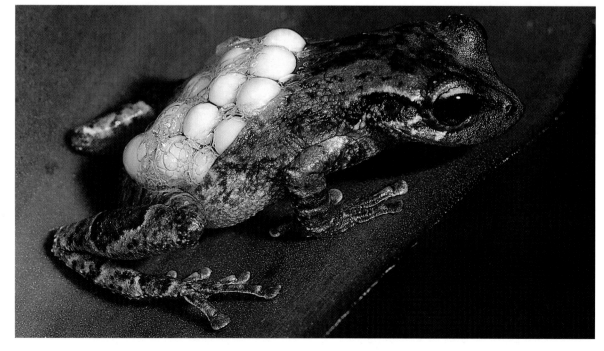

Flectonotus goeldii *(Hylidae) females from southeastern Brazil carry up to 22 eggs on their back. The larvae are deposited in the forks of bromeliad leaves, where they develop into small frogs without requiring any further nutrition.*

Eggs that are laid in sites protected from egg predators have a better chance of survival. The eggs of the gladiator frogs (*Hyla boans* group) have this kind of protection. The males build their own small "swimming pool" by erecting a circular wall out of mud in the shallows of larger bodies of water. The female lays the eggs inside this water-filled nest after deepening it and reinforcing the wall. Rain or rising water levels soon free the hatched tadpoles from this enclosure and release them into the open water.

Other species move even farther away from traditional spawning sites by using minuscule water deposits that form in and on plants (phytotelmata)—e.g., water-filled hollows in trees, bamboo sections and leaf axils on plants such

Egg laying (top) and birth (left) of the marsupial frog Gastrotheca walkeri *(Hylidae).*

as bromeliads (Bromeliaceae) and wild bananas (Musaceae). Eggs laid in these sites are safe from many egg predators. Phytotelmata are also found in areas where there are no still waters—for example, on steep mountain slopes or in regions with porous limestone ground. However, phytotelmata are usually nutrient-poor environments. Brazilian bromeliad tree frogs (*Phyllodytes*) lay very few eggs into leaf axils. Only one larva per axil will survive.

The situation is less dramatic when larvae hatch from large eggs. The yolk is enough to last for the whole larval phase, which means that the larvae require no other food. Non-feeding tadpoles can be observed in some genera of the Microhylidae—for example, the South American *Syncope antenori*, the Madagascan *Anodonthyla*, *Cophyla*, *Platypelis* and *Plethodontohyla*, or *Kalophrynus pleurostigma* from Borneo.

Attending the eggs and transporting tadpoles: Epipedobates tricolor *(Dendrobatidae).*

*Mottled shovel-nosed bur-
rowing frog (Hemisus mar-
moratus) female in exposed
brood cave surrounded by
tadpoles. In time, the female
digs a tunnel and leads her
tadpoles to the next body of
water.*

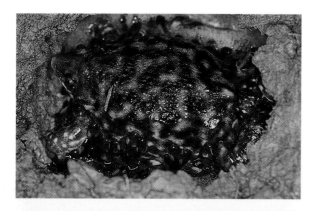

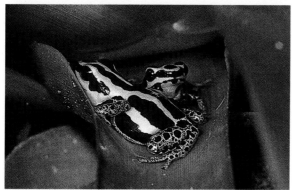

Reproduction of
Dendrobates ventrimacula-
tus *(Dendrobatidae) in
bromeliad leaf axil.*

*Facing page: After mating,
the back-brooding* Stefania
evansi *carries first the eggs,
and later even the young, on
its back.*

drop into the water below or, in some cases, free
themselves actively from their egg envelope and
leap from the broken egg capsules. Leaf frogs
(*Phyllomedusa*) also practise this method. But
they take it one step further and lay their eggs
into a leaf whose edges they wrap around the
eggs and create a leafy cone. Additional eggless
gelatinous capsules store moisture and protect
the fertilized eggs from desiccation. Similar tree
nests can be observed among African banana
frogs (*Afrixalus*). Frog species that construct
foam nests have developed yet another type of
"packaging."

High moisture levels are the prerequisite for egg
development on land without going through an
external larval phase at all. Small, fully formed
frogs hatch directly from the eggs. Direct development is not only a result of a single evolutionary event; it has occurred independently in
various groups—for example, in the rain frogs
(*Eleutherodactylus*), in some toads such as the
Tepui toads (*Oreophrynella*), in pumpkin
toadlets (*Brachycephalus*), and in Indo-
Australian narrow-mouthed frogs.

African live-bearing toads (*Nectophrynoides*)
have a unique reproductive strategy. Two
species (*N. tornieri*, *N. viviparus*) give birth to
live young. As embryos they are not fed
through the maternal body but instead from the
yolk in the egg. They are thus ovoviviparous.
The embryos of two related species
(*Nimbaphrynoides liberiensis*, *N. occidentalis*)
absorb secretions from the maternal oviduct
which has been transformed into a uterus. These
species are thus truly viviparous. Currently only
one other ovoviviparous frog is known, the
neotropical rain frog *Eleutherodactylus jasperi*,
one of some 600 poorly known rain frog
species.

Parental Care of Eggs and Larvae

In several frog species the male stays near the
clutch of eggs. It is not always clear whether
egg attendance represents territorial defense
against conspecifics rather than brood care.
What is certain, however, is that these eggs'
chances of survival are greater. Some male
gladiator frogs (*Hyla rosenbergi*) remain near
their mud nests after the eggs have been laid
and will defend the nest against other males
intending to occupy them. An intruding male
would destroy the surface film of the clutch and
cause the eggs to sink to the bottom and die.

Male glass frogs of the genus *Hyalinobatrachium*
stay near their eggs which are laid onto the
underside of leaves. These are often consumed
by wasps, and some flies also lay their eggs at
the same site. The hatching fly maggots feed on
the frog eggs. *Hyalinobatrachium colymbiphyl-*

Many frogs have moved away for reproduction
from water altogether. They lay their eggs into
moist depressions or cavities. After hatching,
the larvae must make their way to water, as is
the case in the African hyperolid genus
Leptopelis or in the Madagascan golden mantella (*Mantella aurantiaca*). The tadpoles of the
colorful Australian false toadlet (*Pseudophryne*)
hatch only when the eggs are flooded by rising
water levels. Among terrestrial eggs, too, there
are some with sufficient yolk that the hatched
tadpole does not require other food sources.
This means that they no longer need to go in
search of water but can complete their development on land. Among these there is the subterranean genus *Synapturanus*, the rocket frog
Colostethus stepheni, and the African
Phrynodon and *Arthroleptella*.

Several climbing frogs—for example, African
reed frogs (*Hyperolius*), neotropical leaf-
gluing frogs (*Hyla leucophyllata* group), red-
eyed tree frogs (*Agalychnis*), and glass frogs
(Centrolenidae) attach their eggs to vegetation
above water. Upon hatching, the larvae simply

Embryos of the American spotted salamander Ambystoma maculatum *(Ambystomatidae, Pennsylvania, USA) inside their gelatinous envelopes.*

lum is a Central American glass frog whose males stay near the nest only at night. A related species from the same region, *H. valerioi*, stays near the eggs day and night. In the latter species, few eggs are destroyed by wasps and flies.

Other frog parents, especially those species that lay their eggs on land, sit on top of their nests. This may do more than simply moisturize the eggs. Parental skin secretions are probably disinfecting as well. When the narrow-mouthed frog *Cophixalus parkeri* from New Guinea is removed from its nest, fungi attack the egg cases and the embryos. Arthropods and other narrow-mouthed frogs consume the eggs. In the absence of the parent, whose movements would shift the position of the eggs, the yolk inside the egg case remains on one side, where it coagulates and the embryo dies.

Once the larvae have hatched, some adult frogs stay near the larvae—for example, the males of the narrow-mouthed frog *Synapturanus salseri* in a subterranean brood cavity, or *Colostethus stepheni* in a nest under fallen leaves. The males remain until the larvae have completed metamorphosis without requiring more food.

Some large frog species stay near tadpoles that live in water and gather into schools—for example, the females of two South American *Leptodactylus* species and the males of the African giant pyxie (*Pyxicephalus adspersus*). The adults sometimes even guide the larvae and snap at waterfowl that may represent danger. The African mottled shovel-nosed frog (*Hemisus marmoratus*) constructs a subterranean breeding cavity near water. The female stays near the eggs and the larvae, which gather tightly around the female. This obviously keeps the larvae moist. Skin secretions from the female also appear to be bactericidal and fungicidal. After a strong rainfall, the female digs a trench or tunnel to the nearest body of water as a pathway for the larvae. Some larvae are even transported to open water on the mother's back.

Parents Transport Eggs and Young

Transporting larvae on the back, often preceded by guarding the eggs, is quite common among frogs. Male poison-dart frogs (*Allobates, Colostethus, Epipedobates* and *Phyllobates*) spend almost the entire two weeks of the development of their egg clutch near and on top of it. By doing this, they also support the larvae during hatching. The larvae then wriggle onto the parent's back and are transported to water. They are firmly attached and can spend several days in this position. The larvae of the rocket frog *Colostethus degranvillei* and of the Seychelles frog (*Sooglossus seychellensis*) stay on the back of the female until metamorphosis is completed. The males of European midwife toads (*Alytes*) attach the egg string to their hind limbs. Until the larvae hatch, at which time they carry the embryo to a water source, they may spend some time on land and occasionally humidify the eggs.

The Australian kangaroo frog (*Assa darlingtoni*) has skin pouches on both sides of the groin. After hatching from the eggs laid on land, the larvae slip into these pouches, and complete metamorphosis there without ingesting any other food.

All species of the South American egg-brooding frogs (Hemiphractinae) deposit their eggs on the female's back. In species where the eggs are carried openly on top of the back, the female excretes a secretion from the cloaca during mating. The male sits on top of the female's back during amplexus, collects the secretion with its hind limbs, pushes it beneath itself and whips it into bubbles by kicking its limbs back and forth. This frothy mass becomes the egg sac. The eggs then exit from the cloaca. Again the male collects these eggs with its hind limbs and pushes them beneath itself. Within two to three days, the egg sac hardens and the eggs are firmly fixed onto the back of the female. The embryos develop above the yolk. They grow two bell-shaped gills on each side which eventually fully enclose them. After approximately three weeks, some *Flectonotus* species deposit the egg sac into a water-filled bromeliad leaf axil. The larvae burst through the egg envelope and consume the remains of the egg sac, although they are quite independent of food sources because their digestive tract is filled to bursting with yolk. In the genera *Cryptobatrachus, Hemiphractus* and *Stefania*, the development is completed inside the egg.

The young burst through the egg envelope on the back of the female and remain there for some time. They are attached to the mother by two gill filaments which are fused to the mother's back beneath the egg.

Other *Flectonotus* species have developed lateral skin folds that cover the eggs. These species, like the marsupial frogs (*Gastrotheca*), do not form an egg sac. The latter have one or two skin pouches on their back that form out of epidermis folded inside. The male pushes the eggs into these pouches. Some species in the high Andes release up to 150 tadpoles in an advanced stage of development into pools of water after two to three months. In tree-dwelling species, the entire development occurs inside the brooding pouch, from which 20 to 25 fully developed young frogs then "hatch."

A completely different mode of dorsal transportation can be observed in the rain frog *Eleutherodactylus cundalli* in Jamaica. Females lay and guard the eggs up to 285 feet (87 m) deep inside a karst cave, a secure breeding site but one that offers little food. The eggs develop directly into young frogs, which climb onto the mother's back and are carried out of the cave.

Females Feed the Young

Several frog species that deposit their eggs or larvae in water-filled leaf axils or tree hollows feed their young in these nutrition-deficient microenvironments. The males of the Brazilian egg-eating tree frog *Osteocephalus oophagus* attract females to a water-filled plant. The female then chooses the exact site where the eggs are laid. Every five days the pair returns to lay more eggs, which will develop if none have survived from the first clutch or which will be consumed if tadpoles have hatched from the first clutch. If the parents fail to return at least five times, the larvae will starve. The Central American coronated tree frog (*Anotheca spinosa*) has even developed communication between female and tadpoles. When a male has attracted a female to a tree hollow and has coupled with the female, it seeks out a new calling site. The female returns by herself to the breeding location about every five days and feeds the larvae with unfertilized eggs. However, this takes place only if the larvae swim around the female and touch her and communicate by this behavior that they are present and hungry.

In some poison-dart frog species (*Dendrobates histrionicus* group) the parents take on three important roles, as is the case in the Central American strawberry poison-dart frog (*D. pumilio*). The male prevents desiccation in eggs laid on land using moisture from its bladder. After hatching, the female carries each larva on its back, one at a time, and deposits it into a water-filled leaf axil. The female returns every few days. If the tadpole exhibits a special "begging" behavior—it holds itself rigid and vibrates its tail—the female slides down into the leaf axil and feeds the tadpole with unfertilized eggs.

Salamanders and Newts

The most ancestral form of reproduction is found in salamanders who lay their eggs into water. They are fertilized with male sperm in the water. The larval phase also occurs in water. This is observed only in the salamanders of the family Crytobranchidae, in some species of the Hynobiidae and probably in the Sirenidae. All other groups have internal fertilization by means of spermatophores. Eggs and larvae then develop in water in most European species

Urodelans often exhibit complex mating behaviors. The Triturus dobrogicus *male arches its back, displaying its dorsal crest to the female.*

(Salamandridae). The eggs are often laid on land. The larvae hatch and crawl to water. Some eggs hatch only after they have been flooded. Other larvae with sufficient yolk can develop on land without requiring any other source of food. Direct development also occurs: fully developed salamanders hatch from terrestrial eggs. Very few species are viviparous.

Brood Care in Salamanders

Representatives of the European newts (*Triturus*) spend spring and early summer in water. When the female has picked up the spermatophore of the male, the eggs are fertilized in the oviduct. The female then attaches them one by one to water plants, wrapping parts of plants

Top: Ensatina eschscholtzii *(Plethodontidae) with nest.*

Middle: Cynops ensicauda popei *(Salamandridae) during courtship. The cloacal region of the male is clearly visible: the male stands in front of the female and deposits the spermatophores.*

Right: Mispairing of salamanders in a terrarium. The Taricha torosa *male embraces a sharp-ribbed salamander (*Pleurodeles waltl; *both Salamandridae).*

around each egg. The female does not care for the eggs or the larvae in any other manner. This behavior is typical of all Salamandridae. Yet some species carry the eggs longer in the maternal uterus. Fire-bellied salamanders (*Salamandra salamandra*) and the Caucasian salamanders (*Mertensiella caucasica*) deposit fairly developed larvae into water in most of their range. The alpine salamander (*Salamandra atra*) is fully independent of water. Only one egg cell develops in the two uteri; the yolk of other eggs is used to feed the embryos. When it has been used up, the uteri provide additional nutrients. Depending on altitude, gestation may take two to three years. At birth, the young salamanders are fully formed. A similar kind of viviparity is known in the Lykian salamander (*Mertensiella luschani antalyana*).

In most other salamander species at least one parent practices brood care after the eggs have been laid. They take on a variety of tasks. Aquatic hellbenders (*Cryptobranchus*) and waterdogs and mudpuppies (*Necturus*) defend their eggs against egg predators from their own species. Waterdogs use their gill plumes to fan oxygen-rich water around the eggs. Olms (*Proteus anguinus*) agitate the water by moving their tails.

Some salamanders who lay their eggs on land defend them against other predators such as arthropods and other invertebrates. When a female of the dusky salamander *Desmognathus ochrophaeus* is removed from its nest, the eggs

quickly disappear. The female will also remove eggs that show no sign of development or appear to have fallen prey to a fungus, to prevent infection of the healthy eggs; this behavior is also present in other salamanders. In the end, the female places its throat on top of the eggs. The pulsating respiration agitates the eggs and somehow promotes a higher rate of hatching. Another terrestrial species, the palm salamander *Bolitoglossa subpalmata*, rotates its eggs. This behavior probably ensures balanced oxygen supply. It winds its body around the eggs and also places its throat on the eggs. Most likely, its skin toxin is a chemical defense against fungal infection.

Female Cynops orientalis *(Salamandridae) laying eggs.*

Below: Freshly laid eggs of Cynops ensicauda.

Walter Hödl

Amphibian Foam Nests

Foam or froth is frequently used by animals to protect eggs and developmental stages from desiccation, predators and sunlight. Several insects protect their nests with a frothy secretion from accessory glands of their genitalia. Praying mantises lay their eggs into a fan-shaped cocoon made of hardened foam. The eggs of cicada are simply covered in frothed accessory gland secretions. Cicada larvae surround their bodies with a foam cover, the so-called cuckoo saliva. Foam-nest builders exist among labyrinthodont and ostracodermat fishes. Gouramis produce aquatic foam nests by gulping for air at the water's surface and forming air bubbles that are coated with mucus secreted from the palate. Aquatic snails (Janthina spp.) and cirripedic crustaceans (Lepas spp.) manufacture hardened floating bodies from a self-produced frothy mass. Among amphibians, foam nests are a widely spread phenomenon.

Foam-nesting Frogs

In frogs, oviposition in foam nests has evolved independently in at least five families (Hyperoliidae, Hylidae, Leptodactylidae, Myobatrachidae and Rhacophoridae). At least 20 out of the 339 described frog genera contain foam-nesting species. Frogs build foam nests in water, on land or on trees. In most cases, the nesting site is identical with or close to the site for aquatic larval development. Only frogs of the genera *Philautus* (arboreal foam nests), *Adenomera*, *Kyarranus* and *Philoria* (terrestrial foam nests) complete their larval development inside the frothy construct. In all other foam-nesting species known so far, larval development and metamorphosis occur in open water. Froth and foam on the water surface dissolve much more quickly than their equivalent on or in the ground or attached to plant structures at varying heights. Aquatic foam nests usually dissolve within a few days, while terrestrial nests can maintain their frothy consistency up to several weeks. In all species that have been studied in detail, the foam is known to be a product of oviductal secretions at the time of mating. The actual foam-beating motion occurs in axillary (Leptodactylidae, Rhacophoridae) or lumbal amplexus (Myobatrachidae) and varies remarkably among the families. In rhacophorids, the females stir up the foam with their hind limbs; in the leptodactylids, it is the male that takes on this task through rotational movements of the legs. And in the myobatrachids, it is the female that beats oviductal fluids into foam with her arms.

Anuran foam nesting is best documented in the neotropical family Leptodactylidae. The males of foam-nesting leptodactylids perform rotational movements (aquatic foam nests) or sweeping motions (terrestrial foam nests) with

Arboreal foam-nesting in Rhacophorus dulitensis *(Rhacophoridae). Once the foam nest is built, the female remains for some time and uses her hind legs to smooth out the frothy mass during the hardening process (Danum valley, Sabah, Malaysia).*

the legs generating a frothy mass similar in consistency and coloring to whipped egg white. The oviduct secretions, consisting of mucopolysaccharids, are released at the onset of nest construction. In nonfoam-nesting species, the same secretions form the highly hydrophilic jelly matrix surrounding each single egg. This clear, gelatinous mass is whipped by the axillary amplecting male into a foam platform into which eggs are successively deposited. The foam nest is built in alternating phases of activity and rest. Each activity sequence begins with the female taking on a position with a slightly inwardly arched back. This so-called signal position enables the synchronization of the male's behavior of egg uptake, insemination, and foam production with the female's expulsion of secretions and subsequent egg-deposition behavior.

In the well-studied Amazonian species *Physalaemus ephippifer* the whipping sequence begins as soon as the female adopts the lordosis position. The foam-beating phase lasts approximately three seconds and starts out with the male drawing his legs forward and pushing his feet during a pronounced hunched position under the cloaca of the female in order to catch the secretions and the eggs. To prevent the eggs from sinking to the bottom or being swept away (this species is an aquatic breeder), the legs of the male form a basket around the vent of the female during the three-tenths of a second it takes for the eggs to exit from the female cloaca. The eggs—approximately eight per sequence—are moved onto the back of the male from where they are woven into the foam through rapid rotating movements of the male's hind limbs. On average, 80 sequences follow one another with approximately 20-second intervals between each. About half an hour after the foam nesting began, the nest reaches its final shape. The fist-sized, meringue-like mass in which several hundred eggs are imbedded is left by the parents a few minutes after the last whipping sequence has taken place, and they never return to the nest. The initially unpigmented tadpoles leave the foam cover already on the third day. The foam itself dissolves in a further four to six days.

During the early development of *Physalaemus ephippifer*, the foam nest fulfills a multiple protective function. Foam-covered eggs and freshly hatched larvae are safe from desiccation and may withstand several days without rain, which may dry out the shallow breeding puddle. Within the nest, the eggs and larvae are sheltered from aquatic predators such as carnivorous tadpoles and insects. Moreover, the foam probably contains bactericides and fungicides which may contribute to the high survival rate of embryos and early larval stages. Since tropi-

cal waters are often deficient in dissolved salts, the protective foam may also have developed as a means of preventing osmotic desalinization of the cell liquid as a result of salt-free water penetrating through the expandable egg layers. The development of semiterrestrial and terrestrial reproductive modes is interpreted as a reaction to the great number of aquatic predators and the high rate of interspecific competition in breeding ponds. In semiterrestrial foam-nesting species, the embryos and early larval stages occur in foam nests outside of water, while the elder larvae require open water bodies and external sources of food (e.g., South American bull frog, *Leptodactylus knudseni*). In purely terrestrial foam-nesting species, the larvae develop inside the frothy mass produced on land without ingesting any external food (e.g., *Adenomera spp.*). Until metamorphosis, they are nourished exclusively from their internal yolk supply. In some foam-nesting species (e.g., *Leptodactylus fuscus, Rhacophorus schlegelii*), the nests are built by the males inside hollows dug into the ground. The subterranean nests are thus well protected against egg-eating aerial predators (e.g., wasps).

Aquatic foam-nesting in Pleurodema diplolistre (Leptodactylidae), João, Pessoa, Brazil.

Terrestrial foam-nesting in the South American Bull Frog, Leptodactylus kudseni (Leptodactylidae). The nests, up to 20 cm in diameter, are created among fallen leaves near bodies of water at the onset of the rainy season (Reserva Ducke, Manaus, Brazil).

Werner Himstedt

Reproductive Biology in Gymnophiona

All Gymnophiona males have a copulatory organ called phallodeum. A section of the cloacal wall can be everted with the help of a complicated mechanism and is used to transfer the sperm into the cloaca of the female. It is therefore probable that all Caecilian species have internal fertilization. This is in stark contrast to the other two amphibian orders. However, internal fertilization does not necessarily indicate viviparity. In Urodela both oviparity and viviparity are found among families with internal fertilization—one need only remember egg-laying newts and the viviparous alpine salamander. Gymnophiona, too, include oviparous and viviparous species.

Mating Behavior

We have no data on how caecilians find and recognize mating partners. Acoustic communication does not occur in caecilians as it does in most Anura. And the dark habitat of caecilians makes visual partner recognition by means of color signals or skin crests (see mating behavior in newts) virtually impossible. Chemical and tactile signals must therefore play a decisive role, but we have no data to prove this. The mating behavior of caecilians is more difficult to observe and analyze than is that of frogs or salamanders. This behavior has thus far been described only for the aquatic Typhlonectidae (*Chtonerpeton* and *Typhlonectes*).

Copulating Typhlonectes compressicauda.
The partners (a–male; b–female) exhibited contact behavior through touching and embraces. The phallodeum (c) is inserted into the female cloaca (d) and copulation lasts for two to three hours, with the partners holding fairly still. When copulation is completed, the phallodeum withdraws from the female cloaca and remains visible for some minutes. It gradually diminishes in size until it is fully retracted into the male cloaca (after Himstedt, 1996).

Egg-laying Caecilians

Approximately 25 percent of all caecilian species are egg-laying or oviparous. Rhinatrematidae and Ichthyophiidae—i.e., those families considered primitive because of their anatomy—are probably oviparous. Yet the allocation of reproduction mode to specific families is still unknown for many caecilians. The Caeciliidae, for example, include oviparous as well as viviparous species. The entire embryonic development has been studied and understood in only a very few species. There has been only

one instance where a female has been observed laying eggs, and only for a few species have females been discovered near their eggs. Observations of this kind exist for only eight caecilian species from five genera. These are *I. glutinosus*, *I. malabarensis*, and *I. kohtaoensis* from the family Ichthyophiidae and *Hypogeophis rostratus*, *Gegeneophis carnosus*, *Idiocranium russelli*, *Siphonops annulatus* and *S. paulensis* from the family Caeciliidae.

Nests and Parental Care

In all caecilian nests discovered thus far, the eggs were connected by strings. These strings are extensions of the external, gelatinous egg capsule. In freshly deposited eggs, the bundle of strings can still be unwound and one can observe that all eggs were laid onto a continuous string with individual eggs spaced 1/3 inch to 1.2 inches (1 to 3 cm) from one another. It has never been observed how the female winds this long string into a balled-up clutch from which no egg can be lost. This knotting probably also prevents the clutch from falling apart even when one egg is removed, an important factor because dead or infected eggs are devoured by females as part of their brood care behavior.

Right: Ichthyopis glutinosus *(Ichthyophiidae) with nest (after Sarasin and Sarsin, 1887).*

Different species create varying sizes of egg clutches, but again there is little information on intraspecifics variability. Small clutches with only six eggs have been found for *Idiocranium russelli* and *Siphonops annulatus*. *Hypogeophis rostratus* lays 15 to 18 eggs, and *Ichthyophis glutinosus* 25 to 40 eggs. An unusually large nest with 100 eggs was discovered from *I. malabarensis*. In *I. kohtaoensis* clutches have been found with from 9 to 47 eggs, an average of 27 eggs per nest. The eggs are laid into moist ground and the female probably creates a small hollow while knotting the egg string; the female then guards the eggs in this burrow until they hatch. The female remains immobile, wrapped around the knot for many hours each day. Every now and then she rearranges her body position and in doing so also rotates the eggs. It is possible that the eggs need to be regularly rotated for healthy development to take place. Several authors have observed similar behavior in frogs and plethodontid salamanders, which practice brood care on their terrestrial eggs. It is notable that in Anura, Urodela and Gymnophiona, isolated eggs that are no longer guarded and rotated by the mother are attacked by fungi within a matter of days and die. Maternal skin secretions may also play a role. The skin toxin of many amphibians contains substances which have an antibacterial and antimycotic effect. *Ichthyophis* females regularly push their heads into the egg mass during brood care. This leaves one with the impression that the female is controlling and checking on each egg. During this process, the female sometimes consumes individual eggs. It is probable that she identifies infected or dead eggs and removes them from the nest by consuming them. With the exception of eating isolated eggs, the females do not ingest any food during the brood care period.

In addition to protection against infections, brood care is naturally also an important protective measure against predators. This is realized not only by hiding the eggs beneath the maternal body, but also through active defense behavior. When a breeding hollow of *I. kohtaoensis* is opened, one can often observe the female thrusting her head into the opening and biting.

Embryonic Development

In oviparous caecilians, the development of the embryos inside the egg envelope can follow different courses. Similar to other amphibians, there are two principal developmental processes. In one instance, the larvae live a (partially) aquatic life and develop an adult anatomy through metamorphosis alone. In other examples, fully developed juveniles hatch after they have completed their metamorphosis inside the egg envelopes. These so-called directly developing species in caecilians have thus far been found exclusively among Caeciliidae in *Grandisonia brevis*, *G. diminutiva*, *Hyopgeophis rostratus* and *Idiocranium russeli*.

In contrast to other amphibians, caecilian eggs are rich in yolk. Cleavage is therefore not complete as it is in a frog or salamander egg; caecilian cleavage is merobastic. Similarly to fish or bird eggs, a bastodisc forms at the animal pole. In *Ichthyophis* and in *Hypogeophis* the first cell divisions occur in the maternal oviduct prior to egg laying. The subsequent development is largely the same as standard amphibian embryogenesis. After cleavage and gastrulation, organ formation begins with neurulation. The elongated embryo lies on top of the spherical yolk and begins to lift off from the yolk base as it grows. When the embryo reaches approximately 0.6 inch (15 mm) in length, one can recognize the gill buds and the eyecup. The gills grow into three pairs of feathered gills, and lateral line organs form. The gills of embryos are vascularized and therefore most certainly able to function. It is likely that the embryos satisfy their oxygen requirements by means of gill respiration.

As the body continues to grow, the yolk supply is consumed. Finally the body walls grow laterally around the yolk and absorb the ever-decreasing remnant into the intestine. The body can no longer stretch out inside the narrow egg envelope, and it is wound into a tight coil. Prior to hatching, a 2.7-inch (7-cm) caecilian will lie coiled in three loops inside an egg with a diameter of approximately 1/3 inch (1 cm). In *Ichthyophis* the total embryonic development from egg laying to hatching takes 70 to 80 days.

Larvae and Metamorphosis

In *Ichthyophis* the gills regress prior to hatching but the larvae still retain several characteristics necessary for an aquatic mode of life. These are a small tail fin at the end of the body and the lateral line organs. Upon hatching, the larvae are already equipped with fully functional lungs. The remnants of the first and second gills are no longer supplied with blood and fall off on the first or second day of free larval life, although one gill slit remains until metamorphosis. The larvae do not yet have a tentacle. In the past it was assumed that free-swimming caecilian larvae switch to life on land only after metamorphosis and that they live in water like tadpoles or salamander larvae. However, caecilian larvae are found in water only at night. During the day they hide on the shores of small bodies of water above water level, burrowed into damp mud or underneath rocks, leaves and

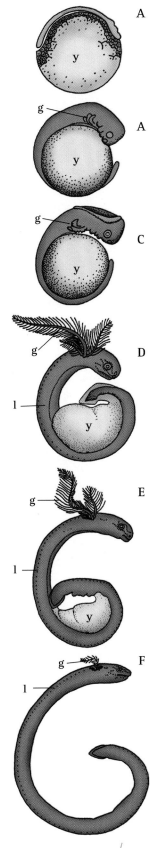

Embryo development in Ichthyophis sp. A–embryo prior to neural tube development; B–at 19 days; C–at 22 days; D–at 40 days; E–at 50 days; F–at 75 days, just prior to hatching; length 2.5 inches (65 mm); y–yolk; g–gill buds and gills; l–lateral line organ (after Himstedt, 1996).

Direct Development

In species with direct development—for example, *Hypogeophis rostratus*, the entire development including metamorphosis occurs within the egg envelope. In general, embryogenesis occurs in much the same way as it does in *Ichthyophis*. The gills are somewhat shorter, and the third gill is especially reduced. Larval organs, which are signs of adaptation to movement and orientation in water for species with free-swimming larvae, are only partially present in *H. rostratus*. Thus lateral line organs form while no tail fin is developed. There is a gill slit. In comparison to larval development, the entire differentiation process seems to take less time. Even prior to hatching from the egg envelope, one can observe that the gills recede, and the lateral line organs disappear altogether. A fully developed, approximately 2.5-inch (65-mm)-long juvenile hatches, fully adapted to the habitat and mode of life of the adults of the species.

Viviparous Species

In contrast to other amphibians, viviparity is the dominant type of reproduction among caecilians. Approximately 75 percent of all caecilian species are viviparous. It seems that viviparity evolved independently in Gymnophiona, because it occurs in several families with different phylogenetic roots on several continents. The paraphyletic family *Caeciliidae*, which is distributed across the Old and the New World, contains both oviparous with free-swimming larvae and direct-developing forms, as well as viviparous species among its group of species. The *Typhlonectidae* in South America and the *Scolecomorphidae* in Africa are almost exclusively viviparous.

As is the case for egg-laying, or oviparous, species, we have little information on the reproduction biology of viviparous caecilians. Research has been carried out mainly on the Central American caeciliid *Dermophis mexicanus* and the South American aquatic caecilian *Typhlonectes compressicaudus*. We cannot determine to which degree the few data can be applied to the other 100 viviparous caecilian species. As is the case for other viviparous amphibians, viviparous caecilians have smaller and fewer eggs. Egg diameters range from 1 to 2 mm, and 10 to 50 eggs develop inside the ovaries. However, the number of embryos is far smaller than the number of ovarian eggs. In *D. mexicanus* 4 to 12 (average value: 7) embryos have been found, in *T. compressicaudus* 2 to 11. It seems probable that viviparous caecilians reproduce in a two-year cycle. In *D. mexicanus* fertilization occurs between June and July and birth between May and June of the following year, after an 11-month gestation period. The

Ichthyophis kohtaoensis female (Ichthyophiidae) with nest.

dense vegetation. All reports on caecilian findings show that the larvae are amphibious rather than aquatic in their mode of life.

Larval development until metamorphosis has been observed for only two *Ichthyophis* species: *I. glutinosus* and *I. kohtaoensis*. In both species, growth is relatively slow. Over the course of 10 to 14 months, the total length of the larva grows from approximately 2.75 inches (70 mm) at hatching to approximately 5.5 to 7 inches (140 to 180 mm) at metamorphosis. Metamorphosis, too, is a slow process in these species and may last several weeks. The anatomical changes that occur are much less dramatic than they are in other amphibians. There is no need for limbs to be formed, and the lungs are already fully developed at hatching. Larval characteristics that disappear as a result of metamorphosis are the gill slits, the tail fin at the end of the body, and the lateral line organs. The tentacle is a new organ, formed during metamorphosis. In some species, the coloring may change. Thus some *Ichthyophis* species are marked by a yellow lateral stripe (e.g., *I. glutinosus*, *I. kohtaoensis* and 10 other species). This bright band of color appears only during metamorphosis. And finally, toward the end of metamorphosis, the shape of the head changes. Metamorphosed specimens have a slightly more pointed mouth than do larvae.

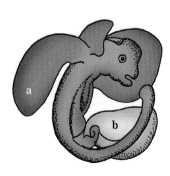

Typhlonectes compressicauda embryo with large gill organs. It is assumed that the large gills, which surround the entire body of the embryo, function as a type of pseudo-placenta. According to this hypothesis, gas exchange and food intake would be realized through the gill epithelium. However, there is no experimental proof of this theory. a–gill; b–yolk (after Himstedt, 1996).

gestation period in *T. compressicaudus* is only 6 to 7 months; obviously fertilization and birth are not as strictly synchronized as they are in *Dermophis*. The morphology of the oviducts changes in the pregnant female. The epithelium, flat and single-layered to begin with, hypertrophies and forms deep folds. From the second month until the end of the gestation period, several cell divisions and secretions take place inside the oviduct epithelium. This material is used to nourish the embryos.

As the embryo grows, the yolk material is consumed. The embryos remain in their egg envelope and can be supplied with oxygen and water only from the mother. When the yolk is used up after two months, the embryos hatch from their egg envelope. Thus the embryo changes into a fetus. It can no longer feed on its own yolk, but depends on nutrition from the mother. A *Dermophis* fetus freshly hatched from the egg envelope is approximately 1.3 inches (35 mm) long. One significant finding is that the jaws are already fully ossified at this point, complete with fetal dentition.

The size at birth can vary greatly in *Dermophis* specimens. Total lengths of 4.25 to 5.9 inches (108 to 151 mm) have been recorded. It is possible that the birth is not induced by having reached a certain length, but by changes in the dentition. Immediately prior to birth, the fetus loses its first dentition and the adult teeth come in. These pointed predator teeth prevent the young from continuing to feed on the epithelium of the maternal oviduct, and they must now adopt an adult mode of life.

The embryos and fetuses of aquatic Typhlonectidae differ from other species in the shape of their gills. All caecilian embryos discussed thus far, egg-laying with freely swimming larvae, directly developing species, or viviparous representatives, have three gill branches with lateral filaments. Typhlonectidae, on the other hand, have only one pair of large, sac-like gills. These gills are permeated by many blood vessels, which are fed by the same three aortic arches as the gills of terrestrial caecilians. These large gills were already interpreted as organs for fetal food intake upon their discovery in the nineteenth century.

The beginning of embryogenesis in *Typhlonectes* is very similar to that in *Ichthyophis*, *Hypogeophis* and *Dermophis*: an elongated embryo forms on top of the yolk. The growth of the embryo depends at first on the rate of yolk consumption. During this yolk-dependent embryonic development inside the egg envelope, the gills form at first as two pairs of evaginations, which subsequently fuse into one large organ on each side. When the yolk supply has been consumed, the *Typhlonectes* embryos leave the egg envelope and become dependent on maternal nutrition as fetuses.

It is possible that the fetuses can ingest food by mouth, because their mouth opening develops at a relatively early stage as it does in other caecilians. Organic substances and cellular material have been found in the intestinal tract of *Typhlonectes* fetuses; this material may originate from various sources: in the epithelium of the oviduct, as in Dermophis; as yolk material of unfertilized eggs; or as dead embryos used to feed their siblings. Since *Typhlonectes* has fetal dentition in a shovel-like form similar to the Caeciliidae, it seems probable that the fetuses of *Typhlonectes* also feed by scraping the oviductal epithelium.

Birth

Typhlonectidae are suited to being raised in aquaria, and it is therefore easier to observe them than terrestrial species, and mating as well as birth have been observed. The birth of several young occurs over the course of several days. One female gave birth to seven young in seven days, another female gave birth to four young in three days. One birth took 10 to 40 minutes. In most cases the young emerge head-first; breech birth was observed in only one case. Generally the large, lobular gills appeared first at 30-minute intervals. At first the gills were still visibly supplied with blood, but after a few minutes blood flow slowed and the gill lobules turned milky white. In one case, a juvenile was already gulping for air while its rear end was still inside the mother's body.

To begin with, the newly born young swam with gills still present, which are somewhat longer than half the total body length at birth. The gills fell off one by one within one to 36 hours after birth. After birth, a massive voiding of the intestine was observed in all specimens. There are no data on excretion during the fetal phase. It is possible that the fetus does not void its intestinal contents inside the oviduct, as this would surely poison the environment inside the oviduct. Therefore the entire intestinal content is probably retained until birth. The fact that the intestine is voided for the first time after birth also supports the theory that food intake in the oviduct cannot be realized through the gills alone and that the fetus must also ingest food by mouth.

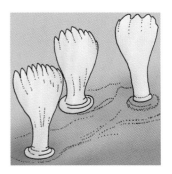

Fetal teeth of Gymnopis multiplicata. *They differ from adult teeth in the shape of the crowns as well as in their maxillar placement. Fetal teeth are shaped like shovels and are not intended for holding onto prey. A caecilian fetus uses its specialized teeth to scrape prolific cells from the internal wall of the maternal oviduct. In other words, the fetus feeds on maternal tissue (after Himstedt, 1996).*

Walter Hödl

Acoustic Communication in Frogs

In an effort to signal both rivals and mating partners, frogs have developed a wide repertoire of acoustic communication strategies. The nocturnal habits of most frogs, coupled with the relatively low energetic cost of information transmission by sound and the high information capacity of the acoustic modality, have led to complex mechanisms underlying acoustic communication in anuran amphibians.

How Do Frogs Call?

Prior to vocalizing, male frogs gulp air through the nostrils by lowering the floor of the buccal cavity while keeping the mouth closed. Next they raise the oral-cavity floor and simultaneously close the nostrils. This forces part of the air volume into the lungs. This process is repeated until the lungs are completely filled with air; at this point the male is ready to call. During the process of calling, air oscillates between the lungs and the oral cavity, while the mouth and nostrils (equipped with annular musculature) are kept closed. Moving between the lungs and oral cavity, air passes through the larynx, setting the vocal chords into vibration, thus creating a sound. In nearly all frog species, vocalizations are produced during the expiratory phase of the calling process.

In most cases the calls are transmitted via inflated gular pouches which may be paired, unpaired, gular or lateral, internal or external. The most common form are singular gular sacs as in the tree-frog genus *Hyla*, toads (Bufonidae) and poison-dart frogs (Dendrobatidae). The call mechanism of European fire-bellied toads (*Bombina spp.*) is one of the rare exceptions to the rule in that sound is emitted during the inspiratory phase. That is, vocalizations are produced during air flow from the oral cavity to the lungs, converting them into functional vocal sacs. The muscle tissue surrounding the lungs and the relatively thick flank skin may be responsible, in part, for the muffled, "soft" character of the fire-bellied toad's call.

What Is the Purpose of Vocal Sacs?

Spherical-shaped vocal sacs radiate sound evenly in all directions. Omnidirectional radiation maximizes the probability of reaching a potential receiver, when location of the receiver is unknown. Spherical vocal-sac morphology may be advantageous to frogs calling from elevated perch sites, in that it allows vocalizing males to maintain a fixed calling position in a structurally intricate environment. It is often assumed, erroneously, that vocal sacs amplify sound. Very little research has been undertaken on the filter characteristics of the sacs; however, recent evidence suggests that the vocal sac in some species acts as a frequency-specific sound radiator and filter. In frogs with internal or without vocal sacs, the buccal musculature is the only antagonist to the air-expelling trunk musculature. The elasticity of the external gular pouches, which are stretched to the extreme during sound production, ensures the rapid return of air to the lungs. In addition to its acoustic function, one could imagine that the vocal sac also acts as a visual signal, although this has not been demonstrated experimentally. Inflatable vocal sacs are present only in sexually mature males.

Frog Calls Are Inherited

Frog calls are inherited and species-specific. As such they are immutable and may serve as a species-identification characteristic as any morphological feature. The hereditary nature of sound parameters is especially evident in the European green-frog species *Rana ridibunda* and *R. lessonae*. Thus the pool frog (*Rana lessonae*) produces long, "snarling" sounds, while the sounds of the marsh frog (*Rana ridibunda*) are more reminiscent of short bursts of human laughter (its scientific name *ridibundus* translates into 'with a laughing voice'). Crossing *R. lessonae* with *R. ridibunda* results in the hybrid edible frog (*Rana kl. esculenta*), whose calls are intermediate and a mixture of both—i.e., edible-frog calls contain both the laughing (narrow-band frequency-modulated) as well as the snarling (broad-band pulsatile) elements. In contrast to birds, which are able to acquire new song elements during a sensitive phase, voice imitation and phenomena such as acoustic imprinting ("dialects") are unknown in frogs. Anuran calls exhibit an

Facing page: Male Green Frogs have relatively large, paired vocal sacs which project outward behind the corners of the mouth. Their intense calls can be heard across great distances. The growling and rasping calls of the hybrid Edible Frog (Rana kl. esculenta) *are a combination of those made by the parental species* Rana ridibunda *and* Rana lessonae. *Frog calls—like morphological characteristics—are inherited and allow for clear species identification.*

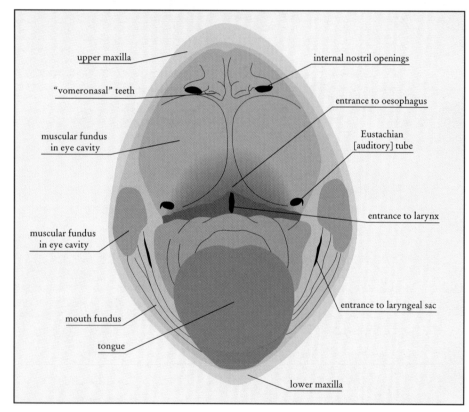

upper maxilla

"vomeronasal" teeth

muscular fundus
in eye cavity

muscular fundus
in eye cavity

mouth fundus

tongue

internal nostril openings

entrance to oesophagus

Eustachian
[auditory] tube

entrance to larynx

entrance to laryngeal sac

lower maxilla

The Amazonian tree frog
Hyla wavrini *emitting a distress call. This is the only anuran call type given with an open mouth. Distress calls are produced by males, females and even juveniles in extreme danger and are considered as a last cry for help (Lago Janauari, Amazonas, Brazil). Illustration after Duellman and Trueb, 1986.*

enormous acoustic diversity. Only a few frogs and toad signals can be onomatopoeically described as "croaking"). The spectrum ranges from dull thunder to squeaking, metallic hammering, laughing, gurgling, tremolo, whistling, bee-like humming, to a plaintive grumble and ox-like bellowing. The vocalizations of tropical frogs are often mistaken for the calls of other animals such as birds, insects or even mammals.

How Do Frogs Hear?

The sound-reception apparatus in frogs consists, on the outside, of a clearly visible round ear drum just behind the eye. The oscillations of this tympanic membrane are transferred through a columnar ossicle to the oval window. Within the inner ear, the amphibian and basilar papillae, two separate hearing organs, differentially respond to specific frequencies transmitted via fluid pathways. Without going into detailed descriptions of the complicated mechanism used to process incoming sound, we can state in general that for most anurans the most sensitive hearing threshold roughly corresponds to the call-note frequencies. Thus, the auditory system resembles an acoustic filter that enhances species-specific sound patterns.

More recently, laser-doppler vibrometers have been used to analyze the minuscule vibrations of the tympanic membrane and the flank surfaces of frogs. Results show that sound reaches the ear drum not only from the outside but also from the inside via the lateral body surface, the lungs, and the Eustachian tube. This mechanism probably ensures that frogs do not damage their own ears as a result of their high-intensity calls. These vocalizations can reach hazardous intensities at the caller's ear, comparable to the sound of a motorcycle at close range. Since the frog's own calls reach the ear drums from the outside and from the inside, phase cancellation can partially reduce their motion. Analyses of the Coqui frog, *Eleutherodactylus coqui*, have shown that the tympanic membrane barely vibrates during calling.

What Is the Function of Frog Calls?

Frog calls—inherited, unique and species-specific—are primarily used for conspecific recognition and synchronization of reproductive effort. Thus, most calls produced by frogs and toads subserve conspecific pair formation. Errors are dealt with harshly in nature, for species interbreeding generally does not produce viable offspring. For successful reproduction, ovulating females must seek out conspecific males within a matter of hours to prevent energy loss by producing eggs that can no longer be reabsorbed. The males, on the other hand, must indicate their reproductive condition to the females as clearly and unmistakably as possible.

Advertisement Calls

Changes in background noise and unpredictability of the receiver's location and receptivity have led to high call-note redundancy in frogs. Males can often be observed monotonously calling for hours, nights or even weeks at a time. Advertisement calls often fulfil a dual function—mate attraction and territorial defence. The advertisement call thus communicates not only the male's reproductive state, but also the readiness to defend the calling site or mating territory. When the minimally acceptable threshold distance, measured indirectly through perceived sound intensity, is exceeded, the resident enters into physical conflict with the intruder.

The dual role of the advertisement call has been illustrated in an impressive manner in two cases of neotropical frog species. In the first, pre-recorded sounds were used to test the reaction of the Coqui frog, *Eleutherodactylus coqui*, to his own calling pattern so aptly captured in its scientific name. In an acoustic playback experiment with calling males, "co" notes above a certain threshold evoked a vocal response in males, while the females only responded to the "qui" note by moving toward the sound source.

The complex function of the composite advertisement call of the male has also been illustrated for the Túngara frog, *Physalaemus pustulosus*. The plaintive first call-note element—the whine—not unlike the mewing of a cat, suffices for intraspecific recognition. The short chucks often following the whine in choruses are attractive to females, especially those chucks containing low dominant frequencies. This means that larger males with a deeper voice—often older, more "experienced" males— are more successful than smaller individuals. Moreover, the females of this species prefer the most acoustically active individuals. But the allure of constant callers takes its toll: *Physalaemus pustulosus* males need 20 times the energy when calling than when at rest. In addition to the high energy expenditure, active callers are also more easily discovered and preyed upon by the frog-eating bat, *Trachops cirrhosus*. Studies of communication biology in the Túngara frog yielded results that when analyzed from a cost-benefit perspective, reveal that the higher the level of conspecific attractiveness, the greater the energy expenditure and predation.

Satellite Males

The high energy consumption and the increased predation risk resulting from continuous calling, as well as the fact that males usually produce their sounds in large groups, have led to the development of alternative pair-formation strategies in some species. In calling assemblages, one can often observe non-calling males in mating condition; since they are silent, they move without hindrance or risk right next to a particularly vocally

active male. The so-called satellite males are non-calling mating parasites that try to intercept females approaching a continuously calling male. It has been reported that individuals are capable of switching from calling to satellite strategy even within one night.

Males often arrive at the breeding site before the females. It is possible that the "sound clouds" generated by the chorus of conspecific males stimulates ovulation. From a biological point of view, it would be nonsensical to release eggs into the body cavity without an abundance of nearby potential mates. Ovulation tends to occur outside the chorus. In the short interval of generally only a few hours between ovulation and oviposition, the females—"blinded by love"—are frantically drawn to the calling assemblage. Nevertheless, it appears that females do not necessarily mate with the first conspecific male encountered, but are in fact quite selective. Females have been shown to be able to assess a male's physical constitution (judged by the persistence of

Sand Toad (Bufo granulosus) with and without inflated vocal sac. Anuran calls function principally to bring the sexes together for mating and reproduction. The spherical shape of the sac radiates sound evenly in all directions (Manaus, Amazonas, Brazil.)

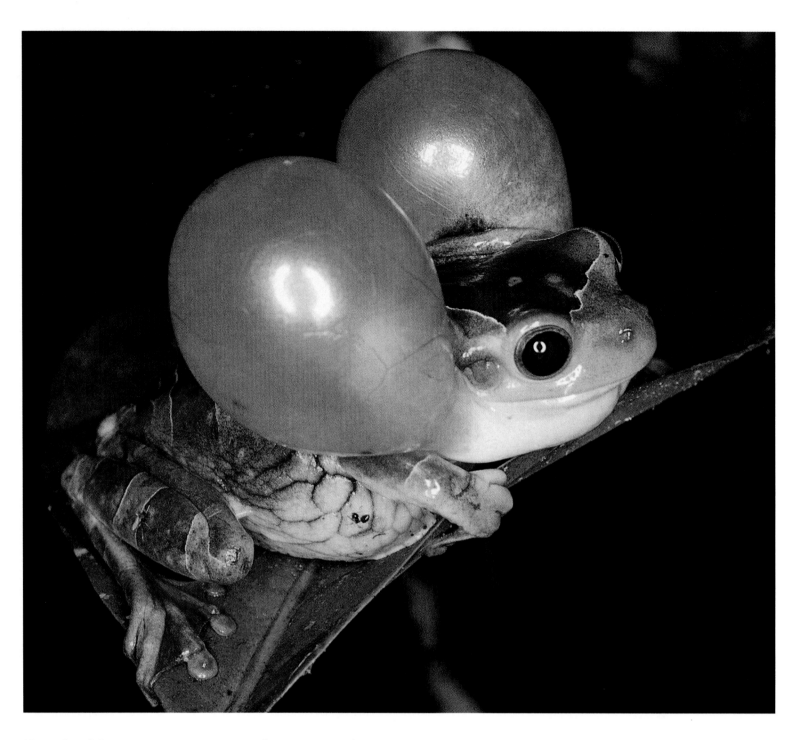

The males of the Amazonian arboreal frog Phrynohyas coriacea *possess large lateral vocal sacs. A separate branch of scientific research, bioacoustics, is devoted to the study of animal acoustic communication (Panguana, Rio Llullapichis, Peru).*

the call and/or its intensity), size and age (reflected by a deep voice relative to the conspecific rivals) and social status (judged by the rank of a caller within a chorus, e.g., "soloist"). Other possible factors to be assessed in choosing a male are the quality of its calling site and/or its territorial size. In this manner, the females may use acoustic information to identify the carrier of the best genes to pass on to their descendants. Although differential attractiveness among competing males has been demonstrated repeatedly by measuring male mating success, the actual process of female mate choice has been only incompletely studied in the field.

Phonotaxis

For most anuran species, acoustic cues guide the females to the male. At short distances,

however, visual, olfactory, and possibly tactile criteria may also be used in mate choice. Phonotactically responsive females are common subjects in acoustic playback experiments. Systematically modified male calls are used as stimuli to test the function of particular call parameters in species recognition, mate selection and acoustic isolation mechanism in frogs. The stereotypical phonotactic reaction in certain highly territorial anuran species also enables to test hearing capacities in male frogs. Male poison-dart frogs (e.g., *Epipedobates femoralis*) are ideal test cases for bioacousticians since their phonotactic sensitivity (i.e., the readiness to approach a loudspeaker playing natural or synthetically altered calls), may last for several weeks. The fast "all or none" response of territorial males allows testing of large series of synthetic calls. Males usually return to their calling stations after playbacks are turned off, and thus do not have to be touched or otherwise disturbed between successive trials.

Other Call Types

In addition to advertisement calls used both to attract females and to keep competitors at a distance, at least four other types of frog calls are known. Mating calls are used exclusively to attract and stimulate the female (especially once the female is close and visible to the caller) and lead to amplexus but never to aggressive behavior. Aggressive calls are produced by frogs prior to or during agonistic interactions. Unlike the advertisement call, aggressive vocalization often exhibits structural gradation that may reflect the level of aggression. Release calls, often accompanied by rapid movements of flank musculature, are produced either by males who have been grasped by other males or by females who are not in mating condition. Distress calls are emitted by both sexes and even by juveniles immediately after an attack by a predator (e.g., birds, snakes). These warning and possibly alarm signals are considered as a last ditch effort for help in moments of mortal danger and are the only sounds frog produce with an open mouth.

Vocalization and Hearing Are Temperature Dependent

Due to the ectothermic physiology of anuran amphibians, call parameters vary with temperature. With rising temperatures, call duration and intercall intervals tend to become shorter, while the call frequency rises. Since the spectral and temporal sensitivity also changes with temperature, experiments undertaken to study acoustics in frogs (e.g., playback experiments with artificial signals) are highly labor-intensive in the temperate zones. Temperature coupling, i.e., the adjustment that takes place in the sound perception apparatus of the female in direct response to temperature-induced changes in the male's call spectrum is an astonishing phenomenon in the bioacoustics of frogs.

Ecoacoustics

The energy in most frog calls lies between 100 Hz and 6 kHz, and is thus well within the human hearing range. In mixed-species assemblages, spectral separation—in analogy to the dedicated carrier frequencies used by individual radio stations—may be one mechanism used to avoid acoustic interference. To be noticed as an individual, neighboring conspecifics in a chorus will often avoid calling at the same time. They wait for a temporal gap in the overall sound and then emit their species-specific call. Usually the potential receivers are separated by no more then a few meters, which means that special spectral adaptations to the abiotic acoustic environment play a minimal role. For communication across long distances, however, frequency-dependent sound propagation through vegetation and weather-dependent sound transmission assume more importance. Because certain frequencies propagate through some plant structures better than others, e.g., frogs calling from widely spaced burrows in tropical rain forests use the so-called Morton's frequency window as a spectral communication channel between approximately 1 kHz and 3 kHz. In this frequency range, or window, long-distance sound propagation is favored since sound absorption and reflection are minimized at ground level. At the same time, broad-band background noises (such as those generated by wind or precipitation) and spectral competitors must be avoided. It has been observed that the Amazonian arboreal frog species *Phrynohyas resinifictrix* does indeed make its long-ranging low-pitched calls from water-filled tree holes exclusively during nights when there is neither wind nor rain in order to ensure transmission across interindividual distances of up to 200 meters.

Seismic Communication in Frogs

Another mode of acoustic communication in frogs utilizes seismic vibrations. The ground-dwelling white-lipped frog, *Leptodactylus albilabris*, found in muddy areas adjacent to Puerto Rican mountain streams, is the first vertebrate known to possess distinct anatomical, neurophysiological and behavioral adaptations for seismic communication. When calling, males of this species create low-frequency substrate vibrations by rhythmic thumping of the vocal sac on the ground. Neuronal reactions to whole-body vibrations suggest that these seismic signals are indeed received and perceived. This is further supported by the fact that the highest vibration sensitivity corresponds to the peak energy of the "thump". The propagation range of the high-frequency airborne signal is limited and all the more so when background noise grows more intense. Thus, the white-lipped frog has evolved a communication system by means of ground vibrations in an environment where high-level ambient noise is ubiquitous.

Walter Hödl

Visual Signaling in Frogs

Compared to acoustic cues, visual signals play a subordinate role in amphibian communication. Although many frog species are brightly colored, the use of color and body structures has barely been studied in frog communication. Most frogs have species-specific coloration that is useful in a variety of ways. Bright colors, as in some poison-dart frogs, may be important in species recognition and may also warn potential predators. Brownish patterns offer good camouflage on the ground and among fallen leaves, while green coloring serves to make other frogs blend in with their environment on bushes and trees. Sexual dimorphism in coloration, which may be present either during the entire adult life or only during the mating season, probably serves as a species-specific in mate selection. Clear visual signals such as limb-flagging ("semaphoring") are known for only a few anuran species.

Males of the noctural arboreal frog Hyla parviceps *attract attention by acoustic and visual means (Note extended hind leg). The unusual markings on the hind legs appear to be visible to rivals or mating partners in low level moonlight (Rio Surumoni, Amazonas, Venezuela).*

Semaphoring Frogs

Some of the documented visual signals serving for intraspecific communication are executed through stereotypic movements with the fore and/or hind limbs. This flagging behavior—analogous to that found in the fiddling crabs (*Uca spp.*)—is interpreted as a signal to indicate the readiness to defend territorial boundaries. Limb waving has probably developed and evolved independently in at least seven anuran families spread across South and Central America, Southeast Asia and Australia.

Semaphoring frogs have so far been recorded only in the tropics with most of them found along mountain streams and creeks. The flagging behavior is best documented in the diurnal frog genera *Staurois* (Malaysia) and *Hylodes* (Brazil), both inhabiting rapidly flowing sections of tropical mountain creeks. The

continuous noise of rushing water unevenly occupies the complete audible sound spectrum of frogs (and humans). Stream-breeding frogs generally produce high squeaky calls to make themselves audibly noticed at all—at the cost of only short-distance sound propagation. The higher the frequency, the better the contrast to the low-frequency dominated noise produced by turbulent waters.

Conspicuousness, i.e., standing out against the background, is a prerequisite for communication. Since constant high background noise along mountain streams renders calling not very effective, semaphoring frogs in cascading waters have developed visual cues in support of their acoustic signals. Whitish feet with widely enlarged toe tips are highly conspicuous during flagging movements. In the Malaysian frog genus *Staurois*, the feet are additionally webbed and brightly colored interdigitally. During

With its upright position (exposing the white throat and chest) and noticeably extended hind leg, a Hylodes asper *male announces its readiness to defend its territory (Picinguaba, São Paulo Brazil).*

calling or even without accompanying vocalizations, the agitated territorium holder—in upright position—repeatedly extends his left and right leg in irregular alteration (*Hylodes asper, H. dactylocinus; Staurois latopalmatus, S. natator, S. tuberilinguis*). In the rock-skipper frog, *S. latopalmatus,* even both hind limbs may be extended simultaneously. When the legs are extended, the splayed feet are tilted forward so that the bright upper sides of the webbed feet face the opponent. The bright (and dynamic) signal of the otherwise inconspicuous foot-flagging frogs contrasts sharply to the dark background of the rock and moss-covered boulders. Thus, the flagging individual, usually positioned on an elevated site, is quickly recognized by its rivals. "Flagging duels" often occur, and it is usually the possessor of a territorium who interrupts the long-range dispute in order to approach the rival. Unless the intruder has not already retreated after perceiving the warning signal of his opponent, he is leaped upon and chased away. The Brazilian torrent frogs *Hylodes asper* and *H. dactylocinus* were observed and filmed for a lengthy period and the results show, that territorial holders will call even when no rivals are present, while flagging signals (with or without accompanying calls) are given only once the presence of a rival is clearly detected, indicated by the defendant's rapid turn toward the intruder.

Most semaphoring frogs known are diurnal. Only some species of the Australian genus *Litoria* and the neotropical tree frogs *Phyllomedusa sauvagii* and *Hyla parviceps* are reported to signal at night. With the exception of *Atelopus spp.* (Bufonidae) and *Brachycephalus ephippium* (Brachycephalidae), which perform flagging movements exclusively with their forelimbs, all other flagging amphibians utilize (primarily) their hind legs for signaling. The phenomenon of semaphoring frogs has yet been insufficiently studied and in most cases only preliminary observation data are available. More quantitative and experimental field studies are needed to better understand the function and evolution of this unusual, remarkable and little-known behavior.

Visual Signaling during Intraspecific Interactions

Visual signals are not only important for intraspecific communication. The neotropical horned frog *Ceratophrys calcarata*, for example, a well-camouflaged sit-and-wait predator lures potential prey (frogs, lizards) with slight movements of their "wormlike" toes to within the range of their fast protrudable tongue. The so-called *unken*-reflex ('Unken' is the German term for the anuran genus *Bombina*), a common behavioral response to perceived threat in the European fire-bellied toads *Bombina bombina* and *B. variegata*, is characterized primarily by lifting all four legs and arching the back, drawing attention to the ventral surface. The term "*unken* reflex" has been used broadly to describe a wide range of similar defensive postures restricted to salamander and frog species with ventral warning coloration. Other visual defense actions in anurans include eyespot display (e.g., in *Pleurodema brachyops*), body inflation, hind parts elevation, noxious gland display, bright glandular secretions and akinesia (feigning death).

Distinctive blue webbing in Staurois natator's *feet enhances the visibility of the foot-flagging motion (Danum Valley, Sabah, Malaysia).*

The intense continuous sound of creeks or waterfalls occupies the full frequency spectrum audible to frogs and is therefore a hindrance to effective acoustic communication. Anurans, that use waving or "flag" signals mostly occur in habitats close to rapidly flowing waters (Danum Valley, Sabah, Malaysia).

Population Biology

Robert Jehle

Studies at the population level are a major component of modern biology. In the 1930s and 1940s the view that all animal and plant species can be treated as groups of populations led to the "modern synthesis" of the evolutionary theory first developed some 150 years ago. In the simplest terms, a population is the sum of all individuals of a species in a certain area, and members of a population are clearly separated in space or time from neighboring populations. As a consequence, within a species some individuals are more likely to mate with each other than others, and due to selection processes each population can, over time, adapt to local conditions. The totality of all individuals in a species is therefore not a uniform entity, but an internally structured, flexible system.

Amphibians Live in Populations

Continents are characterized by landscapes where rainfall exceeds water loss through evaporation, alternating with arid locations that can be virtually free of any humidity. Moreover, some regions are also characterized by rainy and dry seasons. In contrast to all other vertebrates, amphibians have something in common: naked, unprotected skin that makes them more susceptible to dehydration than reptiles, birds or mammals. As amphibians to a large extent depend on the availability of water, they can often be observed in great numbers at certain places or times, or conversely, are not existent or at least lead a very secretive life. Many homeowners who have garden ponds are used to hearing a chorus of frogs, only to wonder during other seasons where all the frogs have gone to when the concert is over. Surprisingly, similar phenomena can be observed even in regions where the climatic conditions stay relatively constant throughout the year; for example, in some tropical rain forests.

In most amphibian species the boundaries between populations are more pronounced than in other animal taxa, and it can often be assumed that all individuals of a species reproducing in a certain water body represent as one population. From this view, amphibians exist as populations in an almost ideal fashion. However, there is no other vertebrate group with a comparable diversity of reproductive strategies. Fifty-four percent of the approximately 350 urodele species known worldwide, for example, use the moisture in the soil or in decomposing plant material for egg deposition and never gather into distinct, water-dependent communities. It is therefore difficult to generalize, but the fact remains that a large number of amphibian species can be clearly separated into populations.

Why and How Do We Study Amphibian Populations?

Individual variability, the prerequisite for evolution to act, provides one of the most fascinating working fields for biologists. Every astute observer of nature is familiar with the experience that even among so-called primitive animal taxa each individual has its own appearance, and behavioral studies often with revealing individual "characters." Since many amphibian populations develop relatively unlinked from each other over many generations, each population has its own characteristics, just as every individual specimen is unique. Amphibian researchers who have focused on particular species in a specific locality are readily able to allocate an individual specimen to a certain locality based only on its phenotype. Revealing population specific traits and their variance is therefore crucial for the understanding of ecological and evolutionary processes. Population studies are also vitally important with respect to the observed worldwide decline of amphibian populations, both in order to better understand the causes and to outline meaningful protection measures.

The main approach for studying amphibian populations in nature is often to capture, count and repeatedly register as many indi-

viduals as possible. Among the most commonly applied methods of catching amphibians is a drift fence with pitfall traps, often erected near breeding ponds. All amphibians migrating to or from this pond encounter the fence and drop into buckets sunk into the ground. These buckets are controlled on a regular basis, captured individuals are registered and subsequently released on the other side of the fence, the presumed direction of migration. For detailed conclusions it is often necessary to compile individual life-histories—an extremely time-consuming and labor-intensive process. External morphological variability, such as spot patterns, can be used to recognize recaptured individuals throughout their postmetamorphic lifetime.

Apart from some phenotypic variation caused by environmental factors such as attaining a large body size when more food is available, the variability of morphological characters is genetically determined. A large amount of this genetic variation is, however, not visible phenotypically, because it has no or very little effect, or for example only influences physiological factors. In the last 30 years various laboratory-based methods for studying genetic variation have revolutionized population biological research in general. In recent years such molecular markers with increasing frequency deal with information that is directly drawn from DNA. Data on genetic

variation can be applied in a variety of ways depending on the study question: closely related species that cannot be unambiguously distinguished from morphological characters can be separated with diagnostic proteins. Genetic fingerprints by means of small tissue or blood samples enable to infer paternity or other levels of relatedness. When applied to amphibian populations, these methods are sure to yield many new findings in the years to come.

Examples from Population Studies

Quantitative population biological studies are meaningful only when basic information about the mode of life has been already acquired for the species under investigation. This knowledge exists with respect to most species living in temperate zones, but the available information about many tropical species is restricted to morphology, systematics and geographical distribution. Therefore the majority of population studies deals with European and North American species. Population biological aspects during the larval phase of amphibians are relatively well studied, as tadpoles and urodele larvae are well suited for experimental settings, either in the laboratory or in the field. Most experiments were conducted with respect to competition for food and space. Caecilians, next to anurans and urodeles the third amphibian

Studies on the European grass frog (Rana temporaria) populations in southern England have shown that in urban areas, where barriers often prevent migrations between populations, the degree of genetic variation is lower than in more interconnected populations in rural areas. Alarmingly, this fact is already expressed by lower fitness parameters at the larval stage. In Germany, studies on the same species have shown that roads which cut through the landscape also can have demonstrable genetic consequences.

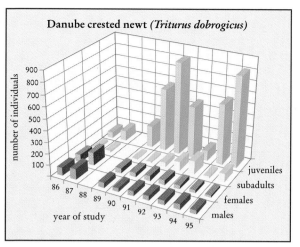

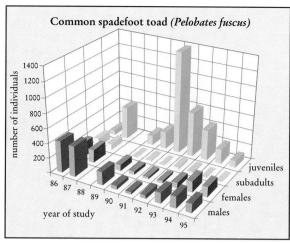

order, are probably the least-studied group of vertebrates. Their subterranean mode of life makes it difficult to observe them, and their population biology is often unknown.

Among the first important studies undertaken on amphibian populations are those conducted in the early seventies on North American urodeles. In some regions of the United States, lungless salamanders (plethodontids) occur in population densities of up to 23,000 individuals per forested hectare. Their biomass—the sum of body weights of all individuals in a designated area—easily surpasses that of birds and mammals together. Despite these impressive densities, which might lead to the assumption that competition for resources would be fierce, there has been relatively little evidence for it to have a major impact on salamander communities. Moreover, urodeles generally have a longer life span than other vertebrates of comparable size, and salamander populations seem to be relatively stable in time.

Individuals on the margin of a species' geographical range may exhibit very different modes of life than those in the center of their distribution area. Studies on alpine newts (*Triturus alpestris*) in the European Alps have shown that in altitudes of over 5,400 feet (1,650 m) above sea level they reach sexual maturity only at approximately ten years of age, while conspecifics from lower altitudes are ready to reproduce at the age of two years. Fire salamanders (*Salamandra salamandra*) from Israel annually lay their eggs into small water deposits after rainfalls in November and December, whereas in mountainous regions of Central Europe fire salamanders tend to reproduce only every second year around June/July.

The size of a population is generally taken to be the total number of animals at a certain

locality. For future generations, however, only those individuals fulfill an important function and are successful in reproduction. Recent studies on the common toad (*Bufo bufo*) in Great Britain, based on a comparison of genetic data between parents and their offspring, have shown that only a small number of individuals (less than 1 percent of all registered adult toads) actually manage to successfully transmit their genes to the next generation. This finding is even more remarkable as many female common toads reproduce only once in their entire lifetime. Current efforts for protecting and sustaining endangered or rare species often focus on the importance of maintaining genetic diversity, for example, in order to avoid the consequences of inbreeding. In this context, the results on the common toad may have far-reaching implications, because even large populations seem to be in high danger of reducing their genetic variation over time.

Long-Term Studies on Amphibian Populations

One of the most detailed long-term studies ever conducted on amphibians took place at an ephemeral pond in South Carolina (USA). Each individual of 13 species (8 anurans and 5 urodeles) entering or leaving the pond was captured and registered over a time span of 16 years (1979–94). The species-specific number of spawning females fluctuated over the study period by up to more than three orders of magnitude. All species reproduced only at irregular intervals, and unsuccessful reproductive periods of several years had to be compensated for with high numbers of offspring in successful years. The most important factor for population regulation was the annual time period the pond was filled with water. Even so, fluctuations in population size were not always synchronized between species, as interspecific competition

during the larval phase also played an important role.

A different picture emerges from a similar study carried out at an artificial pond, filled with water year round, near a former floodplain of the Danube in the vicinity of Vienna (Austria). The twelve species inhabiting this pond were studied over twelve years (1986–97). All members of two species (spadefoot toads, *Pelobates fuscus*, and Danube crested newts, *Triturus dobrogicus*) were recognized on an individual basis. A clear regressive trend became noticeable for these two species, although a certain number of juveniles left the water each year, and although the number of males and females were subject to fluctuations by only one order of magnitude. The silting-up process and the isolation of the study pond is assumed to be the main reason. Remarkably, in both the North American and European study it was impossible to exactly quantify the causes of population fluctuations, although on-site research was undertaken daily over many years.

Metapopulations

In recent years the term "metapopulation" has become a key phrase in amphibian ecology. A metapopulation consists of an assemblage of breeding populations, with a restricted amount of between-population migrations affecting their dynamics and ability to persist. When an amphibian population living at a certain pond due to a catastrophic event, such as an extremely cold winter, becomes extinct, this pond can be successfully recolonized only when an intact population is within the maximum migration distance. If this is not the case, a suitable habitat patch will remain unused. In a metapopulation study of the red-spotted newt (*Notophthalmus viridescens*), a similar finding, the survival of some local populations only through immigration, was already shown in the 1970s. More recently, it has been shown that local populations within a natterjack toad (*Bufo calamita*) metapopulation were maintained only by virtue of immigration from neighboring populations. Especially females migrated between ponds the role of the large annual number of dispersing juveniles has not yet been fully established. For small populations a lack of migration between populations over many generations can also lead to an increased rate of inbreeding, resulting in a decrease of fitness parameters and therefore a higher risk for population extinction. Especially in temperate regions, where amphibians are already very much restricted to habitat remnants, the metapopulation concept has important conservation implications. Many ecologists now hold that the majority of species survive merely as isolated relict populations surrounded by environments that are hostile to their needs. Due to a lack of connectivity between ponds we can therefore in many cases no longer speak of functioning metapopulations. As a result of habitat fragmentation, the danger to the existing amphibian populations in the longer term seems to be far greater than has been assumed previously.

Terrestrial Ecology of Amphibians

Amphibians are often regarded as creatures that live exclusively in or at least near water. Nevertheless, even those species who deposit their eggs and larvae in water spend the majority of their adult lifetime on land. However, locating and observing amphibians in the terrestrial habitat is difficult, and our knowledge of the biology and ecology in this phase is accordingly sketchy. Data are often limited to some information on breeding migrations. The function of terrestrial landscape elements such as meadows, bushes and forests in the life of amphibians, and the question of whether amphibians are able to adapt to human changes of the landscape, which for biological time scales currently take place at a very high pace, is mostly still open. Vast geographical areas can now be recorded and translated into data by means of aerial photographs, topographical maps and satellite images; with the help of GIS systems, these data can be processed on computers. When the distribution of a species in a given area is known, these methods enable to relate the presence or absence of this species to landscape characteristics and/or climate data. When sufficient data are gathered over long time periods, it is also possible to document the impact of landscape changes, for example, as a result of increased agricultural activities, on the distribution range of amphibians. In western France, for example, the local displacement of the marbled newt (*Triturus marmoratus*) by the great crested newt (*Triturus cristatus*) could be directly linked to the disappearance of shrubs and hedgerows as a result of land consolidation.

The Olm *(Proteus anguinus)*
Jakob Parzefall

*One of Europe's most mysterious amphibians is the blind olm (*Proteus anguinus*) occurring exclusively in subterranean bodies of water of the Dinaric karstland. The black species (*P. anguinus parkelj*) with its well-developed eyes was described for the first time in 1994.*

As early as 1768 J. N. Laurenti described the only blind and pale European cave salamander. Today, nearly 250 local reports of *Proteus anguinus anguinus*, the "white" olm, have been recorded. All have been along the Dinaric karst between the river Isonzo (Italy) and eastern Herzegovina in the former Yugoslavia. Some populations have already been completely decimated or are endangered as a result of pollution or changes to the water table. In addition to the nominal species, another subspecies was discovered in 1994, with dark pigmentation and eyes, and described as *Proteus anguinus parkelj*, the "black" olm. Only species from the genus *Necturus* occurring in the rivers and lakes of the eastern and mid-western United States are also listed as members of the family Proteidae.

An allozyme analysis revealed greater genetic differences between some "white" populations than between the "white" and the "black" population. This may indicate that *Proteus* populations were already differentiated into several races prior to karst-formation and the development of local cave habitats.

If the calibration of the molecular clock is correct, pale populations from Planina (near Postojna) and Sticna (30 miles/50 km southeast of Ljubljana) were isolated from one another for 5 to 9 million years, in the Miocene or at the very latest in the Lower Pliocene, long before karst formation took place.

These delicately limbed creatures grow to a total length of 9 to 9.8 inches (23 to 25 cm), with the males always staying somewhat smaller. There are three external gills on either side of the neck. In the "white" populations there is no visible eye. The loss of eyes is irreversible, but when kept under light for months, these specimens can turn black—just like the black subspecies.

The habitat of olms is a labyrinthine cave system varying from the tiniest crack and crevice to large domed chambers, with subterranean rivers and seepage waters coursing through the system and a loamy or clay-covered ground. Olms are rarely observed above ground. The white specimens move through the cave system, where they can be spotted at irregular intervals in certain areas.

Black specimens have until now been observed only at night at spring sources. All populations feed widely on invertebrates. The behavior of olms was studied in cave laboratories. The females attach their eggs to the undersides of stone slabs and guard them. This species reaches sexual maturity at approximately seven years of age and has a relatively high life expectancy: even at 30 to 40 years of age they continue to reproduce on a regular basis.

The individuals leave species-specific signals on the substrate that are perceived when direct contact occurs. Moreover, intraspecific chemicals signals are transmitted in water, and these enable individuals to locate one another for mating. A male ready for reproduction begins to mark his territory with the characteristic waving motion of the tail to chase off competitors. Males in reproductive motivation can sometimes engage in escalated fights resulting in serious injury. As soon as a sexually mature female enters into the territory, the male begins with courtship. It deposits a spermatophore by means of constant back and forth movements of the tail and a "waddling" forward motion. When the female has reached the spermatophore with its cloaca, it hovers above it. The spermata seem to stick to the female's cloacal region. The female then leaves the territory and forms a spawning territory of its own. During this process two to six eggs each are laid over the course of several hours. The entire process takes several days.

Chemical signals also guide olms to their prey. The final "catch" reaction is stimulated by prey that is still alive; adults do not touch dead prey. Experiments with subadult olms showed, however, that they did accept dead chironomid larvae although the time-lapse between finding the prey and grasping it was much longer than with live prey.

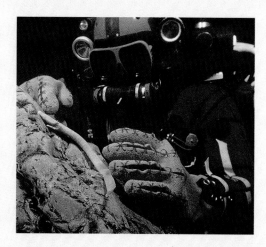

The Pyrenean Salamander *(Euproctus asper)*
Franz Uiblein

*The unusual mating behavior of the Pyrenean mountain newt (*Euproctus asper*). The spermatophore is transmitted by means of direct cloacal contact.*

The Pyrenean salamander *Euproctus asper* (Dugés, 1852) occurs in the French and Spanish Pyrenées mountains and in some isolated areas to the south of the Pyrenées, inhabiting rivers, brooks, lakes, wells, and aquatic caves at elevations ranging from 600 to 1,800 feet (200 to 3,000 m) above sea level. Its closest relatives are the species *E. montanus* in Corsica and *E. platicephalus* in Sardinia. Recent genetic studies carried out using mitochondrial DNA sequences show that the genus *Euproctus* is very closely related to the genus *Triturus*. The division into three species occurred at the time when the Pyrenées separated from the islands of Corsica and Sardinia more than 9 million years ago.

Two subspecies of the Pyrenean salamander are often distinguished: *E. asper asper* (Dugés, 1852) and *E. asper castelmoulensis* (Woltersdorff, 1925). Still, differences in body size, shape, coloring, sexual dimorphism, food, development and reproduction period were recorded among different *E. asper asper* populations. Initial studies on both subspecies and other populations using enzyme electrophoresis show that intraspecies differences in body size, shape and coloring are genetic. Furthermore, the Pyrenean salamander is an amphibian species with a high degree of plasticity and an excellent capacity for ecological adaptation.

Reproduction occurs between April and August in surface above-ground habitats. Time and duration of the reproductive phase vary according to elevation. In cave-dwellers, the gonads may also mature in winter. During the mating season, the males defend their territories, which they mark with chemical signals. Intruders are chased off by means of tail beats or in extreme situations with bites. During courtship, the males maintain a horizontal body position with the tail pointing upward. As soon as it sights a female, the male approaches and holds onto the posterior portion of its body with its tail, while pushing his cloaca opening toward that of the female from behind. During amplexus, shown above, which may last up to several hours, the spermatophore is transferred through direct cloacal contact. The female produces up to 64 eggs. Larvae hatch within a few weeks and usually reach metamorphosis in the following year. Sexual maturity also varies with elevation varying between three and six years of age; the maximum age of males is 20, while females may live to 26 years of age.

The Pyrenean salamander can be described as euryphagous and carnivorous. Its very broad food spectrum includes a number of aquatic insect larvae, small crustaceans, snails, mussels and amphibian larvae (including their own species); even prey of terrestrial origin such as earthworms, spiders and adult insects are consumed, especially in summer. Females are more active feeders than males.

The highly developed adaptive flexibility of the Pyrennean salamander is especially evident in extreme habitats, such as high alpine streams or caves. With a documented distribution ranging from 574 to 9,728 feet (175 to 2,965m) above sea level, this species is distributed across one of the greatest altitudinal gradients of all amphibians. Alpine populations have darker coloring (melanism), which acts as protection against high UV radiation and helps to increase the absorption of heat. In some alpine and cave populations, neoteny (the presence of larval characteristics in adults) has been observed in subadult and adult individuals. Special feeding adaptations exist for life in caves: cave populations that can exist solely on food sources available in the cave or washed in by water and can also survive several months with low food supply or starvation.

Experiments show that individuals from above-ground populations are equally successful in their search for food in the dark. The search behavior changes from a rapid straight approach to the prey to a meandering and slower approach across greater distances in the darkness of the caves. This latter behavior has much in common with the manner in which olms seek out their prey. While their well-developed vision dominates in prey search and selection among Pyrenean salamanders inhabiting well-lit, above-ground areas, olfaction is the key mechanism in caves. Yet this sense is clearly less developed in facultative cave-dwelling species than it is in olms, which are permanent cave-dwellers. Nevertheless, life in caves has clear advantages for the Pyrenean salmander: there are no predators, extreme temperatures, or danger of dehydration, as there are in above-ground habitats.

Today, the Pyrenean salamander is threatened with extinction in many regions. Stocking rivers and brooks with brown trout and rainbow trout has severely stressed local populations. Another factor is increased water pollution as a result of mass tourism. Still, Pyrenean salamander populations continue to thrive in natural bodies of water devoid of predatory fish.

Rudolf Malkmus

Nutrition and Foraging

The prey spectrum varies greatly from one amphibian species to another and ranges from indiscriminate to highly specialized selection of specific food items (monophagy). The more specialized the food requirements are, the greater the impact of nutrition on the distribution patterns and population densities of a species. To best use nutrition resources, regions with high species diversity are characterized by a differentiated blending of species habitats—for example, in the layer of fallen leaves on the ground, in the different forest layers, or at different altitudes on mountain slopes. When such niches are simultaneously utilized by several species, fine-tuned approaches to resource utilization can be observed—for example, different active periods or food specialization.

All Amphibians Are Mainly "Carnivorous"

Most amphibians are opportunistic feeders, following a prey model that could be described as "swallow anything that moves and is smaller than the hunter." Some species, such as the congo eels of the genus *Siren*, the giant toad (*Bufo marinus*), and the American bullfrog (*Rana catesbeiana*), have been observed ingesting plant food from time to time. In general, however, most adult amphibians are exclusively carnivorous and tend to eat a broad spectrum of prey.

Amphibians feed mostly on insects and insect larvae, worms, spiders, snails and pill bugs (Isopoda)—of which they often consume vast quantities. Larger frog species, such as *Caudiverbera*, *Ceratophrys*, *Discodeles* or *Rana*, even consume other frogs, warm-blooded vertebrates (birds, rats, mice), and marine crabs (*Limnonectes cancrivorus*). One African bullfrog (*Pyxicephalus adspersus*) was observed devouring 17 freshly hatched cobras (*Hemachatus*). Large salamanders, such as *Cryptobranchus* and *Dicamptodon*, also hunt fish, crayfish, caecilians, lizards and snakes (Typhlopidae). Hunting for insects, spiders and scorpions that are able

*Many Anura, such as the Green frog (*Lepidobatrachus laevis*) pictured below, have a huge mouth. They can catch other amphibians and even small mammals. When this frog's hind legs are grabbed, it opens its mouth and issues a sound similar to fighting tomcats.*

to defend themselves may result in serious and possibly deadly wounds for the hunter. Some frogs exclusively eat ants and termites, as do several species of the genera *Breviceps*, *Chiasmocleis*, *Dermatonotus*, *Hamptophryne* and *Kaloula* (all Microhylidae), or some shovel-nosed frogs (*Hemisus*), and the Mexican bur-rowing frog (*Rhinophrynus dorsalis*).

Are Some Amphibians Are Also Herbivorous?

In recent years more and more evidence has been compiled that suggests that some amphib-ian species are not only carnivorous, but her-bivorous as well. Some species are herbivorous only during specific periods, while others eat plants year round. The females of the Indian species *Euphlyctis hexadactylus* are predomi-nantly herbivorous during the breeding season; evident, in morphological changes in dentition and intestinal structure. The best-known example, however, is probably the small South American tree frog *Hyla truncata*, found in sand-dune habitats on the southeastern coast of Brazil. This species makes its home in the water-filled cups of bromeliads and feeds mostly on fruit. By this feeding habit, these tree frogs also contribute to the dispersal of plant seeds and do so more effectively than some other fruit-eating animals, such as small lizards. This is because the frogs deposit the plant seed in or near the bromeliads where germination conditions are ideal.

While salamander larvae are carnivorous like their parents and feed predominantly on insect larvae (Coleoptera, Diptera, Ephemeroptera, Trichoptera) and small crustaceans (Crustacea), frog tadpoles chew plants, graze on algae and bacteria, feed on plankton, and sometimes even on carrion: they are omnivorous particle feed-

ers. Some larvae turn into predators under extreme conditions and may devour smaller tadpoles and even adult frogs, as is the case in the larvae of *Scaphiopus hammondi* (Pelobatidae) from the North American Sonora desert. Food specialization can be observed mostly in smaller breeding ponds such as pools in savannas or creeks in tropical rain forests, where species diversity may be very high and larvae of individual species find themselves restricted to extremely small habitat niches. Competition for food is rare as an interspecific, and more common as an intraspecific phenome-non—for example, when the density of individ-uals is high. In many tropical frogs and some salamanders (Plethodontidae), direct develop-ment occurs within the egg envelope without an intermediate free-swimming larval phase. Energy is supplied by nutrients stored in the egg yolk.

A Broad Food Spectrum

A broad food spectrum enables many amphib-ian species to adapt to what each season has to offer, creating numerous food choices over the course of a year. The elements that make up the diet of European newts (*Triturus*), for example, are very different during the months when they live in water from those periods when they live on land. Another example of a fundamental change in feeding habits for developmental rea-sons is the switch from omnivorous tadpole to carnivorous adult frog.

It has been demonstrated that for many species food selection changes with respect to size, taste and nutritive value as amphibians age. Food quantity and quality are also important for lar-val development, for the growth of metamor-phosed specimens, for everything connected to reproduction (territory, yolk production, number of eggs, brood care, etc.), and, finally, for energy storage. The latter is accomplished by fat deposits in the liver, in fat bodies, and in salamanders also in the tail. A drastic reduction of metabolic rate allows them to gradually catabolize these reserves during periods of inactivity, that are usually climate related (hibernation, summer dormancy). In arid regions amphibians survive the dry periods thanks to water reserves in the body cavity, in the bladder, and beneath the skin. Some species build a so-called cocoon that reduces water loss by 50 to 70 percent, as is the case in congo eels (*Siren*) and frogs of the genera *Lepidobatrachus*, *Scaphiopus*, and *Pyxicephalus*. As carnivores, amphibians are secondary consumers that feed on other primary and secondary consumers (plant eaters). They usually occupy a position in the middle of the food chain in their terrestrial habitats, and in aquatic habitats they are often at the end of the food chain, as is the case with large salamanders in creeks (*Siren*, *Ambystoma*, *Dicamptodon*).

The significance of amphibians within the food chain increases with species and individual density. Since many amphibians have a nocturnal, cryptic mode of life, we tend to underestimate their density. From time to time we are made aware of it—for example, when thousands of toads and frogs migrate to their breeding ponds where we may barely see an individual all year long. And when the young step onto land, they do so in such great numbers that the expression "it's raining frogs" has been absorbed into the language of many countries. The individual density of paleoarctic salamander populations can also reach enormous numbers, while in the tropical rain forest individual density is often replaced by species diversity. More than 80 frog species have been recorded in specific areas along the Amazon. Yet further studies show that even in this area high concentrations of individuals may occur. Thus more than 20,000 *Eleuterodactylus coqui* have been counted in a single hectare of forest land in Puerto Rico.

There are few exact data on the total amount of food consumed by amphibian populations. Some estimates do, however, at least offer an insight into the role of amphibians in food webs: one 1,000-member population of northern cricket frogs (*Acris crepitans*) consumes approximately 4 to 5 million arthropods, mostly insects, per year. Amphibian populations therefore play a dominant role worldwide in the natural regulation of invertebrate populations.

Foraging

The impulse to hunt for prey is generally linked to a feeling of hunger and produces—depending on the hunting method—either active search for food (appetence) within a given territory (appetence field) (e.g., Gymnophiona, Urodela, Bufonidae, Dendrobatidae) or else a more passive approach by lying in wait for prey that happens to pass by ("sit and wait" behavior), as is common among most frogs. Some species use both strategies. A successful hunt requires that the prey be recognized in advance and be captured by means of effective hunting equipment and appropriate methods of capture. Most amphibians—especially those that lie in wait—recognize prey visually. Usually an object is perceived and recognized as prey only if it moves neither too quickly nor too slowly and is neither too large nor too small.

The olfactory sense plays a comparatively subordinate role, but it is especially well developed in many Gymnophiona, Urodela, and burrowing toads. The Italian cave newt (*Speleomantes italicus*) locates its prey by means of smell with such precision that it can project its tongue in complete darkness with total efficacy. Gymnophiona have protrusible tentacles on the sides of the head and are therefore equally well equipped for olfactory and tactile recognition. While acoustics play an important intraspecific role for the territorial and mating behavior in Anura, they seem to be unimportant for hunting. *Bufo marinus* and *Bufo woodhousii* are known to attract prey with sound.

The lateral line organ, so common among fish, is also present in amphibian larvae, aquatic frogs (Pipidae) and congo eels (*Siren*). These organs make it possible to perceive tremors in a body of water and provide information about the source, distance and direction of the tremor. This, in turn, allows representatives of these species to localize prey with precision. Amphibian hunters approach their prey either slowly or in big leaps (Ranidae and many tropical tree frogs catch insects even in flight); those that exhibit "sit and wait" behavior allow prey to approach very closely and then capture it. For the latter, the prerequisite to a successful hunt is a good position in which to wait. Anteaters, for example, will position themselves right in the middle of their victims' path. The yellow-striped reed frog (*Hyperolius horstocki*) likes to sit on the blossoms of an Arales (*Zantedeschia*) whose colors match its own coloring, catching insects that approach the plant for pollination. Many frogs transfer their excitement during the hunt into their toes, which begin to vibrate. Horned frogs (*Ceratophrys*) utilize this reflex by lifting their hind limbs, bending their feet with the long, contrastingly colored toes forward, and executing a trembling-undulating movement above their head to attract prey.

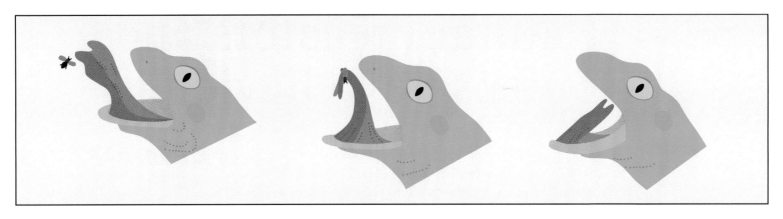

The Vital Role of the Tongue

While teeth (Gymnophiona, Urodela, some Anura) serve to hold and crush prey, the tongue is the essential tool for catching prey. It has evolved in the process of adaptation to life on land. Tongueless frogs (Pipidae), aquatic salamanders and their larvae pull food into their mouth cavity by means of suction created by a sudden opening of the mouth. The Pipidae use their fingers to push larger prey into their mouths. Terrestrial Gymnophiona, Urodela and Anura (Discoglossidae, Leiopelmatidae) with disk-shaped sticky tongues, grab their prey with their jaws; the tongue serves to hold the prey. In many amphibian groups, however, the tongue has evolved into a highly specialized hunting mechanism. Urodela of the genera *Chioglossa*, *Salamandrina*, *Hydromantes* and members of the American family Plethodontidae all possess projectile tongues that can move at lightning speed—on average, 10 milliseconds. It consists of a contractile stalk whose thick end is equipped with glands that produce a sticky secretion used to hold the prey fast to the tongue.

In many frogs and some terrestrial salamanders, the tongue is fused to the front of the lower jaw and lies folded inward when the mouth is closed. As soon as the mouth is opened, the tongue grazes the roof of the mouth, absorbing the sticky secretion of the intermaxillary gland and flips forward and outward at great speed, dropping onto the prey from above. The prey sticks to the tongue, which wraps around it and throws it into the rear of the oral cavity. Larger prey are held fast with the jaws and—whenever present—rows of pointed small teeth on upper jaw. Pieces of the prey that stick out the side, such as extremities or wings, are manipulated out with the fingers. The Papuan genus *Xenobatrachus* has one or two pairs of teeth in the roof of the mouth. Ant- and termite-eating species such as the Mexican burrowing frog (*Rhinophrynus dorsalis*), feature a pipe-like tongue that is fused not at the front, but instead to the middle or rear section of the fundus, and is extended.

Prey is often caught by means of a specific sequence of clearly defined actions, as is the case in newts (*Triturus*): approach–fixation–adjustment–olfactory testing–grabbing. All amphibians generally swallow their prey whole. Swallowing is facilitated by glands in the oral cavity that secrete mucus to make the prey slippery. Finally, the eyeballs, which are retracted during the last swallowing phase, help push the prey into the esophagus. Frog larvae practice a completely different form of food intake. They use two ingestion mechanisms: with sharp, keratinous jaws and rows of minuscule labial teeth, they grasp tiny food particles from plants and detritus; through a pharyngeal basket attached to the branchial arches they also filter plankton and detritus from water drawn into the oral cavity during respiration. *Xenopus* larvae and the Microhylidae have developed such an extensive maxillary filter system that they no longer need either maxillae or labial teeth.

The ability of many amphibian species to survive extended periods without food hunger is an interesting topic. All animals in temperate zones do not feed during hibernation. Their metabolism is extremely reduced during this period. Obviously, amphibians in deserts and semideserts must survive much longer periods. Burrowed deep into the substrate, they await the next life-giving rainfall, with some species becoming aware of impending rain not only through the raindrops, but even through the tremors in the earth caused by drops falling on the surface. If there is no rain in a year, these species must survive one more year underground. During this process, they lose up to 50 percent of their original body weight. In a laboratory setting, the common toad (*Bufo bufo*) was observed successfully surviving a fasting period of 18 months, and a large congo eel (*Siren lacertina*) survived a fast of more than five years in the laboratory.

The tongue plays an important role in food acquisition for most amphibians. Many Anura (top) have a folding tongue used to catch prey. Some Urodela, such as the cave salamander Speleomantes genei (Plethodontidae; below), feature an especially long projectile tongue that "shoots out" to catch prey. The tip of the tongue is thicker and mushroom-shaped; small insects stick to it and are transported into the mouth. In most Urodela, the tongue is fused to the bottom of the oral cavity (after Kabisch, 1990).

Natural Predators and Defensive Behavior

Rudolf Malkmus

In addition to natural predators, amphibians are also threatened by other environmental factors that endanger their existence, such as competing species, pathogens, adverse climate conditions, but more than anything else by "Homo oeconomicus." This chapter focuses on predators who play the most important role in regulating amphibian populations. Predators of pre-adults (egg/larvae) exert far more pressure on populations than predators of fully metamorphosed specimens.

Facing page:
A young Grass snake (Natrix natrix) tries to overcome a Tree frog (Hyla arborea). The lower maxilla of snakes are only loosely connected to the skull and elastic bands allow for maximum flexibility. This enables snakes to gulp down prey that is much thicker than they are. The frog's strategy of inflating itself to its largest possible size offers a poor defense.

Amphibian Enemies

Amphibian eggs often fall prey to aquatic insect larvae, salamanders (for example, *Notophthalmus, Ambystoma, Triturus*) and ducks. Eggs laid on trees by tropical frogs are also consumed by locusts, spiders and snakes. South American annulated (cat-eyed) snakes (*Leptodeira*) often devour the nests of the leaf (*Phyllomedusa*) and glass frogs (*Centrolenidae*). Innumerable predators hunt for amphibian larvae, such as predaceous water insects and their larvae (*Odonata, Coleoptera*), fish, aquatic salamanders, aquatic turtles, snakes (for example, *Thamnophis*), and small mammals.

Adult amphibians are on the "menu" of many mammals (badger, racoon, otter, hedgehog, possum, marten and others). Up to 100 frogs have been found stored in polecat burrows during the winter period: the frogs were still alive but had been rendered immobile by bites. Amphibian remnants have also been found in the stomachs of almost all 100 European bird species, especially in birds of prey, waders and crows. Reptiles such as crocodiles and water snakes, fish, and large invertebrates such as beetles,

praying mantis, spiders and prawns all feed on amphibians. But even large frogs of the genera *Ceratophrys, Cyclorana, Pyxicephalus, Rana,* and others have extremely high food requirements and do not shy away from eating their own relatives for much-needed energy. The stomachs of 10 Hylidae specimens (*Hemiphractus proboscideus*) were found to contain remnants of 15 frogs representing 12 different species.

From time to time, cannibalistic behavior can be observed in amphibians. This is fairly frequent among groups of larvae. Eggs that have been laid too late in the season are often consumed by tadpoles of the same species (egg cannibalism); food shortage caused by high individual densities—for example, as a result of desiccated breeding ponds—can lead to such crowding cannibalism.

Amphibians are generally low on the list of their predators' prey choice. However, some American snake genera (*Heterodon, Xenodon*) and African night adders (*Causus*) meet their food requirements by feeding mostly on Bufonidae; African bush snakes (*Philothamnus*)

A Marsh frog (Rana esculenta) is easy prey for a fully grown Grass snake (Natrix natrix).

The larvae of large Odonata are invertebrate amphibian predators.

feed mostly on Hyperoliidae; and European water snakes (*Natrix*) feed mostly on Ranidae. Even the extremely poisonous alkaloids of *Atelophus* and *Dendrobates* fail to guarantee complete safety; snakes of the genus *Leimadophis* seem to be able to neutralize these poisons.

The most surprising amphibian predator is the bat. Some tropical bat species (*Megoderma*, *Trachops*) hunt tree frogs, localize their calls and are able by some mysterious means to distinguish poisonous from non-poisonous species.

Defensive Behavior

Despite an army of predators, amphibians have proven themselves to be a highly successful group over the course of their evolution. To defend themselves against their predators, they have developed morphological, physiological and behavioral characteristics and mechanisms, which are still largely unknown. Amphibian defense strategies include behavioral responses such as active combat, flight, passive opposition and predator avoidance. Many of these are also characteristic of intraspecific and interspecific interaction—for example, to establish rank within a group. In the absence of effective "combat gear," such as claws, stingers and carnassial teeth, coupled with their small size, amphibians have become masters at passive defense strategies. The obvious method of

*Right: Hirudinea representative (*Haemopis sanguisuga*) are predominantly predators and often feed on amphibian spawn, even catching amphibian larvae or metamorphosizing juveniles nearly ready to leave the aquatic habitat (here* Bufo bufo*).*

escaping from a predator is flight. This requires internal sensors able to detect potential predators in time—usually visual recognition in amphibians—combined with quick reaction times and fast movement, at least across short distances. Aquatic salamanders (for example, Plethodontidae) and frogs (Pipidae, *Conraua*) are excellent swimmers.

When amphibians jump into a body of water with a muddy bottom, their rapid motion stirs up the mud and clouds the water, making it difficult for the predator to spot or chase the prey. Some salamanders (for example, *Chioglossa*)

couple their flight with another trick: should the predator be dangerously close, they cast off their tail by means of muscle contractions (autotomy); while the predator busies itself with the tail, the individual disappears into a hiding place.

Many frogs are capable of impressive escape maneuvers thanks to their long hind limbs which have developed into powerful jumping legs. The small South American *Pseudopaludicola* can leap across a distance that is 50 times its own body length! Predators that use olfaction to find their prey quickly lose the scent as a result of such rapid movement. Frogs in flight tend to jump toward water, either right into the water or else into mud or beneath rocks (for example, *Amolops*, *Astylosternus*, *Litoria* or *Rana*). Species whose habitats are far from water make do with a few leaps, feign death or rely on camouflage. Tree frogs use suction pads to hold onto leaves at the very end of branches, and some Rhacophoridae "glide" away from their hunters by means of "slow-motion" long-distance jumps.

Many tree frogs feature bright yellow spots on their rear flanks, which are covered when they sit and flash only briefly when they jump (flash-colors). Immediately before landing, the flash-colors are once again hidden. This means that the frog disappears from the vision of the predator fixated on the flash-color. Predators are especially confused by leaps not executed in a linear fashion but following a zig-zag course, as does *Amolops*, which inhabit mountain streams.

All forms of flight require energy and may often lead to extreme stress situations. In the case of predators that hunt by sight, the only option for a victim caught off guard and away from a hiding place is to camouflage itself and to remain still. Species in tropical rain forests have an impressive and surprising skill in imitating the structures that surround them in this varied habitat. Coloring and patterning are perfectly adapted to the environment by glandular protrusions or skin processes that imitate leaf

veins, fringes, incisions into leaves made by insects, or bark surfaces. This can be observed in representatives of the genera *Edalorhina*, *Leptobrachium*, *Megophrys*, *Platypelis*, and others. Unusual lichen mimicry is present in *Hyla lancasteri*, *Mantidactylus phantasticus*, *Rhacophorus everetti* and *Theloderma schmardanum*. The camouflage effect is enhanced even further by means of letisimulation (pretending to be dead) during which the animal presses itself against the ground beneath it. Many salamander and frog larvae also possess excellent camouflage colors with somatolytic effect.

The Role of Colors

By contrast, species with highly poisonous secretions tend to exhibit bright warning patterns that signal danger. The most common color patterns are yellow-black and red-black, often combined with a bright blue and green.

Some Urodela (e.g., Taricha torosa, *left) and Anura (e.g.,* Bombina variegata) *are camouflaged on the top, while their abdomens are marked with distinctive signal color combinations. To show off the latter, certain behavior patterns are necessary which are called "rowing position" or "yellow-bellied reflex": the back is held in a concave curve; head and extremities are lifted upwards.*

This bat in Panama, Trachops cirrhosus, *captures a tree frog* Agalychnis callydrias *(after a photograph by M. D. Tuttle; drawing by T. Podlesny).*

These color combinations are present in diurnal, neotropic genera such as *Dendrobates*, *Phyllobates*, *Atelopus* and the Madagascar *Mantella*. The function of such warning colors in nocturnal or predominantly subterranean species (*Ambystoma*, *Pseudotriton*, *Salamandra*, *Tylototriton*) is still disputed.

Colors and color patterns are also actively used in aggressive gestures and evasive maneuvers. The Hylid species *Hemiphractus fasciatus* lifts its head, opening its mouth to show a bright orange tongue and even feigns biting its predator. The leptodactylida *Physalaemus nattereri* raises and presents its posterior, where two large, white eyespots appear, simulating the sudden appearance of a large head.

In the rain forest even large spiders can capture frogs. Here a leaf-frog (Phyllomedusa sp.) *has fallen prey.*

Terrestrial American salamanders assume a variety of positions when faced by predators: they tuck their heads beneath their tails (*Batrachoseps*, *Ambystoma*), bend the torso backwards (*Taricha*) or bend their tails (*Bolitoglossa*). Species of the genera *Bufo*, *Scaphiopus*, and *Leptodactylus* lift their fore-

limbs and pump their lungs full of air to make themselves appear larger. Others, such as the garlic spadefoot (*Pelobates fuscus*) or *Rana septentrionalis*, exude an apparently unpleasant smell. However, we have very little data of how successful these defense strategies are.

The same applies to behavior and color patterns interpreted as mimicry. *Chiasmocleis ventriculata*, a South American microhylid species, spreads its hind limbs out sideways when threatened during amplexus in water; this apparently imitates the webbed feet of an inedible catfish. The calls of *Rhacophorus angulirostris* and *Metaphrynella sundana* are barely distinguishable from the calls of syntopic locusts able to defend themselves (acoustic mimicry).

Active Defense Behavior

Only a few species use active defense behavior such as forceful bites; these are caecilians (Gymnophiona), the ribbed newt (sharp-ribbed salamander) (*Pleurodeles waltl*), congo eels (*Amphiumae*), mole salamanders (*Dicamptodon*), and some frogs (*Ceratophrys*, *Pyxicephalus*). Tusk-like pseudoteeth of some species (*Adoletus brevis*, *Limnonectes corrugatus*) and toe processes (*Ptychadena*, *Limnonectes kuhlii*) also seem to be intended for active defense behavior.

Even inside their predator's mouth, many amphibians continue to fight, and so-called distress calls can often be heard from some frogs (for example, *Rana*, *Leptodactylus*) long after they have disappeared into the gullet of snakes. Inflated ribs, however, can be effective, and the predator may literally choke on its meal, as happens with some newts (for example, *Echinotriton*, *Pleurodeles*) where the ribs actually pierce through the skin. Many frogs also exhibit massive bloating. However, the trump played by many species in fear is to secrete large quantities of poison and mucus, which can cause the predator to spit out its prey.

All these strategies and the circumstances to which they respond are far from fixed or constant. Instead, they are part of an evolutionary process that continues in confrontation with and reaction to the changing factors mentioned at the outset.

Mimicry and Mimesis

Stefan Lötters
and
Miguel Vences

Animals have developed numerous strategies to defend themselves against predators. In species that are less able to defend themselves, deception is a widespread practice. Two types of deceptive behavior are differentiated: mimicry and mimesis (both from the Greek mimesis = imitation). Mimicry can be defined as the imitation of other more powerful or inedible species with distinctive coloration or behavior. Mimesis, on the other hand, refers to detailed imitation of "uninteresting" objects. These may be living or dead plants or parts of plants, other, sometimes larger animals that are not part of the predator's prey pattern, or inanimate objects in the environment such as stones.

When in danger, the South American Physalaemus nattereri (Leptodactylidae) elevates the rear end of its body, displaying large eye spots. Such eye spots as defensive mechanisms are otherwise especially common among butterflies (after a photograph by I. Sazima; Owen, 1980; drawing by: T. Podlesny).

What Is Mimicry?

While animals with mimetic behavior tend to do everything to remain incognito, mimicry is characterized by efforts to be noticed and to frighten the enemy. There are different forms of mimicry and not all are related to protection from predators. For example, there is a known behavior that imitates another conspicuous creature for the purpose of foraging. However, the most common form of mimicry is protective or defensive mimicry, and are Batesian mimicry and Müllersian mimicry. In contrast to insects, where mimicry is common, few examples are known in amphibians. It is also important to note that it is difficult to prove scientifically whether the similarity in camouflage colors of two species represents a form of mimicry or whether it is simply an accident of nature. Mimicry in amphibians has been proven in experiments in only a few cases. Most examples of protective or defensive mimicry among the

Anura and the Urodela discussed in this chapter still need to be critically reviewed.

Bates's Mimicry

This type of mimicry, probably the most familiar, was first discussed by naturalist Henry Bates in the nineteenth century. He had observed in South America that the numerous spotted butterflies of the family Nymphalidae were rarely eaten by birds, despite their conspicuous coloring and slow flight, and that some pierid species

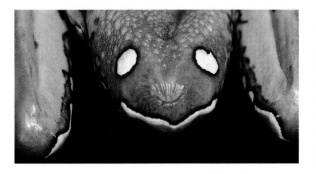

The biological function of these ventral white spots in Phyllomedusa tarsius (Hylidae) from the Reserva Ducke near Manaus, Brazil, is unknown. To date, there are neither published papers nor speculations with respect to these "eye spots."

Megophrys nasuta *(Pelobatidae) from South East Asia is perfectly colored and shaped for camouflage in its habitat.*

looked remarkably similar to the nymphalid. Bates's hypothesis held that if the rare, edible pierids could imitate the more common, inedible nymphalids in appearance and behavior, they would be able to deceive their predators and avoid capture. Bates called this phenomenon mimicry. As a matter of fact, the pierid species collected by Bates (*Dismorphia thenoe*) is edible and imitates the coloring of not one but several distantly related butterfly species of the genus *Ithomia*, which are all inedible.

In amphibians Batesian mimicry has been observed among some frogs and salamanders. Many poisonous frogs of the Dendrobatidae family, found throughout large portions of tropical America, possess potent alkaloid-based neurotoxins. These species "announce" their toxicity or at the very least unpalatability with distinctive warning colors. Some dendrobatid frog species, for example, have so-called dorsolateral stripes on a dark base color, creating a pattern of bright cream-colored to yellow stripes. The pattern extends from the tip of the snout over the eyes, running along the edge of the body between back and flank to the thighs. Dorsolateral stripes of this kind are found, for example, in extremely toxic species such as *Phyllobates aurotaenia* from Colombia and *P. lugubris* from Panama and Costa Rica. *Eleutherodactylus gaigei* of the frog genus Leptodactylidae inhabits the same region as the poisonous frogs mentioned. Although it isn't poisonous, it exhibits similar dorsolateral stripes—even though the Eleutherodactylus species on the whole tend to be more brown in color and inconspicuous. It is assumed that *E. gaigei* imitates *Phyllobates* to protect itself against predators. Some dendrobatid from the Amazon also have bright dorsolateral stripes, such as the moderately toxic *Allobates femoralis*. Here, too, we find another (probably) non-poisonous Leptodactylid frog *Lithodytes*

lineatus, whose pattern greatly resembles that of the poisonous species.

Batesian mimicry is also known among North American salamanders. *Notophthalmus viridescens* (Salamandridae) may spend its entire life in water or can—as it is the common mode in salamanders—switch to life on land in the adult phase. During the terrestrial phase, they secrete a skin toxin and alert potential predators to their toxicity by means of a reddish warning color. In areas where this species is found in the same habitat as the non-poisonous salamander *Plethodon cinereus* (Plethodontidae), the latter will also show a distinctive red dorsal coloration while retaining its typical red and black pattern. Mimicry has also been observed within the Plethodontidae. The inedible *Plethodon jordani* has a red pattern and is imitated by several salamander species of the genus *Desmognathus* in the southern Appalachian mountains. However, the same Desmognathus species occur in other areas where *P. jordani* is absent and then their coloration is plain. Experiments have shown that the inconspicuous *Desmognathus* are more likely to fall prey to predators than are the red mimics.

Müllersian Mimicry

In Müllersian mimicry, two inedible or poisonous species mimic each other. The reciprocal advantage is obvious: predators are more often exposed to the unpleasant experience that an individual with specific coloration or behavior is unfit for consumption. Even if one individual does not survive, it helps protect the entire group with the same warning habit. When two species in one region have a similar warning signal, they both benefit—to put it simply, the total number of victims from both species is only as great as it would otherwise be for one species alone.

Müllersian mimicry is difficult to document in amphibians. Among the Anura, advances in bioacoustical research led to the discovery of an ever-growing number of sibling species, often with similar color patterns. In most cases these are, however, phylogenetic similarities rather than Müllersian mimicry. In the case of Malagasy poison frogs of the genus *Mantella* (Ranidae), which tend to be aposematically colored, one example is difficult to explain by phylogenetic processes alone. The two species *Mantella madagascariensis* and *M. baroni* are syntopic in some areas—a basic prerequisite for Müllersian mimicry. In these syntopic representatives we can observe a near-perfect resemblance in the black-yellow-orange dorsal pattern. Until recently the two taxa had not been distinguished as distinct species. Closer analysis revealed, however, that they are

different in a number of characteristics (e.g., ventral pattern, relative limb length, skeletal character, and not least of all genetically) and can therefore not be regarded as sister species. Both are more closely related to other species with clearly different color pattern. This then may after all be a case of Müllersian mimicry, but final proof—ultimately only possible through experimental analysis of a predator's prey selection—is still required.

North American salamanders may represent another possible example of Müllersian mimicry: the poisonous species *Pseudotriton ruber* and *P. montanus* (Plethodontidae) feature patterning that is very similar to the poisonous *Notophthalmus viridescens*.

In general, however, examples of either Batesian or Müllersian mimicry are extremely rare. It is especially notable that so few imitators of the highly toxic Dendrobatids from the neotropics exist. Moreover, the few examples mentioned in the preceding paragraphs are related to species whose color pattern (bright stripes on dark ground) is much less conspicuous than is the habit of species with red-black, yellow or blue coloration. One interesting aspect is that many Dendrobatid frogs present a high degree of color and pattern polymorphism—at times even within the same population or between neighboring populations. Similar color variations are also found in some species of the Malagasy poison frogs (*Mantella*). In other groups, such as insects, aposematic species are very consistent and similar in their colors and patterns as a rule. This may be an indicator that the warning habits of some amphibians have evolved as a result of different evolutionary mechanisms than is the case for most other aposematic animals.

The mimetic brown coloration of many anuras that live in the fallen leaves on the forest ground offers some protection from predators. This image shows Mantidactylus luteus (Ranidae) from Madagascar.

Above and right: Boophis licheroides *(Rhacophoridae) from Madagascar. The frog is camouflaged by wrapping itself around a branch covered in lichen.*

Left: Mantidactylus ventrimacucatus *(Ranidae) from Madagascar.*

Right: Mantidactylus phantasticus *(Ranidae) from Madagascar.*

Peckhamian Mimicry

The most commonly known example of Peckhamian mimicry or aggressive mimicry are the angler fish, which imitate worms with the help of moving appendages. Unsuspecting prey are drawn to what they mistake for delectable bites of food while the camouflaged angler fish stays immobile. When the prey is close enough to the huge mouth, the trap falls shut. The American freshwater turtle (*Macroclemys temmincki*) has a wriggling lingual tentacle and lies in wait for prey with its mouth wide open. It is interesting that the horned frogs of the genus *Ceratophrys* (Leptodactylidae) have developed a similar behavior. Whenever individuals of the species *Ceratophrys calcarata* or *C. ornata* spot

potential prey, these otherwise inconspicuous frogs lift their hind legs above their back to reveal bright yellow trembling toes. It is interesting to note that the ravenous *Ceratophrys* feed mostly on other frogs and that the behavior described above is mostly exhibited when smaller prey frogs are present. *Ceratophrys* are short-legged and plump with huge mouths, not well equipped for an active hunt. Therefore they probably use their waving toes to coax other frogs to approach, then pounce and devour them with one gigantic, surprising leap.

Encounter Behavior

Several encounter and defensive behaviors have been observed in many amphibians, although their specific meaning is often unclear. Some of these species have markings that can, in combination with the encounter behavior, serve to create a successful illusion of presenting the "face" of a much larger creature. Often these markings are in the shape of large, conspicuous eye spots in the inguinal region (known in the leptodactylid genera *Pleurodema* and *Physalaemus* as well as the Madagascar microhylid *Plethodonotohyla ocellata*).

Mimesis

While mimicry can be understood as exceptions among the limited number of amphibian species with warning colors, the majority of amphibians have inconspicuous colorations and body shapes to remain "invisible" to their many predators. The relationships among color patterns, habitat and life mode are largely unexplored, although a series of correlations are obvious from the many color photographs published in recent years. In frogs, the general color for tree-dwelling species tends to be green—as is the case for the European tree frog (*Hyla arborea*)—while ground-dwelling species are predominantly brown.

In nearly all ground-dwelling species, we find lighter colors on the back and darker colors on the flanks, as well as a usually light-colored stripe on the middle of the back. There is a long list of such examples and in many cases color patterns could be interpreted as mimesis. Green tree frogs spend their days near their base—usually green leaves—and are thus nearly indistinguishable from their surroundings. Many ground-dwelling frogs prefer to pass the day among fallen leaves, and their markings must often be designed to break up the body's outline and to imitate fallen leaves. In many frogs this effect is further enhanced by certain appendicular characteristics in body shape. South American mouth-breeding frogs of the genus *Rhinoderma* have a very pointed snout while other species such as *Ceratobatrachus* or *Bufo*

Extreme mimetic habit of
Scaphiophryne marmorata
(Microhylidae) from
Madagascar.

typhonius have bony crests on the head. Similar features are found in some tree frogs—for example, in *Hemiphractus* and *Polypedates otilophus*. The function of these structures is not always clear; they may serve to make the outline of the head less regular and to make the body contour blend in with the forest floor or tree branches. Some of these species are nearly invisible in their natural environment. Many species also have dermal tubercles on head and body, often as protrusions on the eye. These can be quite bizarre in shape, as in *Megophrys nasuta* or *Bufo superciliaris*. In tree frogs, dermal flaps are also occasionally found on knees and elbows. Some Malagasy *Mantidactylus* species of the

suborder *Spinomantis* have well-developed lateral folds on the limbs, as do species of the neotropical *Hyla lancasteri* group or the Asian rhacophorid genus *Theloderma*. One species, *Mantidactylus aglavei*, has been shown to spend its days literally hugging tree bark, and in this case the folds on the limbs completely diffuse the outline of the frog.

Twig mimesis can be observed in salamanders of the South American genus *Bolitoglossa*. When alarmed, they press their legs close to the body and freeze. In this position they are barely distinguishable from small twigs that have fallen to the ground.

Caecilian Ecology

Werner Himstedt

Caecilians are among the least researched vertebrates because of their cryptic way of life. Terrestrial caecilians have solved the problem that faces all terrestrial amphibians—namely, the danger of dehydration through evaporation—in a relatively simple manner: they live beneath instead of on top of the ground. The aquatic mode of life practiced by the Typhlonectidae, which occur exclusively in South America, is a secondary adaptation from an evolutionary perspective. We can assume that aquatic species are descendants of terrestrial specimens that have moved from the moist, muddy shorelines to aquatic habitats.

Terrestrial Species

Moisture in soil is retained much longer than it is in the open air. There is no wind to blow away moisture from the body surface. Thus the underground caecilian habitat offers conditions that are ideal for amphibians because of the constant high humidity. And the fact that they occur exclusively in tropical and subtropical regions means that other environmental factors tend to be fairly stable as well. Prevailing temperatures in the various habitats of caecilians are constantly high and not subject to annual fluctuations.

Despite this uniformity, the tropics also offer a variety of very different habitats. In mountainous regions, temperatures may be much lower than in the lowland. The distribution of annual precipitation, especially, may drastically change conditions in the environment. In many tropical regions there is a distinct change between dry and rainy seasons.

Caecilian habitats reflect this diversity. And among caecilians themselves, there are enormous differences in the level of adaptation among individual species to various ecological conditions. There are euryecious species that can survive a relatively wide range of variability in environmental factors and there are stenecious species that are specialized in one habitat with narrowly defined conditions. Compared to other amphibians, the ecology of caecilians has hardly been studied. If one caecilian species is known only from one specific site, one cannot extrapolate from this that the same species does not occur in other habitats. All we can do is speak of probabilities, and do so very reservedly. Whenever a number of individuals from one caecilian species are found in different regions, it is safe to assume that this is probably a euryecious species. However, if only one or two representatives of another species are discovered in a specific location, it may be a stenecious species. Euryecious species too have a number of prerequisites that must be fulfilled to ensure their survival. Uppermost is soil quality. It must be neither too dry nor so hard that the individuals are unable to burrow into it. Caecilians are not found in very dry sandy soil, nor in hard soil. Caecilians are found in a variety of tropical soils. They live in inorganic lateritic soil as well as on loamy alluvial soil and in volcanic soil. From a few regions, regularly studied by herpetologists with respect to caecilian fauna, there is some data that allow us to draw conclusions about the ecology of these animals. In what follows, Sri Lanka, Thailand and the Seychelles Islands are used as examples of areas where comparatively detailed studies have been carried out.

Caecilians of the genus *Ichthyophis* occur in Sri Lanka, formerly Ceylon, and these are currently classified into three species. *I. glutinosus* has the widest distribution of these three species and is frequently found on the island. It occurs in the humid plain in the southwest of Sri Lanka, but also in the mountains up to 4,265 feet (1,300 m) above sea level. They tend to live near rivers, creeks and pools, where the soil is moist, but are also found in cultivated soil such as in tea or coffee plantations. Piles of compost and mud are other popular microhabitats. The substrate is usually relatively loose and humid, and no specimen was found more than 20 inches (50 cm) below the surface.

The two other *Ichthyophis* species in Sri Lanka are less widely distributed than *I. glutinosus*, yet they are sympatric with that species. In other words, *I. orthoplicatus* occurs in the same regions as *I. glutinosus*, but is not found in the lowland; the lowest altitude where specimens of this species have been found was 1,509 feet (460 m) above sea level. *I. pseudangularis*, on the other hand, has never been found at altitudes above 3,937 feet (1,200 m), but is commonly found in the lowlands and in hilly regions where *I. glutinosus* also occurs. *I. orthoplicatus* and *I. pseudangularis* also inhabit damp, loose soil, compost heaps and cultivated soil. The habitats of the three species are therefore quite similar, the only difference being altitude.

It is a basic rule of ecology that sympatric species inhabit different ecological niches. Whether this rule applies to the caecilians in Sri Lanka is unclear. But *I. pseudangularis* is significantly smaller than the sympatric *I. glutinosus*. The smaller head may indicate that *I. pseudangularis* catches different types of prey than larger caecilian species, which reduces interspecific competition. Too little is known, however, about the food habits of all three species. And lack of information also makes it impossible to elaborate further on why the ranges are so different. One could imagine that different tolerance levels for temperature fluctuation are the decisive factor. *I. glutinosus* occurs in the hot coastal regions as well as in cooler mountain areas, whereas *I. orthoplicatus* is never found in hot regions and *I. pseudangularis* is never found in the cooler regions. However, other climatic factors may also be responsible for the distribution limits.

Like Sri Lanka, Thailand is home to many caecilian species with a variety of distributions. Here, however, the differences are more clearly defined. Taylor identifies four species of the genus *Ichthyophis* in Thailand's caecilian fauna. Among these *I. kohtaoensis* is the euryecious species distributed across a wide range that encompasses different geographic and climatic

regions, while the other species, *I. acuminatus*, *I. supachaii* and *I. youngorum* are known to occur only within relatively limited boundaries.

I. kohtaoensis occurs throughout Thailand. In the south this species is found in the plain near Surat Thani in coconut plantations, between rice paddies and in vegetable patches. The animals are often very near the surface beneath coconut shells, rocks or wood. The climate in southern Thailand is consistently hot through-

out the year with temperatures ranging from 77 to 86°F (25 to 30°C) and precipitation is high year round. The farther north one travels in Thailand the more distinct is the seasonal shift from dry to rainy seasons. The distribution of *I. kohtaoensis* is not negatively influenced by these changes. This species occurs in alluvial soil in the lowlands of central Thailand (whenever you dig up a garden in Bangkok you find these caecilians) and are equally common in the lateritic soil of the Khorat plateau. Here there are still remnants of primary tropical rain forest, such as in Khao Yai national park. The species has been found in the forest soil, in the shallow layer of humus between tree roots. Yet, this caecilian species seems to survive even when the rain forest is cut down. In the mountain region of Doi Inthanon in northern Thailand, the species occurs at altitudes of 6,562 feet (2,000 m) where forests have been largely destroyed by slashing and burning to gain arable land as well as the cutting of teak trees and other exotic timber. The mountain areas not yet affected by soil erosion are used for agriculture and *I. kohaoensis* is found in the tilled earth. In January temperatures can fall to near freezing. This caecilian therefore seems to have a relatively high tolerance for temperature fluctuations.

Being an egg-laying species with free-ranging larvae, *I. kohaoensis* needs access to permanent bodies of water. Since larval development takes one year and the larvae require water for foraging, the species cannot inhabit areas where water is present only after rainfall. The mountain regions as well as the lowlands offer good habitats where these requirements are met.

Other caecilian species that occur in Thailand are much rarer and have been found only in very specific locations. Moreover, there is no proof that these species still exist. Only four adult and four larval specimens are known of *I. acuminatus*, all collected in 1921. They were all found in the Mae Wang valley in northern Thailand, a region that has long been dedicated to rice and vegetable cultivation. The rather vague location data seem to indicate that some were found in a tea plantation. No other discovery of this species has been reputed since then.

I. youngorum is another species where circumstances are quite similar. In 1957, in northern Thailand Taylor collected 10 adult and 13 larval specimens, which are described as a distinct species. The collecting site is in the rain forest covering Mount Doi Suthep west of the provincial capital Chiang Mai at approximately 3,937 feet (1,200 m) above sea level. For this species, too, no other specimens were ever found. The site is a small valley with a small creek, and Taylor's discoveries were made in the muddy banks of the watercourse.

The fourth caecilian species described in Thailand—*I. supachaii*—was found 623 miles (1,000 km) south of these mountain forests. In 1958 Taylor collected a total of 11 larval, juvenile and adult specimens in the southern provinces of Nakhorn Si Thammmarat and Trang. These caecilians were found in four different sites within a 56-mile (90-km) range. At one of these sites more specimens of *I. supachaii* were discovered 25 years after Taylor. They had made their home in the moist earth on the banks of a small river near an abandoned zinc mine. The original vegetation and thus the natural habitats had been destroyed at this location for decades. The

Schematic overview of habitat and mode of life of Ichthyophis kohtaoensis *(Ichthyophiidae) in Thailand. Adults (a) live just below the surface and are found at the greatest distances from water. Closer to water, one can discover females and their nests (b). The larvae are shown in this illustration in their terrestrial hide-out during the day (c) to indicate their amphibious mode of life. They are found in direct proximity to water (after Himstedt, 1996).*

ground was covered in tall grasses, weeds and bushes. It is impossible to determine at this time whether *I. supachaii* is sympatric with *I. kohtaoensis*. Thus far the two species have not been discovered side by side.

As is the case for *Ichthyophis* in Sri Lanka, it has not been possible to determine why one of the species in Thailand is distributed across an area that covers more than 623 miles (1,000 km) north and south and at least 374 miles (600 km) east and west and encompasses different geographic and climatic regions, while the other three species have very limited distributions despite very similar anatomical characteristics. There are no data on the food of these caecilian species. Hence it is impossible to determine whether these are in fact different adaptations to specific ranges of available prey. Moreover, there is no information on how well these species tolerate temperature and humidity fluctuations or other environmental factors.

Caecilians on the Seychelles Islands

The Seychelles Islands in the Indian Ocean are one region where the caecilian fauna has been comparatively well researched. The occurrence of Gymnophiona on these islands has been known since 1829, when French anatomist and diplomat Georges Cuvier described a new caecilian from the island of Mahé. Many herpetologists have since traveled to the Seychelles to search for caecilians.

Despite this promising research, the data available on the distribution and ecology of caecilians on these islands are incomplete. In the past, many naturalists simply noted "Seychelles" as the collection site; only half of all documents mention the name of the island and even then information on the precise site or descriptions of the habitat are sketchy. The Seychelles archipelago consists of eight larger granite islands (311 to 35,780 acres/126 to 14,480 hectares surface) where amphibians occur. Mahé, the largest island, is mountainous with elevations higher than 2,953 feet (900 m) above sea level and covered in forests. Six of the seven described caecilian species occur on Mahé. Smaller islands with lower mountains and no forests are home to fewer species. Thus only one species, *Hypogeophis rostratus*, is found on the smaller islands of St. Anne, Cerf and Curieuse. This caecilian is obviously relatively euryecious and it occurs on all eight islands colonized by amphibians. The other caecilian species are more specialized in their distribution. *Praslinia cooperi*, for example, only occurs on the islands of Mahé and Praslin. There are also two species that are endemic on one island each. *Grandisonia brevis* occurs

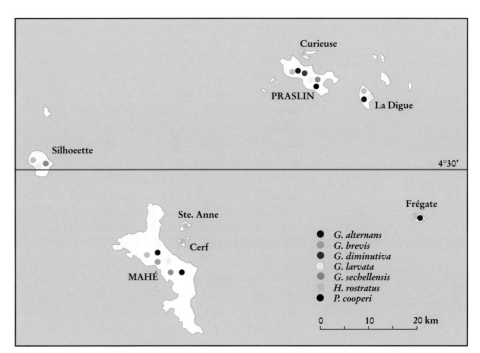

exclusively on Mahé and *G. diminutiva* is found exclusively on Praslin. According to research, all caecilian species on the Seychelles Islands are terrestrial and lay eggs. To date, however, there is no information on their ecology and reproductive biology. In the genus *Grandisonia* the species *alternans*, *larvata* and *sechellensis* have free larval phases, while the species *G. brevis* and *G. diminutiva* have direct development. *Hypogeophis rostratus*, too, develops directly. The species with direct development are independent of water and can therefore occur in habitats that are unsuited to species with free-living larvae.

Regardless of their mode of reproduction, all caecilian species require relatively high soil moisture. From the data gathered thus far, it is evident that on the Seychelles Islands the species cannot be divided according to a geographical profile. While precipitation is higher in the mountains, the lowlands also offer high soil and ground moisture by virtue of the rivers that run through them. All species have been discovered in moist ground, rotten wood, damp fallen leaves, or beneath palm leaves and coconut shells on the ground. Once again the varying levels of caecilian distribution on the Seychelles is yet to be explained. The ubiquitous *H. rostratus*, a species with direct development, is independent of water in its distribution, while the similarly direct developing *G. diminutiva* has a limited distribution on the island of Praslin. Therefore other factors must be responsible for distribution. The impact of environmental factors on caecilians on the Seychelles Islands is not known.

In addition to distribution, population sizes (or estimated frequency of occurrence) of the Seychelles caecilian species is also remarkable. As is the case in Thailand, here, too, there are

Distribution of the seven caecilian species on the Seychelles Islands (after Himstedt, 1996).

Embryo of Ichthyophis kotaoensis *(Ichthyophiidae) with external gills and yolk. These caecilians need access to permanent bodies of water as an egg-laying species with freely developing larvae (after Himstedt, 1996).*

caecilian species that have been sighted only rarely. Only two specimens of *Grandisonia brevis* exist: they were both collected in 1910 and are now housed in museum collections. This was also the year when the three existing museum specimens of *Praslinia cooperi* were collected. Nussbaum writes of his long and unsuccessful search for representatives of these two species. Some caecilian species have been discovered more recently, but the recorded number of individuals is extremely low. These are *Grandisonia diminutiva*, *G. larvata* and *G. sechellensis*. Only *G. alternans* and *Hypogeophis rostratus* occur frequently in the Seychelles.

There is another notable aspect of the ecology of these terrestrial caecilians. Numerous reports indicate that they regularly spend time in water. It is said that all washerwomen on Mahé are aware of these black "Vers de terre" in the ponds where they do their laundry. Nussbaum also mentions that he observed two *H. rostratus* mating in water on the island of La Digue. This terrestrial species seems to be capable of entering aquatic habitats. When *I. kohtaoensis*, the Thailand species, is kept in an aquaterrarium, it can be seen that not only the larvae but the adults, too, enter the water at night to catch prey. Like the larvae, the adults swim with a snake-like movement of their body, or crawl along the bottom among vegetation. They regularly come to the surface for air and then dive back underneath water.

Aquatic Species

In caecilians, the evolutionary step to an aquatic mode of life was not accompanied by any marked anatomical or physiological changes. Since even terrestrial caecilians such as *Hypogeophis* and *Ichthyophis* spend at least some time in water, an aquatic mode of life poses no problem in principle for adult caecilians. In salamanders and frogs, temporary or permanent life in water is also possible without significant anatomical or physiological adaptations.

It would seem that the Typhlonectidae usually do not live permanently in water; instead they tend more toward an amphibious mode of life. Knowing that *Typhlonectes* are often caught in fishermen's nets in the Amazon estuary or can even be caught with fishing rods, one might imagine these creatures constantly swim in water, like carp or catfish. *Typhlonectes* are also successfully kept in aquariums. But in a natural environment, aquatic caecilians do seem to follow a different mode of life than fish.

One of the few works on the ecology of the genus *Typhlonectes* was published by Moodie.

He collected and observed *T. compressicauda* from Amazon tributaries near Manaus. During the day, the animals spent their time on the muddy river banks where they dug out tunnels ranging from 1 to 2 feet (30 to 60 cm) in length and whose exits were level with the water's surface. In the study area, these diurnal hiding places were common and easy to locate. The distance between individual tunnels was 10 to 13 feet (3 to 4 m). This means that the population density of *T. compressicauda* was high in this area. After sunset, the animals left their hiding places and foraged for food in the water. They had an obvious preference for shallow waters which allowed them to easily swim to the surface for air, although they were quite capable of diving for extended periods of time.

Since oxygen requirements for the resting metabolism can be met by skin respiration alone, the air in the lungs needs to be exchanged on a regular basis only during phases of increased activity. Inactive *T. compressicauda* often remain under water for up to 40 minutes before surfacing.

The mode of life for other Typhlondectidae is also not permanently aquatic. The genus *Chthonerpeton*, for example, has several characteristics that have been adapted for life in the water. Their body is laterally compressed, there is no tail fin, and the left lung is reduced as it is in all terrestrial caecilians. In captivity, representatives of the species were successfully kept both in a purely terrestrial setting with damp moss and in an aquaterrarium divided into terrestrial and aquatic sections. In an aquaterrarium with a water basin of 2 to 3 inches (5 to 8 cm) depth, *C. indistinctum* displayed characteristic amphibious behavior. They spent the day hidden in the land section of sandy clay soil and moss; at night they were often observed in the water. They crawled along the ground between the water plants and fed in water, although food was also consumed out of water.

Overall, our knowledge of the habitats and modes of life of caecilians is still very incomplete. However, it appears that it would be inappropriate to differentiate between terrestrial and aquatic species. Rather, many species seem to lead a semiaquatic or amphibious mode of life, switching back and forth between land and water. Much remains to be done in herpetological field research. Observation of caecilians in their natural habitat will yield vital information about this group. If every naturalist and collector who happened to discover a caecilian were to note down specific information about the site, an important step in the right direction would have been made.

How Old Do Amphibians Get?

Joachim Kuhn
and
Doris Gutser

The longevity of amphibians is remarkable, especially when compared to mammals of similar sizes. The record goes to one Japanese giant salamander (Andrias japonicus) that reached 55, or possibly even 62 years of age in captivity. Among the Central European species, a single Fire-bellied salamander (Salamandra salamandra) has broken all other records: without hibernation it lived for 50 years in a terrarium, having already been an adult at the time of capture, or, as the terrarium owner put it, "no longer a baby." Among the Anura, a 36-year-old common toad (Bufo bufo) of unknown sex had been the uncontested "Methuselah" before dying prematurely as a result of an accident. However, the highest age of all was recorded in a Siberian salamander (salamandrella keyserlingii) estimated at 90 years of age (plus/minus 15 years) which was recovered from a 49-foot (15-meter) depth in permafrost and revived by thawing; the animal had spent most of its life frozen.

Amphibians Live Longer in Captivity

The recorded ages reached by amphibians in captivity with optimal care far exceed the ages reached by their relatives in nature. Most amphibians die as a result of the many dangers in the natural environment long before they have realized even a fraction of their life potential. Tree frogs (*Hyla arborea*), for example, which can live up to 22 years in captivity, rarely grow older than 3 to 5 years in nature—provided they even reach sexual maturity, which may occur in the first year of life, but more frequently in the second or third year. An overwhelming majority of all tree frogs reproduce only once in a lifetime.

A comparison of species and species groups reveals several basic trends: first, larger species tend to live longer than smaller species, provided environmental conditions are similar. Second, the Urodela count among their number the longest-living species, and on average, too, urodeles outlive most anurans. Third, species that reach sexual maturity later than others often have long life expectancies, although there are numerous exceptions. Several populations of the same amphibian species often present strikingly different age profiles. Specific genetic factors may contribute to these differences, yet most seem to be the result of environmental influences, with climate playing the decisive role.

Animals whose habitats are high above sea level or in northern latitudes tend to reach sexual maturity later than those in low-lying habitats or southern latitudes. They also tend to live longer. The trend is more evident in altitude than it is with respect to latitude. Some of the record ages shown in the tables for amphibians in their natural environment refer to species whose populations occur in high altitudes (alpine newt 5,390 feet/1,643 m, common toad 6,102 feet/1,860 m, grass frog 6,660 feet/2,030 m above sea level). One table lists the age profile in grass frog (*Rana temporaria*) populations at different altitudes. The differences are even more evident in common toads: in the Netherlands sexually mature females of this species are 3 to 8 years old; in Wales, in Brittany, and in the Bavarian alpine foothills they are 3 to 9; on the northern edge of the Alps they reach 4 to 11 years; in Norway 6 to 11; and highland populations in the Bernese Plateau in Switzerland have a profile ranging from 8 to 21 years. In all common toad populations the sexually mature males are generally younger than the females, and have a lower life expectancy too. With higher elevations, both the minimum age at first reproduction and total life expectancy rise dramatically, as does the absolute age difference between the sexes.

The differences between animals from high- and lowlands, northern and southern latitudes, are, however, diminished to a great degree when data is gathered exclusively for the total duration of actual activity (i.e., not counting winter hibernation which is naturally very long in high altitudes and northern latitudes). This "physio-

Population (Origin)	Height (m above sea level)	Male			Females		
		min.	mod.	max.	min.	mod.	max.
eastern France 1	220 m	2	2	5	2	2	6
eastern France 2	220 m	2	3	5	2	3	5
central Switzerland	600 m	2	4–5	11	2	4–5	8
Swiss Alps	1930 m	4	5	12	4	9	13
French Alps	2030 m	4	8	15	5	8–10	12

Lowest, most common, and highest age of adult Grass frogs (Rana temporaria) captured in spawning area in different French and Swiss populations. The values were established by means of skeletochronological analyses. min. = age of youngest adult specimens; mod. = modal value, most common age among adults; max. = age of oldest adults.

		Maximum age in years	
		in open range	in captivity
Urodela			
Alpine salamander	*Salamandra atra*	(≥ 15*)	?
Fire [European] salamander	*Salamandra salamandra*	> 20	> 50
Alpine newt	*Triturus alpestris*	22*	32
(Great) crested newt	*Triturus cristatus*	18*	28
Palmate newt	*Triturus helveticus*	8*	18
Common [smooth] newt	*Triturus vulgaris*	12*	20
Anura			
Midwife toad	*Alytes obstetricans*	(≥ 8?)	?
Fire-bellied toad	*Bombina bombina*	≥ 13	29
Yellow-bellied toad	*Bombina variegata*	> 16	27
Common spadefoot toad	*Pelobates fuscus*	?	11
Common toad	*Bufo bufo*	21*	≥ 36
Natterjack	*Bufo calamita*	13*	> 16
Green toad	*Bufo viridis*	(≥ 7*)	≥ 15
Common tree frog	*Hyla arborea*	8–9	22
Moor frog	*Rana arvalis*	11*	?
Agile [Dalmation] frog	*Rana dalmatina*	(≥ 5*)	?
Common [grass, brown] frog	*Rana temporaria*	15*	18
Edible frog	*Rana kl. esculenta*	12*	14
Pool frog	*Rana lessonae*	6 (12?)*	(5)
Marsh frog	*Rana ridibunda*	11*	10

Maximum age among amphibians in Central Europe recorded thus far. The values were drawn under consideration of ages recorded throughout the European distribution areas. Values of little-known species are indicated in brackets. Record ages measured by means of skeletonchronology are marked with an asterisk *.

Skeletochronologically recorded age distribution among females of two common toad populations (Bufo bufo) in their first spawning season in the Alpine foothills in Upper Bavaria. The two populations occur at a distance of only 12 miles (20 km); they are indicated by different colors in the graph (after Kuehn, 1997).

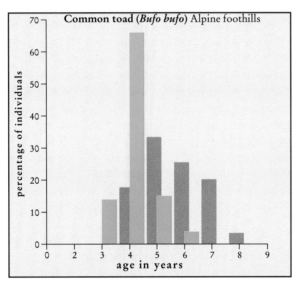

logical life expectancy" (the average "physiological age") of sexual maturity seems to be remarkably constant within a species or subspecies. Perhaps the "life capital" is simply more quickly consumed in different parts of a species range.

Age Profiles in Individual Populations

The age profile of populations of the same amphibian species fluctuates not only on a larger geographical scale but also on a smaller scale, at times even between neighboring populations. Furthermore, the mix of ages within one population can fluctuate from year to year; this is a result, first, of the number of larvae that survive and reach metamorphosis per year; second, of the constant changes in conditions for

growth and thus for developing to sexual maturity; and, third, of the changing mortality rates among juveniles and adults. It is interesting to note that adult populations on the whole are rarely dominated by the youngest age groups, for with the exception of extremely short-lived amphibian species, juveniles and young adults tend to reach maturity in a staggered fashion over the course of several years. Identifying an individual's age has long been a big problem in the field of amphibian biology. For decades body size was used as a yardstick for establishing the age of a specimen. Then records began to show that this method was applicable only in exceptions and was then used only for rough estimates. Age and size of sexually mature amphibians are only marginally related, if at all. This is a result of the fact that growth tends to slow down dramatically once sexual maturity is reached; often growth ceases altogether. Growth and reproduction are factors that are in opposition, and from the point of sexual maturity onward, all else becomes subordinate to reproduction. The resulting drop in growth is usually less evident in males than in females and also less dramatic in the Urodela than in the Anura.

Deeper Insights into the Ecology

In the 1980s a new method of determining the age of amphibians became standard: skeletochronology. Combined with long-term studies, it has dramatically enhanced our insight into the life of amphibians and has revolutionized previous ideas. Thus the common toad, which had always been thought of as enjoying a particularly high life expectancy with reproductive activity extended across many years, turned out to reach sexual maturity relatively late in its development; in addition, evidence showed that in this species, as is the case for many other species, only a small number of individuals ever live long enough to reproduce.

It was believed that the yellow-bellied toad (*Bombina variegata*) was a very short-lived pioneer species inhabiting transitorial habitats. In recent years, it has become clear that in low-lying areas, these toads outlive all other European anurans, although they usually reproduce for the first time at only two to three years of age. Yellow-bellied toads tagged as adults were recaptured as long as 16 years later, and they may live even longer. This "biblical" age, coupled with undiminished fertility, has enabled yellow-bellied toads to survive several years in unfavorable conditions with no reproductive success. Longevity, combined with an extraordinarily effective immune system, thus emerges as a survival strategy even in habitats where unpredictable changes may occur. Amphibians, also, display phenomena of aging, with characteristics ranging from physical changes, weakness and severe deterioration.

Using the Bones of Amphibians to Determine Age
Robert Schabetsberger

Zoologists have been telling each other a strange tale for the past 100 years: Heinrich Schliemann, who discovered Troy, supposedly found two toads under the remains of an exposed wall. Since the walls were nearly 3,000 years old and it appeared as if the toads had been trapped under the rubble, the archeologists had to assume that the amphibians were of biblical age. ...Regardless of whether Schliemann himself believed this story, the fact is that compared to other animals, amphibians do get fairly old

Animals' age is a central factor in any study on population dynamics. Life expectancy, age at the start of sexual maturity, rate of survival and rate of mortality—all of these parameters can be measured only if scientists are able to accurately determine the age of the individual animals in a population. It was initially realized that the exact age of amphibians cannot be determined from their physical size. Animals of the same size may be of different ages, and the largest individuals are not necessarily the oldest.

In the early 1970s, Russian scientists were able to demonstrate that it is possible to determine age by using cross-sections of bones. The bones contain annual growth rings, similar to those of trees, which can be counted. The rings reflect the varying rates of growth of the bone during active and resting phases. During the colder fall season, poikilothermic animals' rate of bone growth slows down and stops completely during the winter. The slowly growing bone is denser and can be seen as a dark line in a histologic cross-section (LAG—line of arrested growth.) Every year a layer of bone is deposited at the outer part of the bone. However, since the shape of a bone changes during growth, it is reconstructed from within the medullary cavity. Only the innermost lines will be partially reabsorbed and bone substance deposited repeatedly from the inside. As soon as an animal reaches sexual maturity, the majority of energy is channeled into reproduction. At this stage, the annual growth rings are set much closer together and it is often difficult to distinguish them, especially in cases where

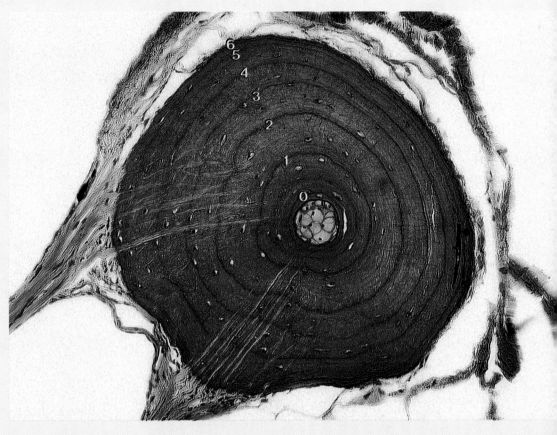

the animals have two annual inactive periods brought on by environmental factors—at which point two rings per year are formed. It takes some practice to be able to make an exact determination of age from these bone cross-sections. Since the 1970s, many species have been examined using this skeletochronological method.

Several conclusions may be drawn from the results. Usually, salamanders attain a greater age than Anura. The age at which amphibians reach sexual maturity and their life expectancy is higher when their breeding grounds are located at higher elevation or latitude. In colder temperatures, growth slows down. Males often reach sexual maturity one to two years earlier than females. Maximum life expectancy tends to be significantly lower in nature than in captivity. A spotted salamander (*Ambystoma maculatum*) from Canada is the oldest amphibian, whose age was determined using the skeletochronological method. Recently there has been increasing information that senescence and senility may even play a role among amphibians living in the wild. This occurs at an age significantly below the maximum age they can reach in captivity.

The image shows a dyed section of a decalcified finger bone of a female common toad (Bufo bufo) at least six years old and spawning for the first time. The tissue surrounding the bone has been partially removed. At the center, the cartilaginous medullary cavity is followed by six successive annual growth rings. Broader, less dense rings form during growth periods; thin, dense rings form during pauses between growth periods: these are called lines of arrested growth (LAG). The innermost basal line (0) developed during metamorphosis; it is followed from the inside out by the winter rings 1 to 6. The finger was amputated in March (spawning season); the most recent winter ring is thus also the outer demarcation of the bone. The interpretation of this image is complicated by two factors: the ring between the metamorphosis line (0) and the first winter ring (1) is not continuous and is visible only in individual sections taken from a comprehensive series that is less clear than the reproduction above. It was therefore not interpreted as a winter ring ("intermediate ring"). Another, also discontinuous, extremely thin ring can be seen on the bone periphery. This may have formed as a result of a longer warm phase during the previous, unusually mild winter ("double ring") (Photo: J. Kuhn).

Almost all vertebrate classes include species that may present a danger to man. Amphibians are the exception: there is not a single amphibian that poses a serious threat to humans. And no amphibian can truly be considered an agricultural pest. On the contrary, amphibians consume enormous quantities of insects and snails and therefore play a vital, and often still unrecognized, role in the ecological network of different habitats. They are also enormously important for science, education and pharmacology. And to tens of thousands of amphibian lovers, they are terrarium pets that they cannot conceive of doing without. In the Third World, they even play an important role as a source of protein in human nutrition. For thousands of years, amphibians have influenced the cultural history of different peoples.

The Meaning of Amphibians for Humankind

Robert Hofrichter

Amphibians in the Cultural Heritage of Peoples Around the World

Some animals have always inspired the human imagination. They have played an important role in witchcraft and magic across the ages. Some tales and superstitious beliefs survived for thousands of years, almost as if they themselves were ageless. In addition to snakes, bats and some other animals, amphibians have always been invested with symbolic power.

Rana grylio (Ranidae) from North America is also called "pig frog." It is distinguished by its calls and its large tympanum.

Progessive frog illustrations in Erdal advertisement (shoe polish) from 1903 to 1971.

A Cultural History

It is difficult to convey a sense of the cultural history of amphibians in only a few pages. Their histories are varied and ancient, not only in Europe but also among peoples in Africa, Asia, Australia and America. Therefore, this chapter makes no claim to presenting a complete overview. There are, however, many well-researched books on various aspects of the cultural history of amphibians and interested readers will find ample opportunity for further study.

The role of amphibians today is quite different from its role in the past. The past decades have brought a gradual change in cultural history, at first nearly unnoticed: amphibians—especially frogs—became popular. While living, real amphibians are severely threatened by any number of factors, their "relatives" in plastic and other materials are ubiquitous.

Frogs have always played an important role in artistic symbolism. A general trend toward commercialization and mass tourism is supplanting true "ethnic art" with "airport kitsch." Entire armies of frogs grin down at shoppers from store shelves: in clay, ceramics, porcelain, glass, rubber, wood, stone, plastic, plaster, wax, metal or even marzipan. On postcards they are depicted in the funniest situations. All these goods are intended to cater to consumer tastes.

What are the psychological reasons behind this frog boom and the efforts of the advertising industry to sell us all kinds of products with the help of frogs as symbols? "Today's frogs" in the form of modern frog products have long lost their original symbolic meaning. They are merely "cute," "adorable," "nice," "friendly," and—here comes the crunch—they sell! This somewhat superficial view of frogs is in contrast to the great historical and cultural legacy of frogs in folklore across the world, as we have already mentioned. To understand modern attitudes toward amphibians, we need to undertake an excursion into their cultural heritage.

Why Are Frogs So Popular?

Next to snakes, amphibians are regarded as belonging to the so-called chthonic domain— that is, the earthy or subterranean domain. The chthonic world with its powers, gods of the earth, and the underworld tended to be regarded negatively. The animals of this domain and their secretive, often hidden, modes of life on the ground, in the earth, in swamps or marshes, provide an ideal "breeding ground" for the creation of many stories. Frogs, toads and salamanders feature in the visual and oral heritage of most cultures, with individual amphibian groups being assigned different levels of importance. Salamanders and toads are often connected with all that is eerie and evil, while frogs are frequently linked with all that is positive and good.

This can be explained in part with the psychological-behavioral phenomenon called the "child syndrome." According to this theory young animals—as well as children—are characterized by large eyes, a large head, round cheeks, rounded body shapes, a soft, smooth skin, and clumsy behavior, characteristics that we spontaneously interpret as "cute" or "lovable," without thinking about the reasons why. They are key stimuli that trigger the parents' brood care mechanism. And some frogs, in Europe above all the common tree frog, tend to correspond this pattern.

In all eras of cultural history and around the world, we encounter symbols, art, stories, fairytales and legends based on frogs. Some of these stories contain an element of truth in that they reflect biological facts about amphibians—

especially the link to rain, water and metamorphosis—while others are based on ignorance, superstition or plain human stupidity—for example, the story about fire salamanders being able to survive in fire unharmed. It documents the longevity of such legends, for from antiquity to modern times, this is a tale that has been told and retold and also believed anew at each telling.

The Multifaceted History of Amphibians

While one of Egypt's goddesses appeared in a frog-like form, in Christianity frogs were seen sometimes as symbols of resurrection and sometimes as "impure" creatures from the world of the devil. Entire peoples were decimated by their poisons—at least, if one is to believe what Pliny the Elder had to say about how dangerous they are. Today, the vocal sacs of frogs are used in images to advertise airbags; Kermit, the lovable and funny playmate and frog hero, became the star of the popular Muppet show on TV and even amused Queen Elizabeth.

In many fairy-tales, frogs are used as figures to illustrate to our children positive and negative ideas. And in laboratories, frogs are used in research in attempts at new breakthroughs. Scientists embark on expeditions into primeval forests, lugging along heavy technical equipment, to study the calls of frogs and their methods of communication, while elsewhere lawsuits

are being fought over the supposedly insufferable noise in a neighbor's frog pond. (The verdict: "The frogs must maintain silence between 10 p.m. and 6 a.m....")

At times they were seen as symbols of fertility and at other times they died in excruciating pain in a magical invocation of weather change. They perform in the circus and are sent into space to find answers to questions about weightlessness and lack of gravity. Some decades ago, common tree frogs were still kept in pickle jars to predict the weather. From pickle jar to space rocket: truly a steep career path! With large corporations choosing frogs to symbolize how environmentally friendly their products are, we can no longer doubt the current popularity of frogs.

Amphibians Mirrored in Quotations

The ugliest of all creatures is the salamander. Others bite only one individual at a time and do not kill Many in one..., but the salamander can kill entire peoples with no one knowing where the calamity has sprung from. When it climbs a tree, all fruit borne by the tree is poisoned and anyone eating of it will die of shivers, as if he had drunk hemlock. When the salamander so much as touches a baking sheet on which bread is being baked, the bread turns to poison; should he fall into a well, the water is poison. Should its spittle drop onto any part of the body, and be it no more than the tip of the toe, then all hair will fall out across the whole body. Nevertheless, this horrible monster is eaten by some animals, such as pigs, for each creature has its enemies. Magicians claim it has the ability to extinguish fire; but this is not true, or else surely one would have noticed it in Rome.

Pliny the Elder (79–23 BC)

The newt is more warm than cold, but its warmth is lost very quickly, and its poison is fatal. In itself the newt is not very dangerous to man while it is alive, but people are killed by its poison if they ingest it. The rest of it is not suitable for healing substances.

Hildegard von Bingen (1098–1179)

Toads are poisonous reptiles, possessing the evil eye. They eat soil and therefore their bodies are heavy.

Peter Candid (1548–1628)

Roadworks authority...complain...that... amphibian conservation is impossible without staff. Activities that are not in direct relation to road construction...should not be taken on. The acceptance of such responsibilities foreign to the authority's mandate, and which quite a few employees can execute only at the cost of sup-

"Frog Rain"

In the past during fertile years, there used to be veritable frog plagues. Of course, this was before the amphibian decline caused by direct and indirect human interference. These "plagues" primarily took place after warmer periods of rain or during the summertime. Hundreds of thousands of little frogs and toads covered paths and meadows and made their way into villages and towns. The concept of the "frog rain" developed, because people noticed that this phenomenon frequently occurred after a rainfall. Under favorable conditions, innumerable tadpoles reach metamorphosis at the same time and crawl out of the water. Since frogs, which have gone through metamorphosis, are vulnerable to dehydration, they opt for wet locations to wait for the best time to leave, which is when there is warm rain. Then large numbers of these juvenile frogs embark on a migration. These days, the term "frog rain" is used in a demystified sense to describe the appearance of a large number of juvenile amphibians after metamorphosis. Nevertheless, the frog rain concept from the Middle Ages is not just a myth. Looking back in history, we find several authentic reports about "fish rain," in which other animals, such as frogs, toads or mice, fell from the sky. Major storms and whirlwinds usually preceded these phenomena. For this reason, it is believed that whirlwinds lifted the animals out of the water, dropping them farther away some time later.

The mass appearance of tiny toads and frogs immediately after metamorphosis became known in folklore as "frog rain." The image shows a young common toad (Bufo bufo) after leaving the breeding pond.

pressing revulsion, should...not be envisaged in consideration of the collective agreement.

Ordinance of the Presiding Committee in Karlsruhe, 1993

Antiquity

Potters in Babylon were undoubtedly aware that frogs live in swamps and mud when they went to dig up their clay. From the fifth millennium onward, many potters' seals and imprints use a

frog image. Mesopotamia, "the land of two rivers," the Tigris and the Euphrates, with its abundance of water, would surely have been an amphibian paradise. The word for frog in many Middle Eastern languages is onomatopoeic. Thus the Egyptian word "krr" or "krwrw" resembled a frog call; similarly the Babylonian "krùru," the Berber "agru" and the Syrian "yaqrúrá." Frogs, or more accurately anurans, for the images make it difficult to surmise which species is represented, were worn as amulets and were also often included as burial gifts.

Egyptian history is especially helpful in understanding the religious or spiritual symbolism of frogs. Religious ideas about frogs are mainly linked to their life in mud and ponds. During and after the Nile floods, people observed how frogs "seemed to appear out of nowhere" when the water returned, immediately launching into their reproductive phase. This contributed to the idea that amphibians were originally created from water and mud, an idea that was still confirmed in subsequent centuries by Greek and Roman authors writing on Egypt.

The frog-shaped goddess Heket (although we cannot distinguish whether she was modeled after a frog or a toad, recent Egyptologists speak of the "toad Heket") played an important role in the Egyptian world of deities. Together with her husband, the ram-headed god of creation Chnum, she is depicted as helping to shape the child in the mother's body. In the Osiris cult, Heket reanimates the limbs of the dead god. In Egypt, frogs are found in a variety of images, among others on the so-called magic knives of the Middle Kingdom that were laid across the belly of pregnant women or on newborns as magical protection. Into the late Middle Ages and even modern times, the frog was adopted from other cultures and religions as a symbol of resurrection.

Greek and Roman Antiquity continued to hold fast to the Egyptian belief that frogs had been created out of water and mud. The image of a "frog rain," which followed later, is known to have first appeared during this era. However, even then some rational voices disagreed with such ideas. One was philosopher Theophrast of Eresos (372–287 BC), who countered this superstition.

The literature of antiquity contains many allusions to loud frog choruses that can disturb humans and gods alike in their sleep. Often frogs are struck dumb as a result, a frequent and popular motif handed down in many oral and written sources. Roman authors were very impressed by the acoustic communication of frogs. Cicero (106–43 BC) and Horaz (65–8 BC) complained about their noisy croaking. Even then, frogs were believed to have meteorological abilities. According to Cicero, "fresh water frogs" especially would announce imminent changes in weather with loud and dissonant croaking.

Frog legs were on the menu even then, although eating them was not encouraged unless they were used as an antidote against snake venom. Frogs and toads played an important role in so-called medicine, which was mostly far-fetched superstition. Several "medications" prepared from different amphibians served as aphrodisiacs and were prescribed as protection against impotence and infertility. Frog tongues were recommended as contraceptives.

"When the tongue is torn out of a living frog without doing other injury to the creature, and if this tongue were placed on the heart of a sleeping woman, she would answer all questions truthfully. When a tube is pushed right through a frog, from its anus to its mouth, and this tube is then dipped into the monthly flow of the woman, then she would come to feel a great distaste for adultery." According to the knowledge of the times, frogs had a "double" liver, one half of which contained an antidote to all other poisons. Frogs and toads were so important in popular magic for thousands of years that Pliny the Elder remarked: "If it were left up to magicians, frogs would be more important to the world than all laws put together." Various frog entrails were used for healing and magic spells. During the Roman Empire, toad lungs were believed to be a means for the "perfect murder of a husband." Frogs and toads were also the subject of obscene and esoteric imagery, with images such as frogs riding a phallus frequently appearing in wall paintings and as sculptures. The old saying "There's nothing new under sun" also applies to Ungerer's "Frog Kamasutra."

Amphibians and Christendom

The attitudes of Christianity toward amphibians has been quite contradictory during its 2,000-year history. On the one hand, the creatures were demonized, especially because of the negative symbolism in the Book of Revelation in the Bible ("impure spirits in the shape of frogs"). Church fathers promoted this negative symbolism: What do frogs and sinners have in common? Their answer: "Both live in dirt!" St. Augustine (354–430) saw the frog as a symbol of prattle or gossip and as a metaphor for boastful hypocrites who refuse to renounce their sins. Demanding silence of frogs remained a popular motif among Christian authors, as it had been in antiquity. Ambrosius (339–397), the bishop of Milan, reported that frog choruses

disturbed the mass, but when the priest commanded it, the frogs fell silent as a gesture of reverence. This was to be taken as an admonishment: if even the most despicable creatures listened to the word of the Lord . . . . Motifs of this nature recur in legends of saints.

Throughout Christendom, attitudes toward the frog remained divided: on the one hand, it is seen as a pleasant water creature, on the other hand as an ugly swamp creature ("*rana horrnes in paludis, decora in acquis*"). This interpretation may be based on an effort to emphasize the healing power of baptismal water. People regarded "swamps" as hostile and useless environments since ecology and the preservation of nature were foreign concepts at that time.

Frogs and toads were usually linked to the forces of evil; they would rarely be cast in a positive role, although popular beliefs sometimes differed from the "official" belief supported by the Church. In popular tales the toad often embodied maternal-protective house spirits that had to be looked after. Their role as guardian of treasures is also well documented. The metamorphosis of a toad from egg to

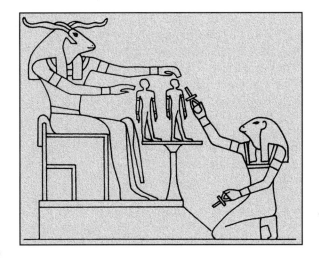

Chnum forms a child on a potter's wheel with the help of his frog-headed assistant Heket. Next, the queen is led into the birth chamber. Detail of relief cycle in the "birth chamber" of the funerary temple of Hatschepsut in Der el-Bahari.

Amphibians in the Bible

5 And the Lord spake unto Moses, Say unto Aaron, Stretch forth thine hand with thy rod over the streams, over the rivers, and over the ponds, and cause frogs to come upon the Land of Egypt. 6...and the frogs came up, and covered the Land of Egypt. [...] 14 And they gathered them together upon heaps: and the land stank... Exodus 8: 5-14. King James translation.

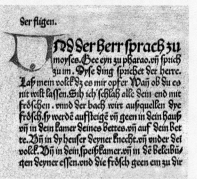

These are the words used in the Bible to describe the second plague that Yahweh, the God of Israel, delivered unto the pharaoh and his land, Egypt, so that the people of Israel could be freed from slavery. Like most of the other ten plagues, this one reflected the Israelites' abhorrence of idolatry in the Egyptian religion. An oversimplified view of the theological controversy between Jews and non-Jews ("heathens") could be summarized as follows: all that was sacred to one people was disgusting and forbidden to the other–and vice-versa. Just as Egyptians worshipped the River Nile, so they worshipped frogs as holy creatures. It is only logical therefore that the Israelites thought frogs were "impure." In fact, according to Moses' law, it was forbidden to eat frogs (3rd Book of Moses 11, 12.). And the Egyptians portrayed their goddess Heket with the head of a frog. The frog-headed Heket is one of the so-called primitive gods of Antiquity and is therefore one of the oldest deities. Egyptian records give little insight into the reasons for the frog cult and its origins. However, people have believed since Antiquity that the sudden appearance of a great number of frogs from the mud of the Nile River after it has flooded is linked to a kind of spontaneous generation. The belief was that under the warm rays of the sun frogs can actually form directly from mud. This is how they came to symbolize the beginning of life.

The country along the Nile River was in fact predestined to become a paradise for frogs, because of its abundance of water. This river flooded annually, ensuring not only a very fertile soil, but also a dynamic habitat with a number of wetlands and smaller bodies of water. The plague of frogs is also mentioned in Psalm 78: 45 and Psalm 105: 30. Some early fathers, such as Origenes (185–254), interpreted the plague of frogs and the entire story about the Exodus as an allegory of the path to God that the human soul takes. The single mention of frogs in the New Testament is less flattering.

The mysterious Book of Revelation compares frogs with "impure ghosts," emerging out of the mouth of a (symbolic) wild animal and false prophet (Revelation 16: 13). The text reflects the Jewish food regulation mentioned above in which the law classifies frogs as "impure" animals.

The second Egyptian plague as shown in the Ninth German Bible *1483, Koberger, Nuremberg. Permission granted by the University Library at Salzburg, Austria.*

tadpole to adult was also a reminder of how heretics turn away from the true faith.

The "Evil" and the "Animal"

In medieval folklore evil is not ascribed only to amphibians. For centuries, all that was "animal" was connected to evil. Having sinned, man has fallen from being made in God's image to being made in the image of the devil. And sin is linked to the body and the "flesh," with the body or the physical in turn being linked to the "animal." Man's soul originating in God is seen in contrast to his sinful, physical, and thus animal nature. Evil in animal form can be traced across the centuries in literature and, above all, in visual depictions. Good, reasonable, human behavior is contrasted with bad, unreasonable, animal behavior. It was believed that it was a task of (Christian Occidental) civilization to overcome the "animal" in man. Natural peoples or people from the past were regarded as being animal in nature and served as a warning example to civilized man. The Western world was surrounded by animal-like "savages," who threatened to turn civilized people into animals. This background of a "philosophical" heritage may help us understand the inhumane behavior of "civilized" Western man in the subjugation, colonization, enslavement and genocide of other peoples and races.

Many aspects of attitudes toward animals–in this case toward amphibians–remain contradictory. The following example is a good illustration: lamps dating from the era of Early Christianity are decorated with crosses and inscriptions of "I am the Resurrection" and often too with images of frogs. Thus the poem "Resurrectio carnis" ("Resurrection of the Flesh") from the sixteenth century:

Like a frog in winter
Lying hidden within the earth
Appearing dead and rotting
As if it had never been alive
Yet in spring
Rises forth all fresh and new
Swims joyfully in the brook:
Thus we Humans also die
And are buried:...
...But if God our Lord
Were to reawaken us from the earth
We would emerge through the clouds
And sing merrily to God the Creator...

The frog as a symbol of rebirth and resurrection? This idea is not new, for the Egyptian goddess Heket was presented as a symbol of rebirth and resurrection. The different stages of development in a frog obviously led to the creation of this symbolism. The Christian symbols of frogs on lamps probably originated in

Egyptian and "pagan" roots, as does so much of the heritage of the Christian church. For this reason this type of lamp was prevalent, especially in the Coptic tradition, because the Egyptian influence of the frog was held "in good memory" in that culture.

Frog lamps were usually found in homes, sometimes in tombs. Some scholars have interpreted the use of lamps with a frog motif as a "means of chasing away the ominous demons of darkness." The connection between frog and light is logical because light was seen as an expression of immortality. Even Mary's virginity is represented not only by the unicorn but also by the salamander—yet another example of a positive role for amphibians. Over the course of time, however, the negative "image" of amphibians became predominant.

The Physiologus

After the Bible, the *Physiologus* (from Greek for "natural scientist") was the most widely read book of the Middle Ages. This theological-allegorical animal book, probably dating from the second century, was translated into Latin in the fourth century. More than any other work, it shaped the mystical and magical thought of scholars. Considered to be the "most important book on animals in the Middle Ages," it also influenced Christian theology and the natural sciences in all matters relating to "animals." In this book, frogs are divided into land frogs and water frogs. The former must endure the heat of the sun and are thus seen as an image of steadfastness, while the latter's ability to flee into water was believed to symbolize vacillating Christians who fled from any danger.

In the alchemistic world of imagery, the toad is a symbol for the watery-earthy portion of the *Ur* matter (or primeval or original matter) intended for purification. This was to be connected with "flight" and therefore many illustrations depict winged toads. The alchemists' goal was to "connect the toad of the earth with the eagle." Some strange and oddly toad-related traditions have survived from the world of alchemy: thus one copperplate engraving shows a toad being placed on a woman's chest. The accompanying text states: "Set a toad upon a woman's breast, so that it may suck, and the woman die, the toad will grow very large from the milk." This bizarre story has the following background: the *Ur* matter on its way to the stone of wisdom must be saturated in the milk of a virgin (philosophical milk, juice of the moon) in order to be nourished. The "child" that is to grow is nursed by its mother, who gives her life in the process; this is called "ablactatio" ("weaning"). This short excursion into alchemy suffices to illustrate that it cannot be understood by rational means.

The common toad (Bufo bufo) plays an important role in folklore. It was often linked to evil or witchcraft, although it was also viewed as a protective maternal house spirit and keeper of wealth.

Amphibians in Folk Medicine

As in Antiquity, frogs and toads played an important role in folk medicine during the Middle Ages. They were especially sought after as aphrodisiacs. The famous mystic Hildegard von Bingen (1098–1179) wrote in some detail about several amphibian species. In *The Book on Animals* she discusses the knowledge of amphibians in her time as well as their possible uses for healing. She was less interested in biological facts than in "recipes and advice for healthy living." Some species, such as newts, fire-bellied toads and common tree frogs, are defined as having little or no medicinal value. The author ascribes greatest importance to the toad:

The toad contains much warmth on the one hand, and a biting sharpness on the other, like a dangerous mass of air when lightning, thunder, and hail break (out of it). In its green it possesses a kind of devilish art; it seeks to dwell on top of the soil and beneath the soil, and so in a certain way keeps company with man, and thus, being near them, sometimes presents a danger to humans.

Some Christian authors of the Middle Ages, however, wrote not only of superstition but also of more exact biological observations: Thomas of Aquinus (1225–1274), the great theologian and philosopher, distinguished between a greenish and a reddish species. He describes the higher volume of calls during the nocturnal mating season and even proclaimed the idea of a nocturnal mating season as a model for humans to follow! Albertus Magnus (1193–1280) is the only one to describe the vocal sac, while the metamorphosis of the tadpole is mentioned by Bartholomew Anglicus. The subterranean hibernation was also known to these authors.

But frogs were also seen as symbols of knowledge and the "cleverness of the little man." In animalia illustrated in the sixteenth and seventeenth centuries they are often shown outwitting larger and more powerful animals, as confirmation of idioms such as "use your brains, not your brawn" or "intellect over brute force."

In addition to moral and ethical teachings, frog parables also include religious elements: the frog as an example of the downfall of the godless. The first verses of this poem are remarkable and of interest as they reflect important biological factors:

The heat, which gives life to the egg
Will cause a frog to die:
And is thus death to the frog, the wet
Creature, which eagerly leaps into water.
When God is well disposed, even though He may
Send us many trials, it only ends well for those
Who are devout: Yet evil ones walk a different path,
For they spoil in God's hand.

Since amphibians were linked to water, rain and humidity, it took only a small mental leap to connect them to meteorological prognoses. The *Historia naturalis ranarum*, a beautifully illustrated work by Renaissance artist Johann Rösel von Rosenhof (1705–1759) includes the following advice:

This frog can be employed instead of a weatherglass, because generally his voice is heard several hours before it rains, calling out "cra cra cra" in his rough tone. If you place him in a glass with damp grass, and supply him now and then with flies, he can be kept alive for a long time. Or else you can put him into a large, tall vessel, for instance a glass containing water and some turf on which can be set a small chair. Cover the opening of the glass just enough to prevent him jumping out but allowing him sufficient air to breathe. As long as he remains sitting on the chair, fine weather will continue; but if he comes down to the turf, you may expect a change in the weather. If he climbs down into the water, you can be certain that the weather will remain rainy and stormy.

Frogs and Weather Spells

The well-known natural scientist Conrad Gesner (1516–1565), often regarded as the founder of scientific zoology, also spoke of the meteorological abilities of frogs by emphasizing that these observations had been confirmed by many authors:

The majority of scribes of old contend that when frogs call out especially loudly, it means [that] storm and rain are sure to follow.

In the context of weather spells, practiced throughout the world and among the most ancient of spells and magic, frogs were often subjected to terrible torture: they were impaled and tortured until they began to scream; weather predictions were then made based on the quality and nature of their screams. A sad highlight in medieval superstition—also in the context of weather spells—was reached in witchcraft, in which frogs and toads played an important role. Witches "brewed" the weather, by tossing snakes and toads into boiling water, invoking evil spells and magic spells while stirring this "toad soup." The Inquisition believed that the devil could appear in the shape of a toad. In direct reference to witchcraft and witch hunts, three witches prepare a poisonous brew from different amphibians in a dark cave in William Shakespeare's (1564–1616) *Macbeth*. And Hieronymus Bosch (1450–1516) depicted toads as a symbol of the devil and hell in his confused and fantastical allegoric art. Toads and other "devilish creatures" feed on skeletons and rotting flesh in his images...

But sometimes the frog can take on a positive, even "apostolic" role. The Styrian visionary Jakob Lorber (1800–1864) claimed to have received the following message from the Lord and Savior: "The frog croaks almost all day in joy of the life [he feels] stirring in his puddle and praises Me with his croaking joy about the gift of life." It could thus serve humankind as a "teaching apostle."

In addition to the literary references to amphibians, rarely true and often full of imagination, many ideas were passed on from generation to generation as oral history. These ideas have survived across the centuries in numerous sayings. Many are based on observation and contain a core of truth, while others can be traced back to the superstition and prejudice that have survived from Antiquity into modern times. We should note at this point that most of these idioms are European and their provenance is based on the observation of European species.

Amphibians in Fairy Tales and Fables

"There is a bit of mankind peeking out of every animal, and the world of animals still tugs every human being by the ear."

Friedrich Rückert

"The pike must surrender to the peaceful frog. See, raw power is overcome with intelligence" (from: Emblemata).

Fairy-tales can be interpreted as projections of the deepest wishes and most secret fears of mankind. They are often moralistic in character: humility and goodness are rewarded, evil and arrogance are punished. No wonder that they have always played such a big role in childhood education. The familiar fable of "The Two Frogs" is clearly pedagogic in nature: two frogs, an optimist and a pessimist, fall into a milk barrel and are at risk of drowning. The pessimist sees death approaching and does nothing but complain and cry. Meanwhile, the optimist does not waste his strength and swims and paddles so powerfully that he churns the milk into butter and is able to save himself.

Notably those fairy-tales and fables that include frogs or toads always include some allusion to "transformation" and also a link to water and rain. Both aspects reflect the two basic biological factors in amphibian life: metamorphosis and their connection to water. This is the reason behind their significant role in "magic and spells on weather" in tropical regions and in Europe. Animal transformation has a different significance in industrial than in non-industrial societies: while it tends to be associated with evil spells, magic or punishment in European latitudes, so-called primitive peoples allow animals to take human form. The transformation from human to animal form is perceived as "normal" or natural because of the human–animal relationships that prevail in those cultures. Frog-related myths also often have an erotic undertone. Marriage to the animal is not seen as indecent and there is no need for the animal to "metamorphose" into a human prior to nuptials or sexual relations. Again, this is in contrast to the European fairy-tales where such an idea is viewed as "sodomy" and rejected as unnatural and undignified for humans.

There is hardly any country without its own amphibian fairy-tale. "How two frogs traveled from Osaka to Kyoto," the Chinese fable "The Drummer Frog," "The Charms of the Lady Frog," "The Frog Who Disappeared," "Miss Frog," "The Tale of the Frog and the Deer," "Rat, Toad, and Cricket in Search of a Bride"—these are just some examples of the worldwide collection of frog fairy-tales. It is interesting to note that Anura—popularly simply referred to as "frogs"—are by far the most popular. There are few fairy-tales with newts and salamanders as protagonists.

In addition to popular fairy-tales, many famous fairy-tale and fable poets and authors return again and again to amphibians as a theme. The fables of Jean de Lafontaine (1621–1695) enjoyed such popularity that a second edition had to be printed even in the first year of publication. Lafontaine harked back to the tradition

of Aesop, a Greek poet of fables from the sixth century BC. "How Frogs Gave Hares Courage" and "How Frog and Rat Deceived Themselves" are among the best known. The tale of "How Frog Wanted to Grow Big" deals with a theme that is also reflected in the saying "*Er ist aufgeblasen wie ein Frosch*" ("He's bloated like a frog." See section on proverbs and idioms). The great Danish author Hans Christian Andersen (1805–1875) made "The Toad" immortal. The Toad of Toadhall in Kenneth Grahame's *The Wind in the Willows* also endures as a literary classic.

The fairy-tale of the fire-bellied toad—the only Grimm's fairy tale with a negative ending—could be interpreted as a warning against the senseless slaughter of animals. A little girl befriends the "domestic fire-bellied toad" in front of her parents' home; it comes crawling out of a crack in the wall every noon and drinks milk from the girl's bowl. When the mother notices this "friendship," she kills the toad without thought. From then on the girl's health deteriorates, and she loses weight and ultimately dies.

The "Frog King"—A Psychological Interpretation

No other frog-related fairy-tale figure is as familiar as the frog king. The story exists in numerous variations and it predates the version authored by the brothers Grimm. The theme can be traced back into Antiquity. The Roman poet Petronius wrote: "*Qui fuit rana nunc rex est*" (what was once a frog is now a king), and the Germanic heritage alone features 35 different version of the frog-king motif. Written sources of the fairy-tale about a girl who accepts all kinds of difficulties for the sake of an

Frog king and princess in Grimm's Fairy and Domestic Tales for Children.

enchanted frog go back to the thirteenth century in Germany. In Scotland the story was recorded in 1549. Slavic versions present the enchanted prince in the shape of a snake, because the word for frog (*zaba*) has a feminine gender. There are also fairy tales in which the enchanted frog is not a prince, but a princess. The spell is broken in the different versions by a kiss or by sleeping at the feet of the bride and groom.

Sigmund Freud's psychoanalysis views the slippery frog who wishes to slip into the bed of the princess as a barely disguised metaphor for the male sexual organ—hardly a surprising view. It must gain its rights through transformation—that is, through acceptance of the marital bond. The distinct sexual character of the story—thus the interpretation—can be seen in the older versions of the tale: "Take me to your little bed, I want to sleep next to you!" Being a "fairy tale for children," Grimm's version has a clearly moral and ethical message: one must keep one's word and one's promise, even if it is difficult.

A slightly less phallic interpretation according to C. G. Jung views the frog–royal child relationship as a metaphor of human maturity. At the beginning of the story, when the promise is made, the frog is a fat, ugly and damp creature. The princess sees in it merely a dumb animal to whom one may give an empty promise: "Listen to the simple frog babbling away, sitting in water with others of his kind and croaking, [...] and surely unfit to be companion to any human." Things get uncomfortable for the princess when the frog comes to demand that she keep her promise. "The king's daughter began to cry, she was afraid of the cold frog, which she dare not touch and which should now sleep in her beautiful, pure bed." Then came the metamorphosis, the transformation from frog to prince. He is accepted by the princess as "beloved companion and husband." Not only the frog transforms himself, but also the princess. The sequence of emotions alludes to the development of a girl once she enters into puberty. The change in attitude toward her own and the opposite sex is the main theme of the fairy tale according to this interpretation. The princess's most precious and favorite toy, the golden sphere, and the site of the games, are rich in libidinous symbolism. The playground is a "large dark forest," where a well stands beneath an old linden tree; "the well was so deep that one could not see its bottom." Only the frog can retrieve the ball, but the frog is enchanted. This enchantment is thus an impediment to the fulfillment of the wish and, from a psychoanalytical perspective, it symbolizes the difficulties experienced in moving from one phase of life into another. The transformation takes place gradually and not without inner

resistance. A new life phase begins: the girl becomes a woman.

According to psychoanalyst Ernst Aeppli, the frog is repulsive to many people as a land–water animal, but as a dream symbol it has a positive meaning. The "human-like [quality] of its webbed hands" and the transformation into a fully mature animal have made it a metaphor for the transformation of the soul. "That is why, in the fairy tale, something that is despised can become something that is admired." Aeppli holds that frogs and toads are valued differently: frogs represent the lively dream animal, while the toad represents heaviness, the female-maternal dream animal.

✎ Amphibians in Poetry and Prose

As in other aspects of the cultural history of amphibians, references to them in poetry are so abundant that we can only touch upon the subject here. One of the most familiar frog rhymes was penned by German humorist and poet Wilhelm Busch (1832–1908):

...] three weeks the frog was so ill,
now, thank the Lord, he smokes again!

The motif of the smoking frog is frequent in caricatures. Eugen Roth (1895–1976) is remarkably precise in his verse with respect to the biology of known frog and toad species.

The tree frog in the pickle jar
Property of not a few green boys
Sat upon his ladder and announced
That the weather would be foul or fair...

While this is hardly a biological fact, these lines reflect old beliefs whose origin in fact have already been discussed. The following observation is more exact:

People rightly say: a wet frog,
For usually it is no water frog.
The green and brown ones are almost alike,
The green frog living more often in a pond,
The brown one more often in a forest brook,
Frogs too have their weaknesses...

Johann Wolfgang von Goethe (1749–1832) also treated frogs in one of his many works:

A large pond was frozen over;
The little frogs lost in its depths,
Could neither croak nor leap,
Yet promised themselves half lost in dream,
If only they could find space up there,
They would jump like nightingales.
Spring winds came, the ice melted,
Now did they paddle and proudly land
And sat upon the shore far and wide
And croaked as of old.

The "War between Frogs and Mice"

One of the strangest works on amphibians in the world's literature dates back to Antiquity: the *Batrachomyomachia,* or the "war between frogs and mice." This parody claimed to be based on Homer's war epic *The Iliad*—most likely in an effort to invest it with literary value by means of attaching itself, however loosely, to the caché of Homer. That Homer would himself create a parody of his own great work is unlikely and it is believed this work was created centuries after Homer. It is dated to the fifth, possibly even the fourth or third century BC. A total of 72 hand-written manuscripts have survived of the *Batrachomyomachia,* with the oldest, probably from the tenth or eleventh century, at Oxford. From the twelfth century onward, the work fell into obscurity and regained prominence only after the invention of printing. Surprisingly, the *Batrachomyomachia* was introduced to a wider public in a Greek-Latin interlinear version in a 1486 edition printed in Venice even before editions of *The Odyssey* and *The Iliad* were printed.
Like mushrooms sprouting after a rainfall, many other editions followed in quick succession—first in Greek, then Latin, Italian, English, French and in 1595 a German version. This work, now forgotten, enjoyed great popularity and ultimately gained importance as a piece that was compulsory reading in schools.
The cause of the battle between frogs and mice is an irretrievable loss that the cowardice of one frog had brought upon the mouse population. While on a leisurely ride on the back of the frog king Physignathos, the mouse Psicharpax had drowned in a lake because the frog king had suddenly dived beneath the water's surface in fear of a hydra. The mice declared war on the frogs and—contributing to the comic character of the work—convened a gathering of the gods for this purpose. Zeus and Athena argued over who should take the side of the frogs and who should side with the mice.
Another famous work is called simply *Frogs* (in Greek *Batrachoi*) by Aristophanes (445–385 BC),

one of Athens' most influential comedic dramatists. His work is a caricature of the conditions prevailing at the time, especially the dissipation of the ancient Hellenistic ideal of life. *Frogs,* created in 405 BC, is a response to the great tragic dramatist Euripides. In this version, the frogs appear as animals from the netherworld whose job is to ward off evil.

The Roman author and imperial biographer Sueton (AD 70–140) tells of an anecdote during which the future emperor Augustus commands the frogs in his grandfather's villa garden to fall silent. Frogs featured too in the story by Roman poet Ovid (43 BC to AD 17) of Latona, mother of Apollo and Diana. In her flight from Juno, she reaches a pond in Lykia and wants to refresh herself with a drink of water. But the peasants of the village deny her the drink and purposely cloud the water by stirring up the mud on the pool bottom. Latona then transforms them into frogs by pronouncing the following sentence: "Forever shall you live in this pond." "Sub aqua, sub aqua maledicere temptant," is the poet's onomatopoeic rendering of the enchanted frogs' noisome croaking even below water.

Rollenhagen's "The Fascinating Tale of Frogs and Mice"

The tradition of satirical frog poems was continued in the work of German humorist and satirist Georg Rollenhagen (1542–1609). In 1595 he penned an animal allegory entitled "Froschmeuseler:"

The Fascinating Tale of Frogs and Mice. For the amusement, erudition and discipline of educated youth as a pretty but also useful instruction [taken] from old poets and rhyme writers and especially from observers of nature of many tame and wild animals of nature and their character. Newly and studiously collected in three volumes never before printed.

Rollenhagen took his material from the pseudo-Homeric "war between frogs and mice." Unlike that work, however, Rollenhagen's was more than satire. He wanted to tell his stories in a way that would teach "wisdom, virtue and good morals." He advises restraining oneself to essentials in the household and in private life, but emphasizes the importance of the Bible as the authoritative book on all religious questions and underscores the role of the king as political authority. The third volume takes a close look at war and the machinery of war, which he criticizes and condemns. Rollenhagen declares himself to be a dedicated pacifist and tries to explain the senselessness of any war to his readers. He also reflects on issues current in his time. Thus the frog Elbmarx (Martin Luther) fights against the deplorable state of affairs in

the spiritual (or religious) regiment of the animal kingdom, against celibacy for priests, and against the moral degeneration in religious communities. A modern variation of the old theme of war between man and beast, set against the troublesome background of rising national socialism and the impending Second World War, is the satirical-utopian work *Der Krieg mit den Molchen* (*The War with the Newts*) by Czech author Karel Čapek (1890–1938). The book tells of the threat to humankind through rising fascism and highly technologized capitalism.

The Internet: A New Chapter in the Cultural History of Amphibians

At the threshold to the new millennium, any excursion into the cultural history of amphibians would be incomplete without taking a look at the Internet. It is enough to simply enter keywords like "amphibians" or "frogs" into any search program to begin a worldwide tour of the curious world of Internet amphibians. North American zoologists, for example, comment on the growing number of malformations in amphibians, while their German colleagues provide a list of all known amphibian species. Species protection is also given its due.

But the flow of information is not restricted to factual topics. Artists creating amphibian-related work have their own sites, as does the world of gastronomy offering "delicious frog legs" and good wine. School classes report on projects and observations carried out at the local pond, publishers' provide their lists, commercial companies list their wares, herpetological societies tell of their activities. Hobbyists and owners of terrariums exchange information and ideas; a three-dimensional, hand-made frog buddha is another offering, as is a frog temple. You can order frog sweaters and the "Bad Frog Brewery & Co." promises the best thirst quencher. On the Internet you can find everything from the serious to the silly.

Proverbs and Idioms

"Frogs are always food for storks, where frogs are, storks are nearby."
While this proverb is based on observation, it isn't quite factual: storks have a varied diet. They consume insects, worms, snails, mice and other small mammals and small birds, and frogs represent only 7 to 10 percent of their food intake. In Europe, 92 bird species, in addition to the stork, are frog predators.

"When the tree frog calls it often rains. Frog chorus at night, rain will follow. The warmer the evening, the louder the frog chorus."

"Weather frog"
Records exist back into Antiquity of a belief that frogs have meteorological abilities. The link between amphibian biology and the presence of water and rain was noticed by people early on. The only European frog that truly does "announce the weather" is the tree frog. However, it does so only for weather patterns that are imminent and not for forecasts of next day's weather. When the sun shines and it is neither too cool nor too windy, tree frogs perch a few yards/meters up on branches and vegetation; when it rains they sit just above the ground. The observation that tree frogs call out more loudly on warm, still evenings than on cold evenings is indeed correct.

"You have to kiss many frogs before you find a prince."
Harks back to the fairy tale about the frog king: one has to try hard to find the right path or to find the solution for a problem.
"A toad is a toad, whether sitting or standing."
African proverb: man cannot pretend to be other than he is.

"Sit a frog on a white chair, and he will jump right back into the mud."
People should stay where they belong; it is difficult for man to change himself. Wilhem Müller after Rollenhagen's *Froschmeuseler*.

"Young frogs learn how to croak from their elders."
Children learn from their parents.
"It's not his fault that frogs have no tails."
Said of the simple-minded. In Jeremias Gotthielf (1797–1854): "They say you are a man with a golden heart but not responsible that frogs have no tail."

"Cold as a frog."
Amphibians are cold-blooded or ectothermic animals and tend to feel cold (to the human touch).

"Don't be a frog."
The same as saying: don't be a coward, offended or indecisive, don't be affected. Encouragement for someone who is frightened.

"To have a frog in one's throat"
To be hoarse, originating in the medical term "ranula" (tumor or swelling in throat or of the tongue). "Frog" is also used to describe a false note produced by a musician playing a wind instrument.

"Blown up like a frog"
When the frog inflates himself to the size of a bull he must burst. Based on Phaedrus' fable "The Burst Frog and the Ox" ("*Rana rupta et bos*"). The frog saw an ox grazing and envied it

© *Metzler Verlag*
The stork, commonly held to be frogs' primary "enemy," feeds on Anura only to a small degree.

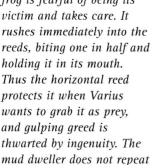

"Varius, the fish in the river Nile, hovers in vain; for the frog is fearful of being its victim and takes care. It rushes immediately into the reeds, biting one in half and holding it in its mouth. Thus the horizontal reed protects it when Varius wants to grab it as prey, and gulping greed is thwarted by ingenuity. The mud dweller does not repeat the plaintive call of old: underlings can fool their masters only by force of numbers." (from: Emblemata).

Right: Frog "school class" from the Musée d'Estavayer-le-Lac.

its size. He began to puff himself up to reach the desired size until he burst. To make more of oneself than one is is boasting. Anurans will often "inflate themselves" when threatened by snakes or other predators, to impress their enemy or to make it more difficult for the snake to swallow them. In the breeding season, their bodies can also appear swollen in size. Ever since Antiquity, (Petronius: "*inflat se tanquam rana*") frogs have been considered as puffed up, boastful, stupid, cowardly and gossipy.

"He's making frog's eyes."

When observing a frog from a "frog's perspective," its bulging eyes are especially noticeable.

"Jump like a frog"
"Jumping like a frog in moonshine"

To move forward in a leaping manner, bit by bit. This idiom is based on one of the most characteristic features of a frog: his ability to jump. The leaping frog can jump across distances that are 20 times its own body length.

"Fire-bellied toad call"
"Don't toad around"

The monotonous, endless, reciprocal toad calls can evoke a melancholy, even depressive mood. Popular belief has always interpreted them in this manner. Hence: to drag something down, to complain.

"He counts his toads."
[Kröte = toad; Kröte *sl.* = money]

To count one's money, to watch one's money. An ancient Bavarian superstition believed that the toad was a protective spirit of homes and guardian of wealth.

"Geldprotz—miser"
[Protz = old Bavarian for toad (see above)]: miser, or someone who boasts with his wealth. Toads were often depicted on wallets and money chests, symbolizing either the avarice of the owner or ensuring the safety of the treasure.

"From the frog's perspective"

Looking at things from the bottom. In film, a camera angle showing an object from below and making it appear larger than it is.

"Giving water to a frog"
"Giving frogs a drink"
"Catching frogs instead of fish"

To bring someone things they do not need, or do something useless. Documented in written records as early as the mystic and theologian Sebastian Franck (1490–1542) and Jakob Ayrer (1543–1605). "Think they have been fishing and instead have caught a frog." The same as "bringing owls to Athens" or "coals to Newcastle."

The Frogs of Estavayer

More than 100 years ago, Francois Perrier, a retired captain from the Vatican's Swiss Guards, amused himself by making figures out of frogs and staging them in settings of everyday human life. The funny models can be admired in a local museum (Musée d'Estavayer-le-Lac) in Estavayer (Stäffis-on-the-Lake) in Switzerland. The captain dissected dead frogs with great dexterity, removing the entrails and filling the empty shell with sand, after which he formed his models. He then dried them, lacquered the models and inserted porcelain eyes and used them to mimic the good citizens of Estavayer in caricatures of village life. The "toads from Nicaragua"—available for little money at the market in Masaya—are like the "frogs from Estavayer." They are prepared in a similar manner and, with models of musical instruments, they are assembled into a toad orchestra.

The Impressive Career of Frogs in Advertising
Walter Hödl

Frogs in advertising are nothing new, as we can see from the pictures in the introduction to this chapter. However, they have become a preferred advertising medium in this industry only in the past few years. In advertisements for cleaning products, there is an obvious connection between the medium and the product: happy frogs like happy people need clean water and a healthy environment. To ensure clean water and a healthy environment, we should use environmentally friendly cleaning products. After all, future generations should also be allowed to experience nature including frogs living in clean water something that used to be a normal experience for every child.

Since advertising reflects the spirit of the times, major international companies must have a reason for using the frog as an advertising vehicle. Perhaps frogs embody our longing for a healthy and whole environment. Or, maybe, as we can see in the advertising for some products, the advertising industry uses the phenomenon of the young child syndrome. Like fairy-tale and cartoon characters, the fact that frogs have big eyes, a large head and rounded body parts endears them to us.

The red frog, probably the most famous amphibian used as an advertising vehicle in German-speaking countries, has promoted Erdal shoe polish, manufactured by the company Werner A. Mertz in Mainz, for more than 80 years. The graphic image of the red frog has been retouched and updated repeatedly during that period. In 1986, the red frog was given a colleague. We can tell by its crown that the red frog was borrowed from the fairy-tale Frog Prince. The use of this other frog, with the friendly green trade mark Frog, which advertises an ecological product line offered by the same company, has led to a major increase in profits.

Phrynohyas resinifictrix, which lives in the canopy of the Amazon rain forest, also came to European television ads. It uses both of its giant laryngeal sacs to promote increased safety with the use of airbags manufactured by the automotive company Mazda. The list of examples of frogs conquering the world of advertising is endless.

Using the beautifully colored green toad (Bufo viridis) was a natural choice for this advertising campaign about "Kröten" (= "toads," German slang for money). Its better known and widely distributed sister species, the common toad, has very bland coloring and would not have made a good subject for advertising purposes.

The Salamander and Fire

Myths of the salamander's invulnerability to fire, already mentioned by Pliny the Elder, were perpetuated in the *Physiologus* mentioned earlier in this chapter. A strange mix of traditions and written records resulted in many fantastic legends about amphibians. "The salamander extinguishes fire per force of its unique power, all the more would it seem appropriate, that the righteous who walk the path of righteousness also extinguish the threatening fire and stuff it into the throat of the lion."

What is probably the strangest passage in the *Physiologus* states that the salamander is "a cold bird... colder than all [other] birds." It was presumed to live inside the volcano Aetna without burning up. This may be a misinterpretation of the legend about the mythical phoenix.

But myths about the salamander's invulnerability to fire were not widespread only among scholars and alchemists—they were part of the popular belief and oral history. According to popular belief only those humans who were somehow "brethren" of fire could come into contact with salamanders. Charcoal burners whose task it was to keep the fires going in remote forests and gorges in order to produce vital fuel fell into this category. When they looked into their element, they saw reflections of the strangest beings. It is possible that every now and then a salamander *did* crawl out from under the wood stacks covered in soil. It may have found a welcome hiding place in the stack and have been startled by the sudden heat. Blacksmiths, alchemists and gipsies were close to

fire and entered into pacts with creatures from other elements.

Young alchemists often wandered from town to town and country to country, propagating their ideas and teachings. Some customs of brotherhoods and student associations may even be derived from such teachings, among them the custom of "calling in the salamander" during which high-proof alcohol is lit and poured down one's throat.

Alchemists knew the European Fire salamander as a symbol for sulphur (the yellow spots of the salamander help explain this link), which in turn stood for all that was combustible. Thus a French alchemist reported: "The salamander, which feeds on fire, and the phoenix, which is reborn out of its own ashes, are the two best-known symbols for sulphur."

When asbestos was discovered, the material was thought of as "salamander's wool" for a long time. Somewhere in Asia, between Tibet, India and Siberia, the so-called "fire worms" were believed to live. They supposely fashioned fire-proof thread, similar to the silk spun by caterpillars. "Women there throw their clothes into fire for cleaning...." A book from 1481 reports: "This salamander carries wool, from which clothes and belts are made which do not burn in fire..."

The salamander in fire can also be a symbol for the purity reached by means of fire: "Look, the salamander walks right through the flames unharmed. Purity always remains unharmed." The poem "The Salamander and a Jealous Human of

"Fire salamander" (from: Emblemata)

*Countless legends about its toxicity and supposed resistance to fire have made the European spotted or fire salamander (*Salamandra salamandra*) one of the best-known European amphibians.*

Fire salamander illustrated in Iconografia della fauna Italica *by C. L. P. Bonaparte, 1841.*

the Same Kind" from the sixteenth century should be interpreted as a metaphor for jealousy and malicious pleasure or gloating at someone else's misfortune:

The salamander shows jealousy
Rejoicing when things go wrong
And when others do well
[He] is miserable and does himself harm…
…Now guard yourself against such feelings
For neither advantage nor gain will they bring;
The jealous heart is its own agony
And always does itself harm…

The eerie world of moors and stagnat, foul water was populated with firey creatures in man's imagination. "City dwellers" had always been opposed to such swamps, but not only in order to gain more firm ground for building. These environments were simply full of occurences for which there seemed to be no explanation. Will o' wisps, fire people, fire snakes, flaming lizards or salamanders, again and again observed by the common people, were later declared as nonsense and superstitions by scholars in the eighteenth and nineteenth century because they could find no rational explanation. Swamp gases (methane) which would spontaneously burst into flames does—or rather, did—exist as a kind of wandering *fata morgana* of light when swamps still stretched across large areas.

Natural philosopher and physician Paracelsus (1493–1541) held that because they were creatures of fire, salamanders could not interact with humans, in contrast to creatures of water which were well-disposed towards humans. In the popular belief of his time, salamanders were neither demons nor symbols of evil, but instead god-sent keepers of the element. In the Renaissance, on the other hand, they were called "vulcanales," and it

was even claimed that less-pure hybrid creatures derived from them (these were called "tinder"). The allegoric poem "The Salamander" by Russian aristrocrat Wladimir Odojewskij (1803–1869), strongly influenced by Paracelsus, contains a remarkable summary of the alchemists' ideas on fire creatures, spirits of the elements and salamanders. In the epic poem, an old Finnish shaman encourages a girl called Elsa to awaken the "salamander," the fire spirit of her soul. The story, one of the best "magical" works in literature, reaches a tragic end that carries within it a warning applicable to the modern world. It warns of the dangers which await megalomaniac civilizations. While they have reached a high level of understanding and knowledge, even incorporating the "magical" wisdom of earlier ages, a lack of love and consideration for nature ultimately prevents man from obtaining any gain from his self-absorbed and self-serving research.

"Two circumstances have long given the newt a bad name, one being the suspicion of poison, the other, the supposed ability to live in fire. The latter is partly true inasmuch as it can remain without harm in a dampened down coal fire for some time by giving off a juice through its mouth and small openings dispersed all across its body, which extinguishes some of the fire and cools the embers a little. In full flames, however, he must perish like all other animals. The written records of the Ancients contain much about the poison of the newt and its effects and there is no basis for this…The usefulness of this creature is that it eats insects. Before it was also often used in the apothecary, where now no one will touch it." (*Krünitzsche Encyclopedia, end of eighteenth century*).

"See, the salamander walks through fire without coming to harm. Purity too is always impervious to injury." (from: Emblemata).

Thomas Schmuck

The Midwife Toad and Human Progress

When Paul Kammerer (1880–1926) discovered a rare toad on his aunt's country estate in Bohemia—unfortunately there is no record of the species—he kissed it reverently on the head. And his aunt promptly fainted. When she recovered, she gave her nephew a nickname which would stick, although he was already in his thirties. She called him a "toadkisser."

Paul Kammerer (1880–1926), famous herpetologist and defender of Lamarckism, already outdated even in his day.

The Tragic Fate of a Herpetologist

Those who are interested in amphibians are familiar with such experiences and the more or less indulgent incomprehension that is often the response—not only from elderly aunts—to herpetology as an occupation.

Yet the amusing anecdote has a deeply tragic end: a few years after this "toad kiss," on September 23, 1926, Paul Kammerer shot himself on a lonely forest path on Mount Schneeberg. He had been a famous scientist, a ladies' man and the center of Viennese "high society." His suicide occurred days before a scheduled journey to Moscow, where he was to assume the directorship of a prestigious Russian research institution. He had become one of the most important herpetologists worldwide. His deed was the final act in one of the greatest criminal cases in science of this century, a philosophical and scientific debate that raged with suspicions, accusations and falsification of scientific results.

Paul Kammerer—who named his daughter Lacerta (lizard)—began his herpetological career with the study of fire-bellied and alpine salamanders, olms and midwife toads. At the "vivarium" in Vienna's Prater, one of the first research installations for experimental biology, young scientists worked under the leadership of Hans Przibram to uncover answers to questions on reproduction, development and heredity. This was the beginning of the twentieth century, a time of triumph for Darwin, of rediscovering of Mendel, and of Ernst Haeckel's controversial writings on evolution.

Kammerer was a talented zoologist and was often the first to succeed in raising many species through several generations, including species which others had failed to keep alive. This fact alone makes his writings about vivaristics fascinating reading. At the same time he successfully carried out several astonishing experiments which proved amphibians' impressive potential for adaptability. He forced the viviparous alpine salamander (*Salamandra atra*) into laying eggs in water, while coercing the fire-bellied salamander (*Salamandra salamandra*) into becoming viviparous. He raised new strands of fire salamanders, all black or pure yellow depending on the base color.

Kammerer kept olms (*Proteus anguinus*) in the dark, moist cellar of his vivarium. He noticed more or less by accident that olms were also able to give birth to live young. This had already been described by Michahelles in 1831. Since olms usually lay eggs, he began to search for a cause for (ovo-) viviparity. He thought that it lay in water temperature, but did not exclude the possibility of other, additional causes. Moreover, he was able to breed dark-pigmented specimens and olms with functional eyes.

Kammerer as Lamarckist

Today we would identify the high adaptive potential of these animals as the cause for this variability in morphology and behavior among olms. On the other hand, we would also consider the fact that these subterranean karst populations have very little interpopulation genetic exchange, which would result in the formation of many unique characters. Black olms as well as olms with eyes have since been discovered in nature. Kammerer, however, interpreted his observations as an indication of how acquired characteristics could become hereditary, and as proof of Lamarckism, which was already considered outdated at that time. Lamarckism taught that acquired characteristics could become inherited. The abilities and characteristics acquired by an individual during its lifetime would, according to Lamarck, find their way into the genetic makeup over the course of several generations until they became hereditary. Even Darwin had not fully excluded the possibility of such hereditary processes.

Kammerer had succeeded in getting midwife toads (*Alytes obstetricans*) to lay their eggs in water by increasing the water temperature; he even managed to shift their mating act into water. It seems that the males redeveloped "mating calluses," which they needed to hold onto the female in water, even though they had previously lost this feature as part of their specialized reproductive strategy. To Kammerer, this was yet another indication of the heredity of acquired characteristics…

Searching for the Meaning of Research

What distinguished Kammerer from many other biologists was that he questioned whether his research had societal relevance: "Despite the most vivid interest in the reproductive process of midwife toads, I could not escape the depressing thought that this minute and detailed research could make no contribution to the wellbeing of society as a whole." He felt that this pursuit was ultimately meaningless.

Only Ernst Haeckel's writings taught him how to look upon scientific research, in all its details, in an overarching biological, philosophical and political context. Every bit of progress in knowledge is beneficial to mankind, "and hence the researcher of nature, absorbed by his original work, need not necessarily be a useless member of human society after all." The step toward Lamarckism, as Kammerer understood it, was only a small one once he had reached this realization.

Kammerer took the Lamarckist model to the extreme. In an analogy to hereditary processes in amphibians, albeit with elevated moral impetus, he held that "every act, yes, in its summation, even every word, be it good or bad, takes on evolutionary significance." If it could be proven that acquired characteristics were hereditary in the animal kingdom, then this would be vitally important with respect to the potential for progress in humans: "Some trace of what we have learned and achieved must transfer organically to our descendants!"

Kammerer's dissatisfaction with a mere theory of selection, in which he saw more "destruction" than "new creation," and his efforts on behalf of the Lamarckist concept, led him on a path from biology into politics. Kammerer was a socialist, but less a strict Marxist than a defender of a diffusive faith in progress that proposed that the misery of the present time would be resolved by a better future. He felt that direct manipulation of the hereditary mate-

rial would be a means of bringing this future about and of helping to actively create and design it. And in this manner he hoped to "liberate the high human potential for progress and development from the yoke of regression."

Kammerer's Tragic End

But the midwife toad would seal Kammerer's fate. The only remaining preserved specimen to support his views—all others had been lost during the First World War—was unmasked as a fake. Ink injections had artificially created false "mating calluses" in the male. Strangely, the very same specimen had previously been presented to leading biologists in England, who were unable to detect any manipulation despite close inspection under the microscope. It is still unclear who was ultimately responsible for the manipulation. All those who knew Kammerer swore that he would never have committed such a deed himself. Nevertheless, his reputation as a scientist lay in ruins and he committed suicide.

Long after Kammerer's death, in the Soviet Union, Lamarckism was declared to be the only correct explanation for evolution and heredity, personally decreed by Stalin. Mendel—suspect because he was a priest—and Morgan—an American—were denounced. The great Russian geneticists died in Siberian concentration camps or fled the country. This is a chapter in the history of natural science that remains to be fully acknowledged even today. But the personal story of Paul Kammerer had been given consideration: the commissioner of culture, Anatoli W. Lunatscharski, a close friend of Lenin, wrote a script for a film about the life of Kammerer. In the film version, the scientist is defeated by dark machinations of titled reactionaries and priests. The film, *Salamandra*, became a hit in Russia. Few herpetologists can lay claim to having their life commemorated in literature and in film.

*The males of the midwife toad (*Alytes obstetricans*) transport fertilized eggs on their back. Paul Kammerer's downfall was caused by supposed mock claspers on the frontal extremities of these amphibians. The claspers enable males in many Anura species to hold onto the back of the female, but they are absent in midwife toads because of their unusual terrestrial reproduction strategy.*

Joseph Schmuck

Amphibians in Human Nutrition

Nutrition can be considered from two perspectives. On the one hand, it has a biological function, which applies equally to humans and animals—namely, to satisfy hunger and supply the elements necessary for life. On the other hand—especially in the so-called civilized world—nutrition serves simply to delight the palate. However, that is mostly the privilege of humans. We are perfectly entitled to make what we eat as tasty as possible, but serious questions must be raised when food is wasted, when our overexploitation of natural resources leads to near-extinction of certain species, or when our nourishment entails unimaginable suffering for animals.

Amphibians as Food

The powerful thigh muscles of many Anura species played a role in the dwindling of their numbers. Large Ranidae (true frogs) are especially at risk due to the high demand in the western world. Below: Marsh frog (Rana ridibunda).

Throughout the ages and all over the globe, humans have eaten amphibians—when they were available. Even today they are an important source of protein in some Third World countries. Anurans are easy to catch, and due to their high reproductive rate—especially in marshy areas of the world—represent a seemingly inexhaustible source of food. In countries where many inhabitants constantly go hungry, almost all parts of frogs are eaten. However, in these countries not a single species of frog has

been endangered or brought to the brink of extinction through traditional nutritional practices!

But the situation looks quite different when we examine the consumption of frogs in Europe or the countries formerly colonized by European powers. In past centuries frog dishes were considered as particularly delicious Lenten fare all over the continent. The clergy, the aristocracy and the rich middle classes have always savored frogs' legs, giving proof of the human ingenuity with which the church's unpopular regulations

for Lent were circumvented. Since meat was forbidden on days of fasting, the church permitted consumption of frogs and fish because of their "coldbloodedness" and amphibious existence. A dozen to twenty pairs of frogs' legs were allotted per person. Only the legs were eaten—the rest of the animal was discarded.

In order to obtain the frogs' legs it was customary—and still is—to sever the rear limbs from the living animals right where they were caught. Still alive, the "refuse" is usually thrown back into the water. The "refuse" is fortunate if a predatory fish or bird of prey is close by to make a grab for it. Otherwise the refuse is condemned to a slow, agonizing and wretched death, which most of the "gourmets" have probably never watched. This cruelty to animals doesn't happen out of necessity but purely to fulfill a questionable "delight of the palate." As cooks in earlier times did under the guise of Lenten dishes, today's "nouvelle cuisine" devises even more fanciful frog offerings. Most self-respecting cookbooks contain recipes for frogs' legs, be it as frog soup, or as breaded, marinated, fried, stewed or steamed dishes.

Consequences of Frog Consumption

Since the loss of amphibian habitat in Europe has been dramatic—most wetlands have been drained—and amphibians are protected in almost all European countries, the enormous demand for frogs' legs is primarily filled from Asia. Every day tons of the animals are caught in the wild in order that European and American chefs may indulge their already-sated clients and further aggravate the illnesses caused by civilization.

It is a fact that the unlimited overexploitation of Asian frogs has dramatically reduced frog populations in many localities. Everyone in Europe, the U.S.A. or in other countries of the western world who eats frogs' legs should therefore consider that by so doing they are

- aggravating the hunger of a generally already hungry population,
- encouraging extreme cruelty to animals,
- contributing to the loss of frogs that previously controlled "harmful" insects, whose populations are now exploding, and simultaneously promoting the production and application of dangerous environmental pollutants instead, as well as
- participating in the extirpation of species.

In addition, suppliers of frogs' legs, already extremely rich, get even richer and the chemical pesticide industry flourishes. Vast amounts of DDT and other environmental poisons, some of which have long been prohibited in developed nations, are now being dumped on Asian rice paddies to deal with increasing insect pests caused by the missing "insecticide"—the frog.

In view of these facts, one can only hope that the exploitation of frogs will be stopped by the authorities, and wish—somewhat maliciously—that these frog delicacies will stick in the craw

Species	Local consumption in	Exported to	Population
(Leptodactylidae)			
Caudiverbera caudiverbera	Central America		
Leptodactylus fallax	Dominican Republic	Guadaloupe	very endangered
L. pentadactylus	South America	–	
(Ranidae)			
Conraua goliath	Equatorial Guinea, Cameroun, Gabun	–	very engangered
Discodeles guppyi	Asia		–
Euphlyctis hexadactylus	Bangladesh, India	Europe, America	endangered
E. cyanophlyctis	Bangladesh, India	Europe, America	endangered
Hoplobatrachus tigerinus	Bangladesh, India	Europe, America	endangered
Limnonectes cancrivorus	Indonesia, Malaysia, Philippines	Europe, America	at risk
L. blythii	Indonesia, Malaysia	Europe, America	at risk
L. grunniens	Indonesia	Europe, America	
L. ibanorum	Indonesia	Europe, America	at risk
L. ingeri	Indonesia, Malaysia	Europe, America	endangered
L. kuhlii	Indonesia	Europe, America	at risk
L. limnocharis	Thailand, Philippines, Bangladesh, India, Indonesia	Europe, America	at risk
L. macrodon	Indonesia	Europe, America	endangered
L. paramacrodon endangered	Indonesia	–	Europe, America
L. raja	South East Asia	–	–
Paa boulengeri	China	–	–
P. liebigii	South East Asia	–	–
P. spinosa	South East Asia	–	–
P. sternosignata	South East Asia	–	–
Pyxicephalus adspersus	Africa	–	–
Rana andersonii	South East Asia	–	–
R. arfaki	Indonesia	Europe, America	–
R. arvalis	Europe	–	endangered
R. catesbeiana	USA, Indonesia	Europe	at risk
*R. crassa**	India	Europe, America	endangered
R. dalmatina	Europe	Europe, America	endangered
R. erythraea	South East Asia	–	–
R. esculenta	Europe	Europe, America	endangered
R. glandulosa	South East Asia	–	–
R. grisea	New Guinea	–	–
R. hosii	South East Asia	–	–
R. jimiensis	New Guinea	–	–
R. lessonae	Europe	Europe, America	endangered
R. livida	South East Asia	–	–
*R. magna**	Indonesia, Philippines	Europe, America	–
*R. malesiana**	Indonesia	Europe, America	–
R. miopus	Indonesia	Europe, America	–
*R. modesta**	China	Europe, America, Asia	endangered
R. nigromaculata	South East Asia	–	–
*R. nitida**	Burma	–	–
R. oatesii	New Guinea	–	–
R. papua	Southwestern Europe	–	endangered
R. perezi	Europe	Europe, America	endangered
R. ridibunda	Malaysia	Europe, America	at risk
*R. rugulosa**	North Africa	–	–
R. saharica	Europe	Europe, America	at risk

Anura species used for human consumption and export and their endangerment status.
* the taxonomic status of these species has changed in recent years.

Frog imports into France from different countries (in tonnes)						
Year	Turkey	India	Indonesia	Bangladesh	Switzerland	Other
1973	103	628	1509	–	–	38
1974	36	440	830	–	–	41
1975	170	521	1024	60	–	139
1976	171	1502	963	30	–	109
1977	190	1369	1306	172	–	114
1978	212	1451	1289	153	–	52
1979	141	1756	1927	151	70	68
1980	126	1761	1635	259	218	47
1981	256	1760	1935	207	226	132
1982	155	1145	902	168	170	88
1983	253	1020	2111	594	130	114
1984	147	723	1638	152	40	43
1985	272	284	2105	161	65	49
1986	297	208	2659	72	29	157
1987	165	8	2303	60	45	450
Total	2694	14576	24136	2239	993	1641

Year (in tonnes)	India	Bangladesh	Indonesia
1963	514	––	––
1964	332	––	––
1965	44	––	––
1966	557	––	––
1967	786	––	––
1968	425	––	––
1969	854	––	––
1970	2545	––	––
1971	1451	––	––
1972	1823	––	––
1973	2698	––	––
1974	1454	––	––
1975	1317	––	––
1976	3170	––	––
1977	2834	372	––
1978	3570	1184	––
1979	3764	987	––
1980	3095	675	1517
1981	4368	1204	1612
1982	2271	(IX 81 – IX 82) 3498	2776
1983	3658	(IX 82 – IX 83) 2587	3262
1984	2834	(IX 83 – IX 84) 2511	2140
1985	2778	1948	2718
1986	680	2471	3690
1987	––	2512	3004

Table, right: Volume of frozen frog legs (in tonnes) exported from the three main export countries– India, Bangladesh and Indonesia.

of their consumers. It is not the same thing for a starving Bangladeshi to devour a frog "with hide and hair"—even if the frog species is possibly endangered—than for some Westerner to gorge ecstatically on a leg of the same species. If we consider the extermination of entire populations and species of frogs and the resulting dire consequences already mentioned above, a dish of "Grenouille sautée à la Bordelaise" is a thoughtless, irresponsible and dubious pleasure.

Frogs' Legs—A Profitable Trade

The frightening statistics cited in the tables will allow the reader to understand the remarks made above, and to realize that they are not just the subjective feelings of a few conservationists. In order to facilitate a deeper understanding we have listed the place where the frog species usually provides an important source of protein, as well as whether that species is exported and to what country. We can hardly raise objections to the local consumption of amphibians, since it does not threaten their

A Latin American restaurant advertises fish as well as frog delicacies (Rana).

existence, as has already been mentioned. The list does not claim to be comprehensive, but most important exported species are included, especially those already endangered by this overexploitation.

To supply the 3,004 tonnes of frogs' legs exported from Indonesia in 1987, 60 to 82 million frogs were killed. This quantity was eaten in at least 5 million servings at European and American gourmet restaurant tables. Only in one year, and counting only the frogs coming from Indonesia! In 1998 the annual consumption rate of frogs' legs was about 200 million pairs.

As the tables make clear, export from Bangladesh and Indonesia only began when the species *Euphlyctis hexadactylus* and *Hoplobatrachus tigerinus* were added to Appendix II (second-highest protective status) of CITES (Convention of International Trade in Endangered Species of wild fauna and flora). The trade then immediately focused on other Asian species. Prime importers and consumers of frogs' legs are the U.S.A., Belgium, Holland and, above all, France. Frog dishes are also offered in restaurants all over Europe and Australia, but not to the same extent as in the four countries listed above. In recent years many Chinese restaurants have increasingly been serving these specialties.

As a non-producing nation, Switzerland is noticeable for agreeing quite vigorously with the trade. This becomes evident when you examine Swiss export figures. Switzerland

imports not only deep-frozen frogs' legs, but also live frogs for consumption. Many of the imported frogs are then re-exported.

The tables show clearly why the representatives of Switzerland and many other nations so vehemently oppose the protection of amphibians at the various conferences for species protection.

Import of frogs into Switzerland (in tonnes)		
Year	live frogs	frog legs
1983	152,5	199,6
1984	160,9	166,6
1985	100,8	143,6
1986	113.3	134,2
1987	127,0	166,0
1988	121,2	170,8
1989	107,8	137,5
1990	124,0	135,2
1991	93,3	137,8
1992	81,9	156,9
1993	no data	no data
1994	84,3	141,0
1995	67,8	151,0

Here, too, business is threatened by the imposition of protection. The paradoxical nature of our society is demonstrated by the fact that in most European countries—even those who are prime consumers of frogs—most or even all indigenous amphibians are protected because they are considered threatened or even highly endangered. Massive harvesting of animals from the wild would be unthinkable here. However, the import of unimaginable quantities of frogs from the Third World in the manner of centuries-old colonial exploitation is deemed quite acceptable.

If we do not succeed in checking the trade in frogs, soon entire populations in many countries, especially in Asia, will be extinct, and the ecological balance will suffer a lasting upheaval. This is already a sad reality in many largely "defrogged" areas.

Many South East Asian markets offer frogs for sale; they are an important nutritional component for the local population.

Christian Proy

Keeping and Breeding Amphibians

Keeping amphibians in captivity has a long tradition in Europe. The first written evidence of frogs as "parlor buddies" is contained in a book entitled Natural History of Household Pets, Amphibians, Frogs, Insects, Worms *by Johann Matthaeus Bechstein (1797). To begin with, a terrarium was a simple container in which to keep the greatest number of collectibles—in this case live amphibians. Attention to the conditions in which the amphibians were kept came at a much later date. Owners tried to care for their specimens in the best possible way and to keep them alive for as long as possible. But the first real turnaround did not occur until the 1930s. Among those who have maintained terrariums, Willy Woltersdorff (1864-1943) and Richard Oeser (1891-1974) are considered the "fathers of keeping and breeding amphibians," for salamanders and frogs, respectively.*

Why Do We Keep and Breed Amphibians as Pets?

There are many reasons why amphibians are kept in captivity. Zoologists, terrarium owners and amphibian "fans" will gladly accept the inconveniences of escaped or lost specimens, loud nocturnal croaking, regular changes of water, and much more, for the benefit of coming in close contact with these creatures. The pets are kept in attractively planted marsh terraria in the living room or in separate rooms designed specifically for more elaborate terrarium installations.

There are those to whom a terrarium is a miniature section of nature, albeit artificially created, inside their home. Their hobby enables them to get in touch with the mysteries of nature. But

Tree frogs (Hylidae) are among the most popular amphibians—and not only with owners of terrariums. The South American genus Phyllomedusa, *here P. hypochondrialis, has many colorful representatives with fascinating behavior patterns.*

are amphibians kept and bred in captivity not only out of biological interest, but also for the purpose of selling them or to exchange with other enthusiasts. Monetary gain is second to trade in caecilians, olms, newts and salamanders. Among Anura, the colorful diurnal Dendrobatidae are especially sought after and accordingly more expensive. You can learn more about the "market situation" by visiting an amphibian show or browsing through specialty journals in which amphibians are sought or offered for sale. National and international laws relating to care, trade and transport should always be observed. Reliable and ethical local hobbyist associations are good sources of information on any of these issues. At the same time, these associations provide a forum for exchanging information on practical experience and scientific discussion through various workshops and special interest groups and their trade publications.

A growing number of terrarium owners are hobby zoologists interested in the natural sciences, but also—and this is especially true for Europe—professional herpetologists. All consciously benefit from the experience of keeping and caring for amphibians in captivity to help decipher the secrets of their biology. The mating behavior, reproduction, egg laying, transporting and feeding of larvae (brood care) of the strawberry poison-dart frog (*Dentrobates pumilio*), for example, were described for the first time through observation in a terrarium.

Amphibian research is often much easier in a terrarium than in the field. Terrestrial caecilians, but also salamanders and frogs, lead a very secretive life. They are difficult to locate in nature and can be observed in a terrarium with much less effort (for example, darkened window

panes to cover the openings into their subterranean tunnels). Another advantage of the terrarium is the individual access to each animal and the certainty of being able to observe it over long periods of time. In this manner, data can be gathered on reproductive rate, ontogenesis, or possible gender transformation, without having to resort to compromising the fitness of the amphibians through toe clipping, dye injections or other methods of marking and tagging.

Individual reaction is the key to researching mating behavior and brood care. Questions such as "Do parents watch over their nest?", "Do they feed the larvae?", "How does intraspecific communication work?" and others can be answered systematically. To do so, simple manipulative measures are required, such as removing a nest, exchanging one mating partner for another, or other clearly traceable experimental arrangements. This precise approach was used to research the brood care of the Central American spine-headed tree frog (*Anotheca spinosa*), a species that lays eggs in tree hollows, by creating artificial situations such as removing the larvae or the male from the breeding basin.

The natural tree hollow, impossible to monitor in nature, was replaced by an artificial hollow with an observation window. In the case of *Ichthyophis kohtaoensis*, a caecilian species from Thailand, a terrarium experiment during which the system of subterranean paths was blocked into sections at different times led to the discovery that the tunnels are used over long periods of time and that the species repeatedly return to designated resting areas.

Much depends on luck in amphibian observation. In the open field, this means "being at the right place at the right time." Generally, both personal and financial efforts are enormous. Because hobbyists tend to spend many hours observing their pets and because they are near them day after day, the probability of chance discoveries and observations is very high. For example, young hatching from the back of the South American Surinam toad *Pipa pipa* were observed for the first time in a terrarium.

Countless questions remain unanswered. Thus some issues related to systematics were solved through cross-breeding experiments in a

Dendrobates reticulatus has impressive coloring. Dendrobatidae are often kept in terrariums. Many aspects of their biology have been studied there.

Struggle for territorial dominance between Dendrobates tinctorius *(top, larger specimen) and* Dendrobates pumilio *(below, smaller specimen). Victory was announced with loud calling.*

Modern food supplements, customized lamps, heating pads, etc. all the way to computer-controlled installations make it possible to respond to all the needs of amphibians in captivity. Despite this array of equipment, don't forget that proper care also requires a basic knowledge of biology and a measure of sensitivity on the part of the keeper.

Outdoor Terrariums and Greenhouses

For amphibians from temperate zones (to some degree also for tropical species during the summer months), outdoor terraria are preferable and highly recommended. Natural influences such as unfiltered sunlight, rain and nightly drops in temperature have a positive effect on health and reproduction. When preparing an outdoor terrarium, ensure that sufficient barriers for burrowing and climbing species are in place. Tree frogs can escape even the highest barriers and can only be kept in terrariums completely surrounded by mesh. An outdoor terrarium can become a focal point in a garden by adding a pond or incorporating a section of a creek, which would also contribute to excellent maintenance and breeding conditions.

Similar factors apply to greenhouses planted with subtropical or tropical plants. A greenhouse provides a more or less oversized terrarium environment with increased space in which to create different structures and microclimates for the amphibians to utilize as the need arises. Another advantage over indoor terraria is the high light intensity that can be achieved, although this also presents a great danger. The greenhouse should be protected against overheating by shading the glazed surfaces or by using customized insulated glass that reflects infrared radiation.

The Indoor Terrarium

Since amphibians constantly require moisture, materials such as glass, acrylic and unplasticized PVC are well suited for building indoor terraria. Silicon in a base of acetic acid can also be used to protect glass panes and to attach various equipment such as rocks and roots. Plastic grilles are more suited for ventilation than metal screens because they allow more light to penetrate into the terrarium. The mesh width should be chosen keeping in mind the smallest animals used for feeding—for fruitflies (*Drosophila*) it should be a maximum of 0.7 mm, for example.

Before constructing a terrarium, decide which species you wish to keep and what their habitat requirements are. For larval phases, as well as the aquatic phases of newts and salamanders or aquatic caecilians and frogs, an aquarium is a

terrarium, and in other instances the species association of larvae was solved by raising them in a terrarium.

Breeding rare, endangered species in terrariums at least offers the potential for recolonization in nature—for example, after local catastrophes. But this only makes sense if the natural habitat is prepared and protected. One example of this kind of action is the protection and reintroduction program for the Majorca midwife toad (*Alytes muletensis*).

Keeping and Breeding Amphibians in Captivity

The practice of keeping and breeding amphibians has become much easier and there is a wide range of support and information available through local pet stores. One need only look at the efforts that Johann von Fischer undertook to heat a terrarium with a spirit stove and thermosiphon, documented in his 1884 volume *The Terrarium: Planting and Populating*.

better choice. It should be as large as possible. Water depth depends on the species, the season and other factors. It may range from an inch or so (a few centimeters) (for fire-bellied toads) to more than 20 inches (half a meter) (for pipas). The aquarium opening must be securely locked as some species (for example, caecilians) leave their aquatic habitat for short periods of time even in nature. It is best to mount the cover on a slant to allow condensation to run off. Islands for basking (for example, for paradox frogs) can be constructed from glass strips or pieces of cork. The openings for ventilation can be set into the side walls or the rear wall above water level, cut out in a circle and covered with mesh.

For terrestrial species, terraria with a fairly shallow basin are best. Burrowing frogs and caecilians require a substrate that is at least 1 foot (30 cm) deep. Tree frogs and climbing salamanders need sufficient height and good ventilation, while ground-dwelling species require a large enough ground surface. Authorities often call for a definition of specific terrarium dimensions for each species, but these are difficult to establish because they depend on too many parameters, such as gender, age and size of the individuals, internal structure of the space. and because most of these factors have not been researched.

For all terraria, experience has shown that it is best to drill holes for water intake and outlet, as well as openings for heating cables, water pump cables, measuring probes or small ventilators. Air intake can be placed directly beneath the viewing panel, and ventilation can be made through the lid. The heat radiating from the lighting installation inside the terrarium creates a temperature gradient inside the terrarium. This

in turn causes air circulation along the surface of the walls, keeping them free of condensation. Another option is to install small ventilators and the corresponding control mechanism to supply the terrarium with cold or warm fresh air.

Fluorescent tubes are best for lighting salamander and newt terraria because they give off very little heat (with an electronic fluorescent lamp ballast). For caecilians, daylight provides sufficient light, as long as the terrarium isn't planted. Fluorescent tubes can be used in frog terraria in combination with mercury vapor

Section of terrarium for Tree frogs and similar species:
1. *drain*
2. *water container*
3. *floor panel*
4. *washable floor panel*
5. *submersible flower pots*
6. *rear wall*
7. *decoration for rear wall (e.g., insulating cork)*
8. *borders*
9. *ventilator*
10. *ventilation (exhaust)*
11. *lamps with reflector (fluorescent tubes)*
12. *HQL or HQI reflector*
13. *sprinkler system (intake duct)*
14. *mounting track, top*
15. *spray nozzle*
16. *viewing panes*
17. *mounting track, bottom*
18. *ventilation (fresh air)*

Dendrobates pumilio, *a colorful Dendrobatidae representative.*

Some enthusiasts even let species such as this Australian green tree frog (Pelodryas caerulea), which tolerates the atmosphere indoors, roam freely inside their homes.

Section of terrarium for newts and salamanders.
1. *drain*
2. *water basin with plants*
3. *caves*
4. *filter*
5. *cork*
6. *drip stones*
7. *drainage layer (e.g., Leca swelling clay)*
8. *ground substrate (e.g., moss, limestone, pieces of cellular or foamed material)*
9. *hideouts (e.g., rocks, bark, plastic foam)*
10. *drain*
11. *ventilation (fresh air intake)*
12. *rear wall*
13. *rear wall decoration*
14. *lighting with reflectors*
15. *ventilation*
16. *hinge*
17. *viewing panes*

lamps or halogen spotlights. Tree frogs need gentle radiant heat and even frogs that live in dark forest floors like to sit in the light of such lamps, which simulate the effect of sunlight filtering through leaves in the terrarium. Reflectors increase the performance of the lamps considerably. Light and dark cycles can be regulated with the help of a timer. If seasonal changes should be required, such as from long to short days, you can program the timer accordingly from week to week. In order to observe nocturnal amphibians during their active phase without disturbing them, install low-wattage red incandescent lamps.

Terrarium air needs to be heated for all tropical or subtropical species or whenever terraria are moved to cool rooms in winter. Silicon-covered heating cables can easily be mounted along the rear wall of the terrarium beneath sticks or

bark, and temperature can be regulated by means of a thermometer and a regulator outside the terrarium. To heat an aquarium or small bodies of water inside a terrarium, you will need special aquarium heaters. The water temperature should always be lower than the air temperature.

Cave and mountain species may need cooler air or water. Terreria with a cooling unit along the rear wall of the terrarium have proven successful. These kinds of customized terraria must be well insulated, and insulated glass should be used to prevent condensation. Newts and salamanders, which require temperatures below 68°F (20°C), should be moved with their terrarium to a cool basement room in summer.

Increased relative humidity can be re-created in a terrarium with the help of artificial miniature

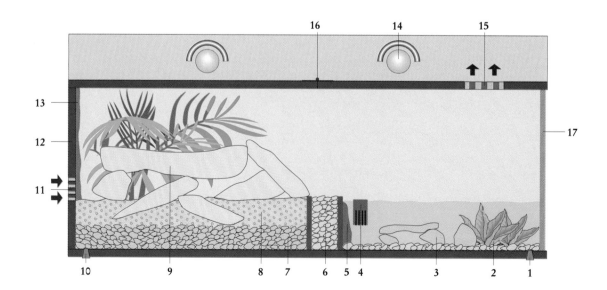

watercourses, air stones in the water basin, or an ultrasound diffuser with external water reservoir. Care must be taken not to create higher relative humidity at the expense of ventilation. Stale air is harmful to amphibians over long periods of time. When several terraria are under one roof, automated sprinkler installations have proven to be the best solution. Aquatic amphibians can be looked after with external and internal filter systems sold for aquariums. Tapwater should be checked for pollution and toxins and be adapted to the needs of the amphibians in captivity.

Basins can be created, keeping in mind functional and aesthetic requirements. PVC tubes are just as useful to caecilians and salamanders as hiding places as are gaps beneath rocks or pieces of bark. Poison-dart frogs will accept empty plastic film containers or small vases in lieu of bromeliads and other phytotelma (water-filled leaf axes). Such non-natural containers have the advantage of being easier to control and to clean. Newts, salamanders and ground-dwelling frogs tolerate insulating cork panels or the swelling clay used in hydroculture. These materials create a good microclimate for amphibians and can take on a natural appearance when covered in moss and foliage. The side walls and rear walls can be covered in cork or various modeling materials (for example, polyurethane foam or tile glue mixed with wood and peat) and then planted. Roots, a small artificial waterfall, climbing branches, etc., can structure the space inside the terrarium and thus meet the needs of amphibians. Any plants that tolerate the climate inside the terrarium and are fairly hardy. Artificial fertilizers for plants should never be used inside terraria to avoid damage to the sensitive amphibian skin. Burrowing frogs and terrestrial caecilians like moss cushions and a loose layer of humus from a beech forest, but also tolerate pieces of foam.

Feeding Amphibians in Captivity

Regular maintenance of a terrarium includes removing excrement, changing the water, misting and feeding. The best food items are live molluscs and insects. Newts, salamanders and caecilians, as well as some aquatic frog species, are also able to smell and "capture" lifeless food such as fish and meat. Of all anurans, only the giant toad (*Bufo marinus*) is known to tolerate canned cat or dog food after having spent some time in captivity. Many amphibians can be coaxed into accepting dead prey by dangling it back and forth on the end of tweezers or a long feeding needle. Depending on the species and size, Collembola, flies, worms, moths, cockroaches, snails, crickets, water fleas, insect larvae, small frogs and infant mice can be used as feeding prey. It is often not necessary to breed

the animals used as food since they can usually be easily purchased. Food should, however, be dusted with a mineral and vitamin powder before being introduced into the terrarium to prevent nutritional deficiencies. The best time for feeding is approximately half an hour after the beginning of the active period of each species. Nocturnal frogs require a small amount of light for orientation and capturing prey.

Breeding Amphibians

To breed amphibians in captivity detailed knowledge of their requirements is needed, especially about factors that trigger reproduction, such as the end of hibernation, dry periods, rain, decrease or increase in temperature, changes in the intensity of light or length of day. It is best to coordinate breeding attempts with natural weather patterns and seasons. One possibility of keeping amphibians in captivity through a winter is to place them inside small cans filled with damp foam and put them in a fridge. Prior to this artificial hibernation, they must have fasted for a period of two weeks and fully voided their intestine. Rain can be simulated with the help of a pump, a pipe and perforated tubes in the terrarium cover, by flooding the terrarium floor or frequent sprinkling. For all species that do not exhibit brood care, it is recommended that eggs, larvae or juveniles be kept away from the parents. The danger of losing some through injuries or parental cannibalism is too great. Nests outside of water must be kept moist.

Water fleas and pieces of earthworms are excellent food sources for newt and salamander larvae. Salamander larvae must not be kept in high densities inside an aquarium as they might injure each other.

Frog larvae feed by grazing on plant or animal matter; they are either obligate or at least facul-

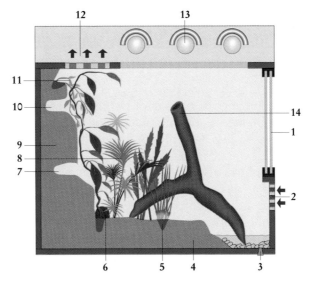

Section of terrarium for "ground-dwelling" frogs.
1. *viewing panes*
2. *ventilation (fresh air intake)*
3. *drain*
4. *floor panel made of insulating cork*
5. *plant holes*
6. *ground holes (e.g., leaves, cork)*
7. *caves in rear wall*
8. *plants*
9. *rear wall decoration*
10. *cave with insert (e.g., empty film container)*
11. *hanging plants*
12. *ventilation (exhaust)*
13. *lighting with reflectors*
14. *root*

A Paradise for Poison-Arrow Frogs (Gerald Benyr)

The Natural History Museum in Vienna boasts a unique terrarium for Colombian poison-arrow frogs. Its base is 48 square feet (4.5 square meters) and its internal height measures 6.5 feet (2 m). All viewing panes are made of insulating glass, and the large frontal pane is heated. The climatic conditions of the Chocó region, where more precipitation falls than anywhere else on the globe, are re-created and simulated inside the terrarium by means of a computer-driven climate control system. This includes a rainwater installation, ultrasound humidifier and five independently regulated heating cables. HQI radiators, fluorescent tubes and a dim nightlight are computer controlled minute by minute and simulate natural light conditions. Ventilators regulate air supply and air currents within the terrarium and also cool the lighting box, if needed.

Plants indigenous to the dense primeval forest in the Chocó create a habitat in this terrarium for *Dendrobates auratus, Dendrobates histrionicus* and *Phyllobates bicolor,* sharing the space with *Gonatodes albigularis fuscus, Gonatodes vittatus* and *Corallus caninus.* Golden poison-arrow frogs and yellow-headed gecko reproduce in the terrarium in a natural manner, without any human intervention or aid.

What makes this terrarium unique is that considering all relevant environmental influences it presents a fine equivalent to the natural habitat of the poison-arrow frogs. Hence, their natural behavior remains unchanged despite their life in captivity. The long mating migrations, during which males lead their females to an appropriate nesting site, are especially impressive to observe.

tative filter feeders. Depending on the type of nutrition and the manner of feeding, fish food, spinach, pieces of carrot, pollen and nettles can be ground into a powder; frozen insect larvae, crushed worm fragments, flaked fish or plankton food can also be used. Anuran larvae, which are usually fed with nutritive eggs from the parents, can sometimes be raised with the help of eggs from other frog species and stored in the deep-freeze. In a few species, the tadpoles require no food at all until the end of metamorphosis. Good water quality is essential for the development of all anuran larvae: if it is too saturated with excrement, crowding effects may occur.

Salamanders and frogs can easily drown during metamorphosis. Containers with shallow water and pieces of moss are one way of preventing this from happening. Amphibian juveniles are very awkward at first in foraging for food. Experience has shown that it is best to raise juveniles in small containers with plenty of food.

The larvae of terrestrial caecilians can be raised in aquaria with shallow water levels (approximately 10 inches/15 cm) and an artificial riverbank section with many hiding places. The juveniles of aquatic species are very susceptible to polluted water. Immediately after birth, they are in danger because the voiding of fetal intestinal contents can easily pollute the small volume of water inside an aquarium. Juvenile caecilians can be fed heart and fish cut into small pieces, but also insect larvae, various types of worms and water fleas.

Prognosis

Keeping a terrarium—keeping and caring for animals without direct reward or return—has a long tradition in many cultures which also tend to place great value on environmental protection. In view of the advancing destruction of ecosystems—and hence of amphibians—we may be justified in questioning whether amphibians should be taken from nature to be kept in a terrarium. Current laws and guidelines make private ownership and the keeping of wild animals exceedingly difficult. And yet daily interaction with amphibians (and with all other animals) promotes better understanding and greater knowledge, as well as more respect for conservation and the laws relating to it.

This is the only way to ensure that people will act responsibly toward amphibians and, by extension, their environment. Children who have never seen a newt in his "wedding dress" or the transformation of a tadpole into a frog will be more likely to act in support of conservation when they are adults. Nature films, no matter how sophisticated, cannot replace the emotional encounter and resulting attachment between man and nature.

The Invasion of the Sugar Cane Toad
Robert Hofrichter

Almost all of the well-intentioned attempts that human beings have made to resettle certain animals or plants in other regions have gone wrong. These kinds of faunal adulteration have almost always created major ecological consequences. In some cases the carelessly introduced species have became plagues to the new environment.

Amphibians are no exception. The best-known import, and internationally probably the most famous toad, is the giant marine toad (*Bufo marinus*). Its habitat used to stretch from Texas to Brazil, exclusively in the New World. Since these amphibians consume a lot of insects, they were brought to settle in other parts of the world. Due to their enormously high rate of reproduction, 25,000 to 30,000 eggs at a time and reproduction possible throughout the year, their rate of distribution in the new habitats was very high. So high in fact that in Australia, for example, their large number turned into a natural disaster. Today giant marine toads can be found not just in Australia and their natural habitat, but also in New Zealand, Hawaii, the Philippines, the Mariana Islands, Cape Salomone, New Guinea, on

many islands in the Caribbean, in Florida and in several other tropical regions. In 1920, the giant marine toad demonstrated its voracity in the sugar-cane fields of Puerto Rico. This encouraged people to export the amphibian to Australia, to serve as a natural pesticide. In Australia, the beetle *Dermolepida albohirtum* was a major problem in sugar-cane plantations. In 1935, the first giant marine toads were loaded onto Australian soil. There were no members of the true toads (*Bufonidae*) on this continent, and critics who warned against importing the toad (pointing to the lack of natural enemies and to the fact that Australia had had bad experiences with the rabbit, also an imported animal) were ignored. It only took a few years for the population of toads to increase to great numbers. Of course, the amphibians did not remain in the sugar-cane fields, but expanded into the surrounding areas and entered human settlements. At certain times and locations it was almost comparable to a biblical frog plague.

Giant marine toads devour anything that is weaker than they are. Their stomachs have been found to contain—besides various invertebrates—mice, young rats, small

*The giant or marine toad (*Bufo marinus*) is the second-largest species among true toads (Bufonidae). These predominantly nocturnal and voracious amphibians have been successfully used for pest control.*

snakes, lizards, other amphibians and even juvenile animals of their own species. This is why, on some Caribbean islands, they were primarily imported to control rats instead of insects. Zoological textbooks frequently present the view that frogs only see moving objects. This is inaccurate. Giant marine toads have even been known to eat cat or dog food if it is available to them. Zoologists now fear that the amphibians will cause massive damage to the indigenous amphibian fauna in Australia. In certain areas, this could lead to the local decimation of some species.

Although in Australia hundreds of thousands of these giant marine toads are processed into leather, used for teaching and research purposes, and exported abroad, it has been almost impossible to decrease their population.

The worldwide decline in amphibian populations has sparked a passionate debate in recent years. Even regions that seem untouched by man are affected. The greenhouse effect and related climate shifts, the diminished ozone layer and increased UV radiation all seem to play a role, as do other factors that remain unclear. These phenomena are, without exception, caused by human activity, and amphibians are not alone in being affected by them. There are other reasons for population decline as well, and these are only too obvious: amphibians react strongly to change and destruction of their natural habitats.

Endangerment
and
Protection

Why Amphibians Are in Danger

Britta Grillitsch

From a global perspective, the extinction of a species means that it disappears forever from Earth. When we look at the Earth's history on a shorter time scale, increased species extinction translates into a loss of biodiversity. Estimates of current rates of extinction point to a dramatic reduction in the diversity of numerous groups of organisms worldwide and thus to a critical situation for the biosphere, known as the biodiversity crisis.

Unchecked deforestation of primeval forests, especially rain forests, endangers countless amphibian species.

The future of amphibians is in the hands of mankind: only global measures can turn the tide of the current crisis in biodiversity.

Species Extinction and the Global Biodiversity Crisis

Advanced decline and its extreme form, extinction—and the evolution of new species—are natural evolutionary processes of life on Earth. It may sound "unfeeling," but it is the natural fate of all species to die out eventually. The average "natural extinction" rate is estimated with the help of paleontological data over the course of geological ages: only one out of 10^5 to 10^7 species that exist simultaneously on Earth would grow extinct per year. Based on this formula, the "natural" extinction of an amphibian species should occur approximately every 1,000 years.

The current rate of extinction—exacerbated by human intervention in nature—is dramatically higher than the estimated natural rate and seems to approach dimensions comparable to the global catastrophes of pre-human ages. Of course, species extinction is not a new phenomenon. What makes species extinction a current "problem," however, is its accelerated rate.

Estimates put the current extinction rate of amphibians at approximately three times above the "paleontological base-rate," excluding the incalculable factor of undiscovered species, which may become extinct before we have had a chance to describe and study them. Experts maintain that only some 10 percent of all extinct or endangered amphibians are actually recorded and listed as such, due to our incomplete knowledge of the true global number of species. Thus the number of known amphibian species has grown from 4,000 to 5,000 in the past eight to ten years alone. New amphibian species are constantly being discovered and described, especially in the tropics—the most diverse and also the most endangered region. The short "appearance on the stage of science" of the gastric brooding frog *Rheobatrachus silus* in Australia, famous for its extraordinary brood-care behavior, illustrates how well-founded these estimates are. The species was discovered as recently as 1973 and was last seen in 1981. Despite intensive searches, it has not been sighted since.

Amphibian Decline

The *Red Book of Threatened Animals*, published by the International Union for the Conservation of Nature (IUCN) in 1996, includes 212 amphibian species in various categories of endangerment; 127 are considered to be at risk of extinction. At least five species are currently thought to have become extinct over the past decades. Another 19 species, among them several that have not been seen for years or even decades, are at critical risk according to the IUCN. Based on the "risk" status in national Red Lists, amphibians are the most endangered vertebrate group in several industrialized nations. For many other amphibian species worldwide, severe population decline and at times even complete disappearance of populations on a local or regional scale has been recorded. It is a great cause for concern that in most cases wholesale human intervention in the land-

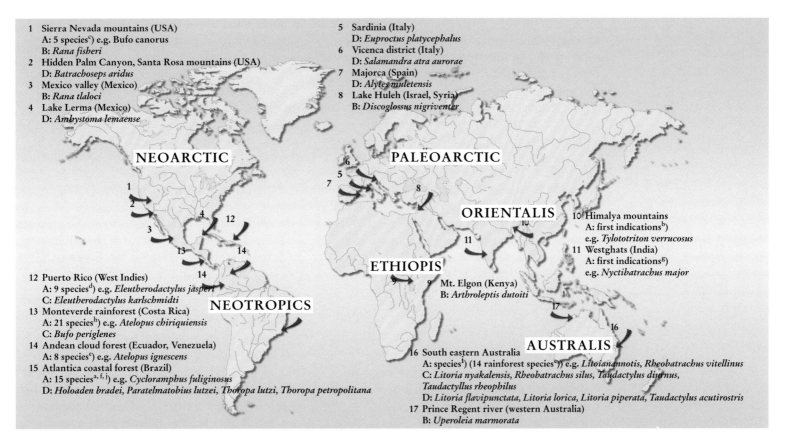

1 Sierra Nevada mountains (USA)
   A: 5 species[c] e.g. *Bufo canorus*
   B: *Rana fisheri*
2 Hidden Palm Canyon, Santa Rosa mountains (USA)
   D: *Batrachoseps aridus*
3 Mexico valley (Mexico)
   B: *Rana tlaloci*
4 Lake Lerma (Mexico)
   D: *Ambystoma lemaense*

5 Sardinia (Italy)
   D: *Euproctus platycephalus*
6 Vicenca district (Italy)
   D: *Salamandra atra aurorae*
7 Majorca (Spain)
   D: *Alytes muletensis*
8 Lake Huleh (Israel, Syria)
   B: *Discoglossus nigriventer*

NEOARCTIC

PALEOARCTIC

ORIENTALIS

10 Himalya mountains
   A: first indications[b]
   e.g. *Tylototriton verrucosus*
11 Westghats (India)
   A: first indications[g]
   e.g. *Nyctibatrachus major*

ETHIOPIS

9 Mt. Elgon (Kenya)
   B: *Arthroleptis dutoiti*

NEOTROPICS

12 Puerto Rico (West Indies)
   A: 9 species[d] e.g. *Eleutherodactylus jasperi*
   C: *Eleutherodactylus karlschmidti*
13 Monteverde rainforest (Costa Rica)
   A: 21 species[h] e.g. *Atelopus chiriquiensis*
   C: *Bufo periglenes*
14 Andean cloud forest (Ecuador, Venezuela)
   A: 8 species[c] e.g. *Atelopus ignescens*
15 Atlantica coastal forest (Brazil)
   A: 15 species[a, f, j] e.g. *Cycloramphus fuliginosus*
   D: *Holoaden bradei, Paratelmatobius lutzei, Thoropa lutzi, Thoropa petropolitana*

AUSTRALIS

16 South eastern Australia
   A: species[i] (14 rainforest species[e]) e.g. *Litoianannotis, Rheobatrachus vitellinus*
   C: *Litoria nyakalensis, Rheobatrachus silus, Taudactyllus diurnus, Taudactyllus rheophilus*
   D: *Litoria flavipunctata, Litoria lorica, Litoria piperata, Taudactylus acutirostris*
17 Prince Regent river (western Australia)
   B: *Uperoleia marmorata*

scape—i.e., habitat destruction—is to blame.

Yet over the past 20 years, observation has revealed declines in areas with seemingly habitats, such as national parks or reserves. The frequency of such observations and the broad geographic and taxonomic range of species believed to be extinct or lost without any "reasonable" explanation is worrisome indeed. Such species share certain characteristics—small ranges, often in middle to high altitudes near creeks in the rain forest, and high degrees of specialization— that in themselves are sufficient to put them at high risk of extinction from natural causes. But other species with larger ranges and higher levels of adaptability are also affected by an inexplicable population decline. This puzzling phenomenon has sparked international debates under headings such as "Amphibian Decline" and "Amphibian Population Decline" and has led to extensive scientific research. In recent years, this phenomenon has emerged as all too real and global in scope, although not universal. Not all regions and not all amphibian species are affected to the same degree. The specific causes are still unknown. In each case, amphibian decline in relatively undisturbed habitats is an indicator of an alarming degree of stress on the environment.

The Declining Amphibian Populations Task Force (DAPTF) was founded in 1991 as a specialized subgroup of the Species Survival Commission (SSC) of the International Union for the Conservation of Nature (IUCN). DAPTF operates through a worldwide network of

regional, national and topical workgroups made up of volunteers from various backgrounds: science, environmental protection agencies and interested laypeople. About 90 nations currently participate in this international cooperative effort. DAPTF's mission is to determine and record the nature, extent and causes of declines and disappearance of amphibians throughout the world, and to promote means by which declines can be halted or reversed.

Several circumstances make it difficult to record amphibian decline: their populations are by nature subject to considerable fluctuations and the conclusion that population growth has taken a permanent downturn can be reached only after many years of observation. In addition, there is not enough historical data for a comparison with current developments. While several indicators permit conclusions about contemporary stress levels on specific populations, the background knowledge necessary to judge the significance of such "measurable" changes is often insufficient. Moreover, insight gained about one species is not necessarily applicable to another.

"Natural" Causes

Many aspects of amphibians' mode of life and individual development, morphology and physiology set them apart from other vertebrates. Some of the amphibian traits—although in evolutionary terms successful across geological ages through persistence and radiation of this vertebrate class—may now constitute the reasons why amphibians are at particular risk from

A: Examples of dramatic amphibian population decline since the mid-seventies in seemingly intact habitats, often concurrent with extraordinary climatic events. The affected species occur predominantly in small ranges or with disjunctive distribution in mid to high elevations and in tropical rain forest areas where they live in close contact with rapidly flowing waters. For each region the total amount of population loss is indicated for the affected species. a) Bertolucci and Heyer, 1995; b) Deuti, 1996; c) Drost and Feller, 1996; d) Hedges, 1993; e) Halliday and Heyer, 1997; f) Heyer et al., 1988; g) Krishnamurthy, 1997; h) Pounds et al., 1997; Lips, 1998; i) Tyler, 1991; j) Weygoldt, 1989; B: Amphibian species grown extinct in the past 50 years (IUCN 1996). C: Critically endangered amphibian species (IUCN 1996) currently lost. D: Critically endangered amphibian species (IUCN 1996).

man-made factors. Such general characteristics of amphibians range from their biphasic life cycle, with reproduction and early development usually taking place in aquatic environments, to their highly permeable skin. Further not mutually exclusive threats that may arise from natural causes are a narrow distribution range of a species (endemism), isolation and low densities of populations or both, a highly specialized mode of life, and a relatively long life span along with a low reproduction rate. Such factors are, in principle, linked to a relatively low ability to survive stresses by means of defense, regulation or compensation mechanisms. Even populations along the vertical and horizontal boundaries of their own species, as well as hybrid systems, are at high natural risk. Hence, not surprisingly, the most striking examples of extinction and population decline in amphibians occur among insular and marginal populations of highly specialized species with restricted distribution ranges. A decrease in genetic variability seems to speed up the death spiral of species.

Man-made Causes

The main anthropogenic threats to amphibians result from land use, combustion of fossil fuels and recent biomass, as well as industrial production. These may lead to monotonous habitats and biological communities, climate changes, acid rain, and increased levels of UV radiation, and fertilizers or persistent chemicals such as heavy metals and certain pesticides. The existence of these global environmental problems is undisputed. However, despite the use of complex and ultra-modern technologies, the ecological impact of these environmental changes can only be estimated in very simplified models such as climate models or ecological risk-assessment models for environmental contaminants.

Fundamental structural changes to natural environments—draining wetlands, for example—are the most serious and also most obvious dangers for amphibians worldwide. Different anthropogenic risk factors may come to bear simultaneously and yet independently of one another. Frequently, however, several such environmental factors interact, and the overall impact may thereby be multiplied. This is the case for some metals like aluminum in combination with acidic water, or certain pesticides and exposure to increased UV-radiation. Different environmental factors can cause similar or even identical effects—many environmental contaminants cause the formation of so-called stress proteins or a characteristic spectrum of abnormalities. Conversely, one and the same environmental factor can be responsible for several different effects, depending on

intensity and duration or frequency of exposure. The impact profile may further vary according to species, gender, age, but also population size and previous stresses. The many potential exogenous and endogenous variables make it difficult to identify the less obvious risks to amphibians. Finally, combinations of several global and local factors are held to be the most probable causes for amphibian decline.

Structural Habitat Changes

All continents are subject to man-made changes in the landscape on a large scale and thus loss of primary habitats. Usually, secondary habitats provide survival conditions only for very few amphibian species, if any at all.

The majority of amphibians rely on aquatic habitats for mating, reproduction and embryonic and larval development. The availability of bodies of water that are conducive to the needs of a species is therefore fundamentally vital for that species to survive. In addition, adequate terrestrial habitats are indispensable as well since a large number of amphibian species spend most of their lifetime on land.

Among the human activities causing primarily structural alterations of both aquatic and terrestrial amphibian habitats, the most severe are land consolidation, draining of wetlands, regulation of flowing waters, and monocultural land use by agriculture and forestry. Apart from direct habitat degradation and destruction such alterations of the landscape all too often indirectly lead to additional loss of amphibian habitats on a larger scale in that they may promote erosion, lowering of groundwater levels, and even climatic changes. In flowing waters, impaired natural water dynamics frequently result in the loss of still water near river banks and ponds and ditches along the margins of flowing waters, and finally, in the absence of flood plains along with the formation of new bodies of water.

Yet even drastic changes rarely destroy the entire habitat of a species and cause its immediate extinction. Instead, they result in habitat fragmentation. Large habitats are split into sections, often far apart. This reduces the overall number of a species and also prevents genetic exchange among individuals from disjunct populations. Populations are isolated when distances between fragmented habitats exceed the critical distance of a species (i.e., the maximum distance individuals of a species are capable of crossing). As an example, severe decline in a critically isolated amphibian population due to catastrophic climatic events—exceptional but still within the normal range of variation—may no longer be compensated for through incoming individuals from neighboring populations. For similar reasons, endemic species with naturally small habitats are especially at risk.

Physical and Chemical Changes

Natural, industrial and technical products can change the physical and chemical properties of the environment. Laboratory studies have shown that many physical and chemical pollutants may be extremely harmful to amphibians. Laboratory tests on the embryos and larvae of the African clawed frog (*Xenopus laevis*) are included in ecological risk-assessment models for environmental chemicals, even though they are less common than the standard tests on aquatic organisms such as algae, Daphnia or fish. Yet, despite common knowledge that amphibians are often subject to severe environmental stresses in the wild, few cause-and-effect studies exist on the sublethal impact of the long-term exposure of amphibian populations to specific environmental stresses. Studies on multiple stressor effects are particularly scarce.

Climatic Changes

Climate and the seasonal variation of these parameters (temperature, humidity, precipitation, air pressure and wind) has an immediate impact on the characteristics of a habitat. For the past decade, global warming has been calculated at approximately 1 degree Fahrenheit (0.6 degrees Celsius). The greenhouse effect is caused by tiny liquid and solid particles (aerosols, dust, steam, etc.) in the atmosphere and gases (above all carbon dioxide, but also methane, fluorocarbons, ozone). The greenhouse factors in the atmosphere are augmented by natural sources (volcanic eruption or brush fires) and anthropogenic sources (combustion of fossil fuels and slash-and-burn clearing), and this increase is the primary cause of the gradual global temperature increase in the atmospheric layers of the atmosphere near the Earth. Climate changes with distinct regional profiles may ultimately result. The interaction between the atmosphere and other components of the global climatic system is extremely complex, and the degree to which human activity contributes to climatic changes is still under investigation.

Intense cultivation of large areas with all related consequences has been a major factor worldwide in the destruction of amphibian habitats and populations. The vital ecological prerequisites to keep a functioning natural balance were given too little consideration in the past, and essential elements such as hedges, groups of trees, moist meadows, small bodies of water, pools, ditches and many more were systematically destroyed.

Studies in England have shown that reproductive cycles of amphibians in moderate latitudes respond to climate changes. Over a period of 17 years (1977–94) the breeding period of the edible frog *Rana* kl. *esculenta* and of the natterjack (*Bufo calamita*) moved forward by ten days in direct relation to temperature increases. A longer active period could be advantageous for amphibian populations. But there are also disadvantages, such as desynchronization with other biologically relevant cycles (for example, the phenology of food organisms). Generally speaking, however, species in temperate climate zones are more resistant to changing climate conditions than those that inhabit regions where natural seasonal changes are minimal. Prospective assessment has identified tropical amphibian species as particularly at risk (especially species in higher altitudes). This is strongly supported by all observations collected to date, and climate changes are major factors responsible for amphibian decline in Costa Rica, southeastern Brazil and Australia.

Other Factors

Ionizing radiation (X-rays, radioactivity and ultraviolet light) is energy-rich and inflicts direct or indirect damage on the DNA; it is one of the most powerful mutagens its levels increased by civilization place an ever-growing burden on the biosphere. Radioactive pollution has been reported to cause an increase in organic, cytological and chromosomal abnormalities in amphibian populations in the eastern Ural Mountains and in the Ukraine where it seems to be a major factor in local population decline.

At least regionally, increased ultraviolet radiation (especially UV B-radiation) is a man-made factor. Fluorocarbons and other industrial organic chlorine compounds add to the transformation of ozone into oxygen and thus reduce the stratospheric ozone layer which absorbs UV radiation. The chlorine content of the stratosphere has increased fivefold as a result of industrial pollution.

UV radiation tends to be highest in regions near the equator and at high altitudes. Furthermore, exposure of water-dwelling amphibians to UV radiation is especially high in shallow, clear, unstructured and unshaded water. Particularly in such habitats amphibians may be subject to harmful UV doses during their most sensitive, early aquatic developmental phases. To which extent the gelatinous egg envelops and pigmentation of embryos and larvae may provide UV protection is still unclear. In addition, UV radiation in itself as well as environmental changes (for example, acidification) can decimate aquatic organisms, especially planktonic organisms. This not only reduces the nutrient supply

for amphibians (directly for anuran larvae) but simultaneously increases the depth to which UV rays can penetrate into the clearer water. In laboratory tests, several amphibian species have demonstrated high levels of sensitivity to UV B-radiation. However, there are few and to some degree contradictory studies on UV-inflicted damage on amphibians in the complex conditions that prevail in the field.

Acid rain, snow or fog (with pH values below 5.6) and to a lesser degree industrial wastewater and road runoff can acidify bodies of water. The worldwide average pH of rainwater has been measured as 4.1 (in industrial areas pH values are often recorded as falling below 3, especially during the first phases of rainfall, and below 2 in fog).

Eutrophication and Its Consequences

Nutrient influx into ecosystems, especially phosphorous and nitrogen compounds from agriculture, set in motion a chain that leads from increased bioproduction to the closely related processes of eutrophication and saprotrophication. These terms refer to increased plant growth and increased microbial degradation processes. Oxygen deficiency is one of the most severe consequences. Mass extinction of fish due to oxygen depletion in the summer months draws public attention to the problem. But oxygen deficiency can also be harmful for amphibian larvae. Even in winter oxygen uptake at the water surface is vitally important. Naturally, bodies of water that freeze in winter cannot be replenished with oxygen in this manner; small, shallow and stagnant bodies of water rich in nutrients and plant growth may therefore be unsuitable hibernation habitats. The mass die-off of amphibians during aquatic hibernation—for example, common frogs (*Rana temporaria*) in the northern areas of Switzerland—has been traced to oxygen deficiency aggravated by over-fertilization and climatic factors. In addition, eutrophication is also an important factor in terrestrialization of bodies of water.

Fertilizers can also harm amphibians in direct ways. Concentrations of ammonium nitrate (10 to 14 mg/L) frequently measured in bodies of water in agricultural settings worldwide have been shown to be highly toxic to amphibian larvae, and ammonium nitrate has also been identified as a harmful substance to both terrestrial and aquatic amphibians in agrarian landscapes.

The Effects of Environmental Chemicals

Chemical pollutants are the most complex environmental problem: approximately 11 million different chemical compounds have been described worldwide (with 400,000 joining the list yearly); 500,000 are used outside of research laboratories; 100,000 different industrial "environmental chemicals" are commonly used according to industry sources (with 2,000 added every year). Approximately 250 (among them cadmium, mercury, cyanide and several pesticides such as atrazine and 2.4-D) have been identified in national and international priority lists as the most dangerous. Yet, there is no list of potentially toxic by-products and degradation products. For amphibians, information on possible harmful effects exists for fewer than 1,000 of all industrially produced chemicals through studies carried out on less than 5 percent of all amphibian species (predominantly robust species with wide distribution). And only a small portion of all these studies takes into account the long-term impact of low pollutant concentrations or pollutant interactions. Furthermore, it is difficult to reach a conclusive interpretation based on the available data because of inconsistency in the test conditions.

It is therefore nearly impossible to assess the actual impact of pollutants on amphibian populations.

Nevertheless, slowly degrading chemicals that may persist in ecosystems for decades—and the majority of the chemicals on the priority lists fall into this category—are undoubtedly extremely hazardous to amphibians. At times, these chemicals even spill directly into the environment in large quantities. A dramatic example is the mercury pollution of rivers in some rain forests of South America (combined with cyanide, arsenic and copper pollution)—a direct result of gold mining. Apart from point-source pollution, water and air may transport chemicals over long distances and even around the world and in potentially damaging concentrations have been found in remote areas such as nature reserves and polar ice fields, far removed from the point of origin. Many of these chemicals can concentrate in the sediment or in suspended particles in water and in microorganisms; the potential of such anorganic

The rain forests of Central and South America are home to most amphibian species worldwide. More than 80 species may occur in an area of only one hectare, twice as many as occur in all of Europe. As rain forests disappear, so do their wondrous and still not fully discovered abundance of flora and fauna.

as lindane). In general, high resistance to pollutants with a high potential to bioaccumulate results in high tissue concentration levels. Thus, amphibians may eventually even constitute a source of intoxication for their predators.

Biological Changes

Humans transport plants and animals—including pathogenic microorganisms—across natural distribution boundaries into all regions of the world. "Exotic" species sometimes encounter very favorable conditions in their new environments where they spread rapidly and affect the indigenous species. As competitors, predators or parasites, the introduced species may be a threat to native species, without being subject to natural control mechanisms themselves. The result is a destabilization of established host–parasite–, nutrient– and predator prey systems that have evolved through the ages.

Exotic competitors and predators that pose a threat to amphibian species are sometimes amphibians themselves. The giant toad (*Bufo marinus*), whose natural range stretches from southern North America to South America, has now been introduced to islands in the Atlantic and the Pacific, to Australia and New Guinea, and has become an infamous case in point. Many other amphibian species can be mentioned in this context: bull frogs (*Rana catesbeiana*), indigenous to eastern North America and now spread across North America, the Antilles, northern Italy and Spain; or the African clawed frog (*Xenopus laevis*), which has spread from its origins in Africa to warm parts of Europe and North America. Some species, released into environments to which they are not indigenous in the interest of conservation— the marsh frog (*Rana ridibunda*) in Switzerland, Italy and England—have proved dominant over the indigenous amphibian fauna.

Many other animals create new conditions in a specific habitat and are a threat to some amphibian species: some widespread salmonids, mosquito fishes and sunfishes; crayfish, such as *Pacifastacus leniusculus* in Sweden or *Procambarus clarkii* in California; birds, too, fall into this category—for example, the pheasant species *Phasianus colchicus*, originally from Asia but now spread across Central and Southern Europe. One of the greatest problems are stocked fish and fish that have escaped from aquaculture. Salmon stock in the Sierra Nevada, released for sport fishing, has been considered a major factor in the disappearance of the mountain yellow-legged frog (*Rana muscosa*).

The larva of the caddisfly *Ptilostomis postica*, a relatively acid-tolerant species, is a good illustration of indirect causes of changes in the

It is the nature of ecological systems that they cannot be strictly divided. Many amphibian species require several habitats to survive— e.g., a spawning site, a summer habitat and a hibernation habitat. The distance between these partial habitats is bridged by means of migration. Man's cultivated landscape is in conflict with these natural needs of amphibians. Countless "borders" and insurmountable barriers have cut the landscape into many small sections.

and organic matter and thus its chemical load to be consumed and concentrated (bioaccumulation), for instance, by microphagous filter feeders such as tadpoles of various amphibian species, is especially high. These chemicals may further be concentrated along food chains (biomagnification). Ultimately, residue levels in organisms of higher trophic levels such as frogs and toads may surpass the initial concentration levels in the surrounding abiotic environment by several degrees.

The amphibian species studied for acute lethal toxicity of environmental chemicals rarely showed to be more sensitive when compared with other aquatic animals (for example, in the case of TFM, trifluoromethyl-nitrophenol, a lampricide); for some chemicals, amphibians appeared to be of average sensitivity (for example, in the case of atrazine, a herbicide); for a number of chemicals in contrast, amphibians were found to be extremely robust (for example, in the case of heavy metals and pesticides such

The unnatural separation of the river as a pulse of life and the surrounding landscape has dire consequences. When river and landscape have no barriers in the natural landscapes, water goes into the ground and the surrounding land, where it naturally collects in many small deposits. Robbed of its natural aquifers, excess water must today be channeled along canalized transportation paths. This has led to the disappearance of many small bodies of water that were once ideal spawning sites for amphibians in the flood plains near rivers and creeks.

environment resulting from an upset in the natural predator–prey equilibrium. In acidified water the larval caddisfly is able to catch more amphibian larvae (wood frogs, *Rana sylvatica*, and mole salamanders, *Ambystoma maculatum* and *A. jeffersonianum*) than usual.

Parasites

Parasites are the cause of most deaths other than from predators. Outbreaks of parasitic disease and high mortality rates have been recorded very recently for several amphibian species, in England (common frog, *Rana temporaria*), in Israel (green toad, *Bufo viridis*), in Australia and Central America (several species).

The primary agents for the diseases in England and Australia have been identified, with varying degrees of certainty, as viral; in Australia and Central America, protozoa may also be involved. Introduced microorganisms may well

be the cause for disease in some areas. Pollution causes immunosuppression and diminished resistance in amphibians and thus a higher degree of susceptibility to disease and a more severe course of disease. Hence, increased mortality among amphibians as a result of pathogenic microorganisms could be the indirect outcome of all or some environmental stresses. Eutrophication in water brought about by fertilizers can contribute indirectly to a shift in the host–parasite equilibrium and to an increase in parasite infestation in amphibians. An example of this "indirect influence" is the reaction set in motion by increased plant growth: it improves the nutrient base for snails, which in turn are intermediate hosts for amphibian trematode parasites. Trematode infestation in tadpoles is thought to be a possible cause for a rise in abnormalities and defects (especially deformations of the legs) that has been observed among amphibians across large areas of North America since 1995.

Amphibians and Water Acidification
Helmut Faber

Over the past few decades, increasing industrialization while improving economic conditions has also had a rising impact on the environment. The negative effects of industrialization, such as acid rain or the deterioration of forests, have received a great deal of public attention. A majority of all amphibians depend on water for reproduction and the increasing acidification of their spawning ponds has had an important impact on their distribution.

The correlation between amphibian distribution and the acidification levels of the spawning ponds was first noticed 40 years ago in the New Jersey pine barrens of the United States. Ponds with high concentrations of acids and corresponding low pH levels were avoided by the more sensitive species. The impact of increasingly acidic precipitation—primarily caused by sulfur dioxide and nitrogen oxides—on impor-

tant sectors such as forestry and fishing industry became obvious at the beginning of the 1970s. Twenty years ago, researchers began showing interest in the possible negative effects of acidification on amphibians, first in North America, then in northern Europe (England, Sweden) and finally in Central Europe (Germany).

What is the effect of the increasing acidification of surface waters, and which stages of development are affected the most? Adult animals can be affected by the declining pH-levels of their terrestrial habitats, but the developmental stages that are dependent on water—eggs and larvae and tadpoles respectively—are the most endangered. The fertilization of eggs can be affected as the mobility of sperm drops rapidly with increasing levels of acidity. The embryonic development is the most critical phase of development and in

Some alpine ponds, pristine on the first glance are at risk because of acid rain, especially where the buffering capacity of the substrate against acids is too weak. As all amphibian species living in the European Alps—with the exception of the alpine salamander (Salamandra atra)—depend on spawning ponds, this determinant means a severe threat to them.

extremely acidic conditions the embryos are damaged directly. The first cleavage stages of the ovum can be interrupted, thus arresting development right from the start. The effects of this sublethal damage during this initial critical phase often becomes visible only at a later stage, specifically, during the development of the three cell layers. Towards the end of this phase, called gastrulation, not all yolked cells can be transferred from the outside into the embryo, and the "yolk plug" literally becomes stuck, resulting in fatal consequences. The impact of the acid also alters the consistency and elasticity of the egg membranes, preventing the gelatinous egg capsules from expanding completely. This reduces the liquid-filled perivitelline space which surrounds the embryo within the egg capsule and places a major restriction on movement. Even animals that have developed in a normal fashion, under less acidic conditions, often fail to hatch under such circumstances. The embryo's movements, a vital aspect of the hatching process, and the production of the hatching enzyme are inhibited at the same time. This, coupled with the major changes in the gelatinous egg capsules, which become less penetrable, can lead to embryonic mortality.

Sublethal damages, which are caused in the embryonic phase, become particularly visible in the larval phase. Due to the reduction of the perivitelline space within the egg capsules, the embryos coil up and show the "curling defect". If hatching follows its normal course, during the larval phase, the animals will often exhibit deformed vertebral spines, as well as other deformities. This leads, for example, to bent tails, which limits movement while swimming and reduces the chance of escaping predators. Finally, after the successful completion of the metamorphosis, damage caused by acidic conditions can result in deformed extremities which is a major disadvantage for catching prey. In general, during their development, larvae and tadpoles show an increasing resistance against the negative effects of water acidification.

Besides direct visible deformities, there is another series of important sublethal damage effects, ranging from an increase in the duration of the larval phase, to reduced growth and detrimental changes of behavior, to finally, an increased risk of infection. For example, eggs which have been damaged by low pH are less resistant to infection by the omnipresent water mould *Saprolegnia* than those not exposed. For the affected animals, all these injuries ultimately result in a reduced probability of survival. Over the long term, this can have a negative effect, not only on individual animals, but on entire populations. Water acidification also results in negative consequences for amphibians by altering their environmental situation. For example, mosses of the genus *Sphagnum* are not only promoted by the increasing acidification of the water, but they accelerate this process. Additionally, they release organic sub-

*Egg-clump of the common frog (*Rana temporaria*) damaged by too low pH levels. In some regions of the world the acidification of surface waters becomes one of the most important threats for amphibians as it strikes the animals at the most sensitive point of their life cycle: during reproduction.*

stances that have also been proven to have a negative impact on amphibian development.

Since low pH levels not only affect amphibians, but other animal and plant species as well, changes in the variety of prey and algae communities can occur. This means that larvae and tadpoles may face an alteration of the food chain which leads to a reduction of their nutrition base. As well, the competition between different species may be changed. Predators that are more resistant to acidic conditions, such as the larvae of dragonflies or waterbeetles, have a greater chance of preying on amphibian larvae that have been impaired by lower pH levels.

For most of the amphibian species studied, the critical level of pH is in the range between 4 and 5, or slightly less. In this context, Urodela are generally more sensitive than Anura. In waters with such low pH levels, toxic ions, like aluminium and other metals can be mobilized, and intensify the negative effect. Explosive breeders spawning in early spring are especially at risk, as the high concentration of pollutants that have accumulated during winter make their way into the spawning ponds when the snow begins to melt. There are not just differences among the various species, but also, as expected—within them. These differences can be genetically determined, especially during the larval

phase. During embryonic development the sensitivity of the embryos to low pH levels increases simultaneously with the size of eggs and egg capsules. Therefore, populations living at higher altitudes or in more northern latitudes are generally more at risk, since they deposit larger eggs, proven, for example, by the widespread common frog (*Rana temporaria*).

Smaller ponds, without sufficient buffering capacity, are often selected as spawning grounds. In smaller ponds, acidic precipitation may cause sudden drops in the pH level resulting in very acidic conditions. Such situations, where the pH level drops to between 3 and 4, have an absolutely lethal effect after only a few hours. The animals that are in the transition from the embryonic to the larval phase are particularly at risk for two reasons. The protection from the egg capsules shortly after hatching no longer exists and the animals are not able to escape predators yet because they are unable to actively swim. Therefore ponds, which at first glance might be considered suitable for amphibian reproduction, are not conducive for reproduction.

In some regions of North America, and in other parts of the world too, amphibian populations have dramatically declined in numbers and some species have become extinct locally. Whether acid precipitation and the resulting acidification of surface waters is the major reason for this phenomenon is still debated. In Scandinavia, observations as early as the late seventies proved that water acidification led to the extinction of local amphibian populations within a few years. In Central Europe, for example, the Black Forest, the Bavarian Forest and parts of the Central Alps are especially at risk. Some populations may have already become extinct due to the reasons discussed, while others have definitely reached their critical limit. If this negative trend continues, harmful effects on a larger ecological scale cannot be excluded.

The quick and effective reduction of air pollutants is of fundamental importance—not only for amphibians, but also for us.

Trade and Species Conservation

Josef Schmuck

No one can deny that animals and plants are more endangered in this century than ever before—and the trend is rising. Human activity is, almost without exception, the cause. Globally, human intervention is responsible for 70 percent of environmental destruction and species loss. We are all familiar with the major factors, among them air, soil and water pollution and loss of habitat. Approximately 30 percent of all destruction is the direct result of human interference, such as harvesting natural resources. The range encompasses many facets, from hunting to trade in timber, animal skins and live animals. The last is a threat to many amphibians.

The Convention on International Trade in Endangered Species of Wild Fauna and Flora

In 1973 the Convention on International Trade in Endangered Species of Wild Fauna and Flora was drafted in Washington. Since then, 136 nations have joined and incorporated its guidelines into their own national laws. CITES, as the agreement is known, aims to control trade in endangered species, to limit and—if necessary—completely banish such trade.

While CITES aims for sustainable species management, it does so only by means of species protection. A species can be "utilized" only as long as it exists and as long as its reproduction is ensured. Simply put, "you can't milk a dead cow." This is the leading motto of CITES—namely, that trade in its many manifestations must be limited or stopped whenever the survival of a species is threatened. The number of specimens removed from nature must not exceed their reproductive abilities.

This theory sounds reasonable, and yet it is rarely translated into practice. The contrast between pure profit motive in world trade and the intent to protect expressed by environmen-

tal NGOs (non-governmental organizations) is nowhere more apparent than on the occasion of international conferences on species protection. These CITES conferences are convened every two and a half years in different host countries under the patronage of the United Nations. At these meetings, the opinions and interests of the individual states are often in conflict. The species protection convention is updated at each CITES conference. New species can be added to the lists if they are proven to be endangered; they are then included in Appendices I, II or III (different categories of endangerment), while others may be deleted from the list if it can be shown that their population numbers have recovered and there is no further need to restrict trade.

In addition to many other groups of animals, many amphibian species have been placed under CITES protection. Amphibians, especially Anura, are a good example of how bitter the battles are that are fought between trade representatives and conservationists both publicly and behind the scenes at each CITES conference. Some nations have a reputation of being hostile to species protection. These countries are Japan, Switzerland, but also Indonesia, Malaysia, China, Norway, Venezuela, South

Species with limited distribution ranges are especially threatened by trade. One of these is Paramesotriton deloustali *(Salamandridae) from Vietnam, whose underside sports impressive coloring.*

Africa, Botswana, Namibia and Zimbabwe. By contrast, countries such as Canada, Germany, Austria, India, Nepal, Israel, Ghana and Hungary are demonstrably in favor of and supportive of species protection. Some nations, such as the United States, Russia and France, are well disposed toward species protection as long as it does not affect their national interests, otherwise they quickly drop the issue. The attitude of many countries' representatives depends on the current political situation in their home country and can change as these conditions change.

The Role of Politics

Politics play an important role in conservation. There are "teams" and "interest groups" that form for each vote and operate quite openly. Switzerland, Norway and Japan could often be described as a whale-killing connection. Japan, South Africa, Namibia, Botswana, Zimbabwe and Switzerland are all supporters of trade in ivory and rhinoceros horns. Japan, Indonesia, Malaysia and Venezuela are unified in their support of harvesting exotic timber. Unfortunately, the EEC plays a rather shameful role as a result of its internal lack of consensus and this is all the more unfortunate as many other states look to the EEC for leadership. In the case of amphibians, the most burning issues are the trade in live specimens and frogs' legs

and these two practices have landed several species on the endangered list. The main reason for trade in live amphibians is the great demand by terrarium owners—above all for brightly colored species. Often small local populations are radically "defrogged" by local gatherers who are encouraged by unscrupulous merchants (wholesale traders). This has and continues to affect the genera *Dendrobates*, *Phyllobates* and *Mantella*.

Atelopus zeteki, the Panamanian golden frog, and *Bufo periglenes*, the golden toad, were often captured for their beauty and are now nearly extinct. Trade was forbidden and both species were included in Appendix I, giving them the highest degree of protection. For the golden toad, these measures seem to be too little too late, and experts are quite certain that the species is extinct, mostly as a result of years of collecting that were exacerbated by other, unknown, factors. The wonderful Panamanian golden frog seems to be gradually recovering, although the survival of the species is by no means certain. *Bufo supercillaris*, the Cameron toad, in Appendix I, and *Bufo retiformis*, the Sonoran green toad, in Appendix II, are terrarium favorites because of their attractive appearance. Since too many were taken from nature and the populations were already damaged, these two species have also been listed in the appendices.

*Many species have been brought to the brink of extinction through trade and mass removal from their natural habitats. The tomato frog (*Dyscophus antongilii*) above is a (still) extant witness to this plundering of nature.* Mantella aurantiaca *(golden mantella or ginger tree frogs), several* Dendrobates *species and many other amphibians are critically endangered as a result of excessive removal from nature.*

The genus *Nectophrynoides*, viviparous African toads, were included in Appendix I, because trade in live specimens seemed to be flourishing, and their habitats and ranges are only a few square miles. Similar circumstances apply to *Rheobatrachus*, gastric-brooding frogs, which are also sought after for medical and pharmacological purposes. Protaglandin E-2, an essential substance in the treatment of stomach ulcers, is produced in the parental stomachs during the development of the young. All *Rheobutrachus* species were included in Appendix II, and only the rarest species, *Rheobatrachus silus*, was entered into the EEC's Appendix A. This unique species has not been seen for nearly two decades.

The fire-engine-red tomato frog was exported *en masse* a few years ago from Madagascar to Europe, the United States and Japan. Because of its localized and limited distribution, this species, too, was awarded the highest protection status in 1987, a step opposed strongly by Switzerland. Often the fate of an entire species or genus depends on chance, trifles and the efforts of an individual delegate in an attempt to achieve the required two-thirds majority vote in favor of their protection.

For ten years, conservationists and species traders have been waging a war over the fate of the genus *Mantella*. The first application to include *Mantella aurantiaca* in Appendix II was submitted by Holland in 1987, which later withdrew the application under pressure from the land of origin, Madagascar, and from Switzerland. Madagascar then promised at the plenary of the CITES conference to include the species in Appendix III. So far, this promise has not been kept.

In 1994, Holland submitted another application for *Mantella aurantiaca*; this time it was to be included in Appendix I since the species was by then severely endangered. Germany submitted an application to include the species in Appendix II and a two-thirds majority was achieved for the German submission. The EEC, whose species-protection agreements are sometimes stricter than CITES, soon after entered the entire genus *Mantella* into Appendix B, which corresponds to Appendix II of CITES. In 1997, Holland tried yet again, this time for the species *Mantella bernhardi*, *M. cowani*, *M. haraldmeieri* and *M. viridis* to be included in Appendix II. Again, the application met strong resistance from Madagascar and Switzerland. Despite powerful lobbying on behalf of the species by the German humane society "Deutsches Tierhilfswerk" and especially the DCSP, the Documentation Center for Species Protection (Austria), the application was rejected. Holland withdrew it not least of all because it had

received very little support from the EEC. Again Madagascar promised that it would include the entire genus *Mantella* in Appendix III.

In reality, a species has to be close to extinction before it can become protected, and the protection can then be implemented gradually, if at all. Anura are often smuggled across borders, which is easily done because each specimen is small and simple to hide. The potential financial gain is great in the case of some species. In many countries, unfortunately including some EEC countries and in North America, enforcement is poor. Illegal trade in protected amphibian species continues through many eastern states that have not joined CITES as members.

The Trade in Frogs' Legs

The trade in frogs' legs has brought several species of *Rana* and other true frogs to the status of endangered. Trade in the legs of six-fingered frogs, *Euphlyctis hexadactylus*, and the Indian bull frog, *Hoplobatrachus tigerinus*, had to be restricted, and the species were listed in Appendix II. In order to meet the demand for this luxury food item, the trade shifted to other species. Consequently, numbers of several Asian Ranidae were dramatically reduced within a matter of years. In 1992, Germany submitted a application for the protection of *Rana arfaki*, *Limnonectes blythii*, *L. cancrivorus* and many other ranids. However, these species were not ultimately awarded protection status.

Germany withdrew the application in reaction to massive pressure from Indonesia, supported by some European countries where frogs' legs are customarily consumed, the leaders being France and Switzerland, as it had become obvious that there was no chance of a two-thirds majority. DCSP was the only organization that supported these species. Elephant, rhino and tiger had completely usurped the protection attention of the other environmental NGOs, for no one seemed to be interested in frogs any more. Some delegates even spoke of those "disgusting Ranidae." *Conraua goliath*, the spectacular giant frog, and *Rana catesbeiana*, the American bullfrog, met with a similar fate. At least they have been included in the EEC list in Appendix B, which restricts the trade in this species, at least in Europe.

Trade in Urodela

The only urodele species protected thus far are members of the genus *Andrias* (Giant salamanders)—and they enjoy the highest protection status. Causes of endangerment are above all habitat loss and, to a lesser degree, trade. These creatures, which many people find somewhat spooky, are mostly exhibited in public facilities.

The average terrarium owner is less interested in them. *Ambystoma dumerilii*, the Lake Patzcuaro salamander, and *A. mexicanum*, the familiar axolotl, are listed in Appendix II because these species are popular as pets and their distribution is limited to one lake in Mexico. The axolotl is also endangered because it is a common food for local residents. Since it has been awarded protected status, the axolotl is being bred in captivity in great numbers.

As the trade in amphibians continues to grow, we can be certain that other species will soon join the list of protected species. Unfortunately, applications are submitted only after wild populations are severely compromised and when numbers are already low. The Ranidae will surely be added to the list because they grow to more than 2 inches (5 cm) in the adult phase (frogs' legs), as will many representatives of the

genus *Leptodactylus*, especially *L. fallax*, the "Mountain Chicken" from the island of Dominica. Moreover, it is to be expected that many frogs from Madagascar, especially *Mantella* species, will soon be included in the appendices. Some species of *Ceratophrys*, the horned frogs, and *Phyllomedusa*, the leaf-frogs, are put under great stress by loss of habitat compounded by ongoing international trade.

Although CITES could easily be criticized and although the enforcement of its rules is lacking in many member states, it must be emphasized that many amphibian species would already be extinct without the protection of the Washington Convention. The only hope is that in the future, the interests of endangered species will be given precedence over the economic interests of individual countries.

Dendrobatidae with beautiful coloring, here Dendrobates histrionicus, are especially sought after for trade.

Martin Kyek

How Many Frogs Does Nature Need?

It is difficult to think of a pond without frogs. Many of us raised tadpoles when we were young and were able to observe the amazing process of metamorphosis in a jar placed on a window sill. The spectacle of amphibian migrations, especially noticeable wherever their paths cross human paths, is a reminder of the existence and also precarious situation of these secretive creatures. Not only the species from the tropical rain forests, but European and North American species, too, are very much endangered. Some options for offering protection to these fascinating animals can be exercised almost literally on our doorstep.

Protective measures, such as the so-called fence-bucket-method, can prevent dramatic losses at critical sites in the short term.

Amphibian Protection Begins at Home

We all know that there are finite amounts of land and soil, and the increasingly intensive use of land by human goes hand in hand with a loss of habitats for wild animals. Amphibians are "earthbound" creatures, usually adapted to a network of specific habitats and can therefore react only to a limited degree to changes in their habitats. This is one reason why amphibians are on the Red List of most industrialized countries in Europe and are usually classified as "endangered," "strongly endangered," or "lost." Amphibians are good indicators that ecologically healthy or intact habitats still exist, and they can help demonstrate what is required in practical environmental protection.

It is up to us to provide amphibians with an acceptable quality of life by giving them the open space they need. We must guard their requirements to such a degree, or re-create these conditions, that toads, frogs and newts are assured long-term survival and that our children's children will still be able to watch the incomparable spectacle of breeding migration.

Where Are the Dangers?

The greatest danger for most local amphibian species is the massive changes to which their habitats are exposed. In Central Europe, very few landscapes have not somehow been utilized and thus changed by man. Even in the Alps, few valleys remain untouched. Natural habitats in valleys, meandering rivers and creeks, alluvial forests with high diversity, or large swamps and marshes have been overrun by human expansion. Man has made the landscape more uniform, the better to use it over the long term. The past hundred years especially have seen intensified use of forests, fields and meadows for agriculture and trade, and this has changed the face of the landscape forever, leading to a great loss of amphibian habitats.

In addition to the increasingly intense use of land for agriculture, the pressure exerted by growing communities and industrial areas play an important role. Construction projects, both residential and industrial, continue to destroy wetlands. At the same time, many smaller bodies of water, such as reservoirs, are filled in, leading to a shortage of suitable water bodies;

the altered dynamics of the landscape prevent new bodies of water from developing naturally. The drain systems have destroyed pools and very small bodies of water, which has compromised the availability of breeding ponds and habitats for yellow-bellied toads (*Bombina variegata*), marsh newts (*Triturus vulgaris*) and grass frogs (*Rana temporaria*). Private garden ponds can usually not compensate for the drastic loss of natural bodies of water, as they are usually concentrated in housing developments where traffic is a problem or other habitats are missing, all factors that prevent the development of larger populations.

In addition to the loss of waters, the increased rate of habitat fragmentation through new roads and higher concentrations of traffic plays a large role. But the destruction of footpaths and hedges also has long-term negative effects on migratory corridors and distribution. Species that depend on microclimatic conditions during migration are strongly restricted in their migratory activity. This is especially serious with respect to the loss of appropriate breeding ponds.

Transitional habitats at forest edges are also increasingly being pushed aside. Cultivated land is frequently extended right up to the forest vegetation without any transition zones, and yet these same areas provide ideal habitats not only for many amphibian and reptile species, but also for other species, especially when they contain structures such as stone walls, fallen wood or piles of wood. Not only forest margins, but the forests themselves have changed dramatically over the past decades through the introduction of monoculture. Monocultures can be equated with loss of diversity. And amphibians are very much in need of habitat diversity.

Changes in water quality and the systematic destruction of food supplies through the use of pesticides are harmful to amphibians in the long term. In areas with insufficient alkalinity that would buffer the acids in water, bodies of water are increasingly acidified and eggs become vulnerable to fungi. Many ponds are overburdened with nutrients. This excess in nutrients can lead to increased oxygen consumption. But when there is too little oxygen in the water, higher life-forms no longer survive in it. Eggs and larvae die even before they have a chance to begin their fascinating transformation into frogs. Fish ponds, recreational bathing and even skating can all pose dangers to amphibians. Natural ponds with healthy populations were often used as fish ponds in the past, and this has destroyed conditions that are favorable for amphibians, such as shallow waters near the banks or submersed vegetation. Moreover, their predators were constantly, artificially, reintroduced into

the water in great numbers. The creation of lucrative bathing lakes for tourism in ecologically valuable wetlands has been another factor that has contributed to the growing uniformity of the landscape. In these cases, the shores tend to be pebbled and cleared, to prevent the growth of reed and other water plants that are a nuisance to bathers. All these influences have rendered these bodies of water unusable by amphibians.

What Can We Do to Help?

Rehabilitation of wetlands and creation of new ponds that resemble natural ponds as much as possible is vitally important, because the lack of breeding ponds and water networks poses the greatest threat to amphibians. When creating "natural" bodies of water, the following guidelines should be considered:

The spawning period is the time when more amphibians are seen than during any other season. In spring, most mature specimens begin with their migration for reproductive purposes. Habitats have been so severely divided and sectioned off that migration has become one of the most serious causes of endangerment. Many animals can be saved from becoming fatalities on the roads with the help of the fence-bucket-method.

Creating new bodies of water—better yet, creating aqueous networks—is an important contribution to amphibian protection, as drainage of moist areas on a large scale and the destruction of spawning waters was one of the major factors in amphibian population decline. Garden ponds, too, can play an important role. The new bodies of water should, however, be created as far away from roads as is possible.

■ The dimension should be at least 35 square yards (30 square meters) and no more than 2,300 square yards (2,000 square meters).

■ It is better to create several small bodies of water than one large body, because negative influences such as drought, toxins and fish may then affect only some of the water bodies.

■ If the water is located right next to intensively farmed land, it is important to create a buffer zone of at least 65 feet (20 m) in order to prevent pesticides leeching into the water, which will lead to eutrophication. The buffer must not be mowed more than once a year and it must not be fertilized.

■ The ratio of deep to shallow water should be 50:50. The shallow water should be no more than 20 inches (50 cm) deep.

■ Shallow water zones should be located on the north side.

■ Access to the habitat must be assured for terrestrial species.

■ It is best not to create new pools within 328 to 546 yards (300 to 500 m) of heavily traveled roads, especially when large forests are located on the far side of the road. Because juvenile frogs tend to wander away from their breeding ponds in all directions, migrations would eventually pass across the traffic artery.

In addition to creating new bodies of waters for amphibians, the following measures should be encouraged:

■ Creating registers of local herpetofauna and their habitats with the goal of implementing conservation by means of targeted environmental care.

■ Researching the life histories of individual species in order to better evaluate how changes in their habitat will affect them.

■ Putting up hedges, wood piles and footpaths to restructure the landscape, especially in open areas.

■ Creating a dense water network, with an average density of two to three bodies of water per square mile/kilometer.

■ Building long-term protective structures near roads, after migratory patterns have been studied, to prevent the isolation of populations.

The question "How many frogs does nature need?" can be answered only in one way: as many as are required for their long-term survival without human help. And when is an amphibian population capable of sustaining itself without human assistance? When it is provided with a good habitat that is subject to certain natural phenomena that will maintain favorable conditions for survival. This habitat may differ for different amphibian species, but its basic parameters apply to all. Not surprisingly, the same characteristics that make landscapes livable for amphibians are also those that promote health and well-being in humans.

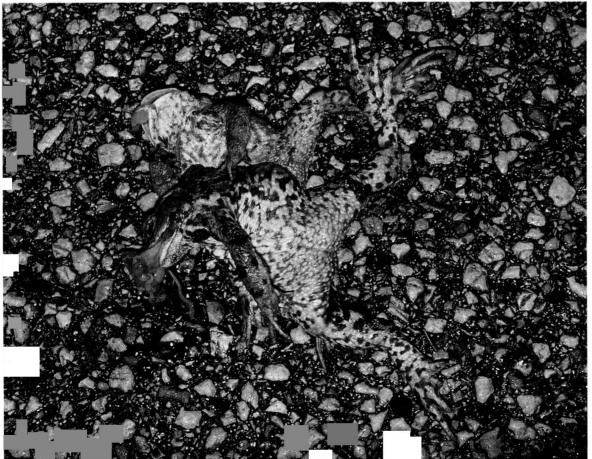

The migratory behavior of European explosive spawners is one of the most impressive phenomena in nature. In Europe alone the total number of amphibians killed during migration—including juveniles, which are difficult to count—lies in the millions. Conservation must ensure the safety of amphibian populations in a changing environment, increasingly cut up by roads and highways. Long-term solutions should be a priority, such as gates and over- and underpasses.

Musings of a Frogkeeper

Rolf Bechter

For more than 30 years, I have been fascinated by the gentle song of the Midwife toad in a Swiss gravel pit as much as by the loud territorial call of the strawberry (poison-dart) frog in a Costa Rican cacao plantation. Today, however, what I hear is less a territorial or mating call than a call for help.

"A true friend of nature is someone with an internal connection to all living things in nature and empathy for the fate of all creatures..."
ALBERT SCHWEITZER

Amphibians are no exception as far as the worldwide threat to wildlife is concerned. Of what use are the cleverest survival strategies of some species? What nature has created in millions of years, its youngest product, the "Homo sapiens" or "wise man," can destroy in just a few years. And if we believe the army of experts, we are on the way to doing just that!

All over the world, economics seems more important than the preservation of an environment without which none of us, including economists, will, in the long run, be able to survive. The hole in the ozone layer; air and water pollution; the fatal waste of raw materials; the clearing, in unimaginable dimensions, of virgin forests—these are catchwords that, as they are repeated over and over, hardly catch anyone's ear any more.

What is left is the individual shrugging his or her shoulders. All of us, whether we want to or not, participate in the general affluence. Because individuals are without power, we delegate our personal responsibility to lawmakers. Mountains of laws, protective measures, lists of species, Red Lists, protocols, conventions, and other such documents litter thousands of offices. Heaps and heaps of paper. But the imposing paper tiger, which swallows millions and millions of dollars, often loses its teeth during its first encounter with economics.

Wherever living beings are protected on paper while their life's necessities are not maintained for economic reasons, laws are but vain alibis; they are meaningless, absurd. What good is it to a fish to be protected by law if it can find neither spawning grounds nor clean water? What help is protection by law to the midwife toad or the natterjack, when gravel pits are being filled to become construction sites? Bats, birds, butterflies, what use is their protective status when they are poisoned by pesticides? Where is the meaning of species-protection legislation, when amateurs with three frogs in their luggage are held up at borders in South and Central America and criminally charged with a $10,000 fine or imprisonment, while at the same time tropical wood is legally being exported by the ton, virgin forests destroyed, depriving thousands and thousands of the same animals of their life habitats?

I am convinced that protection of species can work only in combination with enlightenment. We cannot protect what we do not know. Exhibits with live animals, reports on how to keep and breed them, and illustrations and videos sensitize the larger public much more than corpses in formaldehyde kept on the shelves of scientific institutes will ever do, however important they may be for research purposes.

May this book contribute to the knowledge and understanding of amphibians, for without knowledge there is no conscience, and without awareness no creed. May future generations be able to feel enthusiasm for these gems of nature!

Facing page:
European tree frogs
(Hyla arborea).

Appendix

Photographing Amphibians

Robert Hofrichter

Beginning nature photographers are often satisfied with simply getting a frog or a newt "into the frame." But a good photographer aims much higher: he tries to communicate a personal— and technically and creatively perfect—view of reality. In a good photograph each element in the frame should contribute to the whole image.

Difficulties in Photographing Amphibians

Anyone who has tried their hand at creating good photographs of amphibians soon realizes that this is no easy undertaking. There are several reasons. First is the structure of amphibian skin. Reptiles with their dry scaly skin are usually easier to capture on camera. But the smooth, shiny or slippery skin of amphibians, devoid of hair, scales or other surface features, often reflects flash light in an unfortunate manner. The black spots and stripes of some species, in combination with very light or bright color patterns (fire salamanders and poison-dart frogs) make it difficult to adjust the lighting. The amphibian eye sometimes blurs into a black spot and is no longer recognizable on the photograph; conversely the brightly colored sections of skin may be overexposed as a result of using a flash.

In addition, some amphibian species are quite small and difficult to approach without startling

them into flight; sometimes their habitats may be difficult to reach (ponds, pools, swamps, marshes, flooded forests and in rain forest canopies). The photographer must be able to get up close and must usually be on the same level as the object. The following tips are aimed at photography less as an art than as simple documentation. Many scientists, hobbyists and terrarium owners are not trying to create works of art with their pictures. They are simply capturing a specimen on film—as proof of its occurrence in specific locations, to document a certain coloring or simply as "proof" that the species has even been sighted. This kind of pictorial document has its uses. However, as soon as the print is taken out of the scientific context or the emotional value for the individual photographer and is regarded as a "work of art," its weaknesses are quickly apparent. These can roughly be divided into two areas:

1. **Technical weaknesses:** This includes, above all, lack of focus (e.g., unfocused eyes or poor depth of field) and poor lighting (over- and underexposure, images that are "washed out" by the flash, poor light conduction, shadows, undesirable flash reflections on the skin and in the eyes).

2. **Weaknesses in composition:** Poor image composition, wrong choice of format (landscape or portrait), poor positioning of main subject within the frame, overly animated fore- or background, and similar problems.

Basics of Image Composition

The basics of image composition are derived from fine art (painting) and apply in principle to all graphic media. A good photographer must be able to zero in on the most important elements of image composition—line, color, space and perspective—by looking through the viewfinder, and also to eliminate any detracting factors. Taking a good photograph means exercising self-discipline. Background focus can be verified by pressing the relevant button (most

One common mistake in taking photographs of amphibians is the attempt to do so from a "bird's eye view." Generally, pictures of frogs are best when taken from a "frog perspective." The viewer will then see the surroundings captured in the picture just as a frog sitting on the ground or another one sitting on a tree would. Creating good photographs of amphibians means that the photographer needs to move into the "frog perspective."

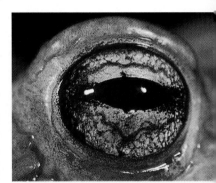

professional-quality cameras are equipped accordingly) to see whether the focus is sufficient and, above all, whether the background interferes with the subject. A branch or blade of grass—possibly lit up by the flash—shouldn't come as a surprise in the print, but rather be identified as a problem through the viewfinder. The photographer must make the right decision, though there is little time to do so in the case of wildlife photography in general, and amphibian photography in particular. "I can't spend all that time thinking about what I'm doing, otherwise the frog will simply be gone," many amateur frog photographers will think upon reading these lines. In response, one could say that a poor photograph in which a small dark spot somewhere within the frame is supposed to represent the frog will hardly capture anyone's interest, is usually useless and ends up in the wastebasket. Therefore the best approach would be to take one or two quick snapshots for documentation (now you've got the subject "in the box") and then take the time to achieve better results.

A good composition can usually be evaluated according to objective criteria: there is a certainty that the image includes all that it should, while omitting anything extraneous. A feeling of balance and harmony defines a good composition. The main motif must be presented without compromise, and there should be no interference through a chaotic or overly animated fore- or background. Often, all that is needed is to move the camera a few inches/centimeters to eliminate unwanted objects from the frame.

The goal should go beyond simply capturing an amphibian on film; it should also capture typical behaviors and movements. It is especially attractive to observe amphibians in their breeding habitat.

The frog should be neither too small nor too large in the picture. Even the most beautiful frog photograph needs to include some background to show off the subject to its best advantage. However, no rule of composition is carved in stone and (sometimes) it should be overthrown. Symmetrical compositions should usually be avoided (for example, with the horizon or another important element right in the middle of the frame) but sometimes complete symmetry can be one of the most powerful means of composing a strong image (e.g., a

Good technical equipment and preparation are essential for photographic expeditions into tropical rain forests. Two cameras, sufficient batteries and film and other equipment are the minimal requirement. Considering the wet habitats of most amphibian species, the photographer must have appropriate clothing and be undaunted by water, mud, swamps, possibly even leeches and other pests.

frontal frog portrait). Diagonal lines in the image—also achieved by simply tilting the camera—are generally preferable to vertical or horizontal lines, but here too exceptions confirm the rule (a leaf frog sitting on a vertical reed among many other vertical reeds, with only some of the reeds brought into full focus; the repetition of vertical lines is the compositional element in this case).

Technical Aspects

One of the most important technical aspects in photographing amphibians is good depth of field and lighting. Here is a rule to which no exception should be made: the eye of the animal must be in focus. Amphibian photography on the whole should have as much depth as possible, the f-stop should be set to 8, 11 or even 16. Ambient light is often insufficient.

Moreover, many amphibian species are nocturnal or live in the dim light of the forest, so flashes are an important tool in amphibian photography.

The Equipment

The best lenses are macrolenses with long focusing ranges (100 to 200 mm) and zoom lenses (possibly with an additional ring) of 200 to 300 mm. Wide-angle lenses with 24, 21 and even 18 mm focal length can produce stunning photographs with unusual perspectives, especially of larger amphibian species. They can only be used for species that have a high flight threshold because you need to be as close as a few inches/centimeters to take the picture. Two flashes are usually required to properly light such wide-angle images.

The advantage of ring flashes is that they are lightweight and easy to handle (important, above all, for expeditions to remote areas) and tend to produce the correct light. Modern ring flashes have TTL-light sensors; they are designed for close-ups and so are not too strong, which means that the usual "wash-out" effect of pictures taken with a flash rarely happens. On the contrary, more care should be taken to avoid underexposure, especially if the animal has dark coloring; several exposures should be taken at different apertures. Another advantage—although this can all too easily become a disadvantage—is even lighting without shadows. The ring flash may produce a "flat" image with unimaginative lighting. One disadvantage of ring flashes in amphibian photography is the unattractive reflection in the eye—most frogs have large eyes and pupils. These ring-flash reflections become the most noticeable aspect of the photograph. After digitization (e.g., for print or for a photo CD) the reflection can be edited out.

When using a flash system, it is best not to attach it directly to the camera—for close-ups shots there wouldn't be enough light in front of the lens—but to set it up at an angle behind the camera. This lighting angle brings out the shape of the body and the texture of the skin. However, the angle should not be too pronounced, otherwise unwanted shadows may result.

In many photographs (here of Agalychnis callydrias) the subject looks away from the camera.

Below: The impressive coloring of this leaf frog Agalychnis annae is wonderfully shown against the black background. When shooting at night, it is important to get the right touch of flashlight: the black background may throw off the camera's light meter and lead to overexposed pictures. The wide open pupil of this specimen confirms that this shot was in fact taken at night.

(Frank Glaw, Jörn Köhler, Robert Hofrichter and Alain Dubois)

Amphibian Systematics: List of Recent Families, Genera, and Species

The following list provides an overview of all currently known species and genera in recent amphibians (status December 31, 1997). New descriptions and other taxonomic changes from 1998 (and after) have not been included. The families are listed in alphabetical order to facilitate locating them. Within each family, genera and species have also been listed in alphabetical order. Rhacophoridae are listed as a separate family for practical reasons, although they are currently classified as a subfamily of true frogs (Ranidae). Even with the utmost effort and every intention to be complete and accurate, a list of this kind may contain some errors for several reasons. For details and comments on systematics, please turn to Chapter 2.

1. Order GYMNOPHIONA (Caecilians)

1. Family Caeciliidae Rafinesque-Schmaltz, 1814

1. Genus *Boulengerula* Tornier, 1897 (5 species, Tanzania, Kenya, Malawi, Rwanda)
Boulengerula boulengeri, B. changamwensis, B. fischeri, B. taitanus, B. uluguruensis
2. Genus *Brasilotyphlus* Taylor, 1968 (1 species, Amazon basin)
Brasilotyphlus braziliensis
3. Genus *Caecilia* Linnaeus, 1758 (32 species, Panama and northern South America)
Caecilia abitaguae, C. albiventris, C. antioquiaensis, C. armata, C. attenuata, C. bokermanni, C. caribea, C. corpulenta, C. crassisquama, C. degenerata, C. disossea, C. dunni, C. flavopunctata, C. gracilis, C. guntheri, C. inca, C. leucocephala, C. marcusi, C. mertensi, C. nigricans, C. occidentalis, C. orientalis, C. pachynema, C. perdita, C. pressula, C. subdermalis, C. subnigricans, C. subterminalis, C. tentaculata, C. tenuissima, C. thompsoni, C. volcani
4. Genus *Dermophis* Peters, 1879 (3 species, southern Mexico to north-western ColumbiaColombia)
Dermophis mexicanus, D. oaxacae, D. parciveps
5. Genus *Gegeneophis* Peters, 1879 (3 species, India)
Gegeneophis camosuscarnosus, G. fulleri, G. ramaswamii
6. Genus *Geotrypetes* Peters, 1880 (3 species, tropical West Africa and western Ethiopia)
Geotrypetes angeli, G. pseudoangeli, G. seraphini
7. Genus *Grandisonia* Taylor, 1968 (5 species, Seychelles Islands)
Grandisonia alternans, G. brevis, G. diminutiva, G. larvata, G. sechellensis
8. Genus *Gymnopis* Peters, 1874 (2 species, Honduras to Panama)
Gymnopis multiplicata, G. syntremus
9. Genus *Herpele*, Peters, 1879 (2 species, tropical West Africa)
Herpele multiplicata, H. squalostoma
10. Genus *Hypogeophis* Peters, 1879 (1 species, Seychelles Islands)
Hypogeophis rostratus
11. Genus *Idiocranium* Parker, 1936 (1 species, Cameroun, Nigeria ?)
Idiocranium russeli
12. Genus *Indotyphlus* Taylor, 1960 (1 species, India)
Indotyphlus battersbyi
13. Genus *Luetkenotyphlus* Taylor, 1968 (1 species, south eastern Brazil)
Luetkenotyphlus brasiliensis
14. Genus *Microcaecilia* Taylor, 1968 (5 species, northern South America)
Microcaecilia albiceps, M. rabei, M. supernumeraria, M. taylori, M. unicolor
15. Genus *Mimosiphonops* Taylor, 1968 (2 species, southeastern Brazil)
Mimosiphonops reinhardti, M. vermiculatus
16. Genus *Oscaecilia* Taylor, 1968 (9 species, Costa Rica, Panama, and northern South America)
Oscaecilia bassleri, O. elongata, O. equatorialis, O. hypereumeces, O. koepckeorum., O. ochrocephala, O. osae, O. polyzona, O. zweifeli
17. Genus *Parvicaecilia* Taylor, 1968 (2 species, northern Colombia)
Parvicaecilia nicefori, P. pricei
18. Genus *Praslinia* Boulger, 1909 (1 species, Seychelles Islands)
Praslinia cooperi
19. Genus *Schistometopum* Parker, 1941 (5 species, Kenya, Tanzania, and islands in the Gulf of Guinea, West Africa)
Schistometopum brevirostre, S. ephele, S. garzonheydti, S. gregorii, S. thomense
20. Genus *Siphonops* Wagler, 1828 (5 species, tropical South America east of the Andes)
Siphonops, annulatus, S. hardyi, S. insulanus, S. leucoderus, S. paulensis
21. Genus *Sylvacaecilia* Wake, 1987 (1 species, Ethiopia)
Sylvocaecilia grandisonae

2. Family Ichthyophiidae Taylor, 1968

1. Genus *Caudacaecilia* Taylor, 1986 (5 species, Malaysia, Sumatra, Borneo, and Philippines)
Caudacaecilia asplenia, C. larutensis, C. nigroflava, C. paucidentula, C. weberi
2. Genus *Ichthyophis* Fitzinger, 1826 (32 species, India, Sri Lanka, Southeast Asia, southern Philippines and western Indonesia)
Ichthyophis acuminatus, I. atricollaris, I. bannanicus I. beddomei, I. bernisi, I. biangularis, I. billitonensis, I. bombayensis, I. dulitensis, I. elongatus, I. glandulosus, I. glutinosus, I. humphreyi, I. hypocyaneus, I. javanicus, I. kohtaoensis, I. laosensis, I. longicephalus, I. malabarensis, I. mindanaoensis, I. monochrous, I. orthoplicatus, I. paucisulcus, I. peninsularis, I. pseudangularis, I. sikkimensis, I. singaporensis, I. subterrestris, I. sumatranus, I. supachaii, I. tricolor, I. youngorum

3. Family Rhinatrematidae Nussbaum, 1977 (Tailed caecilians)

1. Genus *Epicrionops* Boulenger, 1883 (8 species, northwestern South America from Venezuela to Peru)
Epicrionops bicolor, E. columbianus, E. lativittatus, E. marmoratus, E. niger, E. parkeri, E. peruvianus, E. petersi
2. Genus *Rhinatrema* Duméril and Bibron, 1841 (1 species, Guayana region)
Rhinatrema bivittatum

4. Family Scolecomorphidae Taylor, 1969

1. Genus *Crotaphatrema* Nussbaum, 1985 (2 species, Cameroun)
Crotaphatrema bornmuelleri, C. lamottei
2. Genus *Scolecomorphus* Boulenger, 1883 (3 species, Tanzania, Malawi)
Scolecomorphus kirkii, S. uluguruensis, S. vittatus

5. Family Typhlonectidae Taylor, 1968 (Aquatic caecilians)

1. Genus *Atretochoana* Nussbaum and Wilkinson, 1995 (1 species, South America)
Atretochoana eiselti
2. Genus *Chthonerpeton* Peters, 1879 (7 species, southern Brazil and northern Argentina)
Chthonerpeton arii, C. braestrupi, C. exile, C. indistinctum, C. onorei, C. perissodus, C. viviparum
3. Genus *Nectocaecilia* Taylor, 1968 (4 species, Amazon and Orinoko region)
Nectocaecilia cooperi, N. haydee, N. ladigesi, N. petersii
4. Genus *Potomotyphlus* Taylor, 1968 (2 species, Amazon and Orinoko region)
Potomotyphlus kaupii, P. melanochus
5. Genus *Typhlonectes* Peters, 1879 (6 species, northern South America)
Typhlonectes anguillaformis, T. compressicauda, T. cunhai, T. natans, T. obesus, T. venezuelensis

6. Familie Uraeotyphlidae Nussbaum, 1979

1. Genus *Uraeotyphlus* Peters, 1879 (4 species, southern half of Indian subcontinent)
Uraeotyphlus malabaricus, U. menoni, U. narayani, U. oxyurus

2. Order URODELA (Salamanders)

1. Family Ambystomatidae Hallowell, 1856 (Mole salamanders)

1. Genus *Ambystoma* Tschudi, 1838 (28 species, North America to Mexico)
Ambystoma amblycephalum, A, andersoni, A. annulatum, A. barbouri, A. bombypellum, A. cingulatum, A. dumerilii, A. flavipiperatum, A. gracile, A. granulosum, A. jeffersonianum, A. lacustris, A. laterale, A. lermaense, A. mabeei, A. macrodactylum, A. maculatum, A. mexicanum, A. nothagenes, A. opacum, A. ordinarium, A. platineum, A. rosaceum, A. talpoideum, A. taylori, A. texanum, A. tigrinum, A. tremblayi
2. Genus *Rhyacosiredon* Dunn, 1928 (4 species, Mexico)
Rhyacosiredon altamirani, R. leorae, R. rivularis, R. zempoalaensis

2. Family Amphiumidae Gray, 1825 (Amphiumas, congo eels)

1. Genus *Amphiuma* Garden, 1821 (3 species, southeastern USA)
Amphiuma means, A. pholeter, A. tridactylum

3. Family Cryptobranchidae Fitzinger, 1826 (Giant salamander)

1. Genus *Andrias* Tschudi, 1837 (2 species, eastern China, Japan)
Andrias davidianus, A. japonicus
2. Genus *Cryptobranchus* Leuckart, 1821 (1 species, eastern USA)
Cryptobranchus alleganiensis

4. Family Dicamptodontidae Tihen, 1958

1. Genus *Dicamptodon* Strauch, 1870 (4 species, USA)
Dicamptodon aterrimus, D. copei, D. ensatus, D. tenebrosus
2. Genus *Rhyacotriton* Dunn, 1920 (3 species, USA)
Rhyacotriton cascadae, R. kezeri, R. olympicus

5. Family Hynobiidae Cope, 1859 (Asiatic [oriental] salamanders)

1. Genus *Batrachuperus* Boulenger, 1878 (8 species, China, Tibet, Iran and Afghanistan)
Batrachuperus gorganensis, B. karlschmidti, B. longdongensis, B. mustersi, B. persicus, B. pinchonii, B. tibetanus, B. yenyuanensis
2. Genus *Hynobius* Tschudi, 1838 (25 species, East Asia to Japan)
Hynobius abre, H. amjiensis, H. arisanensis, H. boulengeri, H. chinensis, H. dunni, H. formosanus, H. hidamontanus, H. kimurae, H. leechii, H. lichenatus, H. mantschuricus, H. naevius, H. nebulosus, H. nigrescens, H. okiensis, H. retardatus, H. sonani, H. stejnegeri, H. takedai, H. tenuis, H. tokyoensis, H. tsuensis, H. turkestanicus, H. yiwuensis
3. Genus *Liua* Zhao and Hu, 1983 (1 species, China)
Liua shihi
4. Genus *Onychodactylus* Tschudi, 1838 (2 species, northeastern Asia, Japan)
Onychodactylus fischeri, O. japonicus
5. Genus *Pachyhynobius* Fei, Hu and Wu 1983 (1 species, China)
Pachyhynobius shangchengensis
6. Genus *Pseudohynobius* Fei and Ye, 1983 (2 species, China)
Pseudohynobius flavomaculatus, P. tsinpaiensis
7. Genus *Ranodon* Kessler, 1866 (1 species, Russia, China)
Ranodon sibiricus
8. Genus *Salamandrella* Dybowski, 1870 (1 species, large areas of northern Asia)
Salamandrella keyserlingii

6. Family Plethodontidae Gray, 1850 (Lungless salamanders)

1. Genus *Aneides* Baird, 1849 (5 species, USA)
Aneides aeneus, A. ferreus, A. flavipunctatus, A. hardii, A. lugubris
2. Genus *Batrachoseps* Bonaparte, 1841 (9 species, western North America)
Batrachoseps aridus, B. attenuatus, B. campi, B. gabrieli, B. nigriventris, B. pacificus, B. simatus, B. stebbinsi, B. wrighti
3. Genus *Bolitoglossa* Duméril, Bibron and Duméril, 1854 (76 species, Central and South America to central Bolivia)
Bolitoglossa adspersa, B. altamazonica, B. alvaradoi, B. arborescandens, B. biseriata, B. borburata, B. capitana, B. carri, B. celaquae, B. cerroensis, B. chica, B. colonnea, B. compacta, B. conanti, B. cuchumatana, B. cuna, B. decora, B. diaphora, B. digitigrada, B. diminuta, B. dofleini, B. dunni, B. engelhardti, B. epimela, B. equatoriana, B. flavimembris, B. flaviventris, B. franklini, B. gracilis, B. hartwegi, B. helmrichi, B. hermosa, B. hypacra, B. jacksoni, B. lignicola, B. lincolni, B. longissima, B. macrinii, B. marmorea, B. medemi, B. meliana, B. mexicana, B. minutula, B. morio, B. mulleri, B. nicefori, B. nigrescens, B. occidentalis, B. odonnelli, B. orestes, B. palmata, B. pandi, B. peruviana, B. phalarosoma, B. platydactyla, B. porrasorum, B. ramosi, B. riletti, B. robusta, B. rostrata, B. rufescens, B. salvinii, B. savagei, B. schizodactyla, B. schmidti, B. silverstonei, B. sima, B. sooyorum, B. striatula, B. stuarti, B. subpalmata, B. taylori, B. vallecula, B. veracrucis, B. walkeri, B. yucatana
4. Genus *Bradytriton* Wake and Elias, 1983 (1 species, Guatemala)
Bradytriton silus
5. Genus *Chiropterotriton* Taylor, 1944 (9 species, Mexico)
Chiropterotriton arboreus, C. chiropterus, C. chondrostega, C. dimidiatus, C. lavae, C. magnipes, C. mosaueri, C. multidentatus, C. priscus
6. Genus *Dendrotriton* Wake and Elias, 1983 (5 species, Mexico, Guatemala)
Dendrotriton bromeliacia, D. cuchumatanus, D. megarhinus, D. rabbi, D. xolocalcae
7. Genus *Desmognathus* Baird, 1850 (13 species, south eastern Canada and USA)
Desmognathus aeneus, D. apalachicolae, D. auriculatus, D. brimleyorum, D. fuscus, D. imitator, D. monticola, D. ochrophaeus, D. orestes, D. quadramaculatus, D. santeetlah, D. welteri, D. wrighti
8. Genus *Ensatina* Gray, 1850 (1 species, western North America)
Ensatina eschscholtzii
9. Genus *Eurycea* Rafinesque, 1822 (14 species, eastern North America)
Eurycea aquatica, E. bislineata, E. cirrigera, E. junaluska, E. longicauda, E. lucifuga, E. multiplicata, E. nana, E. neotenes, E. quadridigitata, E. sosorum, E. tridentifera, E. tynerensis, E. wilderae
10. Genus *Gyrinophilus* Cope, 1869 (3 species, North America)
Gyrinophilus gulolineatus, G. palleucus, G. porphyriticus
11. Genus *Haideotriton* Carr, 1939 (1 species, southeastern USA)
Haideotriton wallacei
12. Genus *Hemidactylium* Tschudi, 1838 (1 species, eastern North America)
Hemidactylium scutatum
13. Genus *Hydromantes* Gistel, 1848 (3 species, western USA)
Hydromantes brunus, H. platycephalus, H. shastae
14. Genus *Ixalotriton* Wake and Johnson, 1989 (1 species, Mexico)
Ixalotriton niger
15. Genus *Leurognathus* Moore, 1899 (1 species, USA)
Leurognathus marmoratus
16. Genus *Lineatriton* Tanner, 1950 (1 species, Mexico)
Lineatriton lineolus

17. Genus *Nototriton* Wake and Elias, 1983 (12 species, Mexico, Guatemala to Costa Rica)
Nototriton abscondens, N. adelos, N. alvarezdeltoroi, N. guanacaste, N. lignicola, N. major, N. nasalis, N. picadoi, N. richardi, N. sanctibarbarus, N. tapanti, N. veraepacis
18. Genus *Nyctanolis* Elias and Wake, 1983 (1 species, Mexico, Guatemala)
Nyctanolis pernix
19. Genus *Oedipina* Keferstein, 1868 (21 species, southern Mexico to Ecuador)
Oedipina alfaroi, O. alleni, O. altura, O. carablanca, O. collaris, O. complex, O. cyclocauda, O. elongata, O. gephyra, O. gracilis, O. grandis, O. ignea, O. pacificensis, O. parvipes, O. paucidentata, O. poelzi, O. pseudouniformis, O. stenopodia, O. stuarti, O. taylori, O. uniformis
20. Genus *Parvimolge* Taylor, 1944 (1 species, Mexico)
Parvimolge townsendi
21. Genus *Phaeognathus* Highton, 1961 (1 species, USA)
Phaeognathus hubrichti
22. Genus *Plethodon* Tschudi, 1839 (42 species, USA)
Plethodon albagula, P. aureolus, P. caddoensis, P. chattahoochee, P. chlorobryonis, P. cinereus, P. cylindraceus, P. dorsalis, P. dunni, P. elongatus, P. fourchensis, P. glutinosus, P. grobmani, P. hoffmani, P. hubrichti, P. idahoensis, P. jordani, P. kentucki, P. kiamichi, P. kisatchie, P. larselli, P. mississippi, P. neomexicanus, P. nettingi, P. ocmulgee, P. ouachitae, P. petraeus, P. punctatus, P. richmondi, P. savannah, P. sequoyah, P. serratus, P. shenandoah, P. stormi, P. teyahalee, P. vandykei, P. variolatus, P. vehiculum, P. websteri, P. wehrlei, P. welleri, P. yonahlossee
23. Genus *Pseudoeurycea* Taylor, 1944 (32 species, Mexico and Guatemala)
Pseudoeurycea ahuitzotl, P. altamontana, P. anitae, P. bellii, P. brunnata, P. cephalica, P. cochranae, P. conanti, P. exspectata, P. firscheini, P. gadovii, P. galeanae, P. goebeli, P. juarezi, P. leprosa, P. longicauda, P. melanomolga, P. mixcoatl, P. mystax, P. nigromaculata, P. parva, P. praecellens, P. rex, P. robertsi, P. saltator, P. scandens, P. smithi, P. tenchalli, P. teotepec, P. tlahcuiloh, P. unguidentis, P. werleri
24. Genus *Pseudotriton* Tschudi, 1838 (2 species, USA)
Pseudotriton montanus, P. ruber
25. Genus *Speleomantes* Dubois, 1984 (7 species, Italy, Sardinia, southeastern France)
Speleomantes ambrosii, S. flavus, S. genei, S. imperialis, S. italicus, S. strinatii, S. supramontis
26. Genus *Stereochilus* Cope, 1869 (1 species, USA)
Stereochilus marginatus
27. Genus *Thorius* Cope, 1869 (13 species, Mexico)
Thorius arboreus, T. aureus, T. boreas, T. dubitus, T. insperatus, T. macdougalli, T. minutissimus, T. narisovalis, T. pennatulus, T. pulmonaris, T. schmidti, T. smithi, T. troglodytes
28. Genus *Typhlomolge* Stejneger, 1896 (2 species, USA)
Typhlomolge rathbuni, T. robusta
29. Genus *Typhlotriton* Stejneger, 1893 (1 species, USA)
Typhlotriton spelaeus

7. Family Proteidae Gray, 1825 (Olms)

1. Genus *Necturus* Rafinesque, 1819 (5 species, eastern to middle North Amercia)
Necturus alabamensis, N. beyeri, N. lewisi, N. maculosus, N. punctatus
2. Genus *Proteus* Laurenti, 1768 (1 species, northern Italy, Slovenia, Croatia, Bosnia-Herzegovina)
Proteus anguinus

8. Family Salamandridae Goldfuss, 1820 (True salamanders and newts)

1. Genus *Chioglossa* Bocage, 1864 (1 species, Spain, Portugal)
Chioglossa lusitanica
2. Genus *Cynops* Tschudi, 1838 (6 species, China and Japan)
Cynops chenggongensis, C. cyanurus, C. ensicauda, C. orientalis, C. orphicus, C. pyrrhogaster
3. Genus *Echinotriton* Nussbaum and Brodie, 1982 (3 species, China, Japan)
Echinotriton andersoni, E. asperrimus, E. chinhaiensis
4. Genus *Euproctus* Gene, 1838 (3 species, Pyrenees, Sardinia and Corsica)
Euproctus asper, E. montanus, E. platycephalus
5. Genus *Hypselotriton* Wolterstorff, 1934 (1 species, China)
Hypselotriton wolterstorffi
6. Genus *Mertensiella* Wolterstorff, 1925 (2 species, Turkey, Georgia and the Greek Island of Karpathos)
Mertensiella caucasica, M. luschani
7. Genus *Neurergus* Cope, 1862 (4 species, Iran, Iraq, Turkey)
Neurergus crocatus, N. kaiseri, N. microspilotus, N. strauchii
8. Genus *Notophthalmus* Rafinesque, 1820 (3 species, eastern North America)
Notophthalmus meridionalis, N. perstriatus, N. viridescens
9. Genus *Pachytriton* Boulenger, 1878 (2 species, southeastern China)
Pachytriton brevipes, P. labiatus
10. Genus *Paramesotriton* Chang, 1935 (6 species, China, Vietnam)
Paramesotriton caudopunctatus, P. chinensis, P. deloustali, P. fuzhongensis, P. guanxiensis, P. hongkongensis
11. Genus *Pleurodeles* Michahelles, 1830 (2 species, Iberian peninsula, North Africa)
Pleurodeles poireti, P. waltl
12. Genus *Salamandra* Laurenti, 1768 (6 species, Europe, Northwest Africa, western Asia)
Salamandra algira, S. altra, S. corsica, S. infraimmaculata, S. lanzai, S. salamandra
13. Genus *Salamandrina* Fitzinger, 1826 (1 species, Italy)
Salamandrina terdigitata
14. Genus *Taricha* Gray, 1850 (3 species, west coast of North America)
Taricha granulosa, T. rivularis, T. torosa
15. Genus *Triturus* Rafinesque, 1815 (12 species, Europe and Asia Minor to Altai Mountains)
Triturus alpestris, T. boscai, T. carnifex, T. cristatus, T. dobrogicus, T. helveticus, T. italicus, T. karelini, T. marmoratus, T. montandoni, T. vittatus, T. vulgaris
16. Genus *Tylototriton* Anderson 1871 (6 species, India, Nepal, China, Burma, Thailand, Vietnam)
Tylototriton hainanensis, T. kweichowensis, T. shanjing, T. taliangensis, T. verrucosus, T. wenxianensis

9. Family Sirenidae Gray, 1825 (Sirens)

1. Genus *Pseudobranchus* Gray, 1825 (1 species, southeastern USA)
Pseudobranchus striatus
2. Genus *Siren* Österdam, 1766 (2 species, southeastern USA, northeastern Mexico)
Siren intermedia, S. lacertina

3. Order ANURA (Frogs and toads)

1. Family Allophrynidae Goin, Goin and Zug, 1978

1. Genus *Allophryne* Gaige, 1926 (1 species, northeastern South America)
Allophryne ruthveni

2. Family Arthroleptidae Mivart, 1869

1. Genus *Arthroleptis* Smith, 1849 (33 species, subsaharan Africa)
Arthroleptis adelphus, A. affinis, A. adolfifriderici, A. bivittatus, A. breviceps, A. carquejai, A. crusculus, A. francei, A. hematogaster, A. lameerei, A. loveridgei, A. milletihorsini, A. mossoensis, A. nimbaensis, A. phrynoides, A. poecilonotus, A. pyrrhoscelis, A. reichei, A. schubotzi, A. sylvatica, A. spinalis, A. stenodactylus, A. taeniatus, A. tanneri, A. troglodytes, A. tuberosus, A. variabilis, A. vercammeni, A. wahlbergii, A. xenochirus, A. xenodactyloides, A. xenodactylus, A. zimmeri
2. Genus *Astylosternus* Werner, 1898 (11 species, West and Central Africa)
Astylosternus batesi, A. diadematus, A. fallax, A. laurenti, A. montanus, A. nganhanus, A. occidentalis, A. perreti, A. ranoides, A. rheophilus, A. schioetzi
3. Genus *Cardioglossa* Boulenger, 1900 (16 species, West and Central subsaharan Africa)
Cardioglossa aureoli, C. cyaneospila, C. dorsalis, C. elegans, C. escalerae, C. gracilis, C. gratiosa, C. leucomystax, C. liberiensis, C. melanogaster, C. nigromaculata, C. oreas, C. pulchra, C. schiotzi, C. trifasciata, C. venusta
4. Genus *Leptodactylodon* Andersson, 1903 (11 species, West Africa from Nigeria to Cameroun)
Leptodactylodon albiventris, L. axillaris, L. bicolor, L. boulengeri, L. erythrogaster, L. mertensi, L. ornatus, L. ovatus, L. perreti, L. polyacanthus, L. ventrimarmoratus
5. Genus *Nyctibates* Boulenger, 1904 (1 species, Cameroun)
Nyctibates corrugatus
6. Genus *Scotobleps* Boulenger, 1900 (1 species, Nigeria to Zaire)
Scotobleps gabonicus
7. Genus *Trichobatrachus* Boulenger, 1900 (1 species, Nigeria to Zaire)
Trichobatrachus robustus

3. Family Brachycephalidae Günther, 1858 (Saddle-back toads)

1. Genus *Brachycephalus* Fitzinger, 1826 (2 species, southeastern Brazil)
Brachycephalus ephippium, B. nodoterga
2. Genus *Psyllophryne* Izecksohn, 1971 (1 species, southeastern Brazil)
Psyllophryne didactyla

4. Family Bufonidae Gray, 1825 (True toads)

1. Genus *Altiphrynoides* Dubois, 1987 (1 species, Ethiopia)
Altiphrynoides malcolmi
2. Genus *Andinophryne* Hoogmoed, 1985 (3 species, Ecuador, Colombia)
Andinophryne atelopoides, A. colomai, A. olallai
3. Genus *Ansonia* Stoliczka, 1870 (20 species, Southeast Asia)
Ansonia albomaculata, A. fuliginea, A. guibei, A. hanitschi, A kamblei, A. latidisca, A. leptopus, A. longidigita, A. malayana, A. mcgregori, A. minuta, A. muelleri, A. ornata, A. penagensis, A. platysoma, A. rubrigina, A. siamensis, A. spinulifer, A. tiomanica, A. torrentis
4. Genus *Atelophryniscus* McCranie, Wilson and William, 1989 (1 species, Honduras)
Atelophryniscus chrysophorus
5. Genus *Atelopus* Duméril and Bibron, 1841 (65 species, Costa Rica to Bolivia)
Atelopus arsyecue, A. arthuri, A. balios, A. bomolochos, A. boulengeri, A. carauta, A. carbonerensis, A. carrikeri, A. certus, A. chiriquiensis, A. chocoensis, A. coynei, A. cruciger, A. chryscorallus, A. ebenoides, A. elegans, A. erythropus, A. eusebianus, A. exiguus, A. famelicus, A. farci, A. flavescens, A. franciscus, A. galactogaster, A. glyphus, A. halihelos, A. ignescens, A. laetissimus, A. leoperezii, A. limosus, A. longibrachius, A. longirostris, A. lynchi, A. mindoensis, A. minutulus, A. mucubajiensis, A. muisca, A. nahumae, A. nepiozomus, A. nicefori, A. oxyrhynchus, A. pachydermus, A. palmatus, A. pedimarmoratus, A. peruensis, A. pictiventris, A. pinangoi, A. planispina, A. quimbaya, A. sanjosei, A. seminiferus, A. senex, A. sernai, A. simulatus, A. sonsonensis, A. sorianoi, A. spumarius, A. spurrelli, A. subornatus, A. tamaense, A. tricolor, A. varius, A. walkeri, A. willimani, A. zeteki
6. Genus *Bufo* Laurenti, 1768 (225 species, worldwide with the exception of Australia, New Zealand, Madagascar, the South Sea islands and polar regions; *B. marinus* has been imported to many areas, e.g. Australia).
Bufo abatus, B. achalensis, B. ailaoanus, B. alvarius, B. amatolicus, B. amboroensis, B. americanus, B. anderssoni, B. andrewsi, B. angusticeps, B. arborescandens, B. arenarum, B. arquipensis, B. arunco, B. asmarae, B. asper, B. atakamensis, B. atukoralei, B. bankorensis, B. beddomii, B. beiranus, B. berghei, B. biporcatus, B. blanfordii, B. blombergi, B. bocourti, B. boreas, B. brauni, B. brevirostris, B. brongersmai, B. buchneri, B. bufo, B. burmanus, B. caeruleostictus, B. calamita, B. camerunensis, B. campbelli, B. canaliferus, B. canorus, B. castaneoticus, B. cavifrons, B. celebensis, B. ceratophrys, B. chappuisi, B. chlorogaster, B. chudeaui, B. claviger, B. coccifer, B. cognatus, B. compactilis, B. coniferus, B. cophotis, B. corynetes, B. cristatus, B. cristiglans, B. crucifer, B. cruciger, B. cryptotympanicus, B. cycladen, B. cyphosus, B. danatensis, B. danielae, B. dapsilis, B. debilis, B. dhufarensis, B. diptychus, B. dodsoni, B. dombensis, B. dorbignyi, B. exsul, B. fastidiosus, B. fenoulheti, B. fergusonii, B. fernandezae, B. fissipes, B. flavolineatus, B. fuliginatus, B. funereus, B. gabbi, B. galeatus, B. gallardoi, B. gargarizans, B. gariepensis, B. garmani, B. gemmifer, B. glabberimus, B. gnustae, B. gracilipes, B. grandisonae, B. granulosus, B. guttatus, B. gutturalis, B. hadramautinus, B. haematiticus, B. hemiophrys, B. himalayanus, B. hoeschi, B. holdrigei, B. hololius, B. houstonensis, B. hypomelas, B. ibarrai, B. icterics, B. inca, B. intermedius. B. inyangae, B. iserni, B. japonicus, B. justinianoi, B. juxtasper, B. kabischi, B. kassasii, B. kavangensis, B. kavirensis, B. kelaartii, B. kelloggi, B. kerinyagae, B. kisoloensis, B. kotagamai, B. koynayensis, B. langanoensis, B. latastei, B. latifrons, B. lemairii, B. limensis, B. lindneri, B. lonnbergi, B. lughensis, B. lytkenii, B. macrocristatus, B. macrotis, B. maculatus, B. manicorensis, B. marinus, B. marmoreus, B. mauritanicus, B. mazatlanensis, B. melanochloris, B. melanogaster, B. melanopleura, B. melanostictus, B. microscaphus, B. microtympanum, B. minshanicus, B. nasicus, B. nesiotes, B. occidentalis, B. ocellatus, B. olivaceus, B. orientalis, B. pageoti, B. paracnemis, B. pardalis, B. parietalis, B. parkeri, B. parvus, B. pentoni, B. periglenes, B. peripatetes, B. perplexus, B. perreti, B. poeppigii, B. poweri, B. punctatus, B. pygmaeus, B. quadriporcatus, B. quechua, B. quercicus, B. raddei, B. rangeri, B. reesi, B. regularis, B. retiformis, B. robinsoni, B. rubropunctatus, B. rufus, B. rumbolli, B. schmidti, B. schneideri, B. scortecci, B. shaartusiensis, B. siachinensis, B. sibiliai, B. silentvalleyensis, B. simus, B. speciosus, B. spiculatus, B. spinulosus, B. steindachneri, B. stejnegeri, B. sternosignatus, B. stomaticus, B. stuarti, B. sulfureus, B. sumatranus, B. superciliaris, B. surdus, B. tacanensis, B. taitanus, B. terrestris, B. tibetanus, B. tienhoensis, B. togoensis, B. torrenticola, B. trifolium, B. tuberculatus, B. tuberosus, B. turkanae, B. tutelarius, B. typhonius, B. urunguensis, B. uzunguensis, B. valhallae, B. valliceps, B. variegatus, B. vellardi, B. veraguensis, B. verrucosissimus, B. vertebralis, B. villiersi, B. viridis, B. vittatus, B. wazae, B. wolongensis, B. woodhousii, B. xeros
7. Genus *Bufoides*, Pillai and Yazdani, 1973 (1 species, India)
Bufoides meghalayanus
8. Genus *Capensibufo* Grandison, 1980 (2 species, South Africa)
Capensibufo rosei, C. tradouwi
9. Genus *Crepidophryne* Cope, 1889 (1 species, Panama, Costa Rica)
Crepidophryne epiotica
10. Genus *Dendrophryniscus* Jiménez De La Espada, 1871 (7 species, South America)
Dendrophryniscus berthalutzae, D. bokermanni, D. brevipollicatus, D. carvalhoi, D. leucomystax, D. minutus, D. stawiarskyi
11. Genus *Didynamipus* Andersson, 1903 (1 species, Cameroun)
Didynamipus sjostedti
12. Genus *Frostius* Cannatella, 1986 (1 species, Brazil)
Frostius pernambucensis
13. Genus *Laurentophryne* Tihen, 1960 (1 species, Zaire)
Laurentophryne parkeri
14. Genus *Leptophryne* Fitzinger, 1843 (2 species, Southeast Asia)
Leptophryne borbonica, L. cruentata
15. Genus *Melanophryniscus* Gallardo, 1961 (9 species, South America)
Melanophryniscus cambaraensis, M. devincenzii, M. macrogranulosus, M. moreirae, M. orejasmirandai, M. rubriventris, M. sanmartini, M. stelzneri, M. tumifrons
16. Genus *Mertensophryne* Tihen, 1960 (1 species, Zaire to Tanzania and Kenya)
Mertensophryne micranotis
17. Genus *Metaphryniscus* Señaris, Ayarzagüena and Gorzula, 1994 (1 species, South America)
Metaphryniscus sosai
18. Genus *Nectophryne* Buchholz and Peters, 1875 (2 species, Nigeria to Zaire)
Nectophryne afra, N. batesii
19. Genus *Nectophrynoides* Noble, 1926 (5 species, mountains in East Africa)
Nectophrynoides cryptus, N. minutus, N. tornieri, N. viviparus, N. wendyae
20. Genus *Nimbaphrynoides* Dubois, 1987 (2 species, Guinea, Ivory Coast, Liberia)
Nimbaphrynoides liberiensis, N. occidentalis
21. Genus *Oreophrynella* Boulenger, 1895 (6 species, Guayana, Venezuela)
Oreophrynella cryptica, O. hubneri, O. macconnelli, O. nigra, O. quelchii, O. vasquezi
22. Genus *Osornophryne* Ruiz and Hernandez, 1976 (6 species, Colombia, Ecuador)
Osornophryne antisana, O. bufoniformis, O. guacamayo, O. percrassa, O. sumacoensis, O. talipes
23. Genus *Pedostibes* Günther, 1876 (6 species, southern India, Southeast Asia)
Pedostibes everetti, P. hosii, P. kempi, P. maculatus, P. rugosus, P. tuberculosus
24. Genus *Pelophryne* Barbour, 1938 (9 species, Southeast Asia)
Pelophryne albotaeniata, P. api, P. brevipes, P. guentheri, P. lighti, P. macrotis, P. misera, P. rhodophilius, P. scalpta
25. Genus *Peltophryne* Fitzinger, 1843 (9 species, Greater Antilles)
Peltophryne cataulaciceps, P. empusa, P. fluviatica, P. guentheri, P. gundlachi, P. lemur, P. longinasus, P. peltocephala, P. taladai
26. Genus *Pseudobufo* Tschudi, 1838 (1 species, Malaysia, Sumatra, Borneo)
Pseudobufo subasper
27. Genus *Rhamphophryne* Trueb, 1971 (9 species, Panama to Ecuador, Brazil)
Rhamphophryne acrolopha, R. festae, R. lindae, R. macrorhina, R. nicefori, R. proboscidea, R. rostrata, R. tenrec, R. truebae
28. Genus *Schismaderma* Smith, 1849 (1 species, Tanzania and Zaire to South Africa)
Schismaderma carens
29. Genus *Spinophrynoides* Dubois, 1987 (1 species, Ethiopia)
Spinophrynoides osgoodi
30. Genus *Stephopaedes* Channing, 1978 (2 species, Tanzania, Mozambique, Zimbabwe)
Stephopaedes anotis, S. loveridgei
31. Genus *Torrentophryne* Yang, Liu and Rao, 1997 (2 species, China)
Torrentophryne aspinia, T. tuberospina
32. Genus *Truebella* Graybeal and Cannatella, 1995 (2 species, Peru)
Truebella skoptes, T. tothastes
33. Genus *Werneria* Posch, 1903 (4 species, Togo, Cameroun)
Werneria bambutensis, W. mertensiana, W. preussi, W. tandyi
34. Genus *Wolterstorffina* Mertens, 1939 (2 species, Nigeria, Cameroun)
Wolterstorffina mirei, W. parvipalmata

5. Family Centrolenidae Taylor 1951 (Glass frogs)

1. Genus *Centrolene* Jiménez De La Espada, 1872 (36 species, Central and South America)
Centrolene acanthidiocephalum, C. altitudinatis, C. andinum, C. antioquiensis, C. audax, C. bacatum, C. ballux, C. buckleyi, C. fernandoi, C. geckoideum, C. gemmatum, C. gorzulai, C. grandisonae, C. guanacarum, C. helodermatum, C. hesperium, C. huilense, C. hybrida, C. ilex, C. lemniscatum, C. lentiginosum, C. litoralis, C. lynchi, C. medemi, C. muelleri, C. notostictum, C. paezorum, C. peristictum, C. petrophilum, C. pipilatum, C. prosoblepon, C. quindianum, C. robledoi, C. sanchezi, C. savagei, C. scirtetes
2. Genus *Cochranella* Taylor, 1951 (61 species, Central and South America)
Cochranella adiazeta, C. albomaculata, C. ametarsia, C. anomala, C. armata, C. azulae, C. balionota, C. bejaranoi, C. cariticommata, C. chami, C. chancas, C. cochranae, C. cristinae, C. croceopodes, C. daidalea, C. duidaensis, C. euhystrix, C. euknemos, C. flavopunctata, C. garciae, C. geijskesi, C. granulosa, C. griffithsi, C. helenae, C. ignota, C. luminosa, C. luteopunctata, C. mariae, C. megacheira, C. megistra, C. midas, C. nephelophila, C. nola, C. ocellata, C. ocellifera, C. orejuela, C. orenympha, C. oyampiensis, C. phenax, C. pluvialis, C. posadae, C. prasina, C. punctulata, C. puyoensis, C. ramirezi, C. resplendens, C. ritae, C. riveroi, C. rosada, C. ruizi, C. savagei, C. saxiscandens, C. siren, C. solitaria, C.

spiculata, C. spilota, C. spinosa, C. susatamai, C. tangarana, C. truebae, C. xanthocheridia

3. Genus *Hyalinobatrachium* Ruiz-Carranza and Lynch, 1991 (29 species, southern Mexico to Bolivia and northeastern Argentina)
Hyalinobatrachium antisthenesi, H. aureoguttatum, H. bergeri, H. cardiacalyptum, H. chirripoi, H. colymbiphyllum, H. crurifasciatum, H. crybetes, H. duranti, H. eurygnathum, H. fleischmanni, H. fragilis, H. iaspidiensis, H. lemur, H. loreocarinatum, H. munozorum, H. orientalis, H. ostracodermoides, H. pallidum, H. parvulum, H. pellucidum, H. pleurolineatum, H. pulveratum, H. revocatum, H. talamancae, H. taylori, H. uranoscopum, H. valerioi, H. vireovittatum

6. Familie Dendrobatidae Cope, 1865 (Poison-arrow frogs)

1. Genus *Allobates* Zimmermann and Zimmermann, 1988 (1 species, northern South America)
Allobates femoralis

2. Genus *Aromobates* Myers, Paollilo and Daly, 1991 (1 species, Venezuela, Andes)
Aromobates nocturnus

3. Genus Colostethus Cope, 1866 (105 species, Costa Rica to Brazil and Bolivia) Colostethus abditaurantius, C. agilis, C. alacris, C. alagoanus, C. anthracinus, C. argyrogaster, C. atopoglossus, C. awa, C. ayarzaguenai, C. beebei, C. betancuri, C. bocagei, C. brachistriatus, C. breviquartus, C. bromelicola, C. brunneus, C.capixaba, C. capurinensis, C. carioca, C. cevallosi, C. chalcopis, C. chocoensis, C. citreicola, C. degranvillei, C. delatorreae, C. edwardsi, C. elachyhistus, C. exasperatus, C. faciopunctulatus, C. fallax, C. festae, C. flotator, C. fraterdanieli, C. fugax, C. fuliginosus, C. furviventris, C. goianus, C. guanayensis, C. guatopoensis, C. humilis, idiomelus, C. imbricola, C. infraguttatus, C. inguinalis, C. intermedius, C. jacobuspetersi, C. juanii, C. kingsburyi, C. lacrimosus, C. latinasus, C. lehmanni, C. leopardalis, C. littoralis, C. machalilla, C. maculosus, C. mandelorum, C. maquipucuna, C. marchesianus, C. marmoreoventris, C. mcdiarmidi, C. mertensi, C. mittermeieri, C. murisipansis, C. mystax, C. nexipus, C. nubicola, C. olfersioides, C. palmatus, C. parcus, C. parimae, C. parkerae, C. peculiaris, C. peruvianus, C. pinguis, C. poecilonotus, C. praderioi, C. pratti, C. pulchellus, C. pumilus, C. ramosi, C. ranoides, C. roraima, C. ruizi, C. ruthveni, C. saltuensis, C. sanmartini, C. sauli, C. shrevei, C. shuar, C. silvaticus, C. stepheni, C. subpunctatus, C. taeniatus, C. talamancae, C. tamacuarensis, C. tergogranularis, C. thorntoni, C. toachi, C. torrenticola, C. trilineatus, C. utcubambensis, C. vergeli, C. vertebralis, C. whymperi, C. yaguara

4. Genus *Dendrobates* Wagler, 1830 (29 species, Nicaragua to Brazil and Peru)
Dendrobates arboreus, D. auratus, D. azureus, D. biolat, D. captivus, D. castaneoticus, D. fantasticus, D. galactonotus, D. granuliferus, D. histrionicus, D. imitator, D. labialis, D. lamasi, D. lehmanni, D. leucomelas, D. mysteriosus, D. occultator, D. pumilio, D. quinquevittatus, D. reticulatus, D. rufulus, D. sirensis, D. speciosus, D. tinctorius, D. truncatus, D. vanzolinii, D. variabilis, D. ventrimaculatus, D. vicentei

5. Genus *Epipedobates* Myers, 1987 (23 species, tropical South America)
Epipedobates andinus, E. azureiventris, E. bilinguis, E. bolivianus, E. boulengeri, E. braccatus, E. cainarachi, E. erythromos, E. espinosai, E. flavopictus, E. hahneli, E. ingeri, E. macero, E. maculatus, E. myersi, E. parvulus, E. petersi, E. pictus, E. pulchripectus, E. rubriventris, E. smaragdinus, E. tricolor, E. zaparo

6. Genus *Mannophryne* Lamarca, 1992 (8 species, Venezuela, Trinidad, Tobago)
Mannophryne collaris, M. herminae, M. neblina, M. oblitteratus, M. olmonae, M. riveroi, M. trinitatis, M. yustizi

7. Genus *Minyobates* Myers, 1987 (9 species, Panama and northwestern South America)
Minyobates abditus, M. altobueyensis, M. bombetes, M. fulguritus, M. minutus, M. opisthomelas, M. steyermarki, M. viridis, M. virolinensis

8. Genus *Nephelobates* Lamarca, 1994 (8 species, Venezuela)
Nephelobates alboguttatus, N. duranti, N. haydeeae, N. mayorgai, N. meridensis, N. molinarii, N. orostoma, N. serranus

9. Genus *Phobobates*, Zimmermann and Zimmermann, 1988 (3 species, northern South America)
Phobobates bassleri, P. silverstonei, P. trivittatus

10. Genus *Phyllobates* Duméril and Bibron 1841 (5 species, Costa Rica, Panama, Colombia)
Phyllobates aurotaenia, P. bicolor, P. lugubris, P. terribilis, P. vittatus

7. Family Discoglossidae Günther, 1859 (Disk-tongued frogs)

1. Genus *Alytes* Wagler, 1829 (4 species, central, western and southern Europe, northern Africa)
Alytes cisternasii, A. dickhilleni, A. muletensis, A. obstetricans

2. Genus *Barbourula* Taylor and Noble, 1924 (2 species, Borneo and Palawan)
Barbourula busuangensis, B. kalimantanensis

3. Genus *Bombina* Oken, 1816 (7 species, Europe to East Asia)
Bombina bombina, B. fortinuptialis, B. lichuanensis, B. maxima, B. microdeladigitora, B. orientalis, B. variegata

4. Genus *Discoglossus* Otth, 1837 (5 species, southern Europe, northwestern Africa, Syria?, Israel?)
Discoglossus galganoi, D. montalentii, D. nigriventer, D. pictus, D. sardus

8. Family Heleophrynidae Noble, 1931 (Ghost frogs)

1. Genus *Heleophryne* Sclater, 1898 (5 species, South Africa)
Heleophryne hewitti, H. natalensis, H. purcelli, H. regis, H. rosei

9. Family Hemisotidae Cope, 1867 (Shovel-nosed frogs)

1. Genus *Hemisus* Günther, 1859 (8 species, subsaharan Africa)
Hemisus brachydactylus, H. guineensis, H. guttatus, H. marmoratus, H. microscaphus, H. olivaceus, H. perreti, H. wittei

10. Family Hylidae Rafinesque, 1815 (Tree frogs)

1. Genus *Acris* Duméril and Bibron, 1841 (2 species, eastern North America)
Acris crepitans, A. gryllus

2. Genus *Agalychnis* Cope, 1864 (8 species, southern Mexico to Peru)
Agalychnis annae, A. calcarifer, A. callidryas, A. craspedopus, A. litodryas, A. moreletii, A. saltator, A. spurrelli

3. Genus *Anotheca* Smith, 1939 (1 species, Mexico and Central America)
Anotheca spinosa

4. Genus *Aparasphenodon* Miranda-Ribeiro, 1920 (3 species, northern South America)
Aparasphenodon bokermanni, A. brunoi, A. venezolanus

5. Genus *Aplastodiscus* Lutz, 1950 (1 species, Brazil)
Aplastodiscus perviridis

6. Genus *Argenteohyla* Trueb, 1970 (1 species, Argentina, Paraguay, Uruguay)
Argenteohyla siemersi

7. Genus *Calyptahyla* Trueb and Tyler, 1974 (1 species, Jamaica)
Calyptahyla crucialis

8. Genus *Corythomantis* Boulenger, 1896 (1 species, northeastern Brazil)
Corythomantis greeningi

9. Genus Cryptobatrachus Ruthven, 1916 (3 species, Colombia)
Cryptobatrachus boulengeri, C. fuhrmanni, C. nicefori

10. Genus Cyclorana Steindachner, 1867 (13 species, Australia)
Cyclorana australis, C. brevipes, C. cryptotis, C. cultripes, C. longipes, C. maculosa, C. maini, C. manya, C. novaehollandiae, C. platycephala, C. slevini, C. vagitus, C. verrucosa

11. Genus *Duellmanohyla* Campbell and Smith, 1992 (8 species, Mexico to Panama)
Duellmanohyla chamulae, D. ignicolor, D. lythrodes, D. rufioculis, D. salvavida, D. schmidtorum, D. soralia, D. uranochroa

12. Genus Flectonotus Miranda-Ribeiro, 1926 (5 species, Venezuela, Colombia, Brazil, Trinidad and Tobago)
Flectonotus fissilis, F. fitzgeraldi, F. goeldii, F. ohausi, F. pygmaeus

13. Genus *Gastrotheca* Fitzinger, 1843 (46 species, South America)
Gastrotheca abdita, G. andaquiensis, G. angustifrons, G. antomia, G. argenteovirens, G. aureomaculata, G. bufona, G. christiani, G. cornuta, G. crysosticta, G. dendronastes, G. dunni, G. espeletia, G. excubitor, G. fissipes, G. galeata, G. gracilis, G. griswoldi, G. guentheri, G. helenae, G. humbertoi, G. lateonota, G. lauzuricae, G. litonedis, G. longipes, G. marsupiata, G. microdisca, G. monticola, G. nicefori, G. ochoai, G. orophylax, G. ovifera, G. pacchamama, G. peruana, G. plumbea, G. pseustes, G. psychrophila, G. rebeccae, G. riobambae, G. ruizi, G. splendens, G. testudinea, G. trachyceps, G. walkeri, G. weinlandii, G. williamsoni

14. Genus *Hemiphractus* Wagler, 1828 (5 species, Panama, northwestern South America)
Hemiphractus bubalus, H. fasciatus, H. johnsoni, H. proboscideus, H. scutatus

15. Genus *Hyla* Laurenti, 1768 (305 species, Europe, palaeoarctic Asia, South, Central and North America, in Africa only north of the Sahara)
Hyla acreana, H. albofrenata, H. alboguttata, H. albolineata, H. albomarginata, H. albonigra, H. albopunctata, H. albopunctulata, H. albosignata, H. albovittata, H. alemani, H. allenorum, H. altipotens, H. alvarengai, H. alytolylax, H. americana, H. anataliasiasi, H. anceps, H. andersonii, H. andina, H. angustilineata, H. annectans, H. aperomea, H. arborea, H. arborescandens, H. arenicolor, H. arianae, H. arildae, H. armata, H. aromatica, H. astartea, H. atlantica, H. auraria, H. avivoca, H. baileyi, H. balzani, H. battersbyi, H. benitezi, H. berthalutzae, H. bifurca, H. biobeba, H. bipunctata, H. bischoffi, H. bistincta, H. boans, H. bocourti, H. bogertae, H. bogotensis, H. bokermanni, H. branneri, H. brevifrons, H. bromeliacia, H. caingua, H. calcarata, H. callipeza, H. callipygia, H. calvicollina, H. calypsa, H. carinata, H. carnifex, H. carvalhoi, H. catracha, H. caucana, H. cavicola, H. celata, H. cembra, H. chaneque, H. charadricola, H. charazani, H. chimalapa, H. chinensis, H. chlorostea, H. chryses, H. chrysoscelis, H. cinerea, H. circumdata, H. claresignata, H. clepsydra, H. columbiana, H. colymba, H. crassa, H. crepitans, H. cyanomma, H. cymbalum, H. debilis, H. decipiens, H. dendroscarta, H. dentei, H. denticulenta, H. dolloi, H. dutrai, H. ebraccata, H. echinata, H. elegans, H. euphorbiacea, H. eximia, H. faber, H. fasciata, H. femoralis, H. fimbrimembra, H. fluminea, H. fuentei, H. fusca, H. garagoensis, H. geographica, H. giesleri, H. godmani, H. gouveai, H. graceae, H. grandisonae, H. granosa, H. gratiosa, H. gryllata, H. guentheri, H. haddadi, H. hadroceps, H. hallowellii, H. haraldschultzei, H. hazelae, H. heilprini, H. helenae, H. hobbsi, H. hutchinsi, H. hylax, H. hypselops, H. ibitiguara, H. ibitipoca, H. imitator, H. inframaculata, H. inparquesi, H. insolita, H. intermedia, H. intermixta, H. izecksohni, H. jahni, H. japonica, H. juanitae, H. kanaima, H. karenanneae, H. koechlini, H. labedactyla, H. labialis, H. lancasteri, H. lanciformis, H. langei, H. larinophygion, H. lascinia, H. leali, H. lemai, H. leptolineata, H. leucophyllata, H. leucopygia, H. limai. H. lindae, H. loquax, H. loveridge, H. luctuosa, H. luteoocellata, H. lynchi, H. marginata, H. marianae, H. marianitae, H. marmorata, H. martinsi, H. mathiassoni, H. melanargyrea, H. melanomma, H. melanopleura, H. melanorhabdota, H. meridensis, H. meridionalis, H. microcephala, H. microderma, H. microps, H. miliaria, H. minera, H. minima, H. minuscula, H. minuta, H. miotympanum, H. mixe, H. mixomaculata, H. miyatai, H. molitor, H. multifasciata, H. musica, H. mykter, H. nahderei, H. nana, H. nauzae, H. novaisi, H. nubicola, H. oliveirai, H. ornatissima, H. pacha, H. pachyderma, H. padreluna, H. palaestes, H. palliata, H. palmeri, H. pantosticta, H. pardalis, H. parviceps, H. pauiniensis, H. pelidna, H. pellita, H. pellucens, H. pentheter, H. perkinsi, H. phlebodes, H. phyllognatha, H. picadoi, H. piceigularis, H. pieta, H. pictipes, H. picturata, H. pinima, H. pinorum, H. platydactyla, H. plicata, H. polytaenia, H. praestans, H. prasina, H. psarolaima, H. pseudopseudis, H. pseudopuma, H. ptychodactyla, H. pugnax, H. pulchella, H. pulchrilineata, H. punctata, H. quadrilineata, H. raniceps, H. rhodopepla, H. riveroi, H. rivularis, H. robertmertensi, H. robertsorum, H. roeschmanni, H. roraima, H. rosenbergi, H. rossalleni, H. rubicundula, H. rubracyla, H. rufitela, H. ruschii, H. sabrina, H. salvaje, H. sanchiangensis, H. sarampiona, H. sarayacuensis, H. sarda, H. sartori, H. savignyi, H. sazimai, H. schubarti, H. secedens, H. semiguttata, H. senicula, H. sibleszi, H. simmonsi, H. simplex, H. siopela, H. smaragdina, H. smithii, H. soaresi, H. squirella, H. staufferorum, H. stingi, H. subocularis, H. sumichrasti, H. surinamensis, H. suweonensis, H. taeniopus, H. thorectes, H. thysanota, H. tica, H. timbeba, H. tintinnabulum, H. torrenticola, H. triangulum, H. tritaeniata, H. truncata, H. trux, H. tsinlingensis, H. tuberculosa, H. uruguaya, H. valancifer, H. varelae, H. vasta, H. versicolor, H. vigilans, H. viridifusca, H. virolinensis, H. walfordi, H. walkeri, H. warreni, H. wavrini, H. weygoldti, H. wilderi, H. xanthosticta, H. xapuriensis, H. xera, H. zeteki, H. zhaopingensis

16. Genus *Hylomantis* Peters, 1872 (2 species, Brazil)
Hylomantis aspera, H. granulosa

17. Genus *Litoria* Tschudi, 1838 (112 species, Australia and Tazmania, New Guinea and surrounding islands, imported to New Zealand and New Caledonia)
Litoria adelaidensis, L. alboguttata, L. albolabris, L. amboinensis, L. andiirrmalin, L. angiana, L. arfakiania, L. aruensis, L. aurea, L. becki, L. bicolor, L. booroolongensis, L. brevipalmata, L. brongersmai, L. bulmeri, L. burrowsi, L. capitula, L. chloris, L. chloronata, L. citropa, L. congenita, L. contrastens, L. cooloolensis, L. coplandi, L. cyclorhynchus, L. dahlii, L. darlingtoni, L. dentata, L. dorsalis, L. dorsivena, L. electrica, L. eucnemis, L. everetti, L. ewingii, L. exophthalmia, L. fallax, L. flavipunctata, L. freycineti, L. genimaculata, L. gracilenta, L. graminea, L. havina, L. impura, L. inermis, L. infrafrenata, L. iris, L. jenolanensis, L. jervisiensis, L. jeudii, L. kinghorni, L. latopalmata, L. lesueurii, L. leucova, L. littlejohni, L. longicrus, L. longirostris, L. lorica, L. louisiadensis, L. lutea, L. majikthise, L. meiriana, L. microbelos, L. micromembrana, L. modica, L. moorei, L. mucro, L. multiplica, L. mystax, L. nannotis, L. nappaea, L. nasuta, L. nigrofrenata, L. nigropunctata, L. nyakalensis, L. obtusirostris, L. oenicolen, L. ollauro, L. olongburensis, L. pallida, L. paraewingi, L. pearsoniana, L. peronii, L. personata, L. phyllochroa, L. piperata, L. pratti, L. pronimia, L. prora, L. pygmaea, L. quadrilineata, L. raniformis, L. revelata, L. rheocola, L. rothii, L. rubella, L. sanguinolenta, L. speceri, L. spinifera, L. subglandulosa, L. thesaurensis, L. timida, L. tornieri, L. tyleri, L. umbonata, L. vagabunda, L. verreauxi, L. vinosa, L. vocivincens, L. watjulumensis, L. wisselensis, L. wollastoni, L. xanthomera

18. Genus *Nyctimantis* Boulenger 1882 (1 species, Ecuador)
Nytimantis rugiceps

19. Genus *Nyctimystes* Stejneger, 1916 (24 species, New Guinea, Moluccas, Australia)
Nyctimystes avocalis, N. cheesmani, N. dayi, N. daymani, N. disruptus, N. fluviatilis, N. foricula, N. granti, N. gularis, N. humeralis, N. kubori, N. montanus, N. narinosus, N. obsoletus, N. oktediensis, N. papua, N. perimetri, N. persimilis, N. pulcher, N. rueppelli, N. semipalmatus, N. trachydermis, N. tyleri, N. zweifeli

20. Genus *Osteocephalus* Steindachner, 1862 (12 species, tropical South America)
O. ayarzaguenai, Osteocephalus buckleyi, O. cabrerai, O. elkejungingerae, O. langsdorffii, O. leprieurii, O. oophagus, O. pearsoni, O. planiceps, O. subtilis, O. taurinus, O. verruciger

21. Genus *Osteopilus* Fitzinger, 1843 (3 species, Greater Antilles, Bahamas, Florida)
Osteopilus brunneus, O. dominicensis, O. septentrionalis

22. Genus *Pachymedusa* Duellman, 1968 (1 species, western Mexico)
Pachymedusa dacnicolor

23. Genus *Pelodryas* Günther, 1858 (3 species, Australia, New Guinea, imported to New Zealand)
Pelodryas caerulea, P. cavernicola, P. splendida

24. Genus *Phasmahyla* Cruz, 1990 (4 species, Brazil)
Phasmahyla cochranae, P. exilis, P. guttata, P. jandaia

25. Genus *Phrynohyas* Fitzinger, 1843 (5 species, Mexico to Argentina)
Phrynohyas coriacea, P. imitratix, P. mesophaea, P. resinifictrix, P. venulosa

26. Genus *Phrynomedusa* Miranda-Ribeiro, 1923 (5 species, Brazil)
Phrynomedusa appendiculata, P. bokermanni, P. fimbriata, P. marginata, P. vanzolinii

27. Genus *Phyllodytes* Wagler, 1830 (7 species, South America)
Phyllodytes acuminatus, P. auratus, P. brevirostris, P. kautskyi, P. luteolus, P. melanomystax, P. tuberculosus

28. Genus *Phyllomedusa* Wagler, 1830 (29 species, Costa Rica to Argentina and Paraguay)
Phyllomedusa atelopoides, P. ayeaye, P. baltea, P. bicolor, P. boliviana, P. buckleyi, P. burmeisteri, P. centralis, P. coelestis, P. danieli, P. distincta, P. duellmani, P. ecuatoriana, P. hulli, P. hypocondrialis, P. iheringii, P. lemur, P. medinai, P. palliata, P. perinesos, P. psilopygion, P. rohdei, P. sauvagei, P. tarsius, P. tetraploidea, P. tomopterna, P. trinitatis, P. vaillanti, P. venusta

29. Genus *Plectrohyla* Brocchi, 1877 (16 species, Central America)
Plectrohyla acanthodes, P. avia, P. chrysopleura, P. dasypus, P. glandulosa, P. guatemalensis, P. hartwegi, P. ixil, P. lacertosa, P. matudai, P. pokomchi, P. pychnochila, P. quecchi, P. sagorum, P. teuchestes, P. tecunumani

30. Genus *Pseudacris* Fitzinger, 1843 (11 species, eastern North America)
Pseudacris brachyphona, P. brimleyi, P. cadaverina, P. clarkii, P. crucifer, P. nigrita, P. ocularis, P. ornata, P. regilla, P. streckeri, P. triseriata

31. Genus *Pternohyla* Boulenger, 1882 (2 species, western Mexico and Arizona)
Pternohyla dentata, P. fodiens

32. Genus *Ptychohyla* Taylor, 1944 (11 species, Central America)
Ptychohyla erythromma, P. ethysanota, P. hypomykter, P. legleri, P. leonhardschultzei, P. macrotympanum, P. merazi, P. panchoi, P. salvadorensis, P. sanctaecrucis, P. spinipollex

33. Genus *Scarthyla* Duellman and De SΣ, 1988 (1 species, Peru)
Scarthyla ostinodactyla

34. Genus *Scinax* Wagler, 1830 (82 species, Central and South America)
Scinax acuminatus, S. agilis, S. albicans, S. alcatraz, S. alleni, S. argyreornatus, S. ariadne, S. atratus, S. auratus, S. baumgardneri, S. berthae, S. blairi, S. boesemani, S. boulengeri, S. caldarum, S. canastrensis, S. cardosoi, S. carnevallii, S. castroviejoi, S. catharinae, S. centralis, S. chiquitanus, S. crosspedospilus, S. cruentommus, S. cuspidatus, S. cynocephalus, S. danae, S. duartei, S. ehrhardti, S. elaeochrous, S. epacrorhinus, S. eurydice, S. exiguus, S. flavoguttatus, S. funerus, S. fuscomarginatus, S. fuscovarius, S. garbei, S. goinorum, S. hayii, S. heyeri, S. hiemalis, S. humilis, S. ictericus, S. jureia, S. kautskyi, S. kennedyi, S. lindsayi, S. littoralis, S. littorea, S. longilineus, S. luizotavioi, S. machadoi, S. maracaya, S. melloi, S. nasicus, S. nebulosus, S. obtriangulatus, S. opalinus, S. oreites, S. pachychrus, S. parkeri, S. pedromedinai, S. perereca, S. perpusillus, S. proboscideus, S. quinquefasciatus, S. ranki, S. rizibilis, S. rostratus, S. ruber, S. similis, S. squalirostris, S. staufferi, S. strigilatus, S. sugillatus, S. trachythorax, S. trilineatus, S. v-signatus, S. vauterii, S. wandae, S. x-signatus

35. Genus *Smilisca* Cope, 1865 (6 species, Texas to South America)
Smilisca baudinii, S. cyanosticta, S. phaeota, S. puma, S. sila, S. sordida

36. Genus *Sphaenorhynchus* Tschudi, 1838 (11 species, tropical South America)
Sphaenorhynchus bromelicola, S. carneus, S. dorisae, S. lacteus, S. orophilus, S. palustris, S. pauloalvini, S. planicola, S. platycephalus, S. prasinus, S. surdus

37. Genus *Stefania* Rivero, 1968 (13 species, northeastern South America)
Stefania evansi, S. ginesi, S. goini, S. marahuaquensis, S. oculosa, S. percristata, S. riae, S. riveroi, S. roraimae, S. satelles, S. schuberti, S. tamacuarina, S. woodleyi

38. Genus *Tepuihyla* Ayarzagüena, Señaris and Gorzula, 1992 (7 species, South America)
Tepuihyla aecii, T. edelcae, T. galani, T. luteolabris, T. rimarum, T. rodriguezi, T. talbergae

39. Genus *Trachycephalus* Tschudi, 1838 (3 species, eastern Brazil, coastal regions in northwestern South America)
Trachycephalus atlas, T. jordani, T. nigromaculatus
40. Genus *Triprion* Cope, 1866 (2 species, western Mexico, Yucat‡n)
Triprion petasatus, T. spatulatus

11. Family Hyperoliidae Laurent, 1943 (Hyperoliidae)

1. Genus *Acanthixalus* Laurent, 1944 (1 species, Nigeria and Cameroun to Zaire)
Acanthixalus spinosus
2. Genus *Afrixalus* Laurent, 1944 (29 species, subsaharan Africa)
Afrixalus aureus, A. brachycnemis, A. clarkei, A. crotalus, A. dabagae, A. delicatus, A. dorsalis, A. enseticola, A. equatorialis, A. fornasinii, A. fulvovitatus, A. knysnae, A. lacteus, A. laevis, A. leucostictus, A. lindholmi, A. nigeriensis, A. orophilus, A. osorioi, A. paradorsalis, A. pygmaeus, A. schneideri, A. spinifrons, A. stuhlmanni, A. sylvaticus, A. uluguruensis, A. vittiger, A. weidholzi, A. wittei
3. Genus *Alexteroon* Perret, 1988 (1 species, Cameroun)
Alexteroon obstetricans
4. Genus *Arlequinus* Perret, 1988 (1 species, Cameroun)
Arlequinus krebsi
5. Genus *Callixalus* Laurent, 1950 (1 species, Zaire, Rwanda)
Callixalus pictus
6. Genus *Chlorolius* Perret, 1988 (1 species, Cameroun, Gabon)
Chlorolius koehleri
7. Genus *Chrysobatrachus* Laurent, 1951 (1 species, Zaire)
Chrysobatrachus cupreonitens
8. Genus *Cryptothylax* Laurent and Combaz, 1950 (2 species, Cameroun to Zaire)
Cryptothylax greshoffii, C. minutus
9. Genus *Heterixalus* Laurent, 1944 (9 species, Madagascar)
Heterixalus alboguttatus, H. andrakata, H. betsileo, H. boettgeri, H. luteostriatus, H. madagascariensis, H. punctatus, H. rutenbergi, H. tricolor
10. Genus *Hyperolius* Rapp, 1842 (113 species, subsaharan Africa)
Hyperolius acutirostris, H. adametzi, H. albifrons, H. albofrenatus, H. albolabris, H. alticola, H. angolanus, H. argus, H. atrigularis, H. balfouri, H. baumanni, H. benguellensis, H. bicolor, H. bobirensis, H. bocagei, H. bolifambae, H. bopeleti, H. brachiofsciatus, H. castaneus, H. chabanaudi, H. chlorosteus, H. chrysogaster, H. cinereus, H. cinnamomeoventris, H. concolor, H. cystocandicans, H. dermatus, H. destefanii, H. diaphanus, H. discodactylus, H. endjami, H. erythromelanus, H. erythropus, H. fasciatus, H. ferreirai, H. ferrugineus, H. fimbriolatus, H. frontalis, H. fusciventris, H. ghesquieri, H. gularis, H. guttulatus, H. horstocki, H. houyi, H. inornatus, H. kachalolae, H. kibarae, H. kivuensis, H. kuligae, H. lamottei, H. lateralis, H. laticeps, H. laurenti, H. leleupi, H. leucotaenius, H. lucani, H. maestus, H. marmoratus, H. minutissimus, H. mitchelli, H. montanus, H. mosaicus, H. nasutus, H. obscurus, H. occidentalis, H. ocellatus, H. orkarkarri, H. pardalis, H. parkeri, H. phantasticus, H. pickersgilli, H. picturatus, H. pictus, H. platyceps, H. polli, H. polystictus, H. protchei, H. puncticulatus, H. punctulatus, H. pusillus, H. pustulifer, H. quadratomaculatus, H. quinquevittatus, H. raveni, H. reesi, H. rhizophilus, H. riggenbachi, H. robustus, H. rubrovermiculatus, H. sankuruensis, H. schoutedeni, H. seabrai, H. semidiscus, H. sheldricki, H. soror, H. spinigularis, H. steindachneri, H. stenodactylus, H. sylvaticus, H. tanneri, H. thoracotuberculatus, H. tornieri, H. torrentis, H. tuberculatus, H. tuberilinguis, H. vilhenai, H. viridiflavus, H. viridigulosus, H. viridis, H. wermuthi, H. xenorhinus, H. zavattarii, H. zonatus
11. Genus *Kassina* Girard, 1853 (13 species, subsaharan Africa)
Kassina arboricola, K. cassinoides, K cochranae, K. decorata, K. fusca, K. kuvangensis, K. lamottei, K. maculata, K. maculosa, K. mertensi, K. parkeri, K. senegalensis, K. somalica
12. Genus *Kassinula* Laurent, 1940 (1 species, Zaire and Zambia)
Kassinula wittei
13. Genus *Leptopelis* Günther, 1859 (49 species, subsaharan Africa)
Leptopelis anchietae, L. argenteus, L. aubryi, L. barbouri, L. bequaerti, L. bocagei, L. boulengeri, L. breviceps, L. brevirostris, L. broadleyi, L. bufonides, L. calcaratus, L. christyi, L. concolor, L. cynnamomeus, L. fenestratus, L. fiziensis, L. flavomaculatus, L. gramineus, L. hyloides, L. jordani, L. karissimbensis, L. kivuensis, L. lebeaui, L. macrotis, L. marginatus, L. millsoni, L. modestus, L. mossambicus, L. natalensis. L. nordequatorialis, L. notatus, L. occidentalis, L. ocellatus, L. omissus, L. oryi, L. palmatus, L. parbocagii, L. parkeri, L. parvus, L. ragazzii, L. rufus, L. susanae, L. uluguruensis, L. vannutellii, L. vermiculatus, L. viridis, L. xenodactylus, L. yaldeni
14. Genus *Nesionixalus* Perret, 1976 (2 species, Gulf of Guinea)
Nesionixalus molleri, N. thomensis
15. Genus *Opisthothylax* Perret, 1966 (1 species, Nigeria to Cameroun)
Opisthothylax immaculatus
16. Genus *Paracassina* Peracca, 1907 (2 species, Ethiopia)
Paracassina kounhiensis, P. obscura
17. Genus *Phlyctimantis* Laurent and Combaz, 1950 (4 species, tropical West Africa and Tanzania)
Phlyctimantis boulengeri, P. keithae, P. leonardi, P. verrucosus
18. Genus *Semnodactylus* Hoffman, 1939 (1 species, South Africa)
Semnodactylus wealii
19. Genus *Tachycnemis* Fitzinger, 1843 (1 species, Seychelles Islands)
Tachycnemis seychellensis

12. Family Leiopelmatidae Mivart, 1869 (Tailed frogs)

1. Genus *Ascaphus* Stejneger, 1899 (1 species, USA, Canada)
Ascaphus truei
2. Genus *Leiopelma* Fitzinger, 1861 (3 species, New Zealand)
Leiopelma archeyi, L. hamiltoni, L. hochstetteri

13. Family Leptodactylidae Werner, 1896 (Southern frogs)

1. Genus *Adelophryne* Hoogmoed and Lescure, 1984 (6 species, northeastern South America)
Adelophryne adiastola, A. baturitensis, A. gutturosa, A. maranguapensis, A. pachydactyla, A. tridactyla
2. Genus *Adenomera* Steindachner, 1867 (7 species, tropical South America)
Adenomera andreae, A. bokermanni, A. diptyx, A. hyleadactyla, A. lutzi, A. marmorata, A. martinezi
3. Genus *Alsodes* Bell, 1843 (10 species, southern Argentina and Chile)
Alsodes barrioi, A. gargola, A. illotus, A. laevis, A. monticola, A. nodosus, A. tumultuosus, A. vanzolinii, A. verrucosus, A. vittatus
4. Genus *Atelognathus* Lynch, 1978 (7 species, Patagonia and Wellington Island)
Atelognathus grandisonae, A. nitoi, A. patagonicus, A. praebasalticus, A. reverberii, A. salai, A. solitarius
5. Gattung *Atopophrynus* Lynch and Ruíz, 1982 (1 species, Colombia)
Atopophrynus syntomopus
6. Genus *Barycholos* Heyer, 1969 (2 species, Ecuador, Brazil)
Barycholos pulcher, B. savagei
7. Genus *Batrachophrynus* Peters, 1873 (1 species, Peru)
Batrachophrynus macrostomus
8. Genus *Batrachyla* Bell, 1843 (5 species, southern Argentina and Chile)
Batrachyla antartandica, B. fitzroya, B. leptopus, B. nibaldoi, B. taeniata
9. Genus *Caudiverbera* Laurenti, 1768 (1 species, Chile)
Caudiverbera caudiverbera
10. Genus *Ceratophrys* Wied-Neuwied, 1824 (8 species, South America)
Ceratophrys aurita, C. calcarata, C. cornuta, C. cranwelli, C. joazeirensis, C. ornata, C. stolzmanni, C. testudo
11. Genus *Chacophrys* Reig and Limeses, 1963 (1 species, Argentina, Bolivia, Paraguay)
Chacophrys pierottii
12. Genus *Crossodactylodes* Cochran, 1938 (3 species, Brazil)
Crossodactylodes bokermanni, C. izecksohni, C. pintoi
13. Genus *Crossodactylus* Duméril and Bibron, 1841 (9 species, Brazil, Argentina)
Crossodactylus aeneus, C. bokermanni, C. caramaschii, C. dantei, C. dispar, C. gaudichaudii, C. lutzorum, C. schmidti, C. trachystomus
14. Genus *Cycloramphus* Tschudi, 1838 (25 species, Brazil)
Cycloramphus asper, C. bandeirensis, C. bolitoglossus, C. boraceiensis, C. brasiliensis, C. carvalhoi, C. catarinensis, C. cedrensis, C. diringshofeni, C. dubius, C. duseni, C. eleutherodactylus, C. fuliginosus, C. granulosus, C. izecksohni, C. jordanensis, C. juimirim, C. lutzorum, C. migueli, C. mirandaribeiroi, C. ohausi, C. rhyakonastes, C. semipalmatus, C. stejnegeri, C. valae
15. Genus *Dischidodactylus* Lynch, 1979 (2 species, Venezuela)
Dischidodactylus colonnelloi, D. duidensis
16. Genus *Edalorhina* Jiménez De La Espada, 1870 (2 species, Amazon)
Edalorhina nasuta, E. perezi
17. Genus *Eleutherodactylus* Duméril and Bibron, 1841 (601 species, southern USA, Mexico, Central America to northern Argentina, West Indies)
Eleutherodactylus aaptus, E. abbotti, E. acatallelus, E. acerus, E. achatinus, E. acmonis, E. actites, E. acuminatus, E. acutirostris, E. adamastus, E. aemulatus, E. affinis, E. alalocophus, E. alberchi, E. albipes, E. albolabris, E. alcoae, E. alfredi, E. altae, E. altamazonicus, E. alticola, E. amadeus, E. amplinympha, E. anatipes, E. anciano, E. andi, E. andicola, E. andrewsi, E. angelicus, E. angustidigitorum, E. anolirex, E. anomalus, E. anonymus, E. anotis, E. antillensis, E. aphanus, E. apiculatus, E. apostates, E. appendiculatus, E. armstrongi, E. atkinsi, E. atratus, E. audanti, E. augusti, E. aurantigattus, E. auriculatoides, E. auriculatus, E. aurilegulus, E. avius, E. azueroensis, E. babax, E. bacchus, E. bakeri, E. balionotus, E. barlagnei, E. bartonsmithi, E. baryecuus, E. batrachylus, E. bearsei, F. bellona, E. berkenbuschii, E. bernali, E. bicolor, E. bicumulus, E. bilineatus, E. binotatus, E. biporcatus, E. bockermanni, E. boconoensis, E. bocourti, E. bogotensis, E. bolbodactylus, E. boulengeri, E. bransfordii, E. bresslerae, E. brevifrons, E. brevirostris, E. briceni, E. brittoni, E. brocchi, E. bromeliaceus, E. buccinator, E. buckleyi, E. bufoniformis, E. cabrerai, E. cacao, E. cadenai, E. cajamarcensis, E. calcaratus, E. calcarulatus, E. caliginosus, E. cantitans, E. caprifer, E. caribe, E. carmelitae, E. carranguerorum, E. carvalhoi, E. caryophyllaceus, E. cavernibardus, E. cavernicola, E. celator, E. cerasinus, E. cerastes, E. ceuthospilus, E. chac, E. chalceus, E. charlottevillensis, E. cheiroplethus, E. chiasonotus, E. chloronotus, E. chlorophenax, E. chlorosoma, E. chrysozetes, E. citriogaster, E. cochranae, E. colodactylus, E. colomai, E. colostichos, E. condor, E. conspicillatus, E. cooki, E. coqui, E. cornutus, E. corona, E. cosnipatae, E. counouspeus, E. crassidigitus, E. cremnobates, E. crenunguis, E. cristinae, E. croceoinguinis, E. crucifer, E. cruentus, E. cruralis, E. cruzi, E. cryophilius, E. cryptomelas,E. cuaquero, E. cubanus, E. cundalli, E. cuneatus, E. curtipes, E. cystignathoides, E. danae, E. darlingtoni, E. daryi, F. decoratus, E. degener, E. delicatus, E. delius, E. dennisi, E. devillei, E. diadematus, E. diaphonus, E. diastema, E. dilatus, E. dimidiatus, E. discoidalis, E. dissimulatus, E. dixoni, E. dolomedes, E. dolops, E. dorsopictus, E. douglasi, E. duellmani, E. eileenae, E. elassodiscus, E. elegans, E. emcelae, E. emiliae, E. eneidae, E. epipedus, E. epochthidius, E. eremitus, E. eriphus, E. ernesti, E. erythromerus, E. erythropleura, E. escoces, E. etheridgei, E. eunaster, E. eurydactylus, E. fecundus, E. fenestratus, E. fitzingeri, E. flavescens, E. fleischmanni, E. floridus, E. fowleri, E. frater, E. fraudator, E. furcyensis, E. fuscus, E. gaigei, E. galdi, E. ganonotus, E. gentryi, E. ginesi, E. gladiator, E. glamyrus, E. glandulifer, E. glanduliferoides, E. glandulosus, E. glaphycompus, E. glaucoreius, E. glaucus, E. gollmeri, E. gossei, E. grabhami, E. gracilis, E. grahami, E. grandiceps, E. grandis, E. grandoculis, E. greggi, E. greyi, E. griphus, E. gryllus, E. gualteri, E. guanahacabibes, E. guantanamera, E. guentheri, E. guerreoensis, E. gularis, E. gundlachi, E. guttilatus, E. gutturalis, E. haitianius, E. hamiotae, E. hectus, E. hedricki, E. helonotus, E. heminota, E. hernandezi, E. heterodactylus, E. hobartsmithi, E. hoehnei, E. holti, E. hybotragus, E. hylaeformis, E. hypostenor, E. iberia, E. ignicolor, E. illotus, E. imitatrix, E. incanus, E. incomptus, E. ingeri, E. inguinalis, E. inoptatus, E. insignitus, E. intermedius, E. interorbitalis, E. inusitatus, E. ionthus, E. izecksohni, E. jaimei, E. jamaicensis, E. jasperi, E. johannesdei, E. johnstonei, E. johnwrighti, E. jorgevelosai, E. jota, E. jugans, E. juipoca, E. junori, E. karcharias, E. karlschmidti, E. katoptroides, E. kirklandi, E. klinikowskii, E. labiosus, E. lacrimosus, E. lacteus, E. lamprotes, E. lancinii, E. lanthanites, E. lasalleorum, E. latens, E. laticeps, E. laticlavius, E. laticorpus, E. latidiscus, E. lauraster, E. leberi, E. lentiginosus, E. lentus, E. leoncei, E. leoni, E. leprus, E. leptolophus, E. leucopus, E. librarius, E. lichenoides, E. limbatus, E. lindae, E. lineatus, E. lirellus, E. lividus, E. locustus, E. longipes, E. longirostris, E. loustes, E. lucioi, E. luscombei, E. luteolateralis, E. luteolus, E. lutitus, E. lymani, E. lynchi, E. lythrodes, E. maculosus, E. malkini, E. manezinho, E. mantipus, E. mariposa, E. marmoratus, E. marnockii, E. martiae, E. martinicensis, E. matudai, E. maurus, E. maussi, E. medemi, E. megalops, E. megalotympanum, E. melacara, E. melanoproctus, E. melanostictus, E. memorans, E. mendax, E. mercedesae, E. meredonensis, E. merostictus, E. mexicanus, E. milesi, E. mimus, E. minutus, E. miyatai, E. modestus, E. modipeplus, E. molybrignus, E. mondolfii, E. monensis, E. monnichorum, E. montanus, E. moro, E. muricatus, E. museosus, E. myersi. E. nasutus, E. necerus, E. necopinus, E. neodreptus, E. nervicus, E. nicefori, E. nigriventris, E. nigrogriseus, E. nigrovittatus, E. nitidus, E. nivicolimae, E. noblei, E. nortoni, E. nubicola, E. nyctophylax, E. obmutescens, E. occidentalis, E. ocellatus, E. ockendeni, E. ocreatus, E. octavioi, E. oeus, E. omiltemanus, E. omoaensis, E. orcesi, E. orcutti, E. orestes, E. orientalis, E. ornatissimus, E. orocostalis, E. orpacobates, E. orphnolaimus, E. oxyrhynchus, E. pallidus, E. palmeri, E. pantoni, E. parabates, E. paramerus, E. paranaensis, E. parapelates, E. pardalis, E. parvillus, E. parvus, E. pastazensis, E. patriciae, E. paulodutrai, E. paulsoni, E. paululus, E. pecki, E. pentasyringos, E. peraticus, E. percultus, E. permixtus, E. peruvianus, E. petrobardus, E. petrophilus, E. pezopetrus, E. phasma, E. philipi, E. phoxocephalus, E. phragmipleuron, E. piceus, E. pictissimus, E. pinarensis, E. pinchoni, E. pipilans, E. pituinus, E. planirostris, E . platychilus, E. platydactylus, E. pleurostriatus, E. plicifer, E. pluvicanorus, E. podiciferus, E. polychrus, E. polymniae, E. poolei, E. portoricensis, E. pozo, E. principalis, E. probolaeus, E. prolatus, E. proliroxdiscus, E. proserpens, E. pruinatus, E. psephosypharus, E. pseudoacuminatus, E. pteridophilus, E. pugnax, E. pulidoi, E. pulvinatus, E. punctariolus, E. pusillus, E. pycnodermis, E. pygmaeus, E. pyrrhomerus, E. quaquaversus, E. quinquagesimus, E. racemus, E. racenisi, E. ramagii. E. randorum, E. raniformis, E. rayo, E. repens, E. reticulatus, E. restrepoi, E. rhabdolaemus, E. rhodesi, E. rhodopis, E. rhodpolichus, E. richmondi, E. ricordii, E. ridens, E. riveroi, E. riveti, E. ronaldi, E. rosadoi, E. roseus, E. rostralis, E. rozei, E. rubicundus, E. rubrimaculatus, E. ruedai, E. rufescens, E. rufifemoralis, E. rugulosus, E. ruidus, E. ruizi, E. ruthae, E. ruthveni, E. salaputium, E. saltator, E. saltuarius, E. samaipatae, E. sanctaemartae, E. sanmartinensis, E. sartori, E. satagius, E. savagei, E. saxatilis, E. schmidti, E. schultei, E. schwartzi, E. sciagraphus, E. scitulus, E. scolobleharus, E. scolodiscus, E. scopaeus, E. semipalmatus, E. sernai, E. sierramaestrae, E. signifer, E. silverstonei, E. silvicola, E. simonbolivari, E. simoteriscus, E. simoterus, E. siopelus, E. sisyphodemus, E. skydmainos, E. sobetes, E. spanios, E. spatulatus, E. spilogaster, E. spinosus, E. stejnegerianus, E. stenodiscus, E. sternothylax, E. stuarti, E. subsigillatus, E. sulcatus, E. sulculus, subsigillatus, E. sulcatus, E. sulculus, E. supernatis, E. surdus, E. symingtoni, E. syristes, E. taeniatus, E. talamancae, E. tamsitti, E. tarahumaraensis, E. taurus, E. taylori, E. tayrona, E. tenebrionis, E. terestres, E. terraebolivaris, E. tetajulia, E. thectopternus, E. thomasi, E. thorectes, E. thymalopsoides, E. thymelensis, E. tigrillo, E. toa, E. toftae, E. tonyi, E. trachyblepharis, E. trachydermus, E. trepidotus, E. tribulosus, E. truebae, E. tubernasus, E. turquinensis, E. turumiquirensis, E. unicolor, E. unistrigatus, E. uno, E. uranobates, E. urichi, E. vanadisae, E. variabilis, E. varians, E. varleyi, E. veletis, E. venancioi, E. ventrilineatus, E. ventrimarmoratus, E. verecundus, E. verrucipes, E. verruculatus, E. versicolor, E. vertebralis, E. vicarius, E. vidua, E. vilarsi, E. vinhai, E. viridicans, E. viridis, E. vocalis, E. vocator, E. w-nigrum, E. walkeri, E. warreni, E. weilandi, E. wetmorei, E. wiensi, E. wightmanae, E. williamsi, E. xestus, E. xucanebi, E. xylochobates, E. yaviensis, E. yucatanensis, E. zeuctotylus, E. zeus, E. zimmermanae, E. zongoensis, E. zugi, E. zygodactylus
18. Genus *Euparkerella* Griffiths, 1959 (4 species, eastern Brazil)
Euparkerella brasiliensis, E. cochranae, E. robusta, E. tridactyla
19. Genus *Eupsophus* Fitzinger, 1843 (8 species, southern Argentina and Chile)
Eupsophus calcaratus, E. contulmoensis, E. emiliopugini, E. insularis, E. migueli, E. nahuelbutensis, E. roseus, E. vertebralis
20. Genus *Geobatrachus* Ruthven, 1915 (1 species, northern Colombia)
Geobatrachus walkeri
21. Genus *Holoaden* Miranda-Ribeiro, 1920 (2 species, southeastern Brazil)
Holoaden bradei, H. luederwaldti
22. Genus *Hydrolaetare* Gallardo, 1963 (1 species, Amazon)
Hydrolaetare schmidti
23. Genus *Hylodes* Fitzinger, 1826 (18 species, southeastern Brazil)
Hylodes asper, H. babax, H. charadranaetes, H. glabrus, H. heyeri, H. lateristrigatus, H. malgalhaesi, H. meridionalis, H. mertensi, H. nasus, H. ornatus, H. otavioi, H. perplicatus, H. phyllodes, H. pulcher, H. regius, H. sazimai, H. vanzolinii
24. Genus *Hylorina* Bell 1843 (1 species, Chile)
Hylorina sylvatica
25. Genus *Insuetophrynus* Barrio, 1970 (1 species, Chile)
Insuetophrynus arcapicus
26. Genus *Ischnocnema* Reinhardt and Lütken, 1862 (5 species, tropical South America)
Ischnocnema quixensis, I. sanctaecrucis, I. saxatilis, I. simmonsi, I. verrucosa
27. Genus *Lepidobatrachus* Budgett, 1899 (3 species, Paraguay, Bolivia and Argentina)
Lepidobatrachus asper, L. laevis, L. llanensis
28. Genus *Leptodactylus* Fitzinger, 1826 (59 species, southern Texas to Argentina, Hispaniola, Antilles)
Leptodactylus albilabris, L. bolivianus, L. bufonius, L. camaquara, L. chaquensis, L. colombiensis, L. cunucularius, L. dantasi, L. didymus, L. diedrus, L. elenae, L. fallax, L. flavopictus, L. furnarius, L. fuscus, L. geminus, L. gracilis, L. griseigularis, L. hallowelli, L. insularum, L. jolyi, L. knudseni, L. labialis, L. labrosus, L. labyrinthicus, L. laticeps, L. latinasus, L. lithonaetes, L. longirostris, L. macrosternum, L. marambaiae, L. melanonotus, L. myersi, L. mystaceus, L. mystacinus, L. nesiotus, L. notoaktitis, L. ocellatus, L. pascoensis, L. pentadactylus, L. plaumanni, L. podicipinus, L. poecilochilus, L. pustulatus, L. rhodomystax, L. rhodonotus, L. rhodostima, L. riveroi, L. rugosus, L. sabanensis, L. silvanimbus, L. spixii, L. stenodema, L. syphax, L. tapiti, L. troglodytes, L. ventrimacalatus, L. viridis, L. wagneri
29. Genus *Limnomedusa* Fitzinger, 1843 (1 species, Brazil, Argentina, Uruguay)
Limnomedusa macroglossa
30. Genus *Lithodytes* Fitzinger, 1843 (1 species, northern South America)
Lithodytes lineatus
31. Genus *Lynchophrys* Laurent, 1984 (1 species, Peru)
Lynchophrys brachydactyla
32. Genus *Macrogenioglottus* Carvalho, 1946 (1 species, eastern Brazil)
Macrogenioglottus alipioi
33. Genus *Megaelosia* Miranda-Ribeiro, 1923 (3 species, southern Brazil)
Megaelosia bocainensis, M. goeldii, M. lutzae
34. Genus *Odontophrynus* Reinhardt and Lütken, 1862 (9 species, South America)
Odontophrynus achalensis, O. americanus, O. barrioi, O. carvalhoi, O. cultripes, O. lavillai, O. maratoi,

O. occidentalis, O. salvatori

35. Genus *Paratelmatobius* Lutz and Carvalho, 1958 (3 species, southeastern Brazil)
Paratelmatobius gaigeae, P. lutzei, P. poecilogaster

36. Genus *Phrynopus* Peters, 1874 (21 species, Colombia to Bolivia)
Phrynopus adenobrachius, P. bagrecitoi, P. bracki, P. brunneus, P. columbianus, P. cophites, P. flavomaculatus, P. juninensis, P. kempffi, P. laplacai, P. lucida, P. montium, P. nanus, P. nebulanastes, P. parkeri, P. peraccai, P. pereger, P. peruanus, P. peruvianus, P. simonsii, P. wettsteinii

37. Genus *Phyllonastes* Heyer, 1977 (4 species, South America)
Phyllonastes heyeri, P. lochites, P. lynchi, P. myrmecoides

38. Genus *Physalaemus* Fitzinger, 1826 (39 species, Mexico to Argentina)
Physalaemus aguirrei, P. albifrons, P. albonotatus, P. barrioi, P. biligonigerus, P. bokermanni, P. caete, P. centralis, P. cicada, P. coloradorum, P. crombiei, P. cuqui, P. cuvieri, P. deimaticus, P. enesefae, P. ephippifer, P. evangelistai, P. fernandezae, P. fischeri, P. fuscomaculatus, P. gracilis, P. henselii, P. jordanensis, P. krojeri, P. lisei, P. maculiventris, P. moreirae, P. nanus, P. nattereri, P. obtectus, P. olfersii, P. pertersi, P. pustulatus, P. pustulosus, P. riograndensis, P. rupestris, P. santafecinus, P. signifer, P. soaresi

39. Genus *Phyzelaphryne* Heyer, 1977 (1 species, Brazil)
Phyzelaphryne miriamae

40. Genus *Pleurodema* Tschudi, 1838 (12 species, Panama to Argentina and Chile)
Pleurodema bibroni, P. borellii, P. brachyops, P. bufonium, P. cinereum, P. diplolistre, P. guayapae, P. kriegi, P. marmoratum, P. nebulosum, P. thaul, P. tucumanum

41. Genus *Proceratophrys* Miranda-Ribeiro, 1920 (12 species, Brazil, Argentina, Paraguay)
Proceratophrys appendiculata, P. avelinoi, P. bigibbosa, P. boiei, P. cristiceps, P. cristinae, P. fryi, P. goyana, P. laticeps, P. moehringi, P. palustris, P. schirchi

42. Genus *Pseudopaludicola* Miranda-Ribeiro, 1926 (11 species, South America)
Pseudopaludicola boliviana, P. ceratophyes, P. falcipes, P. llanera, P. mineira, P. mirandae, P. mystacalis, P. pusilla, P. riopiedadensis, P. saltica, P. ternetzi

43. Genus *Scythrophrys* Lynch, 1971 (1 species, southeastern Brazil)
Scythrophrys sawayae

44. Genus *Somuncuria* Lynch, 1978 (1 species, Patagonia)
Somuncuria somuncurensis

45. Genus *Telmalsodes* Díaz, 1989 (2 species, Chile, Argentina)
Telmalsodes montanus, T. pehuenche

46. Genus *Telmatobius* Wiegmann, 1835 (46 species, Ecuador to Argentina and Chile)
Telmatobius albiventris, T. arequipensis, T. atacamensis, T. atahualpai, T. bolivianus, T. brevipes, T. brevirostris, T. carrillae, T. ceiorum, T. cirrhacelis, T. colanensis, T. contrerasi, T. crawfordi, T. culeus, T. degener, T. edaphonastes, T. halli, T. hauthali, T. huayra, T. hypselocephalus, T. ignavus, T. intermedius, T. jahuira, T. jelzkii, T. laticeps, T. latirostris, T. marmoratus, T. mayoloi, T. necopinus, T. niger, T. oxycephalus, T. pefauri, T. peruvianus, T. pinguiculus, T. platycephalus, T. rimac, T. schreiteri, T. scrocchii, T. simonsi, T. stephani, T. thompsoni, T. truebae, T. vellardi, T. verrucosus, T. yuracare, T. zapahuirensis

47. Genus *Telmatobufo* Schmidt, 1952 (3 species, Chile)
Telmatobufo australis, T. bullocki, T. venustus

48. Genus *Thoropa* Cope, 1865 (5 species, southeastern Brazil)
Thoropa lutzi, T. megatympanum, T. miliaris, T. petropolitana, T. saxatilis

49. Genus *Vanzolinius* Heyer, 1974 (1 species, Amazon)
Vanzolinius discodactylus

50. Genus *Zachaenus* Cope, 1866 (3 species, southeastern Brazil)
Zachaenus carvalhoi, Z. parvulus, Z. roseus

14. Family Microhylidae Noble, 1931 (Narrow-mouthed toads)

1. Genus *Adelastes* Zweifel, 1986 (1 species, Venezuela)
Adelastes hylonomus

2. Genus *Albericus* Burton and Zweifel, 1995 (3 species, New Guinea)
Albericus darlingtoni, A. tuberculus, A. variegatus

3. Genus *Altigius* Wild, 1995 (1 species, Amazon)
Altigius alios

4. Genus *Anodonthyla* Müller, 1892 (4 species, Madagascar)
Anodonthyla boulengerii, A. montana, A. nigrigularis, A. rouxae

5. Genus *Aphantophryne* Fry, 1917 (3 species, Papua-New Guinea)
Aphantophryne minuta, A. pansa, A. sabini

6. Genus *Arcovomer* Carvalho, 1954 (1 species, Brazil)
Arcovomer passarellii

7. Genus *Asterophrys* Tschudi, 1838 (2 species, New Guinea)
Asterophrys leucopus, A. turpicola

8. Genus *Balebreviceps* Largen and Drewes, 1989 (1 species, Ethiopia)
Balebreviceps hillmani

9. Genus *Barygenys* Parker, 1936 (7 species, Papua-New Guinea)
Barygenys atra, B. cheesmanae, B. exsul, B. flavigularis, B. maculata, B. nana, B. parvula

10. Genus *Breviceps* Merrem, 1820 (13 species, southern Africa)
Breviceps acutirostris, B. adspersus, B. fuscus, B. gibbosus, B. macrops, B. maculatus, B. montanus, B. mossambicus, B. namaquensis, B. poweri, B. rosei, B. sylvestris, B. verrucosus

11. Genus *Calluella* Stoliczka, 1872 (6 species, Southeast Asia to Borneo)
Calluella brooksi, C. flava, C. guttulata, C. smithi, C. volzi, C. yunnanensis

12. Genus *Callulina* Nieden, 1910 (1 species, Tanzania)
Callulina kreffti

13. Genus *Callulops* Boulenger, 1888 (14 species, New Guinea region, Moluccas)
Callulops boettgeri, C. doriae, C. dubia, C. eurydactyla, C. fusca, C. glandulosa, C. humicola, C. kopsteini, C. personata, C. robusta, C. sagittatus, C. slateri, C. stictigaster, C. wilhelmana

14. Genus *Chaperina* Mocquard, 1892 (1 species, Malaysia, Borneo, Philippines)
Chaperina fusca

15. Genus *Chiasmocleis* Méhely, 1904 (15 species, Panama, South America)
Chiasmocleis albopunctata, C. anatipes, C. atlantica, C. bassleri, C. capixaba, C. carvalhoi, C. centralis, C. hudsoni, C. leucosticta, C. mehelyi, C. panamensis, C. schubarti, C. shudikarensis, C. urbanae, C. ventrimaculata

16. Genus *Choerophryne* Van Kampen, 1915 (1 species, New Guinea)
Choerophryne rostellifer

17. Genus *Cophixalus* Boettger, 1892 (28 species, New Guinea, Moluccas, Australia)
Cophixalus ateles, C. biroi, C. bombiens, C. cheesmanae, C. concinnus, C. crepitans, C. cryptotympanum, C. daymani, C. exiguus, C. hosmeri, C. infacetus, C. kaindiensis, C. mcdonaldi, C. montanus, C. monticola, C. neglectus, C. nubicola, C. ornatus, C. parkeri, C. peninsularis, C. pipilans, C. riparius, C. saxatilis, C. shellyi, C. sphagnicola, C. tagolensis, C. variegatus, C. verrucosus

18. Genus *Cophyla* Boettger, 1880 (1 species, Madagascar)
Cophyla phyllodactyla

19. Genus *Copiula* Méhely, 1901 (5 species, New Guinea)
Copiula fistulans, C. minor, C. oxyrhinus, C. pipiens, C. tyleri

20. Genus *Ctenophryne* Mocquard, 1904 (2 species, tropical South America)
Ctenophryne geayi, C. minor

21. Genus *Dasypops* Miranda-Ribeiro, 1924 (1 species, Brazil)
Dasypops schirchi

22. Genus *Dermatonotus* Méhely, 1904 (1 species, Brazil, Argentina, Bolivia, Paraguay)
Dermatonotus muelleri

23. Genus *Dyscophus* Grandidier, 1872 (3 species, Madagascar)
Dyscophus antongili, D. guineti, D. insularis

24. Genus *Elachistocleis* Parker, 1927 (4 species, Panama, South America)
Elachistocleis bicolor, E. ovalis, E. piauiensis, E. surinamensis

25. Genus *Gastrophryne* Fitzinger, 1843 (5 species, USA to Costa Rica)
Gastrophryne carolinensis, G. elegans, G. olivacea, G. pictiventris, G. usta

26. Genus *Gastrophrynoides* Noble, 1926 (1 species, Borneo)
Gastrophrynoides borneensis

27. Genus *Genyophryne* Boulenger, 1890 (1 species, Papua-New Guinea)
Genyophryne thompsoni

28. Genus *Glyphoglossus* Günther, 1868 (1 species, Southeast Asia)
Glyphoglossus molossus

29. Genus *Hamptophryne* Carvalho, 1954 (1 species, Amazon)
Hamptophryne boliviana

30. Genus *Hoplophryne* Barbour and Loveridge, 1928 (2 species, Tanzania)
Hoplophryne rogersi, H. uluguruensis

31. Genus *Hylophorbus* Macleay, 1878 (1 species, Papua-New Guinea)
Hylophorbus rufescens

32. Genus *Hyophryne* Carvalho, 1954 (1 species, Brazil)
Hyophryne histrio

33. Genus *Hypopachus* Keferstein, 1867 (2 species, USA to Costa Rica)
Hypopachus barberi, H. variolosus

34. Genus *Kalophrynus* Tschudi, 1838 (11 species, southern China to Borneo and Philippines)
Kalophrynus baluensis, K. bunguranus, K. heterochirus, K. intermedius, K. menglienicus, K. nubicola, K. palmatissimus, K. pleurostigma, K. punctatus, K. robinsoni, K. subterrestris

35. Genus *Kaloula* Gray, 1831 (10 species, Korea, China, Southeast Asia to Sri Lanka)
Katoula baleata, K. borealis, K. conjuncta, K. mediolineata, K. picta, K. pulchra, K. rigida, K. rugifera, K. taprobanica, K. verrucosa

36. Genus *Madecassophryne* Guibé, 1974 (1 species, Madagascar)
Madecassophryne truebae

37. Genus *Mantophryne* Boulenger, 1897 (3 species, region of New Guinea)
Mantophryne infulata, M. lateralis, M. lousiadensis

38. Genus *Melanobatrachus* Beddome, 1878 (1 species, India)
Melanobatrachus indicus

39. Genus *Metaphrynella* Parker, 1934 (2 species, Malaysia, Borneo)
Metaphrynella pollicaris, M. sundana

40. Genus *Microhyla* Tschudi, 1838 (24 species India, Sri Lanka, China, Japan, Southeast Asia to Bali)
Microhyla achatina, M. annamensis, M. annectens, M. berdmorei, M. borneensis, M. butleri, M. chakrapanii, M. erythropoda, M. fowleri, M. fusca, M. heymonsi, M. karunaratnei, M. maculifera, M. mixtura, M. okinavensis, M. ornata, M. palmipes, M. perparava, M. petrigena, M. picta, M. pulchra, M. rubra, M. superciliaris, M. zeylanica

41. Genus *Micryletta* Dubois, 1987 (2 species, Burma, China to Malaysia and Sumatra)
Micryletta inornata, M. steinegeri

42. Genus *Myersiella* Carvalho, 1954 (1 species, Brazil)
Myersiella microps

43. Genus *Nelsonophryne* Frost, 1987 (2 species, Costa Rica, Panama, Colombia, Ecuador)
Nelsonophryne aequatorialis, N. atterima

44. Genus *Oreophryne* Boettger, 1895 (24 species, Philippines to New Guinea)
Oreophryne albopunctata, O. annulata, O. anthonyi, O. biroi, O. brachypus, O. brevicrus, O. celebensis, O. crucifera, O. flava, O. frontifasciata, O. geislerorum, O. idenburgensis, O. inornata, O. insulana, O. jeffersoniana, O. kampeni, O. moluccensis, O. monticola, O. nana, O. parkeri, O. rookmaakeri, O. variabilis, O. wolterstorffi, O. zimmeri

45. Genus *Otophryne* Boulenger, 1900 (1 species, northern South America)
Otophryne robusta

46. Genus *Paradoxophyla* Blommers-Schlösser and Blanc, 1991 (1 species, Madagascar)
Paradoxophyla palmata

47. Genus *Parhoplophryne* Barbour and Loveridge, 1928 (1 species, Tanzania)
Parhoplophryne usambarica

48. Genus *Pherohapsis* Zweifel, 1972 (1 species, Papua-New Guinea)
Pherohapsis menziesi

49. Genus *Phrynella* Boulenger, 1887 (1 species, Malaysia, Sumatra)
Phrynella pulchra

50. Genus *Phrynomantis* Peters, 1867 (5 species, subsaharan Africa)
Phrynomantis affinis, P. annectens, P. bifasciatus, P. microps, P. somalicus

51. Genus *Platypelis* Boulenger, 1882 (9 species, Madagascar)
Platypelis alticola, P. barbouri, P. cowanii, P. grandis, P. milloti, P. occultans, P. pollicaris, P. tsaratananaensis, P. tuberifera

52. Genus *Plethodontohyla* Boulenger, 1882 (12 species, Madagascar)
Plethodontohyla alluaudi, P. bipunctata, P. brevipes, P. coudreaui, P. guentherpetersi, P. inguinalis, P. laevipes, P. minuta, P. notosticta, P. ocellata, P. serratopalpebrosa, P. tuberata

53. Genus *Probreviceps* Parker, 1931 (3 species, East Africa)
Probreviceps macrodactylus, P. rhodesianus, P. uluguruensis

54. Genus *Ramanella* Rao and Ramanna, 1925, (8 species, India, Sri Lanka)
Ramanella anamalaiensis, R. minor, R. montana, R. mormorata, R. obscura, R. palmata, R. triangularis, R. variegata

55. Genus *Relictivomer* Carvalho, 1954 (1 species, Panama, Colombia)
Relictivomer pearsei

56. Genus *Rhombophryne* Boettger, 1880 (1 species, Madagascar)
Rhombophryne testudo

57. Genus *Scaphiophryne* Boulenger, 1882 (6 species, Madagascar)
Scaphiophryne brevis, S. calcarata, S. gottlebei, S. madagascariensis, S. marmorata, S. pustulosa

58. Genus *Spelaeophryne* Ahl, 1924 (1 species, Tanzania)
Spelaeophryne methneri

59. Genus *Sphenophryne* Peters and Doria, 1878 (18 species, northern Australia, New Guinea)
Sphenophryne adelphe, S. brevicrus, S. brevipes, S. cornuta, S. crassa, S. dentata, S. fryi, S. gracilipes, S. hooglandi, S. mehelyi, S. mocrorhyncha, S. palmipes, S. pluvialis, S. polysticta, S. pusilla, S. rhododactyla, S. robusta, S. schlaginhaufeni

60. Genus *Stereocyclops* Cope, 1870 (1 species, Brazil)
Sterocyclops incrassatus

61. Genus *Stumpffia* Boettger, 1881 (7 species, Madagascar)
Stumpffia gimmeli, S. grandis, S. psologlossa, S. pygmaea, S. roseifemoralis, S. tetradactyla, S. tridactyla

62. Genus *Synapturanus* Carvalho, 1954 (3 species, Colombia, Brazil)
Synapturanus mirandaribeiroi, S. rabus, S. salseri

63. Genus *Syncope* Walker, 1973 (2 species, Ecuador, Peru)
Syncope antenori, S. carvalhoi

64. Genus *Uperodon* Duméril and Bibron, 1841 (2 species, India, Sri Lanka)
Uperodon globulosus, U. systoma

65. Genus *Xenobatrachus* Peters and Doria, 1878 (17 species, New Guinea)
Xenobatrachus anorbis, X. arfakianus, X. bidens, X. fuscigula, X. giganteus, X. huon, X. macrops, X. mehelyi, X. multisica, X. obesus, X. ocellatus, X. ophiodon, X. rostratus, X. scheepstrai, X. schiefenhoeveli, X. subcroceus, X. tumulus

66. Genus *Xenorhina* Peters, 1863 (6 species, New Guinea)
Xenorhina bouwensi, X. eiponis, X. minima, X. oxycephala, X. parkerorum, X similis

15. Family Myobatrachidae Schlegel, 1850

1. Genus *Adelotus* Ogilby, 1907 (1 species, eastern Australia)
Adelotus brevis

2. Genus *Arenophryne* Tyler, 1976 (1 species, southwestern Australia)
Arenophryne rotunda

3. Genus *Assa* Tyler, 1972 (1 species, Australia)
Assa darlingtoni

4. Genus *Bryobatrachus* Rounsevell, Ziegeler, Brown, Davies and Littlejohn, 1994 (1 species, Tazmania)
Bryobatrachus nimbus

5. Genus *Crinia* Tschudi, 1838 (14 species, Australia, Tazmania, eastern New Guinea)
Crinia bilingua, C. deserticola, C. georgiana, C. glauerti, C. insignifera, C. parinsignifera, C. pseudinsignifera, C. remota, C. riparia, C. signifera, C. sloanei, C. subinsignifera, C. tasmaniensis, C. tinnula

6. Genus *Geocrinia* Blake, 1973 (7 species, southern Australia)
Geocrinia alba, G. laevis, G. leai, G. lutea, G. rosea, G. victoriana, G. vitellina

7. Genus *Heleioporus* Gray, 1841 (5 species, southern Australia)
Heleioporus australiacus, H. barycragus, H. eyrei, H. inornatus, H. psammophilus

8. Genus *Kyarranus* Moore, 1958 (3 species, eastern Australia)
Kyarranus kundagungan, K. lovreridgei, K. sphagnicola

9. Genus *Lechriodus* Boulenger, 1882 (4 species, eastern Australia, New Guinea, Aru Islands)
Lechriodus aganoposis, L. fletcheri, L. melanopyga, L. platyceps

10. Genus *Limnodynastes* Fitzinger, 1843 (12 species, Australia, Tazmania, New Guinea)
Limnodynastes convexiosculus, L. depressus, L. dorsalis, L. dumerilii, L. fletcheri, L. interiois, L. ornatus, L. peronii, L. salmini, L. spenceri, L. tasmaniensis, L. terraereginae

11. Genus *Megistolotis* Tyler, Martin and Davies, 1979 (1 species, northwestern Australia)
Megistolotis lignarius

12. Genus *Metacrinia* Parker, 1940 (1 species, Australia)
Metacrinia nichollsi

13. Genus *Mixophyes* Günther, 1864 (6 species, eastern Australia, New Guinea)
Mixophys balbus, M. fasciolatus, M. fleayi, M. hihihorlo, M. iteratus, M. schevilli

14. Genus *Myobatrachus* Schlegel, 1850 (1 species, western Australia)
Myobatrachus gouldii

15. Genus *Neobatrachus* Peters, 1863 (9 species, southern and western Australia)
Neobatrachus aquilonius, N. centralis, N. fulvus, N. kunapalari, N. pelobatoides, N. pictus, N. sudelli, N. sutor, N. wilsmorei

16. Genus *Notaden* Günther, 1873 (4 species, northern and southeastern Australia)
Notaden bennettii, N. melanoscaphus, N. nichollsi, N. weigeli

17. Genus *Paracrinia* Heyer and Liem, 1976 (1 species, southeastern Australia)
Paracrinia haswelli

18. Genus *Philoria* Spencer, 1901 (1 species, Australia)
Philoria frosti

19. Genus *Pseudophryne* Fitzinger, 1843 (13 species, Australia, Tazmania)
Pseudophryne australis, P. bibronii, P. coriacea, P. corroboree, P. covacevichae, P. dendyi, P. douglasi, P. guentheri, P. major, P. occidentalis, P. pengilleyi, P. raveni, P. semimarmorata

20. Genus *Rheobatrachus* Liem, 1973 (2 species, Australia)
Rheobatrachus silus, R. vitellinus

21. Genus *Spicospina* Roberts, Horwitz, Wardell-Johnson, Maxson and Mahony, 1997 (1 species, Australia)
Spicospina flammocaerulea

22. Genus *Taudactylus* Straughan and Lee, 1966 (6 species, Australia)
Taudactylus acutirostris, T. diurnus, T. eungellensis, T. liemi, T. pleione, T. rheophilus

23. Genus *Uperoleia* Gray, 1841 (24 species, Australia, southern New Guinea)
Uperoleia altissima, U. arenicola, U. aspera, U. borealis, U. capitulata, U. crassa, U. fusca, U. glandulosa, U. inundata, U. laevigata, U. lithomoda, U. littlejohni, U. marmorata, U. martini, U. micromeles, U. mimula, U. minima, U. mjobergi, U. orientalis, U. rugosa, U. russelli, U. talpa, U. trachyderma, U. tyleri

16. Family Pelobatidae Bonaparte, 1850 (Spadefoots)

1. Genus *Leptobrachella* Smith, 1931 (7 species, Borneo and surrounding islands)
Leptobrachella baluensis, L. brevicrus, L. mjobergi, L. natunae, L. palmata, L. parva, L. serasanae
2. Genus *Leptobrachium* Tschudi, 1838 (12 species, southern China and Southeast Asia)
Leptobrachium ailaonicum, L. boringii, L. chapaense, L. gunungense, L. hainanense, L. hasseltii, L. hendricksoni, L. leishanense, L. liui, L. montanum, L. nigrops, L. pullus
3. Genus *Leptolalax* Dubois, 1980 (12 species, southern China and Southeast Asia)
Leptolalax alpinus, L. arayai, L. bourreti, L. dringi, L. gracilis, L. hamidi, L. heteropus, L. liui, L. maurus, L. pelodytoides, L. pictus, L. ventripunctatus
4. Genus *Megophrys* Kuhl and Van Hasselt, 1822 (34 species, China, India, Southeast Asia)
Megophrys aceras, M. baluensis, M. boettgeri, M. carinensis, M. daweimontis, M. dringi, M. edwardinae, M. feae, M. gigantica, M. glandulosa, M. intermedia, M. jingdongensis, M. kempii, M. kobayahsii, M. kuatunensis, M. lateralis, M. longipes, M. mangshanensis, M. medogensis, M. minor, M. montana, M. nankiangensis, M. nasuta, M. omeimontis, M. pachyproctus, M. palpe-pralespinosa, M. parva, M. platyparieta, M. robusta, M. shapingensis, M. spinata, M. wuliangshanensis, M. wushanensis, M. zhangi
5. Genus *Ophryophryne* Boulenger, 1883 (3 species, Southeast Asia)
Ophryophryne microstoma, O. pachyproctus, O. poilani
6. Genus *Oreolalax* Myers and Leviton, 1962 (16 species, China)
Oreolalax chuanbeiensis, O. granulosus, O. jingdongensis, O. liangbeinsis, O. lichuaensis, O. major, O. multipunctatus, O. omeimontis, O. pingii, O. popei, O. puxiongensis, O. rhodostigmatus, O. rugosus, O. schmidti, O. weigoldi, O. xiangchengensis
7. Genus *Pelobates* Wagler, 1830 (4 species, Europe, West Asia, North Africa)
Pelobates cultripes, P. fuscus, P. syriacus, P. varaldii
8. Genus *Scaphiopus* Holbrook, 1836 (3 species, North America)
Scaphiopus couchii, S. hammondii, S. holbrookii
9. Genus *Scutiger* Theobald, 1868 (15 species, China, India)
Scutiger adungensis, S. boulengeri, S. chintingensis, S. glandulatus, S. gongshanensis, S. liupanensis, S. maculatus, S. mammatus, S. nepalensis, S. ningshanensis, S. nyingchiensis, S. pingwuensis, S. ruginosus, S. sikimmensis, S. tuberculatus
10. Genus *Spea* Cope, 1866 (3 species, North America)
Spea bombifrons, S. intermontana, S. multiplicata

17. Family Pelodytidae Bonaparte, 1850 (Mud divers)

1. Genus *Pelodytes* Fitzinger, 1838 (2 species, Western Europe and Southwest Asia)
Pelodytes caucasicus, P. punctatus

18. Family Pipidae Gray, 1825 (Tongueless frogs)

1. Genus *Hymenochirus* Boulenger, 1896 (4 species, western equatorial Africa)
Hymenochirus boettgeri, H. boulengeri, H. curtipes, H. feae
2. Genus *Pipa* Laurenti, 1768 (7 species, Panama, northern South America to Brazil and Bolivia)
Pipa arrabali, P. aspera, P. carvalhoi, P. myersi, P. parva, P. pipa, P. snethlageae
3. Genus *Pseudhymenochirus* Chabanaud, 1920 (1 species, Guinea, Sierra Leone)
Pseudhymenochirus merlini
4. Genus *Silurana* Gray, 1864 (2 species, tropical West Africa)
Silurana epitropicalis, S. tropicalis
5. Genus *Xenopus* Wagler, 1827 (15 species, subsaharan Africa)
Xenopus amieti, X. andrei, X. borealis, X. boumbaensis, X. clivii, X. fraseri, X. gilli, X. laevis, X largeni, X. longipes, X. muelleri, X. pygmaeus, X. ruwenzoriensis, X. vestitus, X. wittei

19. Family Pseudidae Fitzinger, 1843

1. Genus *Lysapsus* Cope, 1862 (1 species, South America)
Lysapsus limellus
2. Genus *Pseudis* Wagler, 1830 (2 species, South America)
Pseudis minuta, P. paradoxa

20. Family Ranidae Rafinesque-Schmaltz, 1814 (True frogs)

1. Genus *Amolops* Cope, 1865 (36 species, India, Nepal, China and Southeast Asia)
Amolops amoropalamus, A. cavitympanum, A. chapaensis, A. chunganensis, A. daiyunensis, A. formosus, A. gerbillus, A. granulosus, A. hainanensis, A. hongkongensis, A. javanus, A. jerboa, A. kaulbacki, A. kinabaluensis, A. larutensis, A. liangshanensis, A. lifanensis, A. loloensis, A. longimanus, A. macrophthalmus, A. mantzorum, A. marmoratus, A. mengyangensis, A. monticola, A. nasicus, A. nepalicus, A. orphnocnemis, A. phaeomerus, A. poecilus, A. rickettii, A. sumatranus, A. tormotus, A. torrentis, A. viridimaculatus, A. whiteheadi, A. wuyiensis
2. Genus *Anhydrophryne* Hewitt, 1919 (1 species, South Africa)
Anhydrophryne rattrayi
3. Genus *Arthroleptella* Hewitt, 1926 (4 species, South Africa)
Arthroleptella drewesii, A. hewitti, A. lightfooti, A. ngongoniensis
4. Genus *Arthroleptides* Nieden, 1910 (2 species, Kenya, Tanzania)
Arthroleptides dutoiti, A. martiensseni
5. Genus *Aubria* Boulenger, 1917 (2 species, Zaire, West Africa)
Aubria masako, A. subsigillata
6. Genus *Batrachylodes* Boulenger, 1887 (8 species, Salomone Islands)
Batrachylodes elegans, B. gigas, B. mediodiscus, B. minutus, B. montanus, B. trossulus, B. vertebralis, B. wolfi
7. Genus *Cacosternum* Boulenger, 1887 (7 species, eastern and southern Africa)
Cacosternum boettgeri, C. capense, C. leleupi, C. namaquense, C. nanum, C. poyntoni, C. striatus
8. Genus *Ceratobatrachus* Boulenger, 1884 (1 species, Salomone Islands)
Ceratobatrachus guentheri
9. Genus *Chaparana* Bourret, 1939 (6 species, India, China to Thailand and Vietnam)
Chaparana aenea, C. delacouri, C. fansipani, C. quadranus, C. sikimensis, C. unculuanus
10. Genus *Conraua* Nieden, 1908 (6 species, tropical Africa)
Conraua alleni, C. beccarii, C. crassipes, C. derooi, C. goliath, C. robusta
11. Genus *Dimorphognathus* Boulenger, 1906 (1 species, Cameroun, Gabun, Zaire)
Dimorphognathus africanus
12. Genus *Discodeles* Boulenger, 1918 (5 species, Salomone Islands, Admirality Island and Bismarck Archipelago)
Discodeles bufoniformis, D. guppyi, D. malukana, D. opisthodon, D. vogti
13. Genus *Ericabatrachus* Largen, 1991 (1 species, Ethiopia)
Ericabatrachus baleensis
14. Genus *Euphlyctis* Fitzinger, 1843 (4 species, northeastern Africa, Arabian Peninsula to Nepal, India, Sri Lanka and Malaysia)
Euphlyctis cornii, E. cyanophlyctis, E. ehrenbergi, E. hexadactylus
15. Genus *Hildebrandtia* Nieden, 1907 (3 species, subsaharan Africa)
Hildebrandtia macrotympanum, H. ornata, H. ornatissima
16. Genus *Hoplobatrachus* Peters, 1863 (4 species, sections of Africa including Angola, Sudan, Ethiopia and Zambia as well as Southeast Asia to Thailand)
Hoplobatrachus crassus, H. occipitalis, H. rugulosus, H. tigerinus
17. Genus *Indirana* Laurent, 1986 (9 species, India, Malaysia)
Indirana beddomii, I. bachytarsus, I. diplosticta, I. gundia, I. leithii, I. leptodactyla, I. phrynoderma, I. semipalmata, I. tenuilingua
18. Genus *Ingerana* Dubois, 1987 (5 species, Southeast Asia)
Ingerana baluensis, I. mariae, I. sariba, I. tasanae, I. tenasserimensis
19. Genus *Lanzarana* Clarke, 1983 (1 species, Somalia)
Lanzarana largeni
20. Genus *Limnonectes* Fitzinger, 1843 (67 species, Central Africa, Asia from Pakistan, Nepal, India to Japan, Philippines, Sri Lanka, Greater and Lesser Sunda Islands to Timor)
Limnonectes acanthi, L. andamanensis, L. arathooni, L. blythii, L. brevipalmatus, L. cancrivorus, L. corrugatus, L. dabanus, L. dammermani, L. diuata, L. doriae, L. finchi, L. fragilis, L. fujianensis, L. greenii, L. grunniens, L. gyldenstolpei, L. heinrichi, L. ibanorum, L. ingeri, L. kenepaiensis, L. keralensis, L. khammonensis, L. khasianus, L. kirtisinghei, L. kohchangae, L. kuhlii, L. laticeps, L. leytensis, L. limnocharis, L. macrocephalus, L. macrodon, L. macrognathus, L. magnus, L. malesianus, L. mawlyndipi, L. mawphlangensis, L. micrixalus, L. microdiscus, L. microtympanum, L. modestus, L. murthii, L. namiyei, L. nepalensis, L. nilagirica, L. nitidus, L. orissaensis, L. palavanensis, L. paramacrodon, L. parambikulamana, L. parvus, L. pierrei, L. pileatus, L. plicatellus, L. raja, L. rufescens, L. sauriceps, L. shompenorum, L. syhadrensis, L. teraiensis, L. timorensis, L. toumanoffi, L. tweediei, L. verruculosus, L. visayanus, L. vittiger, L. woodworthi
21. Genus *Liurana* Dubois, 1987 (5 species, China)
Liurana alpina, L. liui, L. medogensis, L. reticulata, L. xizangensis
22. Genus *Mantella* Boulenger, 1882 (12 species, Madagascar)
Mantella aurantiaca, M. baroni, M. bernhardi, M. betsileo, M. cowani, M. crocea, M. expectata, M. haraldmeieri, M. laevigata, M. madagascariensis, M. pulchra, M. viridis
23. Genus *Mantidactylus* Boulenger, 1895 (62 species, Madagascar)
Mantidactylus aerumnalis, M. aglavei, M. albofrenatus, M. albolineatus, M. alutus, M. ambohimitombi, M. ambreensis, M. argenteus, M. asper, M. bertini, M. betsileanus, M. bicalcaratus, M. biporus, M. blommersae, M. boulengeri, M. brevipalmatus, M. cornutus, M. corvus, M. curtus, M. decaryi, M. depressiceps, M. domerguei, M. eiselti, M. elegans, M. femoralis, M. fimbriatus, M. flavobrunneus, M. grandidieri, M. grandisonae, M. granulatus, M. guibei, M. guttulatus, M. horridus, M. kely, M. klemmeri, M. leucomaculatus, M. liber, M. lugubris, M. luteus, M. madecassus, M. majori, M. malagasius, M. massi, M. microtympanum, M. mocquardi, M. opiparis, M. peraccae, M. phantasticus, M. plicifer, M. pseudoasper, M. pulcher, M. punctatus, M. redimitus, M. rivicola, M. silvanus, M. spinifer, M. thelenae, M. tornieri, M. ulcerosus, M. ventrimaculatus, M. webbi, M. wittei
24. Genus *Micrixalus* Boulenger, 1888 (6 species, India, Sri Lanka)
Micrixalus fuscus, M. gadgili, M. nudis, M. phyllophilus, M. saxicola, M. silvaticus, M. thampii
25. Genus *Microbatrachella* Hewitt, 1926 (1 species, South Africa)
Microbatrachella capensis
26. Genus *Nannophrys* Günther, 1869 (3 species, Sri Lanka)
Nannophrys ceylonensis, N. guentheri, N. marmorata
27. Genus *Nanorana* Günther, 1896 (3 species, Tibet, Nepal, China)
Nanorana parkeri, N. pleskei, N. ventripunctata
28. Genus *Natalobatrachus* Hewitt and Methuen, 1913 (1 species, South Africa)
Natalobatrachus bonebergi
29. Genus *Nothophryne* Poynton, 1963 (1 species, Malawi, Mozambique)
30. Genus *Nyctibatrachus* Boulenger, 1882 (12 species, India)
Nyctibatrachus aliciae, N. beddomii, N. deccanensis, N. humayuni, N. kempholeyensis, N. major, N. minor, N. modestus, N. pygmaeus, N. sanctipalustris, N. sylvaticus, N. vasanthi
31. Genus *Occidozyga* Kuhl and Van Hasselt, 1822 (1 species, India to China and Southeast Asia)
Occidozyga lima
32. Genus *Paa* Dubois, 1975 (26 species, Afghanistan, Pakistan, India, Nepal to China, Thailand and Vietnam)
Paa anandalii, P. arnoldi, P. blanfordii, P. boulengeri, P. bourreti, P. chayuensis, P. conaensis, P. ercepeae, P. exilispinosa, P. fasciculispina, P. feae, P. hazarensis, P. jiulongensis, P. liebigii, P. liui, P. maculosa, P. minica, P. polunini, P. rara, P. robertingeri, P. rostandi, P. shini, P. sichuanensis, P. spinosa, P. sternosignata, P. vicina, P. yunnanensis
33. Genus *Palmatorappia* Ahl, 1927 (1 species, Salomone Islands)
Palmatorappia solomonis
34. Genus *Petropedetes* Reichenow, 1874 (7 species, Sierra Leone to Cameroun, Fernando Po Island)
Petropedetes cameronensis, P. johnstoni, P. natator, P. newtoni, P. palmipes, P. parkeri, P. perreti
35. Genus *Phrynobatrachus* G∏nther, 1862 (67 species, subsaharan Africa)
Phrynobatrachus accraensis, P. acridoides, P. acutirostris, P. albomarginatus, P. alleni, P. alticola, P. annulatus, P. anotis, P. asper, P. auritus, P. batesii, P. bequarerti, P. bottegi, P. calcaratus, P. congicus, P. cornutus, P. cricogaster, P. cryptotis, P. dalcqui, P. dendrobates, P. dispar, P. elberti, P. feae, P. francisci, P. fraterculus, P. gastoni, P. ghanensis, P. giorgii, P. graueri, P. guineensis, P. gutturosus, P. hylaios, P. keniensis, P. kinangopensis, P. krefftii, P. liberiensis, P. mababiensis, P. manengoubensis, P. minutus, P. moorii, P. nanus, P. natalensis, P. ogoensis, P. pakenhami, P. parkeri, P. parvulus, P. perpalmatus, P. petropedetoides, P. plicatus, P. pygmaeus, P. rouxi, P. rungwensis, P. scapularis, P. sciangallarum, P. steindachneri, P. stewartae, P. sulforeogularis, P. taiensis, P. tellinii, P. tokba, P. ukingensis, P. uzungwensis, P. versicolor, P. villiersi, P. vogti, P. werneri, P. zavattarii
36. Genus *Phrynodon* Parker 1935 (1 species, Cameroun and Fernando Po Island)
Phrynodon sandersoni
37. Genus *Phrynoglossus* Peters, 1867 (9 species, Southeast Asia from southern China to Philippines, Sunda Islands to Flores)
Phrynoglossus baluensis, P. borealis, P. celebensis, P. diminutivus, P. floresianus, P. laevis, P. magnapustulosus, P. martenssii, P. semipalmatus
38. Genus *Platymantis* Günther, 1859 (44 species, Philippines, New Guinea and various South Sea Islands)
Platymantis acrochordus, P. aculeodactylus, P. akarithymus, P. banahao, P. batantae, P. boulengeri, P. cheesmanae, P. cornutus, P. corrugatus, P. dorsalis, P. gilliardi, P. guentheri, P. guppyi, P. hazelae, P. ingeri, P. insulatus, P. isarog, P. laevigatus, P. lawtoni, P. luzonensis, P. macrops, P. macrosceles, P. magnus, P. mimicus, P. mimulus, P. myersi, P. neckeri, P. negrosensis, P. nexipus, P. panayensis, P. papuensis, P. parkeri, P. pelewensis, P. polillensis, P. punctata, P. rabori, P. rhipiphalcus, P. schmidti, P. solomonis, P. spelaeus, P. subterrestris, P. vitianus, P. vitiensis, P. weberi
39. Genus *Poyntonia* Channing and Boycott, 1989 (1 species, Cape region, South Africa)
Poyntonia paludicola
40. Genus *Ptychadena* Boulenger, 1917 (47 species, Egypt, subsaharan Africa, Madagascar, Seychelles and Mascarenes Islands)
Ptychadena aequiplicata, P. anchietae, P. ansorgii, P. arnei, P. broadleyi, P. bunoderma, P. christyi, P. chrysogaster, P. cooperi, P. erlangeri, P. filwoha, P. floweri, P. grandisonae, P. guibei, P. harenna, P. ingeri, P. keilingi, P. largeni, P. longirostris, P. maccarthyensis, P. mahnerti, P. mapacha, P. mascareniensis, P. mossambica, P. nana, P. neumanni, P. newtoni, P. obscura, P. oxyrhynchus, P. perplicata, P. perreti, P. porosissima, P. pujoli, P. pumilio, P. retropunctata, P. schillukorum, P. schubotzi, P. stenocephala, P. straeleni, P. submascareniensis, P. subpunctata, P. superciliaris, P. taenioscelis, P. tournieri, P. trinodis, P. upembae, P. uzungwensis
41. Genus *Pyxicephalus* Tschudi, 1838 (3 species, subsaharan Africa)
Pyxicephalus adspersus, P. edulis, P. obbianus
42. Genus *Rana* Linnaeus, 1758 (242 species, worldwide with the exception of large areas in Australia)
Rana adenopleura, R. albolabris, R. albotuberculata, R. altaica, R. alticola, R. amamiensis, R. amieti, R. amnicola, R. amurensis, R. andersonii, R. angolensis, R. anlungensis, R. aragonensis, R. archotaphus, R. areolata, R. arfaki, R. arvalis, R. asiatica, R. asperata, R. asperrima, R. aurantiaca, R. aurora, R. bannanica, R. baramica, R. barmoachensis, R. bedriagae, R. berlandieri, R. bergeri, R. bhagmandlensis, R. blairi, R. bonaespei, R. boylii, R. brownorum, R. bwana, R. caldwelli, R. camerani, R. cascadae, R. catesbeiana, R. celebensis, R. cerigensis, chalconota, R. chaochiaoensis, R. chapaensis, R. chensinensis, R. chevronta, R. chiricahuensis, R. clamitans, R. cordofana, R. crassiovis, R. cretensis, R. cubitalis, R. curtipes, R. daemeli, R. dalmatina, R. danieli, R. darlingi, R. daunchina, R. debussyi, R. demarchii, R. desaegeri, R. dracomontana, R. dunni, R. dybowskii, R. elberti, R. emeljanowi, R. epeirotica, R. erythraea, R. kl. esculenta, R. everetti, R. fasciata, R. fisheri, R. florensis, R. forreri, R. fukienensis, R. fuscigula, R. galamensis, R. garoensis, R. garritor, R. ghoshi, R. glandulosa, R. gracilis, R graeca, R. kl. grafi, R. grahami, R. grandocula, R. grayii, R. grisea, R. grylio, R. guentheri, R. heckscheri, R. hejiangensis, R. kl. hispanica, R. holsti, R. holtzi, R. hosii, R. huanrenensis, R. huanrensis, R. hubeiensis, R. humeralis, R. hymenopus, R. iberica, R. ijimae, R. ishikawae, R. italica, R. japonica, R. jimiensis, R. johnsi, R. johnstoni, R. juliani, R. kampeni, R. khare, R. kreffti, R. kuangwuensis, R. kurtmuelleri, R. latastei, R. lateralis, R. latouchii, R. lemairii, R. leptoglossa, R. lepus, R. lessonae, R. livida, R. longicrus, R. longipes, R. luctuosa, R. lungshengensis, R. luzonensis, R. macrocnemis, R. macrodactyla, R. macroglossa, R. macrops, R. maculata, R. magnaocularis, R. malabarica, R. maosonensis, R. margaretae, R. margariana, R. melanomenta, R. miadis, R. milleti, R. minima, R. miopus, R. moellendorffi, R. moluccana, R. montezumae, R. montivaga, R. multidenticulata, R. muscosa, R. narina, R. neovolcanica, R. nicobariensis, R. nigrolineata, R. nigromaculata, R. nigrotympanica, R. nigrovittata, R. novaeguineae, R. oatesii, R. occidentalis, R. okaloosae, R. okinavana, R. omeimontis, R. omiltemana, R. onca, R. ornativentris, R. palmipes, R. palustris, R. papua, R. parkeriana, R. perezi, R. persimilis, R. pipiens, R. pirica, R. plancyi, R. pleuraden, R. porosa, R. pretiosa, R. psaltes, R. pueblae, R. pustulosa, R. pyrenaica, R. raniceps, R. rhacoda, R. ridibunda, R. rugosa, R. ruwenzorica, R. saharica, R. sakuraii, R. sanguinea, R. sangzhiensis, R. sauteri, R. schmackeri, R. scutigera, R. semelvella, R. senchalensis, R. septentrionalis, R. shqiperica, R. shuchinae, R. siberu, R. sierramadrensis, R. signata, R. similis, R. spectabilis, R. sphenocephala, R. spinidactyla, R. spinulosa, R. springbokensis, R. subaquavocalis, R. subaspera, R. supragrisea, R. supranarina, R. susana, R. swinhoana, R. sylvatica, R. tagoi, R. taipehensis, R tarahumarae, R. taylori, R. temporalis, R. temporaria, R. terentievi, R. tiannanensis, R. tientaiensis, R. tlaloci, R. trilobata, R. tsushimensis, R. tuberculata, R. utsunomiyaorum, R. vaillanti, R. vandijki, R. varians, R. versabilis, R. vertebralis, R. vibicaria, R. virgatipes, R. wageri, R. warschewitschii, R. weiningensis, R. wittei, R. wuchuanensis, R. yavapaiensis, R. zhenhaiensis, R. zweifeli
43. Genus *Staurois* Cope, 1865 (3 species, Borneo, Philippines)
Staurois latopalmatus, S. natator, S. tuberilinguis
44. Genus *Taylorana* Dubois, 1987 (2 species, India to Vietnam and Java)
Taylorana hascheana, T. limborgii
45. Genus *Tomopterna* Duméril and Bibron, 1841 (14 species, subsaharan Africa, Madagascar, India, Sri Lanka, Nepal)
Tomopterna breviceps, T. cryptotis, T. delalandii, T. dobsonii, T. krugerensis, T. labrosa, T. leucorhynchus, T. marmorata, T. natalensis, T. rolandae, T. strachani, T. swani, T. tandyi, T. tuberculosa

21. Family Rhacophoridae Hoffman, 1932

1. Genus *Aglyptodactylus* Boulenger, 1919 (1 species, Madagascar)
Aglyptodactylus madagascariensis
2. Genus *Boophis* Tschudi, 1838 (41 species, Madagascar)
Boophis albilabris, B. albipunctatus, B. andohahela andreonei, B. anjanaharibeensis, B. ankaratra, B. blommersae, B. boehmei, B. brachychir, B. burgeri, B. difficilis, B. elenae, B. englaenderi, B. erythrodactylus, B. goudotii, B. guibei, B. hillenii, B. idae, B. jaegeri, B. laurenti, B. luteus, B. madagascariensis, B. majori, B. mandraka, B. marojezensis, íB. microtis,Ó B. microtympanum, B. miniatus, B. opisthodon, B. pauliani, B. periegetes, B. rappiodes, B. reticulatus, B. rhodoscelis, B. rufioculis, B. septentrionalis, B. sibilans, B. tephraeomystax, B. viridis, B. williamsi, B. xerophilus
3. Genus *Buergeria* Tschudi, 1838 (4 species, Japan,

Taiwan)
Buergeria buergeri, B. japonica, B. pollicaris, B. robusta
4. Genus *Chirixalus*, Boulenger, 1893 (8 species, Southeast Asia)
Chirixalus doriae, C. eiffingeri, C. hansenae, C. idiootocus, C. laevis, C. nongkhorensis, C. simus, C. vittatus
5. Genus *Chiromantis*, Peters, 1854 (3 species, tropical Africa)
Chiromantis petersii, C. rufescens, C. xerampelina
6. Genus *Nyctixalus* Boulenger, 1882 (3 species, India?, Southeast Asia)
Nyctixalus margaritifer, N. pictus, N. spinosus
7. Genus *Philautus* Gistel, 1848 (87 species, India, Sri Lanka, China and Southeast Asia)
Philautus acutirostris, P. acutus, P. adspersus, P. albopunctatus, P. alticola, P. amoenus, P. andersoni, P. annandalii, P. aurantium, P. aurifasciatus, P. banaensis, P. beddomii, P. bombayensis, P. bunitus, P. carinensis, P. chalazodes, P. charius, P. cherrapunjiae, P. cornutus, P. crnri, P. disgregus, P. dubius, P. elegans, P. emembranatus, P. eximius, P. femoralis, P. flaviventris, P. garo, P. glandulosus, P. gracilipes, P. gryllus, P. hassanensis, P. hosii, P. hypomelas, P. ingeri, P. jacobsoni, P. jerdonii, P. jinxiuensis, P. kempiae, P. kerangae, P. kottigeharensis, P. leitensis, P. leucorhinus, P. lissobrachius, P. longchuanensis, P. longicrus, P. maosonensis, P. medogensis, P. melanensis, P. menglaensis, P. microtympanum, P. mjobergi, P. namdaphaensis, P. narainensis, P. nasutus, P. noblei, P. ocellatus, P. pallidipes, P. palpebralis, P. parkeri, P. parvulus, P. petersi, P. pleurostictus, P. poecilus, P. pulcherrimus, P. refugii, P. rhododiscus, P. romeri, P. sanctisilvaticus, P. saueri, P. schmackeri, P. shillongensis, P. shyamrupus, P. signatus, P. similis, P. stictomerus, P. surdus, P. surrufus, P. swamianus, P. tectus, P. temporalis, P. travancoricus, P. tytthus, P. umbra, P. variabilis, P. vermiculatus, P. williamsi
8. Genus *Polypedates* Tschudi, 1838 (16 species, tropical Southeast Asia, Japan, eastern China)
Polypedates colletti, P. cruciger, P. dennysii, P. dugritei, P. eques, P. feae, P. insularis, P. leucomystax, P. longinasus, P. macrotis, P. maculatus, P. megacephalus, P. mutus, P. omeimontis, P. otilophus, P. zhaojuensis
9. Genus *Rhacophorus* Kuhl and Van Hasselt, 1822 (62 species, Southeast Asia, India, China, Japan)
Rhacophorus angulirostris, R. annamensis, R. appendiculatus, R. arboreus, R. arvalis, R. aurantiventris, R. baluensis, R. bimaculatus, R. bipunctatus, R. bisacculus, R. calcadensis, R. calcaneus, R. cavirostris, C. chenfui, R. depressus, R. dulitensis, R. edentulus, R. everetti, R. fasciatus, R. fergusonianus, R. gauni, R. georgii, R. gongshanensis, R. harrissoni, R. hecticus, R. hungfuensis, R. javanus, R. kajau, R. leucofasciatus, R. macropus, R. malabaricus, R. maximus, R. modestus, R. moltrechi, R. monticola, R. namdaphaensis, R. nigropalmatus, R. nigropunctatus, R. notater, R. owstoni, R. oxycephalus, R. pardalis, R. poecilonotus, R. prasinatus, R. prominanus, R. reinwardtii, R. rhodopus, R. robinsoni, R. rufipes, R. schlegelii, R. taeniatus, R. taipeianus, R. taroensis, R. translineatus, R. tuberculatus, R. tunkui, R. turpes, R. verrucopus, R. verrucosus, R. viridis, R. yaoshanensis, R. zed
10. Genus *Theloderma* Tschudi, 1838 (11 species, China, Myanmar, Southeast Asia)
Theloderma asperum, T. bicolor, T. corticale, T. gordoni, T. horridum, T. kwangsiense, T. leporosa, T. moloch, T. phrynoderma, T. schmardanum, T. stellatum

22. Family Rhinodermatidae Bonaparte, 1850 (Mouth-brooding frogs)

1. Genus *Rhinoderma* Duméril and Bibron, 1841 (2 species, southern Chile and Argentina)
Rhinoderma darwinii, R. rufum

23. Family Rhinophrynidae Günther, 1858 (Burrowing toads)

1. Genus *Rhinophrynus* Duméril and Bibron, 1841 (1 species, southern USA Mexico to Costa Rica)
Rhinophrynus dorsalis

24. Family Sooglossidae Noble, 1931 (Seychelles frogs)

1. Genus *Nesomantis* Boulenger, 1909 (1 species, Seychelles)
Nesomantis thomasseti
2. Genus *Sooglossus* Boulenger, 1906 (2 species, Seychelles)
Sooglossus gardineri, S. sechellensis

Bibliography

Books and General Works

ARAK, A., 1983: Male-male competition and male choice in anuran amphibians. In: BATESON, P. (Ed.): Mate choice. Cambridge Univ. Press, Cambridge.

ARNOLD, E. N. & J. A. BURTON, 1979: Pareys Reptilien- und Amphibienführer Europas. Verlag Paul Parey, Hamburg, Berlin.

BARBADILLO ESCRIVA, L. J., 1987: La Guia de Incafo de los anfibios y reptiles de la peninsula Iberica, Islas Baleares y Canarias. INCAFO, Madrid.

BARUS, V., O. OLIVA et al., 1992: Fauna CSFR. Obojzivelnici (Amphibia). Academia, Prague.

BEEBEE, T. J. C., 1996: Ecology and conservation of amphibians. Chapman Hall, London.

BENTON, M. J., 1990: Vertebrate paleontology. Harper Collins Academic, London.

BEREITER-HAHN, J., A. G. MATOLTSY & K. S. RICHARDS (eds.), 1986: Biology of the integument. 2. Vertebrates. Springer Verlag, Berlin, Heidelberg, New York, Tokyo.

BLAB, J., 1986: Biologie, Ökologie und Schutz von Amphibien. Schriftenreihe für Landschaftspflege und Naturschutz 18, Kilda, Bonn-Bad Godesheim.

BLÜM, V., 1985: Vergleichende Reproduktionsbiologie der Wirbeltiere. Springer Verlag, Berlin, Heidelberg, New York.

BREHMS, TIERLEBEN, 1876-1878: Allgemeine Kunde des Thierreichs. Leipzig.

CAPULA, M., 1995: Anfibi e Repttili. Biologia, Abitudini di vita. Ambienti e distribuzione. Arnoldo Mondadsori Editore, Milano.

CARROLL, R. L., 1993: Paläontologie und Evolution der Wirbeltiere. Georg Thieme Verlag, Stuttgart and New York.

CARROLL, R. L., 1997: Patterns and processes of vertebrate evolution. Cambridge Paleobiology Series, Cambridge University Press, Cambridge.

CORBETT, K., 1989: The conservation of European reptiles and amphibians. Christopher Helm, London.

COTT, H.B., 1957: Adaptive coloration in animals. Methuen & Co. Ltd., London.

DEVILLERS, J. & J. M. EXBRAYAT, 1992: Ecotoxicity of chemicals to amphibians. Gordon and Breach, Philadelphia.

DIESENER, G., J. REICHHOF, R. DIESENER, 1995: Lurche und Kriechtiere. Mosaik Verlag, Munich.

DUDEL, J., R. MENZEL & R. F. SCHMIDT, 1996: Neurowissenschaft: Vom Molekül zur Kognition. Springer Verlag, Berlin, Heidelberg, New York.

DUELLMAN, W. E. & L. TRUEB, 1986: Biology of amphibians. McGraw-Hill Book Company, New York, St. Louis, San Francisco.

DUELLMAN, W. E., 1993: Amphibian species of the world: additions and corrections. The University of Kansas, Lawrence.

EGGER, F., 1936: Frosch und Kröte bei den alten Ägyptern. Geographisch-Ethnologische Gesellschaft, 4, Basel.

ELDREDGE, N., 1992: The Miner's Canary. Virgin Books, London.

ELKAN, E., 1976: Pathology in the amphibian. In: Lofts B. (ed.): Physiology of the Amphibian. Academic Press Inc. NY, San Francisco, London.

ENGELMANN, W. E., 1986: Lurche und Kriechtiere Europas. Deutscher Taschenbuch Verlag. F. Enke Verlag, Stuttgart.

FEDER, M. E. & W. W. BURGGREN (eds.), 1992: Environmental physiology of the amphibians. The University of Chicago Press, Chicago, London.

FERRARI, M., 1993. Farben im Tierreich - Tarnen, Täuschen, Überleben. Stürtz-Verlag Würzburg.

FREEDMAN, M., 1995: Environmental ecology. The ecological effects of pollution, disturbance, and other stresses. Academic Press, San Diego.

FRIEDRICH, U. & W. VOLLAND, 1992: Futtertierzucht. Lebendfutter für Vivarientiere. Ulmer, Stuttgart.

FRITSCH, B., M. J. RYAN, V. WILCZYNSKI, T. E. HETHERINGTON & W. WALKOWIAK (eds.), 1988: The evolution of the amphibian auditory system. John Wiley & Sons. New York.

FROST, D. R. (ed.), 1985: Amphibian species of the world. Allen Press Inc. and Ass. of Systematics Collections, Lawrence.

GOUDIE, A., 1997: The human impact reader. Blackwell, Oxford.

GREEN, D. M., 1997: Amphibians in decline: Canadian studies of a global problem. Society for the Study of Amphibians and Reptiles, Saint Louis.

GRIFFITHS, R. A., 1996: Newts and salamanders of Europe. Poyser Natural History, London.

GRZIMEKS TIERLEBEN, 1993: Enzyklopädie des Tierreichs in 13. Bänden. [encyclopaedia of the animal world in 13 volumes] Fische 2, Lurche. DTV, Munich.

GÜNTHER, R., 1990: Die Wasserfrösche Europas (Anura, Froschlurche). Die Neue BREHM Bücherei 600. A. Ziemen Verlag, Wittenberg Lutherstadt.

GÜNTHER, R., 1996: Die Amphibien und Reptilien Deutschlands. Gustav Fischer Verlag, Jena.

HAIRSTON, N. G., 1987: Community ecology and salamander guilds. Cambridge University Press, Cambridge.

HALLIDAY, T. R. & K. ADLER, 1987: The encyclopedia of reptiles and amphibians. Facts on File Inc., New York.

HENLE, K. & M. VEITH (eds.), 1997: Naturschutzrelevante Methoden der Feldherpetologie. Mertensiella 7, Rheinbach.

HERRMANN, H.-J., 1994: Amphibien im Aquarium. Ulmer, Stuttgart.

HEYER, W. R., M. A. DONNELLY, R. W. McDIARMID, L.-A. HAYEK & M. S. FOSTER, 1994: Measuring and monitoring of biological diversity. Standard methods for amphibians. Smithsonian Institution Press, Washington and London.

HIMSTEDT, W., 1996: Die Blindwühlen. Westarp Wissenschaften. Die Neue Brehm Bücherei, Vol. 630, Magdeburg.

HIRSCHBERG, W., 1988: Frosch und Kröte in Mythos und Brauch. Böhlau Verlag, Vienna, Cologne, Graz.

HÖDL, W., 1993: Amazonien aus der Froschperspektive. In: AUBRECHT, G., M. BRANDS, F. GUSENLEITNER, F. SPETA, & S. WEIGL (eds.): Amerika - Zur Entdeckung Kulturpflanzen - Lebensraum Regenwald. Kataloge des OÖ Landesmuseum, NF- 61, 499-545.

HÖDL, W. & G. AUBRECHT, 1996: Frösche, Kröten, Unken: Aus der Welt der Amphibien. Stapfia 37, Linz.

HÖDL, W., R. JEHLE & G. GOLLMANN (eds.), 1997: Populationsbiologie von Amphibien: Eine Langzeitstudie auf der Wiener Donauinsel. Stapfia. 51, Linz.

HONEGGER, E. H., 1981: Threatened amphibians and reptiles in Europe. Suppl. In: BÖHME, W. (ed.): Handbuch der Amphibien und Reptilien Europas. Aula, Wiesbaden.

HOUCK, L. D., 1977: Life history patterns and reproductive biology of Neotropical salamanders. In: TAYLOR, D. H. & S. I. GUTTMAN (eds.): The reproductive biology of amphibians. Plenum Press, New York.

IUCN, The World Conservation Union, 1996: The IUCN Red List of threatened animals. IUCN Publications Service Unit, Cambridge.

JARVIK, E., 1980: Basic structure and evolution of vertebrates. Vols. 1 and 2. Academic Press, London.

JEDICKE, E., 1994: Biotopverbund: Grundlagen und Maßnahmen einer neuen Naturschutzstrategie. 2nd revised and expanded edition. Verlag Ulmer, Stuttgart.

JEFFRIES, M. J., 1997: Biodiversity and conservation. Routledge, London.

KABISCH, K., 1990: Wörterbuch der Herpetologie. Gustav Fischer Verlag, Jena.

KAULE, G., 1991: Arten- und Biotopschutz. 2nd revised edition. Verlag Ulmer, Stuttgart.

KLINGELHÖFFER, W., 1956: Terrarienkunde. Part Two: Lurche. Alfred Kernen Verlag, Stuttgart.

KÜSTER, H., 1995: Geschichte der Landschaft Mitteleuropas. Verlag C. H. Beck, Munich.

KUZMIN, S. L., 1995: Die Amphibien Rußlands und angrenzender Gebiete. Die Neue Brehm-Bücherei Vol. 627; Westarp Wissenschaften, Magdeburg.

KUZMIN, S. L., C. K. DODD & M. M. PIKULIK (eds.), 1995: Amphibian populations in the Comm. of Ind. States: Current status and declines. Pensoft, Moscow.

LANDIS, W.G. & MING-HO YU, 1995: Introduction to environmental toxicology. Impacts of chemicals upon ecological systems. Lewis Publishers, Boca Raton.

MARCUS, L. C., 1983: Amphibien und Reptilien in Heim, Labor und Zoo. F. Enke-Verlag, Stuttgart.

MASURAT, G. & W. R. GROSSE, 1991: Vermehrung von Terrarientieren. Lurche. Urania Verlag, Leipzig, Jena, Berlin.

MATTISON, C., 1987: Frogs & toads of the world. Blanford Press, Poole, New York, Sydney.

MATZ, G. & D. WEBER, 1983: BLV Bestimmungsbuch Amphibien und Reptilien. BLV Verlagsgesellschaft, Munich, Vienna, Zurich.

McDIARMID, R. W., 1978: Evolution of parental care in frogs, 127-147. In: BURKHARDT, G. M. & M. BEKOFF (eds.): The development of behavior: Comparative and evolutionary aspects. STPM Press, New York.

MEBS, D., 1989: Gifttiere. Wissenschaftliche Verlagsgesellschaft, Stuttgart.

MEHLHORN, H., D. DÜWEL & W. RAETHER, 1986: Diagnose und Therapie der Parasiten von Haus-, Nutz- und Heimtieren. Gustav Fischer Verlag. Stuttgart, New York.

NIETZKE, G., 1989: Die Terrarientiere 1. Schwanzlurche und Froschlurche. Ulmer, Stuttgart.

NIEUWENHUYS, R., H. J. DONKELAAR & C. NICHOLSON, 1997: The central nervous

system of vertebrates, Vol. 2. Springer Verlag, Berlin, Heidelberg, New York.
NÖLLERT, A. & C. NÖLLERT, 1992: Die Amphibien Europas. Bestimmung, Gefährdung, Schutz. Franckh-Kosmos, Stuttgart.
NOWAK, E., J. BLAB & R. BLESS, 1994: Rote Liste der gefährdeten Wirbeltiere in Deutschland: Mit kommentierten Artenverzeichnissen und Synopsen der Roten Listen der Bundesländer. Schriftenreihe für Landschaftspflege und Naturschutz, 24. Kilda, Greven.
OWEN, D., 1982: Camouflage and mimicry. University of Chicago Press, Chicago.
PAPI, F. (ed.), 1992: Animal homing. Chapman and Hall, London and New York.
PARKER, H. W. & A. BELLAIRS, 1972: Die Amphibien und Reptilien. Die Enzyklopädie der Natur, Vol. X. Editions Recontre Lausanne.
PHILLIPS, K., 1994: Tracking the vanishing frogs. Penguin Books, Harmondsworth.
POWER, T., K. L. CLARK, A. HARFENIST & D. B. PEAKALL, 1989: A review and evaluation of the amphibian toxicology literature. Technical report series, 61, Canadian Wildlife Service, Ottawa.
RAND, G. M., 1995: Fundamentals of aquatic toxicology. Taylor & Francis, Bristol.
REGÖS, J., 1987: Die grüne Hölle - ein bedrohtes Paradies. Bericht aus dem Regenwald. Parey, Hamburg.
RIMPP, K., 1985: Salamander und Molche. Schwanzlurche im Terrarium. Ulmer, Stuttgart.
ROTH, G., 1987: Visual behavior in salamanders. Springer Verlag, Berlin, Heidelberg, New York.
RÖDEL, M.-O., 1996: Amphibien der westafrikanischen Savanne. Edition Chimaira, Frankfurt on Main.
RUNDQUIST, E. M., 1995: Reptile and amphibian parasites. T. F. H. Publications Inc. Neptune, NJ.
RYAN, M. J., 1985: The Túngara Frog. A study in sexual selection and communication. University of Chicago Press, Chicago.
SALTHE, S. N. & W. E. DUELLMAN, 1973: Quantitative constraints associated with reproductive modes in anurans. 229-249. In: VIAL, J. L. (ed.): Evolutionary biology of the anurans: Contemporary research on major problems. University of Missouri Press, Columbia.
SCHMALHAUSEN, I. I., 1968: The origin of terrestrial vertebrates. Academic Press, New York and London.
SCHULTE, R., 1984: Frösche und Kröten. Tropische und einheimische Froschlurche im Terrarium. Eugen ULMER, Stuttgart.
SEMLITSCH, R. D., D. E. Scott, J. H. K. PECHMANN & J. W. GIBBONS, 1996: Structure and dynamics of an amphibian community: evidence from a 16-year study of a natural pond. 217-250. in: CODY, M. L. & J. A. SMALLWOOD (eds): Long-term studies of vertebrate communities. Academic Press, San Diego.
SHISHKIN, M. A., 1973: The morphology of the early amphibia and some problems of the lower tetrapod evolution. Nauka, Moscow.
SINSCH, U., 1998: Biologie und Ökologie der Kreuzkröte. Laurenti Verlag, Bochum.
STARCK, D., 1982: Vergleichende Anatomie der Wirbeltiere, Vol. 3: Organe des aktiven Bewegungsapparates, der Koordination, der Umweltbeziehung, des Stoffwechsels und der Fortpflanzung. Springer Verlag, Berlin, Heidelberg, New York.
STEBBINS, R. C. & N. W. COHEN, 1995: A natural history of amphibians. Princeton University Press, Princeton.
STORCH, V. & U. WELSCH, 1991: Systematische Zoologie. 4th edition. Gustav Fischer Verlag, Stuttgart, New York.
SUTER, G. W., 1993: Ecological risk assessment. Lewis Publishers, Michigan.
TYLER, M. J., 1989: Australian frogs. Penguin Books Australia, Victoria.
VIAL, J. L & L. SAYLOR, 1993: The status of amphibian populations. A compilation and analysis. IUCN/SSC Declining Amphibian Task Force. Working Document No. 1. The World Conservation Union (IUCN), Species Survival Commission (SSC).
WATERMAN, A. J., B. E. FRYE, K. JOHANSEN, A. C. KLUGE, M. L. MOSS, C. R. NOBACK, I. D. OLSEN & G. R. ZUG, 1971: Chordate structure and function. The Macmillan Company, New York
WELLS, K. D., 1981: Parental behavior in male and female frogs. 184-197. In: ALEXANDER, D. R. & D. W. TINKLE (eds.): Natural selection and social behavior: Recent research and new theory. Chiron Press, Newton.
WILSON, E. O., 1992: The diversity of life. Harvard University Press, Harvard.
ZISWILER, V., 1976: Die Wirbeltiere. Vol 1. DTV and G. Thieme, Stuttgart.

Original Works

ARNOLD, A., 1983: Zur Veränderung des pH-Wertes der Laichgewässer einheimischer Amphibien. Archives. Naturschutz u. Landschaftsforsch., Berlin, 23 (1), 35-40.
BAGNARA, J. T., J. D. TAYLOR & M. E. HADLEY, 1968: The dermal chromatophore unit. J. Cell Biol., 38, 67-79.
BERGER, L., 1983: Western palearctic water frogs (Amphibia, Ranidae): Systematics, genetics, and population compositions. Experientia, 39, 127-130. BERTOLUCI, J. & W. R. HEYER, 1995: Boracéia update. Froglog, 14, 8.
BLAUSTEIN, A. R. & D. B. WAKE, 1990: Declining amphibian populations. A global phenomenon? Trends Ecol. Evolut., 5, 203-204.
BÖHMER, J. & H. RAHMANN, 1990: Influence of surface water acidification on amphibians. In: HANKE, W. (ed.): Biology and physiology of amphibians. Fortschr. Zool., 38, 287-309.
BRANDON, R. A. & J. E. HUHEEY, 1981: Toxicity in the plethodontid salamanders *Pseudotriton ruber* and *Pseudotriton montanus* (Amphibia, Caudata). Toxicon, 19, 25-31.
BRODIE, E. D. Jr. & E. D. BRODIE III, 1980: Differential avoidance of mimetic salamanders by free-ranging birds. Science, 208, 181-183.
BRODIE, E. D. Jr., 1977: Salamander antipredator postures. Copeia, 1977, 523-535.
CABELA, A. & F. TIEDEMANN, 1985: Atlas der Amphibien und Reptilien Österreichs, Stand 1984. Neue Denkschriften des Naturhistorischen Museums in Wien, Verlag Ferdinand Berger & Söhne, Vienna - Horn, 4, 80.
CACCONE, A., M. C. MILINKOVITCH, V. SBORDONI & J. R. POWELL, 1997: Mitochondrial DNA rates and biogeography in European newts (Genus *Euproctus*). Syst. Biol., 46, 126-144.
CAPRANICA, R. R., L. S. FRISHKOPF & E. NEVO, 1973: Encoding of geographic dialects in the auditory system of the cricket frog. Science, 182, 1272-1275.
CLAUSNITZER, H.-J., 1979: Durch Umwelteinflüsse gestörte Entwicklung beim Laich des Moorfrosches *(Rana arvalis* L.). Beitr. Naturk. Niedersachsens, 32, 68-78.
DEUTI, K., 1996: The Himalayan salamander. Cobra, 23, 35-37.
DOURNON, C., C. HOUILLON & C. PIEAU, 1990: Temperature sex reversal in amphibians and reptiles. Int. J. Dev. Biol., 34: 81-92.
DROST, C. A. & G. M. FELLERS, 1996: Collapse of a regional frog fauna in the Yosemite area of the Sierra Nevada, USA. Conserv. Biol., 10, 414-425.
DUBOIS, A. & R. GÜNTHER, 1982: Klepton and Synklepton: Two new Evolutionary Systematic Categories in Zoology. Zool. Jb. Syst., 109, 290-305.
DUBOIS, A., 1983: Classification et nomenclature supragenerique des amphibiens anoures. Bul[letin] Men[suel] Soc[iété] Linnéenne Lyon, 52, 270-276.
DUELLMAN, W. E. & R. THOMAS, 1996: Anuran amphibians from a seasonally dry forest in southeastern Peru and comparisons of the anurans among sites in the upper Amazon basin. Occ. Pap. Nat. Hist. Mus. University [of] Kansas, Lawrence, 180, 1-34.
DUELLMAN, W. E., 1975: On the classification of frogs. Occ. Pap. Mus. Nat. Hist. University [of] Kansas, 42, 1-14.
DUNSON, W. A., R. L. WYMAN & E. S. CORBETT, 1992: A Symposium on Amphibian Declines and Habitat Acidification. J. Herpetol., 26 (4), 349-352.
EWERT, J.-P., 1997: Neural correlates of key stimulus and releasing mechanism: a case study and two concepts. TINS, 20, 332-338.
FEDER, M. E. & W. W. BURGGREN, 1986: Hautatmung bei Wirbeltieren. Spektrum der Wissenschaft, 1, 86-95.
FORREST, T. G., 1994: From sender to receiver: propagation and environmental effects on acoustic signals. Amer. Zool., 34, 644-654.
FREDA, J., 1986: The influence of acidic pond water on amphibians: a review. Water, Air and Soil Pollution, 30, 439-450.
GANS, C., 1973: Sound production in the Salientia: mechanism and evolution of the emitter. Amer. Zool., 13, 1179-1194.
GASSER, F. & M. CLERGUE-GAZEAU, 1981: Les Protéines sériques de l'urodèle *Euproctus asper* (DUGES). Éléments de différenciation génétique dans les Prépyrenées espagnoles. Vie Milieu, 31, 297-302.
GEBHARDT, H., K. KREIMES, & M. LINNENBACH, 1987: Untersuchungen zur Beeinträchtigung der Ei- und Larvalstadien von Amphibien in sauren Gewässern. Natur und Landschaft, 62 (1), 20-23.
GERLACH, G. & A. BALLY, 1992: Das Grasfroschsterben in der Nord-Schweiz. Bundesamt für Umwelt, Wald und Landschaft, Bern.
GITTINS, S. P., J. E. STEEDS & R. WILLIAMS, 1982. Population age-structure of the common toad *(Bufo bufo)* at a lake in Mid-Wales determined from annual growth rings in the phalanges. British Journal of Herpetology, 6, 249-252.
GLAW, F. & J. KÖHLER (in print): Amphibian species diversity exceeds that of mammals. Herpetological Review.
GLAW, F. & M. VENCES, 1997a: Neue Daten über die *Mantidactylus*-Untergattung *Spinomantis* aus Madagaskar, mit Beschreibung einer neuen Art. Salamandra, 32 (4), 243-258.
GLAW, F. & M. VENCES, 1997b: A review of anuran eye colouration: definitions, taxonomic implications and possible functions. In: BÖHME, W., W. BISCHOFF & T. ZIEGLER (eds.): Herpetologia Bonnensis (Proc. of the 8th ord. gen. meet. of the Soc. Herp. Eur.), Bonn (SEH), 125-138.
GOSNER, K. L. & I. H. BLACK, 1957: The effects of acidity on the development and hatching of New Jersey frogs. Ecology, 38 (2), 256-262.
GRAF, J.-D. & M. POLLS-PELAZ, 1989: Evolutionary genetics of the *Rana esculenta* complex. In: DAWLEY, R. M. & J. P. BOGART (eds.): Evolution and ecology of unisexual vertebrates. Bulletin, 466, 289-301. N.Y. State Museum, Albany, New York.
GRILLITSCH, B. & A. CHOVANEC, 1995: Heavy metals and pesticides in anuran spawn and tadpoles, water and sediment. Toxicol. Environ. Chem., 50, 131-155.
GUILFORD, T. & M. S. DAWKINS, 1993: Are warning colors handicaps? Evolution, 47 (2), 400-416.
HAGSTRÖM, T., 1977: Grodornas försvinnande i en försurad sjö. Sver[ige] Nat., 11 (6), 367369.
HAGSTRÖM, T., 1980: Reproductive strategy and success of amphibians in waters acidified by atmospheric pollution. Proc. Euro. Herp. Symp. C.W.L.P. Oxford, 5557.
HALL, R. J. & B. M. MULHERN, 1984: Are anuran amphibians heavy metal accumulators? In: Vertebrate ecology and systematics. (eds.): SEIGEL, R. A., L. E. HUNT, J. L. KNIGHT, L. MALARET & N. L. ZUSCHLAG. Spec. Publ. Univ. Kansas Mus. Nat. Hist., 123-133. University of Kansas, Lawrence.
HALL, R. J. & P. F. P. HENRY, 1992: Review: Assessing effects of pesticides on amphibians and reptiles: Status and needs. Herpetol. J., 2, 65-71.
HALLIDAY, T. R. & W. R. HEYER, 1997: The case of the vanishing frogs. Technol. Rev., May/June 1997, 56-62.
HARDING, K. A., 1982: Courtship display in a Bornean frog. Proc. Biol. Soc. Washington, 95, 621-624.
HEDGES, S. B., 1993: Global amphibian declines: A perspective from the Caribian. Biodivers. Conserv., 2, 290-303.
HEMELAAR, A., V. CLAESSEN & W. WIJNANDS, 1987: Enkele karakteristieken van een voortplantingspopulatie van de gewone pad (*Bufo bufo*) uit het gebergte van Zwitserland. Lacerta, 45, 129-144.
HENLE, K.,1996: Möglichkeiten und Grenzen der Analyse von Ursachen des Artenrückganges aus herpetofaunistischen Kartierungsdaten am Beispiel einer langjährigen Erfassung. Z. Feldherpetol., 3, 73-101.
HENLE, K. & B. STREIT, 1990: Kritische Betrachtungen zum Artenrückgang bei Amphibien und Reptilien und zu dessen Ursachen. Natur & Landschaft, 65, 347361.
HEYER, W R., A. S. RAND, C. A. GONCALVEZ DA CRUZ & O. L. PEIXOTO, 1988: Decimations, extinctions, and colonizations of frog populations in southeast Brazil and their evolutionary implications. Biotropica, 20, 230-235.
HÖDL, W., 1977: Call differences and calling site segregation in anuran species from Central Amazonian floating meadows. Oecologia, 28, 351-363.
HÖDL, W, 1990: An analysis of foam-nest construction in the neotropical frog *Physalaemus ephippifer* (Leptodactylidae). Copeia, 1990, 547-554.
HÖDL, W., 1990: Reproductive diversity in Amazonian lowland frogs. In: HANKE, W. (ed.): Biology and physiology of amphibians. Fortschr. Zool., 38, 41-60.
HÖDL, W., 1991: *Phrynohyas resinifictrix* (Hylidae, Anura) - Calling behaviour. Wiss. Film, 42, 63-70.
HÖDL, W., 1992: Reproductive behaviour in the neotropical foam-nesting trog *Pleurodema diplolistris* (Leptodactylidae). Amphibia-Reptilia, 13, 263-274.
HÖDL W., & G. GOLLMANN, 1986: Distress calls in neotropical frogs. Amphibia-Reptilia, 7, 11-21.
HÖLDL, W., M. T. RODRIGUES, G. M. ACCACIO, P. H. LARAP, D. PAVAN, L. C. SCHIESARI & G. SKUK, 1997: Foot-flagging display in the Brazilian stream-breeding frog *Hylodes asper* (Leptodactylidae). Scientific film C 2703. ÖWF Vienna.
HOWARD, R. R. & E. D. BRODIE Jr., 1973: Experimental study of Batesian mimicry in the salamanders *Plethodon jordani* and *Desmognathus ochrophaeus*. Amer. Midl. Nat., 60, 38-46.
JARVIK, E., 1996: The Devonian tetrapod *Ichthyostega.* Fossils and Strata, 40, 1-213, Oslo.
JUNGFER, K.-H. & P. WEYGOLDT (in print): Biparental care - a primitive reproductive mode in the Amazonian treefrog *Osteocephalus oophagus.* Amphibia-Reptilia.
JUNGFER, K.-H., 1996: Reproduction and parental care of the coronated treefrog, *Anotheca spinosa* (STEINDACHNER, 1864) (Anura, Hylidae). Herpetologica, 52, 25-32.
KRISHNAMURTHY, S. V., 1997: *Nyctibatrachus major* in Malnad, India. Froglog, 20, 5.
KUHN, J., 1994: Lebensgeschichte und Demographie von Erdkrötenweibchen *Bufo bufo bufo* (L.). Zeitschrift für Feldherpetologie, 1, 3-87.
KUHN, J., 1997: Die Erdkröte: eine biologische Porträtskizze und die Lebensgeschichte der Weibchen. Biologie in unserer Zeit, 27, 76-86.
KUZMIN, S. L., 1994: The geographical range *of Salamandrella keyserlingii* DYBOWSKI, 1870: Ecological and histor-

ical implications. - Abhandlungen und Berichte für Naturkunde, 17 (special edition), 177-183.

KYEK, M., 1995: Amphibienschutz an Straßen in Österreich. Empfehlungen für den Straßenbau. LÖBF-Mitteilungen, 1, 3440.

KYEK, M, 1997: Tod auf der Straße - Anmerkungen zum Amphibienschutz an Straßen in Österreich. Mitt. Haus der Natur, 13, 26-29.

KYEK, M., 1997: Empfehlungen zum Amphibienschutz an Straßen in Österreich - Zusammenarbeit von Naturschutz und Straßenbau, Rethicus, 3, 167-168.

KYEK, M., N. WINDING & M. PALZEN-BERGER, 1997: Habitatpräferenzen der Erdkröte *(Bufo bufo)* - eine telemetrische Untersuchung. In: HENLE, K. & M. VEITH (eds.): Naturschutzrelevante Methoden der Feldherpetologie. Mertensiella, Rheinbach, 7, 185-202.

LAMOTTE, M. & J. LESCURE, 1977: Tendances adaptives à l'affranchisement du milieu aquatique chez les amphibiens anoures. Terre et Vie, 31, 225-312.

LENGVENUS, W. & J. PARZEFALL, 1992. The role of the visual reaction in the behaviour of an epigean and a cave living population of *Euproctus asper* Duges (Salamandridae, Urodela). Mém. Biospéol., 19, 111-115.

LESCURE, J., V. MARTY, C. MARTY & M. AUBERTHOMAY, 1996: Contribution à l'étude des amphibiens de Guyane française XI. Les *Phrynohyas* (Anura, Hylidae). Revue française d'aquariologie herpetologie, 23 (1-2), 69-76.

LINDQUIST, E. D. & T. E. HETHERINGTON, 1996: Field studies on visual and acoustic signaling in the "earless" Panamanian golden frog, *Atelopus zeteki*. J. Herpetol., 30, 347-354.

LINNENBACH, M. & H. GEBHARDT, 1987: Untersuchungen zu den Auswirkungen der Gewässerversauerung auf die Ei- und Larvalstadien von *Rana temporaria* LINNAEUS, 1758 (Anura: Ranidae). Salamandra, 23 (213), 153-158.

LOWCOCK, J. A., L. E. LICHT & J. P. BOGART, 1987: Nomenclature in hybrid complexes of *Ambystoma* (Urodela, Ambystomatidae): No case for the erection of hybrid "species". Syst. Zool., 36, 328336.

MALKMUS, R.,1982/83: Soziale Thermoregulation bei Larven des Grasfrosches *(Rana temporaria)*. Abh. Naturwiss. Ver. Würzburg, 23/24, 109-118.

MALKMUS, R., 1989: Beobachtungen an einer Überwinterungskolonie des Grasfrosches *(Rana temporaria)*. Nachr. Naturwiss. Mus. Aschaffenburg, 95, 43-66.

MIAUD, C., 1991: La squelettochronologie chez les *Triturus* (Amphibiens, Urodèles) à partir d'une étude de *T. alpestris, T. helveticus* et *T. cristatus* du sud-est de la France. In: "Tissus durs et âge individuel

des vertébrés." Colloque National, Bondy, France, 4-6 Mars 1001. BAGLINIÈRE, J. L., J. CASTANET, F. CONAND & F. J. MEUNIER (eds.): Colloques et Séminaires ORSTOM-INRA.

MITTWOCH, U., 1996: Sex-determining mechanisms in animals. Trend. Ecol. Evol., 11, 63-67.

MÜLLER, H. & D. STEINWARZ, 1987: Landschaftsökologische Aspekte der Jungkrötenwanderung. Untersuchungen an einer Erdkrötenpopulation *(Bufo bufo* L.) im Siebengebirge. Natur und Landschaft, W. KOHLHAMMER, 62 (11), 473-476.

MÜLLER, H. J., 1964: The relation of mutation to mutational advance. Mutat. Res., 1, 29.

MURPHY, J. B., 1976: Pedal luring in the leptodactylid trog *Ceratorphrys calcarata* Boulenger. Herpetologica, 32, 339-341.

MYERS, C. W. & J. W. DALY, 1983: Dart-poison frogs. Scientific American, 248 (2), 120133.

NARINS, P., 1990: Seismic communication in anuran amphibians. BioScience, 40, 268-274.

NARINS, P., 1995: Frog communication. Scientific American, August 1995, 62-67.

NARINS, P. & R. R. CAPRANICA, 1978: Communicative significance of the two-note call of the treefrog *Eleutherodactylus coqui*. J. Comp. Physiol., A 127, 1-9.

NELSON, C. E. & G. A. MILLER, 1971: A possible case of mimicry in frogs. Herpetological Review, 3, 109.

NOTT, M. P., E. ROGERS. & S. PIMM, 1995: Modern extinctions in the kilo-death range. Current Biology, 5 (1), 14-17.

PERRILL, S. A., H. C. GERHARDT & R. DANIEL, 1982: Mating strategy shifts in male green treefrogs *(Hyla cinerea):* an experimental study. Animal Behaviour, 30, 43-48.

PIEAU, C., M. DORIZZI & C. DOURNON, 1989: Influence of environmental factors on sexual differentiation in vertebrates: evolutionary aspects. Geobios, 12, 303-311.

PIERCE, A. P., 1985: Acid Tolerance in Amphibians. BioScience, 35 (4), 239-243.

POUNDS, J. A., M. P. L. FOGDEN, J. M. SAVAGE & G. C. GORMAN, 1997: Tests of null models for amphibian declines on a tropical mountain. Conserv. Biol., 11, 1307-1322.

LIPS, [is this out of order or should it be Pips?]K. R., 1998: Decline of a tropical montane amphibian fauna. Conserv. Biol., 12, 106-117.

PROY, C., 1996: Zur Bedeutung der Terraristik bei der Erforschung der Biologie von Fröschen. In: HÖDL, W. & G. AUBRECHT: Frösche, Kröten, Unken. Aus der Welt der Amphibien. Stapfia, 47, 219-226.

RADCLIFFE, C. W. & D. CHISZAR, K. ESTEP,

J. B. MURPHY & H. M. SMITH, 1986: Observations on pedal luring and pedal movements in leptodactylid frogs. J. Herpetology, 20 (3), 300-306.

ROTH, G., K. C. NISHIKAWA, C. NAUJOKS-MANTEUFFEL, A. SCHMIDT & D. WAKE, 1993: Paedomorphosis and Simplification in the Nervous System of Salamanders. Brain Behav. Evol., 42, 137-170.

SALTHE, S. N., 1969: Reproductive modes and the number and sizes of ova in the urodeles. Amer. Midl. Natural., 81, 467-490.

SCHABETSBERGER, R. & A. GOLDSCHMID, 1994: Age structure and survival rate of Alpine newts *(Triturus alpestris)* at high altitude. Alytes, 12, 41-47.

SCHERZINGER, W., 1991: Problemgruppe Lurche im Bereich des Nationalparks Bayerischer Wald. Schriftenreihe Bayerisches Landesamt für Umweltschutz, 11 3, 1336.

SCHMID, M., 1983: Evolution of sex chromosomes and heterogametic systems in Amphibia. Differentiation, 23, 13-22.

SCHULTZ, R. J., 1969: Hybridization, unisexuality and polyploidy in the teleost *Poeciliopsis* (Poeciliidae) and other vertebrates. Amer. Nat., 103, 605-619.

SCHUYTEMA, G. S. & A. V. NEBEKER, 1996: Amphibian toxicity data for water quality criteria chemicals. EPA/600/R-96/124, U.S. Environmental Protection Agency, Corvallis.

SESSIONS, S. K., 1982: Cytogenetic of diploid and triploid salamanders of the *Ambystoma jeffersonianum* complex. Chromosoma, 84, 599-621.

SINSCH, U., 1989: Behavioural thermoregulation in the Andean toad *(Bufo spinulosus)* at high altitudes. Oecologia, 80, 3238.

SINSCH, U., 1990a: Froschlurche (Anura) der zentralperuanischen Anden: Artdiagnose, Taxonomie, Habitate, Verhaltensökologie. Salamandra, 26, 177-214.

SINSCH, U., 1990b: Migration and orientation in anurae amphibians. Ethology, Ecology & Evolution, 2, 65-79.

SINSCH, U., 1991: Mini-review: Orientation behaviour in amphibians. Herpetological Journal, 1, 541-544.

SMIRINA, E. M., 1994: Age determination and longevity in amphibians. Gerontology, 40, 133-146.

TIEDEMANN, F. & M. HÄUPL, 1994: Rote Liste der in Österreich gefährdeten Kriechtiere und Lurche. In: GEPP, J., 1994: Rote Listen gefährdeter Tiere Österreichs, 2, 67-74. Grüne Reihe des Bundesministeriums für Umwelt, Jugend und Familie. Styria Medienservice, Verlag Ulrich Moser, Graz.

TUNNER, H. G. & S. HEPPICH-TUNNER, 1991: Genome exclusion and two strategies of chromosome duplication in oogenesis of a hybrid frog. Naturwissenschaften, 78, 32-34.

TYLER, M. J., 1991: Declining amphibian populations - a global phenomenon? An Australian perspective. Alytes, 9, 43-50.

UIBLEIN, F., 1992: Prey choice behaviour in light and darkness in a facultative cave dweller, the Pyrenean salamander *Euproctus asper*. Alytes, 10, 131-136.

UIBLEIN, F., J. P. DURAND, C. JUBERTHIE & J. PARZEFALL, 1992: Predation in caves: the effects of prey immobility and darkness on the foraging behaviour of two salamanders, *Euproctus asper* and *Proteus anguinus*. Beh. Proc., 28, 33-40.

UIBLEIN, F., S. ENGELKE & J. PARZEFALL, 1995: Trade-off between visual detectability and nutrient content in patch choice of the Pyrenean salamander *Euproctus asper*. Ethology, 101, 39-45.

UZZELL, T., 1970: Meiotic mechanisms of naturally occuring unisexual vertebrates. Amer. Nat., 104, 433-445.

VEITH, M. & M. KLEIN, 1996: Zur Anwendung des Metapopulations-konzeptes auf Amphibienpopulationen. Zeitschrift für Ökologie und Naturschutz, 5, 217-228.

VENCES, M., F. GLAW & W. BÖHME (in print): Systematic revision of the genus *Mantella* (Anura, Ranidae, Mantellinae): colour pattern variability, biogeography and conservation of Malagasy poison frogs. Alytes.

VRIJENHOEK, R. C., 1978: Coexistence of Clones in a Heterogeneous Enviroment. Science, 199, 549-552.

VRIJENHOEK, R., R. M. DAWLEY, CH. J. COLE & J. P. BOGART, 1989: A list of the known unisexual vertebrates. In: R. M. DAWLEY & J. P. BOGART (eds.): Evolution and ecology of unisexual vertebrates. Bulletin, 466, 19-23. New York State Museum, Albany, New York, USA.

WALKOWIAK, W. & H. MÜNZ, 1985: The significance of water surface waves in the communication of fire-bellied toads. Naturwissenschaften, 72, 49-50.

WALLACE, H.,1987: Abortive development in the crested newt *Triturus cristatus*. Development, 100, 65-72.

WEYGOLDT, P., 1980: Complex brood care and reproductive behavior in captive poison-arrow frogs, *Dendrobates pumilio*. O. Schmidt. Behav. Ecol. Sociobiol., 7, 329-332.

WEYGOLDT, P., 1987: Evolution of parental care in dart poison frogs (Amphibia: Anura: Dendrobatidae). Z. zool. Syst. Evol.-forsch., 25, 51-67.

WEYGOLDT, P., 1989: Changes in the composition of mountain stream frog communities in the Atlantic mountains of Brazil: Frogs as indicators of environmental deteriorations? Studies on Neotropical Fauna and Environment, 243, 249-255.

WUNDER, W., 1932: Nestbau und Brutpflege bei Amphibien. Ergebnisse d. Biol., 8, 180-220.

Photo Credits

Index

(bold page numbers indicate illustrations)